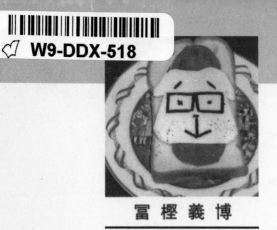

冨樫義博

Please help yourself.

Yoshihiro Togashi

Yoshihiro Togashi's manga career began in 1986 at the age of 20, when he won the coveted Osamu Tezuka Award for new manga artists. He debuted in the Japanese **Weekly Shonen Jump** magazine in 1989 with the romantic comedy **Tende Shôwaru Cupid**. From 1990 to 1994 he wrote and drew the hit manga **YuYu Hakusho**, which was followed by the dark comedy science-fiction series **Level E**, and finally this adventure series, **Hunter x Hunter**, available from VIZ Media's SHONEN JUMP Advanced imprint. In 1999 he married the manga artist Naoko Takeuchi.

HUNTER X HUNTER Volume 13
SHONEN JUMP ADVANCED Manga Edition

STORY AND ART BY
YOSHIHIRO TOGASHI

English Adaptation & Translation/Lillian Olsen
Touch-up Art & Lettering/Mark Griffin
Cover Design/Amy Martin
Graphic Design/Matt Hinrichs
Editor/Urian Brown

HUNTERxHUNTER © POT (Yoshihiro Togashi) 2001. All rights
reserved. First published in Japan in 2001 by SHUEISHA Inc., Tokyo.
English translation rights arranged by SHUEISHA Inc.

The stories, characters and incidents mentioned in this publication are
entirely fictional.

Printed in the U.S.A.

Published by VIZ Media, LLC
P.O. Box 77010
San Francisco, CA 94107

10 9 8 7 6 5 4 3 2
First printing, March 2007
Second printing, January 2016

www.viz.com

PARENTAL ADVISORY
HUNTER X HUNTER is rated T+ for Older Teen
and is recommended for ages 16 and up.
Contains realistic violence and mature language.
ratings.viz.com

www.shonenjump.com

SHONEN JUMP ADVANCED MANGA

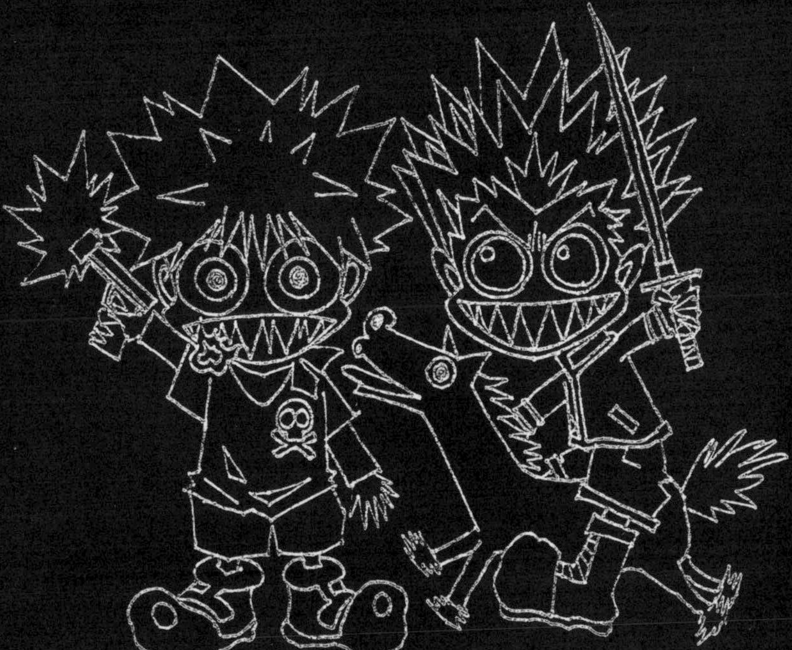

HUNTER × HUNTER

ハンター × ハンター

Story & Art by
Yoshihiro Togashi

Volume 13

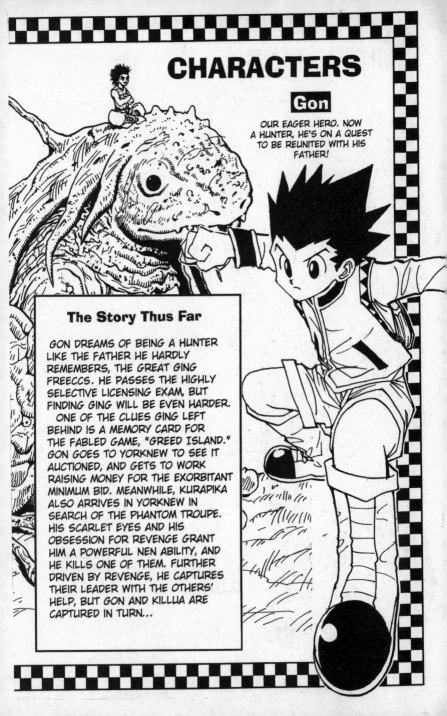

CHARACTERS

Gon

OUR EAGER HERO. NOW A HUNTER, HE'S ON A QUEST TO BE REUNITED WITH HIS FATHER!

The Story Thus Far

GON DREAMS OF BEING A HUNTER LIKE THE FATHER HE HARDLY REMEMBERS, THE GREAT GING FREECSS. HE PASSES THE HIGHLY SELECTIVE LICENSING EXAM, BUT FINDING GING WILL BE EVEN HARDER.

ONE OF THE CLUES GING LEFT BEHIND IS A MEMORY CARD FOR THE FABLED GAME, "GREED ISLAND." GON GOES TO YORKNEW TO SEE IT AUCTIONED, AND GETS TO WORK RAISING MONEY FOR THE EXORBITANT MINIMUM BID. MEANWHILE, KURAPIKA ALSO ARRIVES IN YORKNEW IN SEARCH OF THE PHANTOM TROUPE. HIS SCARLET EYES AND HIS OBSESSION FOR REVENGE GRANT HIM A POWERFUL NEN ABILITY, AND HE KILLS ONE OF THEM. FURTHER DRIVEN BY REVENGE, HE CAPTURES THEIR LEADER WITH THE OTHERS' HELP, BUT GON AND KILLUA ARE CAPTURED IN TURN...

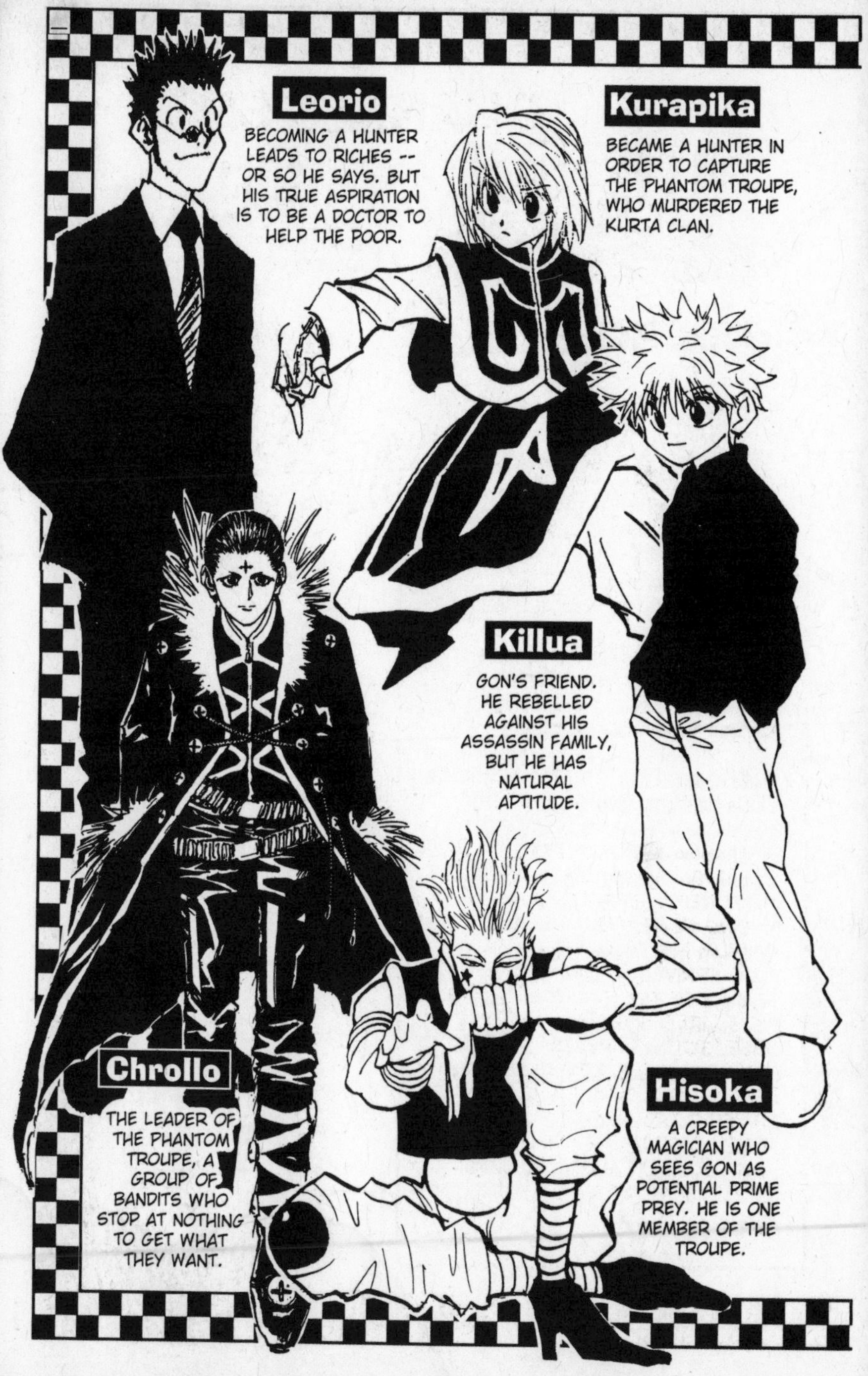
Kurapika
BECAME A HUNTER IN ORDER TO CAPTURE THE PHANTOM TROUPE, WHO MURDERED THE KURTA CLAN.
Leorio
BECOMING A HUNTER LEADS TO RICHES -- OR SO HE SAYS. BUT HIS TRUE ASPIRATION IS TO BE A DOCTOR TO HELP THE POOR.
Killua
GON'S FRIEND. HE REBELLED AGAINST HIS ASSASSIN FAMILY, BUT HE HAS NATURAL APTITUDE.
Hisoka
A CREEPY MAGICIAN WHO SEES GON AS POTENTIAL PRIME PREY. HE IS ONE MEMBER OF THE TROUPE.
Chrollo
THE LEADER OF THE PHANTOM TROUPE, A GROUP OF BANDITS WHO STOP AT NOTHING TO GET WHAT THEY WANT.

HUNTER×HUNTER

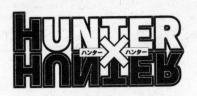

Volume 13

CONTENTS

READ THIS WAY

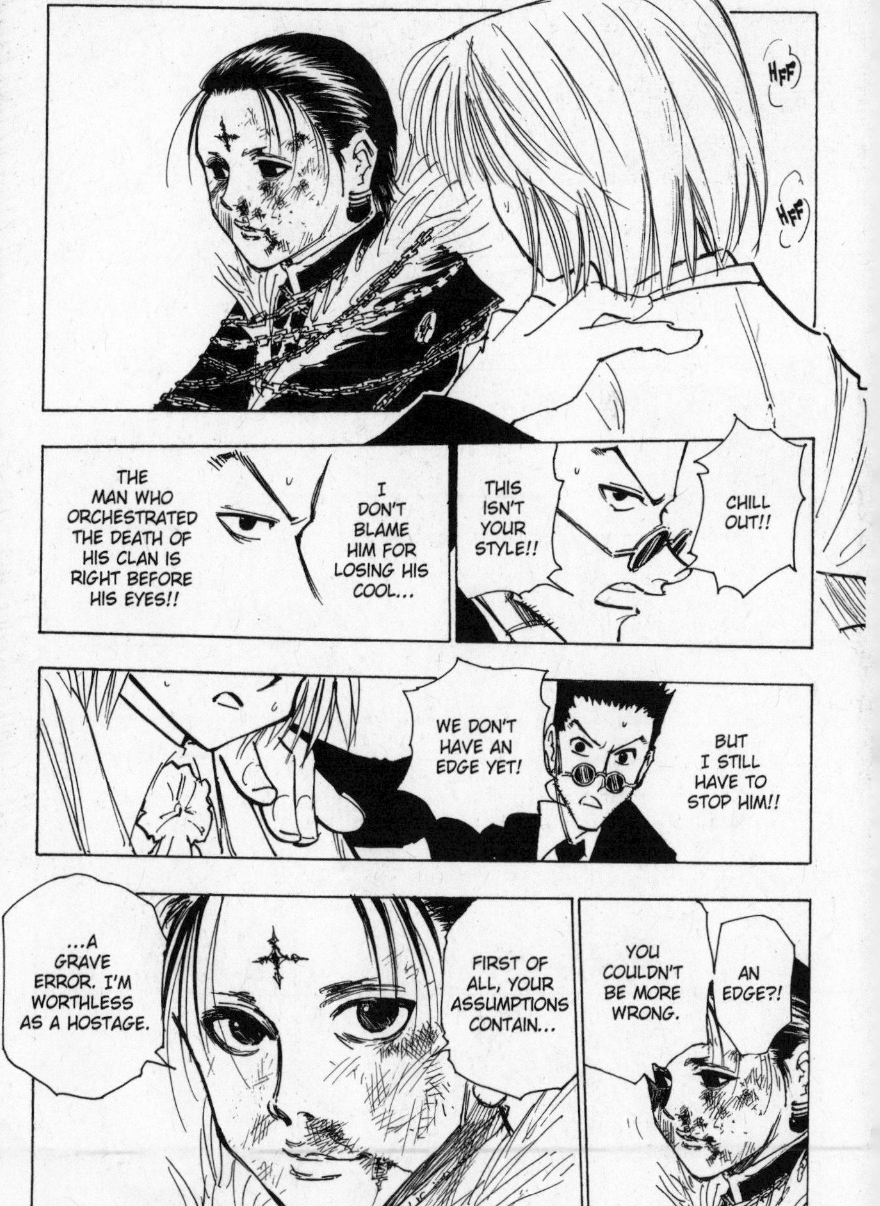
HFF
HFF
CHILL OUT!!
THIS ISN'T YOUR STYLE!!
I DON'T BLAME HIM FOR LOSING HIS COOL...
THE MAN WHO ORCHESTRATED THE DEATH OF HIS CLAN IS RIGHT BEFORE HIS EYES!!
BUT I STILL HAVE TO STOP HIM!!
WE DON'T HAVE AN EDGE YET!
AN EDGE?!
YOU COULDN'T BE MORE WRONG.
FIRST OF ALL, YOUR ASSUMPTIONS CONTAIN...
...A GRAVE ERROR. I'M WORTHLESS AS A HOSTAGE.

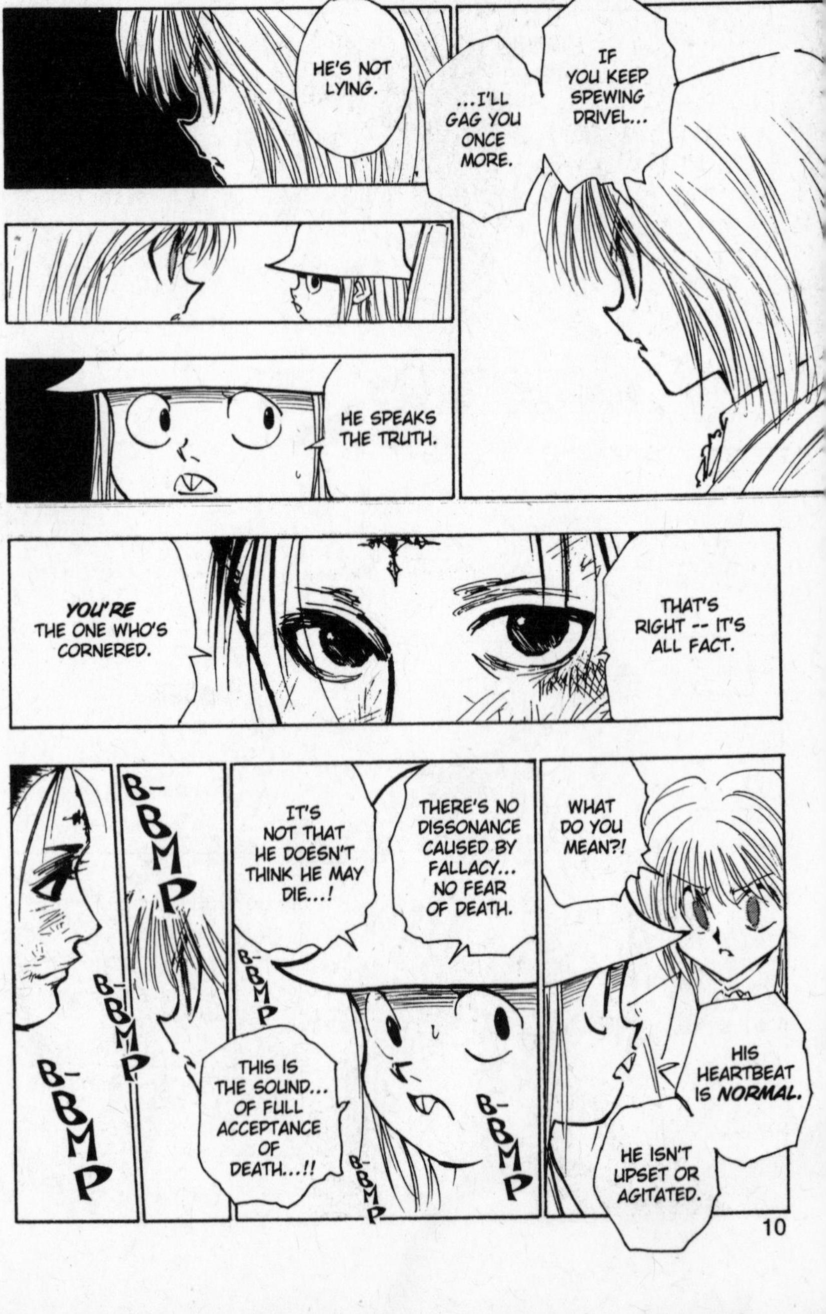
IF YOU KEEP SPEWING DRIVEL...
...I'LL GAG YOU ONCE MORE.
HE'S NOT LYING.
HE SPEAKS THE TRUTH.
THAT'S RIGHT -- IT'S ALL FACT.
YOU'RE THE ONE WHO'S CORNERED.
WHAT DO YOU MEAN?!
HIS HEARTBEAT IS ***NORMAL.***
HE ISN'T UPSET OR AGITATED.
THERE'S NO DISSONANCE CAUSED BY FALLACY... NO FEAR OF DEATH.
IT'S NOT THAT HE DOESN'T THINK HE MAY DIE...!
B-BMP
B-BMP
THIS IS THE SOUND... OF FULL ACCEPTANCE OF DEATH...!!
B-BMP
B-BMP
B-BMP
B-BMP

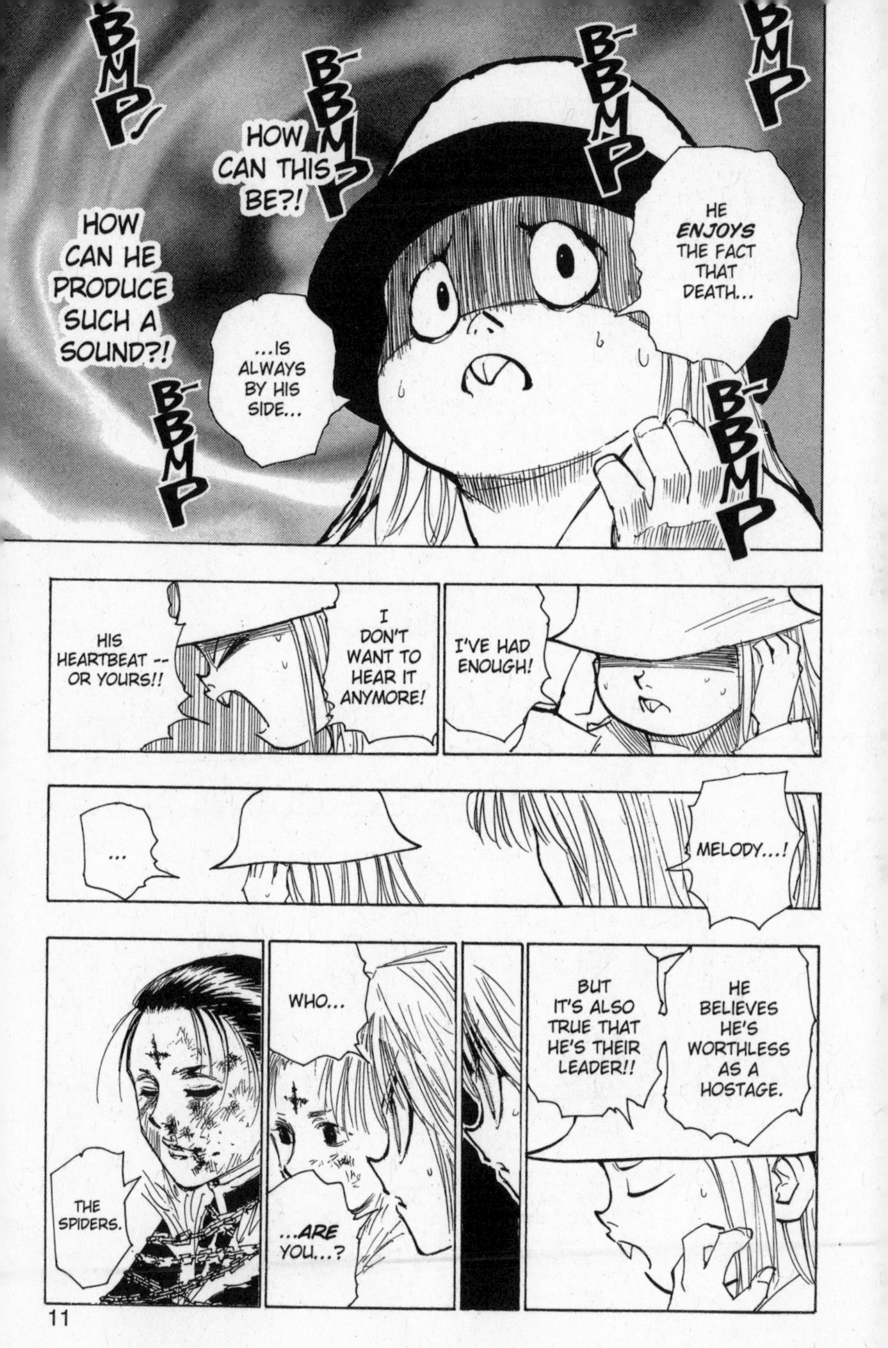
BMP
HE *ENJOYS* THE FACT THAT DEATH...
B-BMP
B-BMP
HOW CAN THIS BE?!
...IS ALWAYS BY HIS SIDE...
BMP!
HOW CAN HE PRODUCE SUCH A SOUND?!
B-BMP
B-BMP
I'VE HAD ENOUGH!
I DON'T WANT TO HEAR IT ANYMORE!
HIS HEARTBEAT -- OR YOURS!!
MELODY...!
...
HE BELIEVES HE'S WORTHLESS AS A HOSTAGE.
BUT IT'S ALSO TRUE THAT HE'S THEIR LEADER!!
WHO...
...*ARE* YOU...?
THE SPIDERS.

WERE YOU THE LEADER FIVE YEARS AGO WHEN...
...YOU SLAUGHTERED THE KURTAS FOR THE SCARLET EYES?
ANSWER ME.
IS THAT THE CHAIN...
...YOU USED TO KILL UVO?
!
WHAT DID HE SAY TO YOU...
...BEFORE HE DIED?

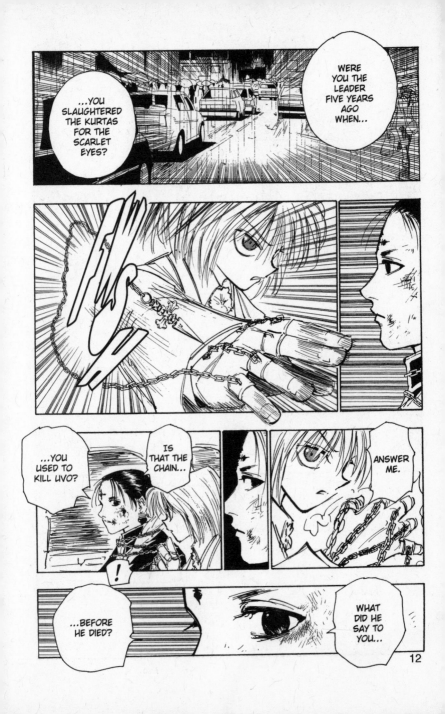

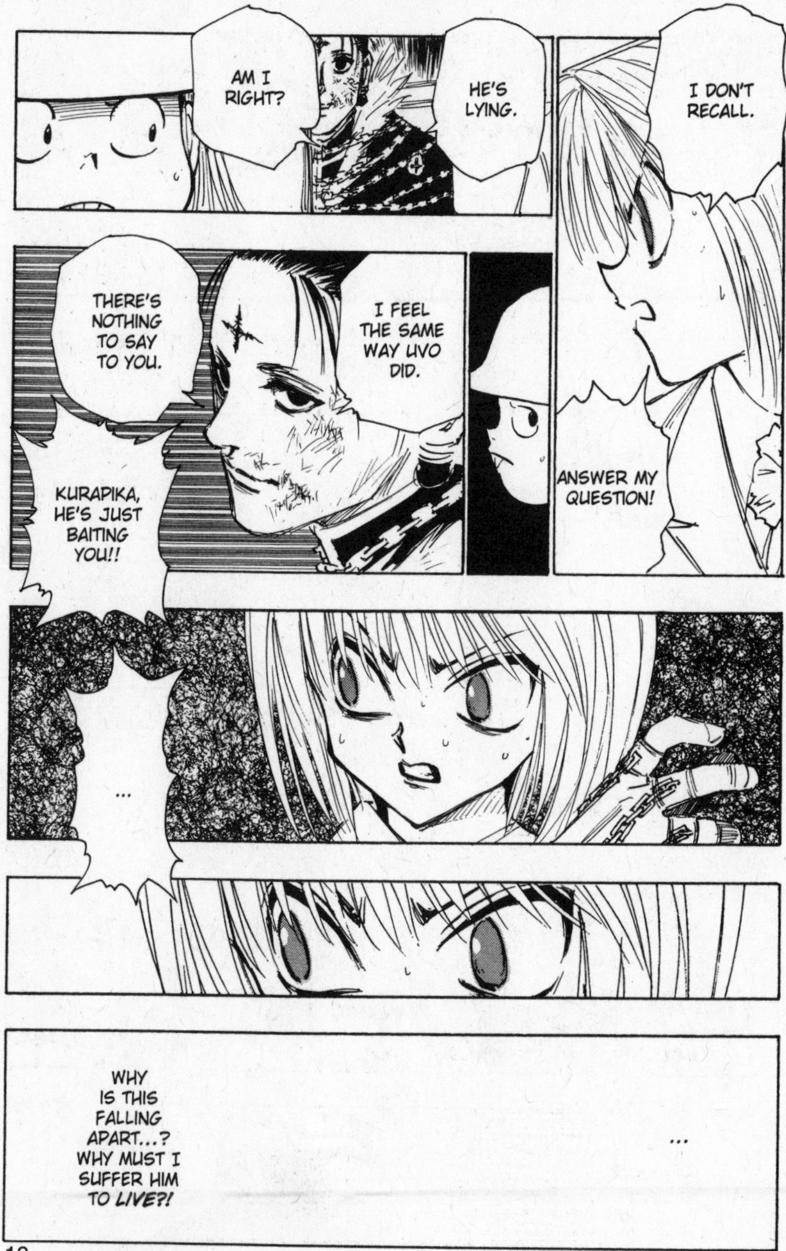
I DON'T RECALL.
ANSWER MY QUESTION!
HE'S LYING.
AM I RIGHT?
I FEEL THE SAME WAY UVO DID.
THERE'S NOTHING TO SAY TO YOU.
KURAPIKA, HE'S JUST BAITING YOU!!
...
...
WHY IS THIS FALLING APART...? WHY MUST I SUFFER HIM TO *LIVE*?!

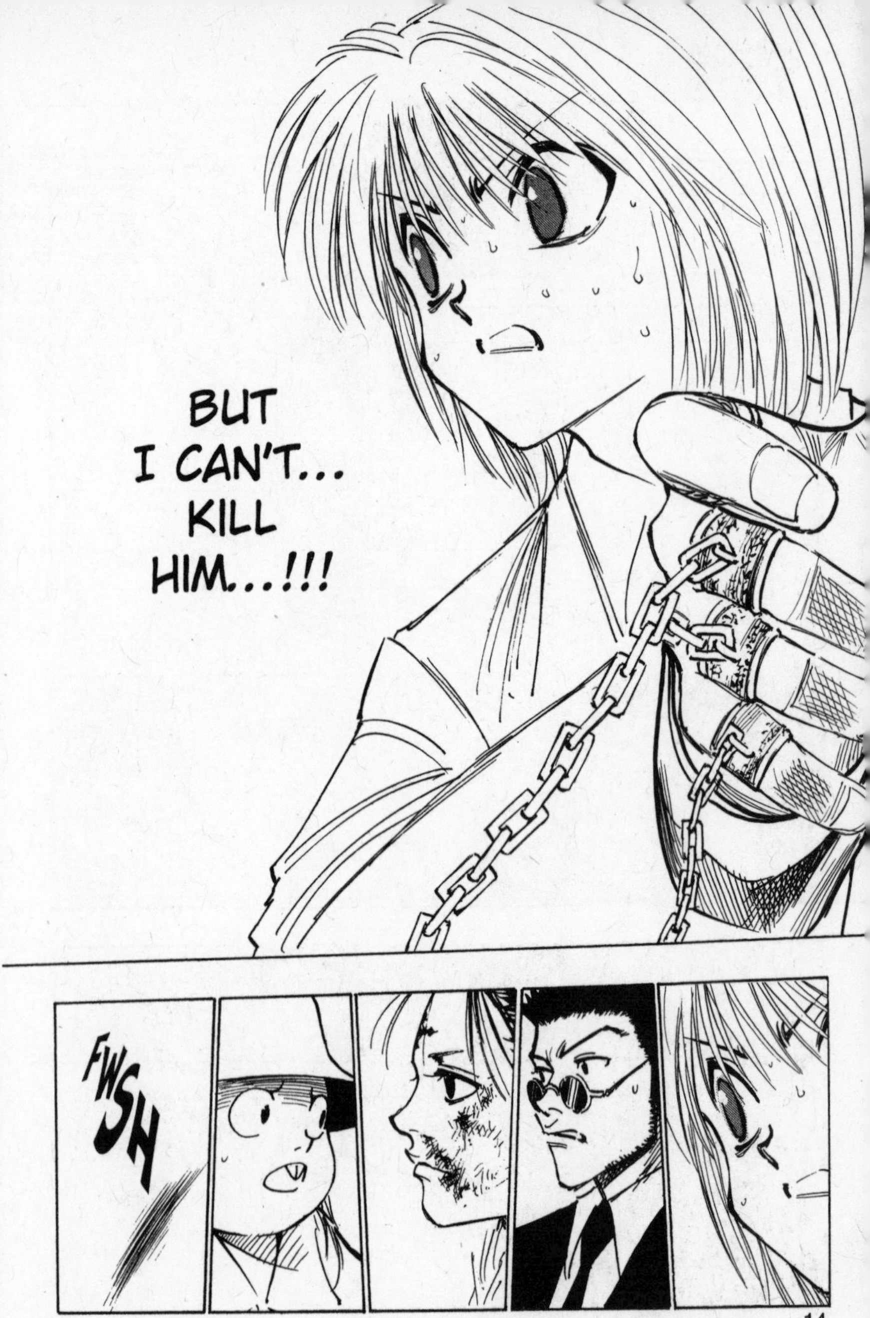
BUT I CAN'T... KILL HIM...!!!
FWSH

READ THIS WAY

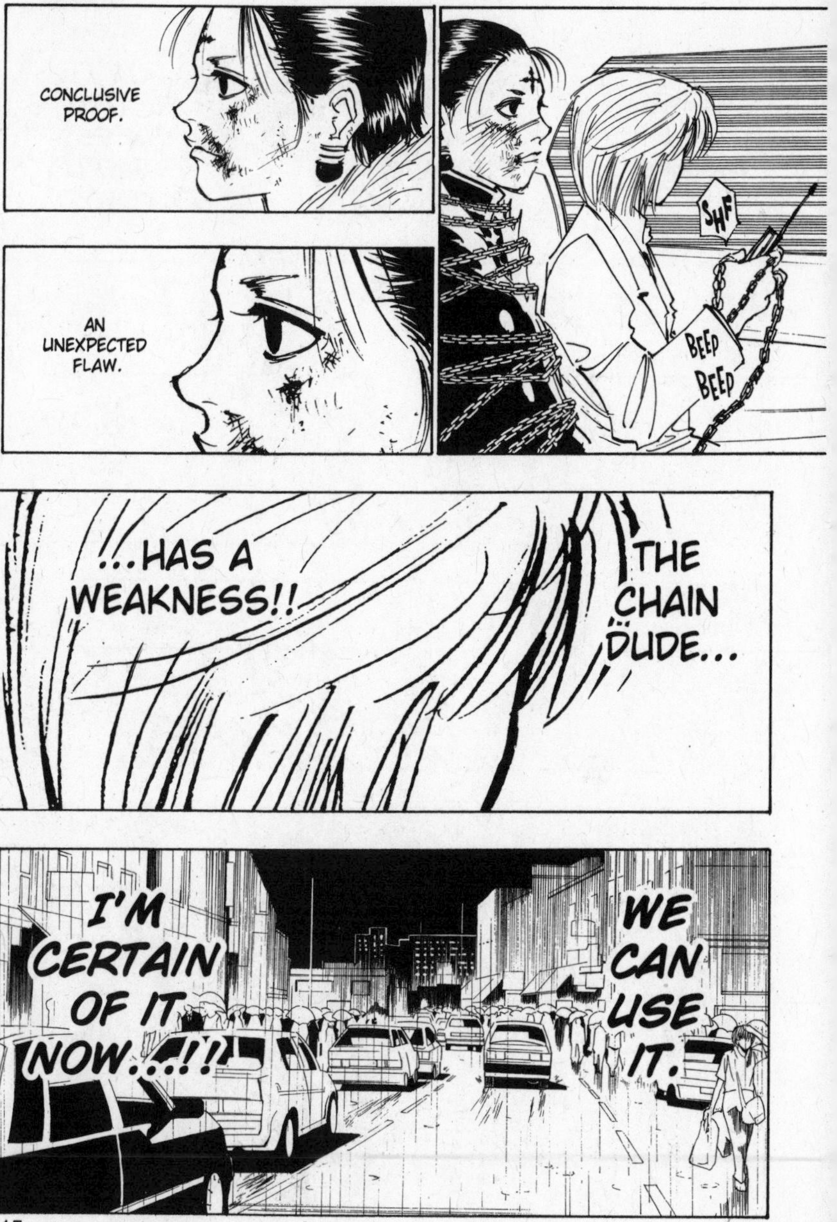
SHF
BEEP BEEP
CONCLUSIVE PROOF.
AN UNEXPECTED FLAW.
THE CHAIN DUDE...
...HAS A WEAKNESS!!
WE CAN USE IT.
I'M CERTAIN OF IT NOW...!!

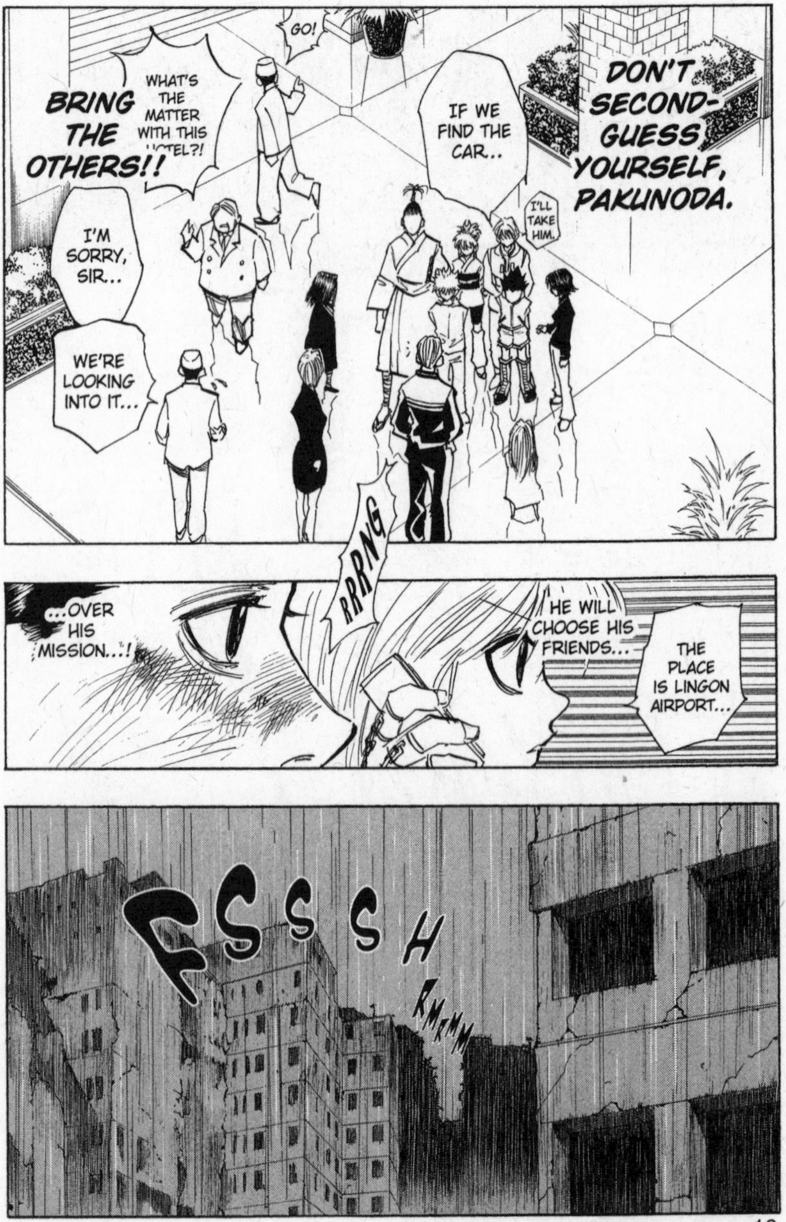
DON'T SECOND-GUESS YOURSELF, PAKUNODA.
I'LL TAKE HIM.
IF WE FIND THE CAR...
GO!
WHAT'S THE MATTER WITH THIS HOTEL?!
BRING THE OTHERS!!
I'M SORRY, SIR...
WE'RE LOOKING INTO IT...
RRRNG
THE PLACE IS LINGON AIRPORT...
HE WILL CHOOSE HIS FRIENDS...
...OVER HIS MISSION...!
FSSSH
RMRMM

READ THIS WAY

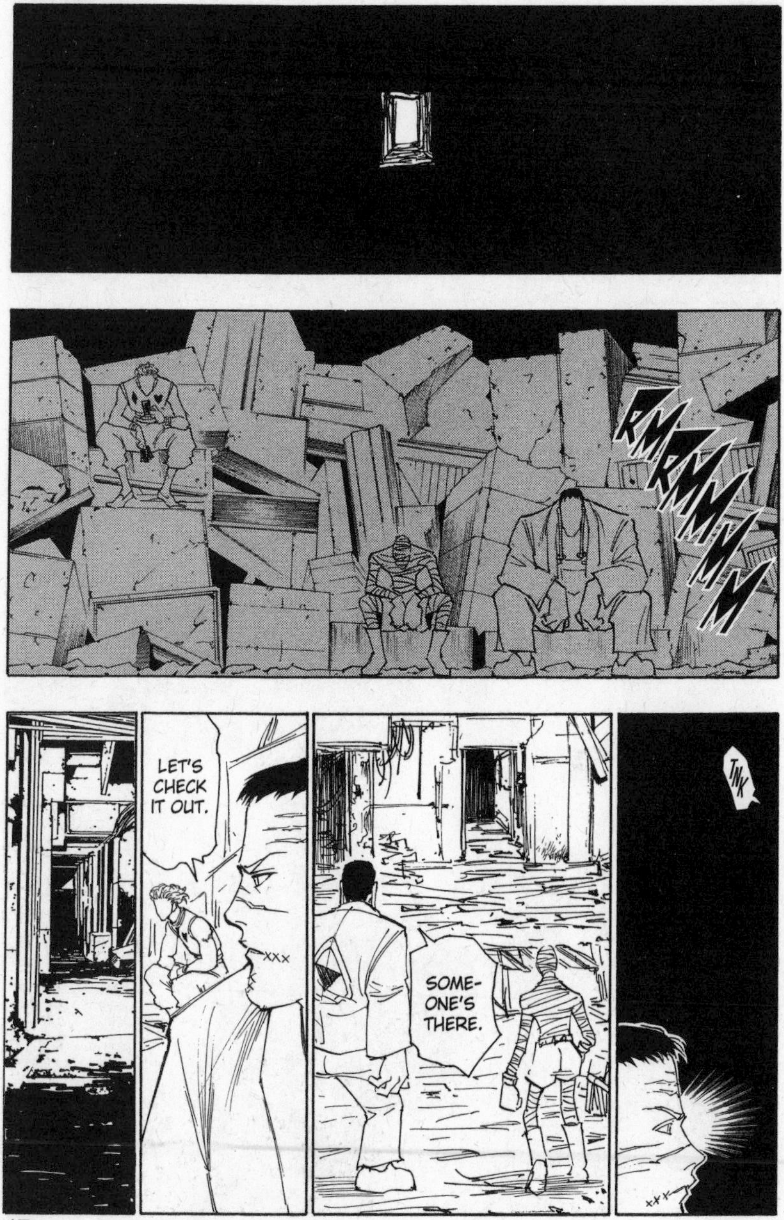
RMRMMMMM
TNK
SOME-ONE'S THERE.
LET'S CHECK IT OUT.

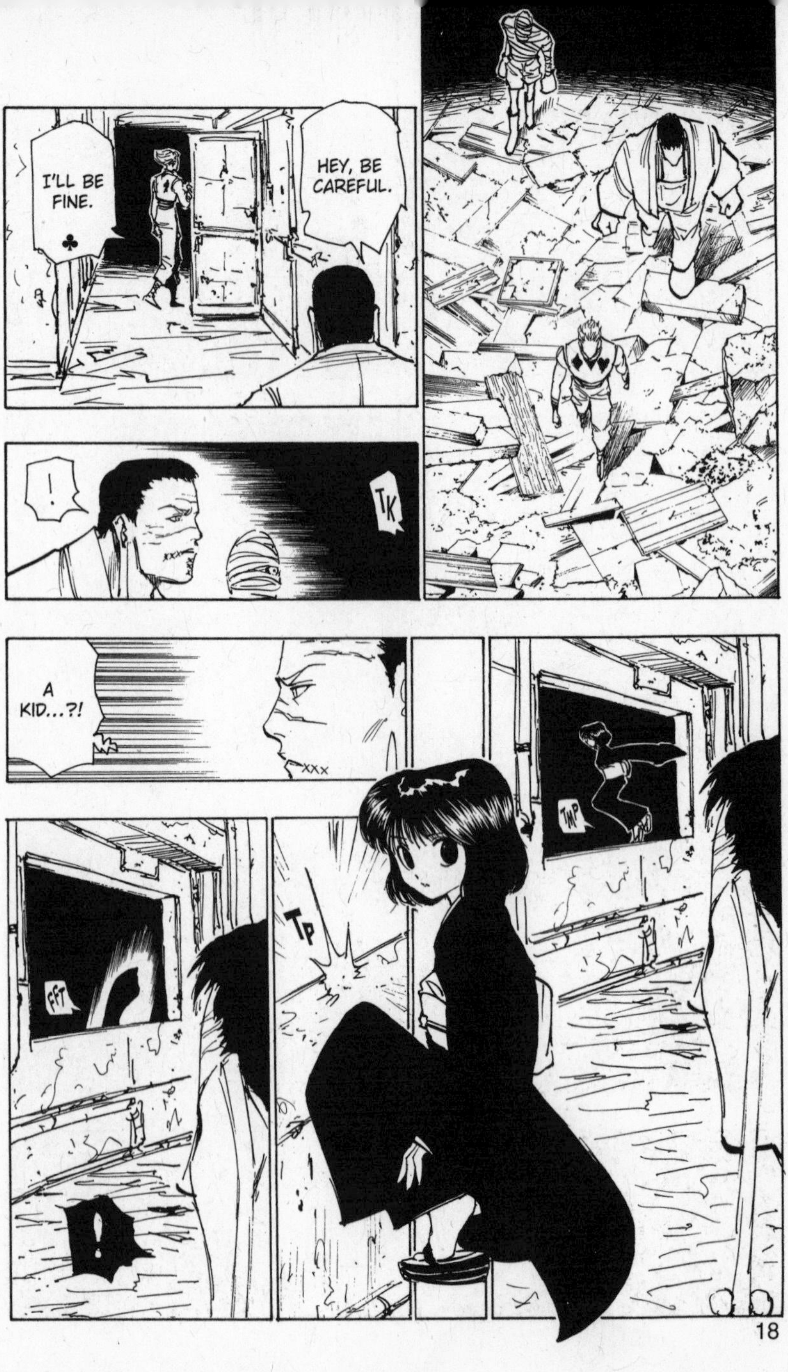

HEY, BE CAREFUL.
I'LL BE FINE. ♣
TK
!
TMP
A KID...?!
TP
FFT
!

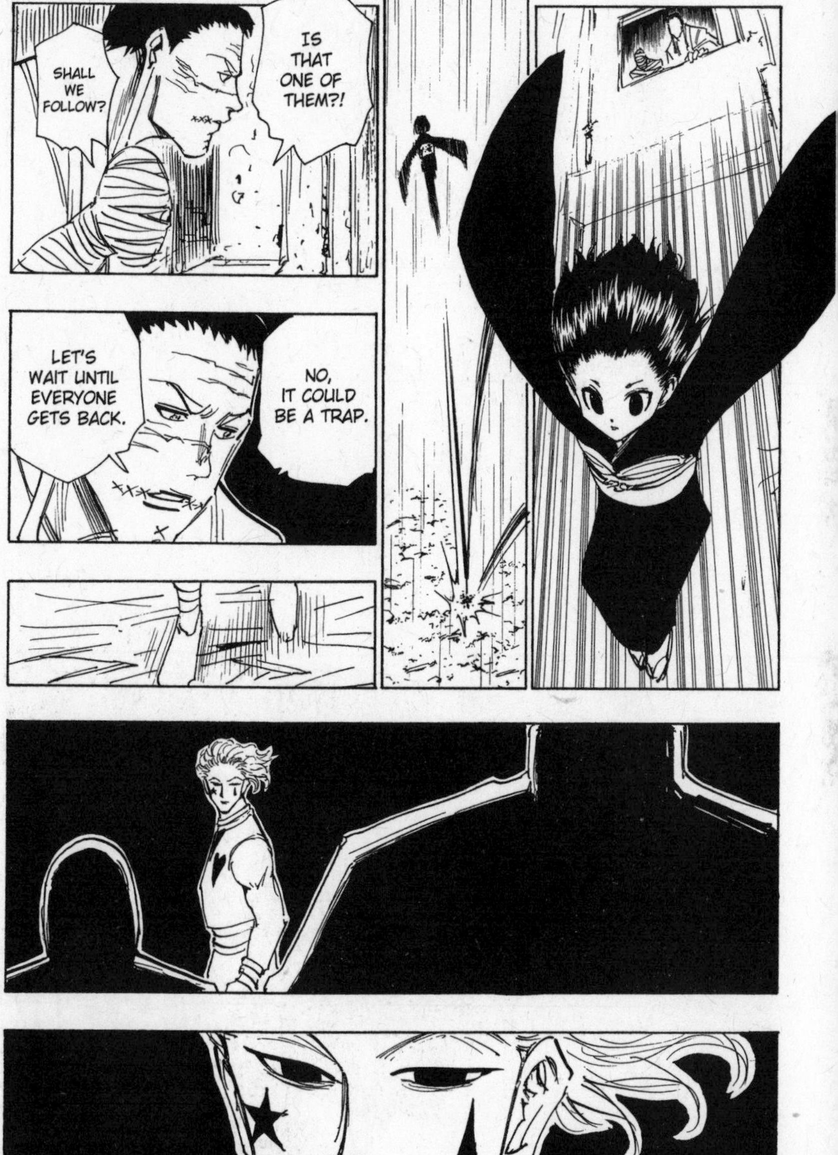
IS THAT ONE OF THEM?!
SHALL WE FOLLOW?
NO, IT COULD BE A TRAP.
LET'S WAIT UNTIL EVERYONE GETS BACK.

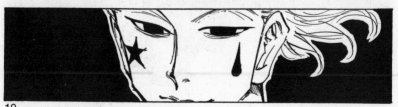

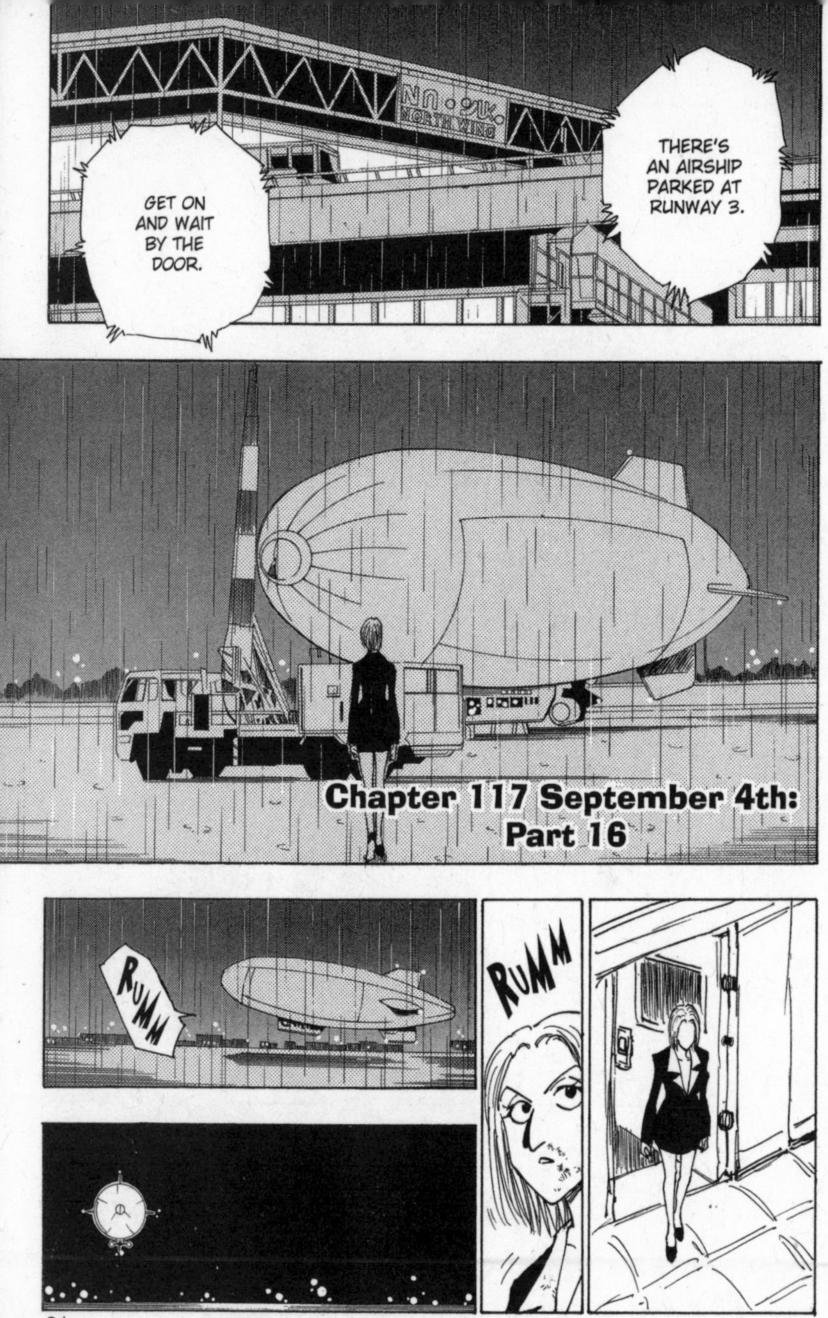
NORTH WING
THERE'S AN AIRSHIP PARKED AT RUNWAY 3.
GET ON AND WAIT BY THE DOOR.
Chapter 117 September 4th: Part 16
RUMM
RUMM

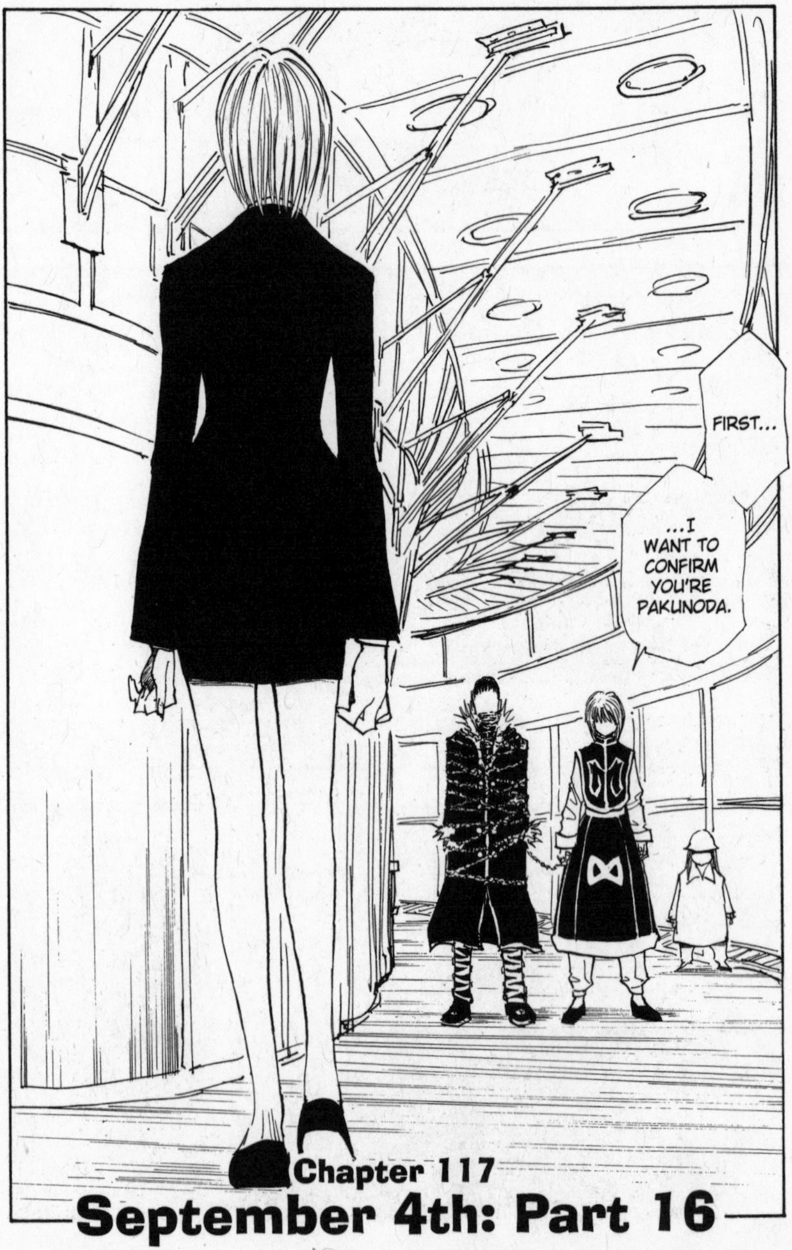
FIRST...
...I WANT TO CONFIRM YOU'RE PAKUNODA.

Chapter 117
September 4th: Part 16

READ THIS WAY

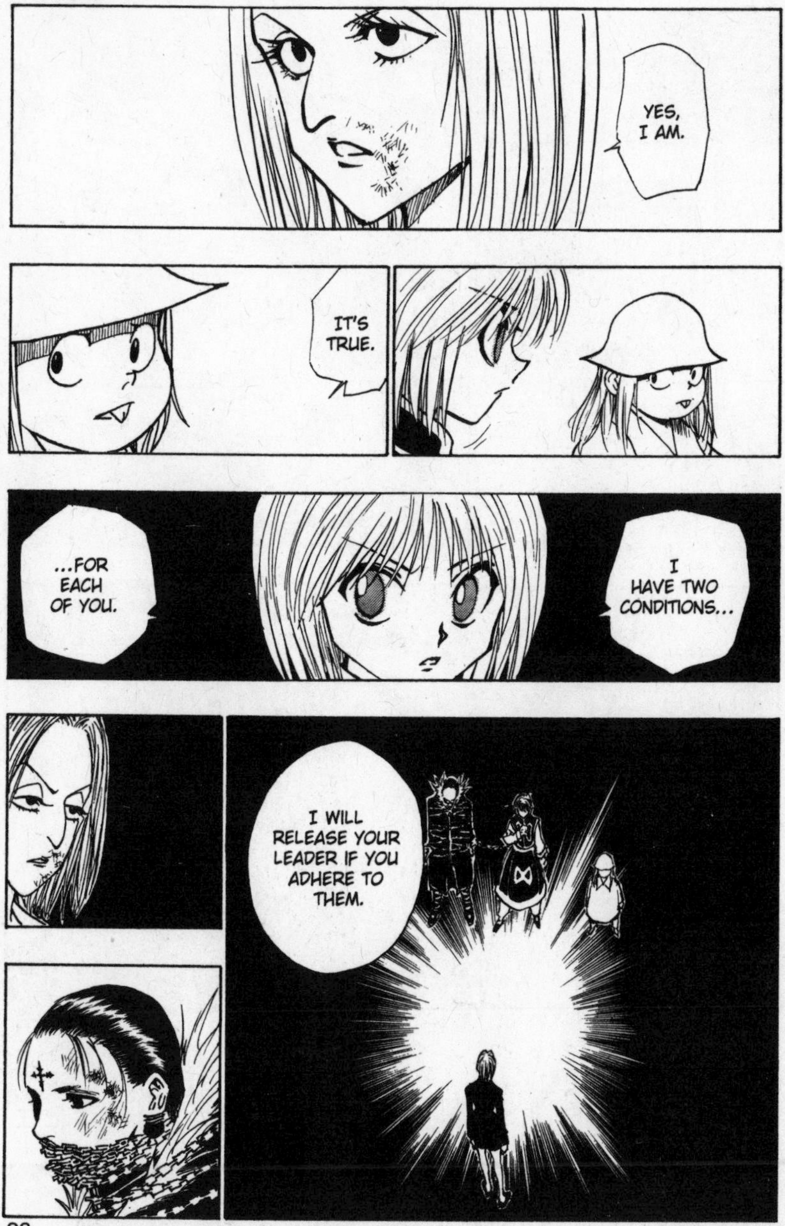
YES, I AM.
IT'S TRUE.
I HAVE TWO CONDITIONS...
...FOR EACH OF YOU.
I WILL RELEASE YOUR LEADER IF YOU ADHERE TO THEM.

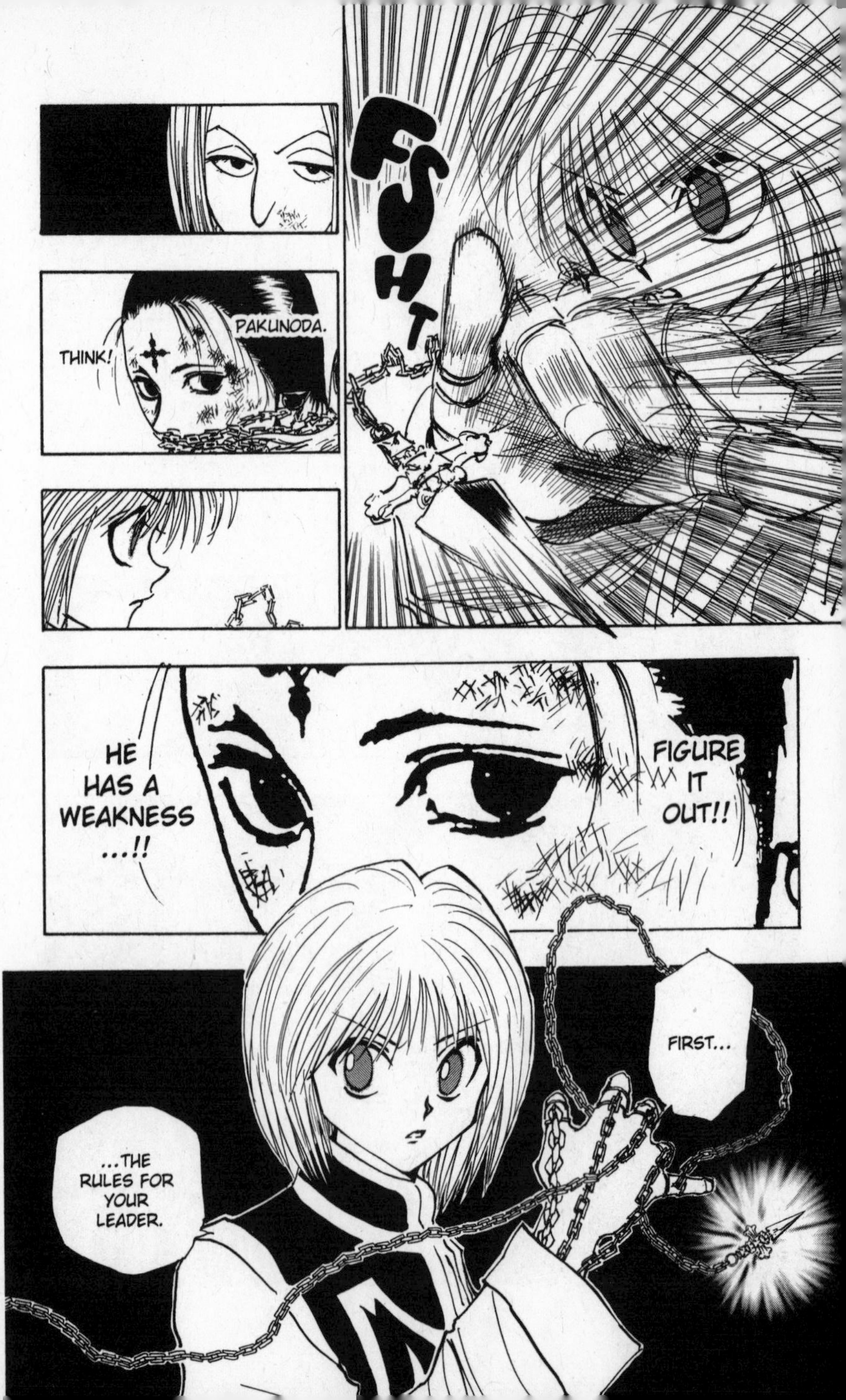
FSHT
PAKUNODA.
THINK!
FIGURE IT OUT!!
HE HAS A WEAKNESS ...!!
FIRST...
...THE RULES FOR YOUR LEADER.

READ THIS WAY

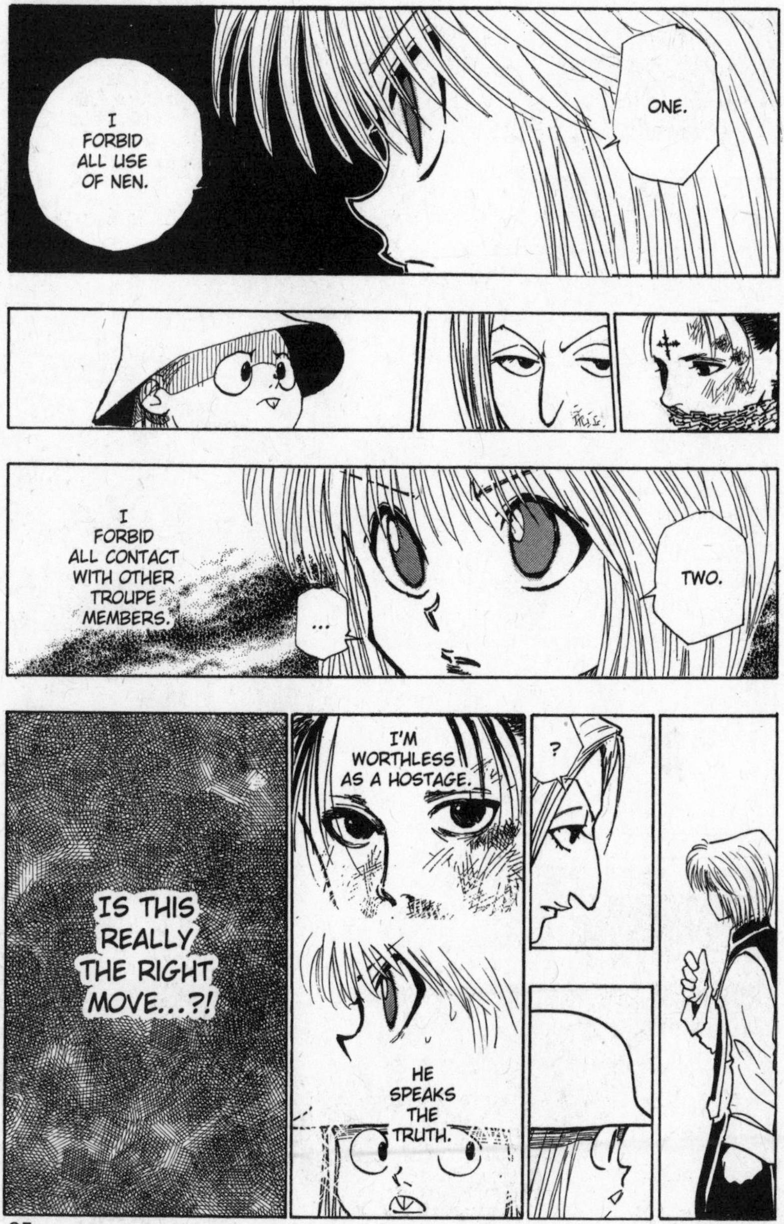
ONE.
I FORBID ALL USE OF NEN.
TWO.
...
I FORBID ALL CONTACT WITH OTHER TROUPE MEMBERS.
?
I'M WORTHLESS AS A HOSTAGE.
HE SPEAKS THE TRUTH.
IS THIS REALLY THE RIGHT MOVE...?!

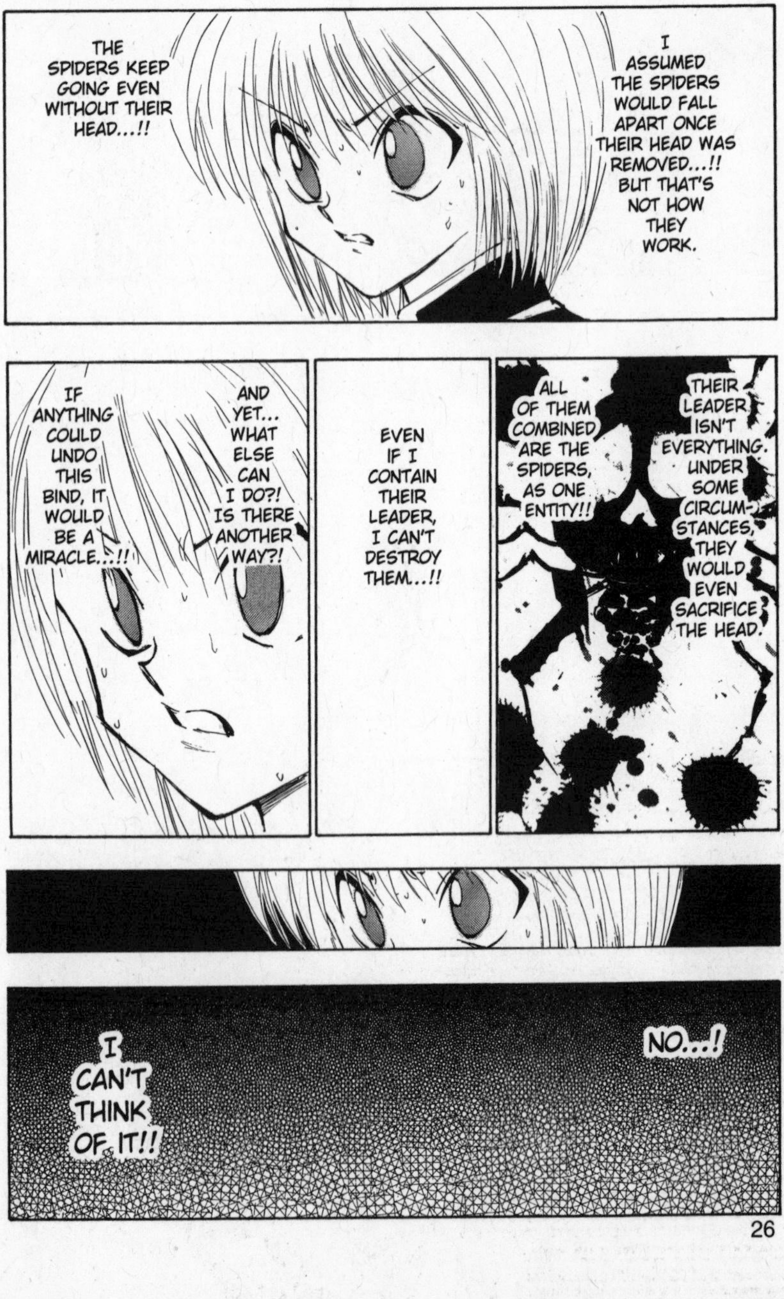
I ASSUMED THE SPIDERS WOULD FALL APART ONCE THEIR HEAD WAS REMOVED...!! BUT THAT'S NOT HOW THEY WORK.
THE SPIDERS KEEP GOING EVEN WITHOUT THEIR HEAD...!!
THEIR LEADER ISN'T EVERYTHING. UNDER SOME CIRCUMSTANCES, THEY WOULD EVEN SACRIFICE THE HEAD.
ALL OF THEM COMBINED ARE THE SPIDERS, AS ONE ENTITY!!
EVEN IF I CONTAIN THEIR LEADER, I CAN'T DESTROY THEM...!!
AND YET... WHAT ELSE CAN I DO?! IS THERE ANOTHER WAY?!
IF ANYTHING COULD UNDO THIS BIND, IT WOULD BE A MIRACLE...!!
NO...!
I CAN'T THINK OF IT!!

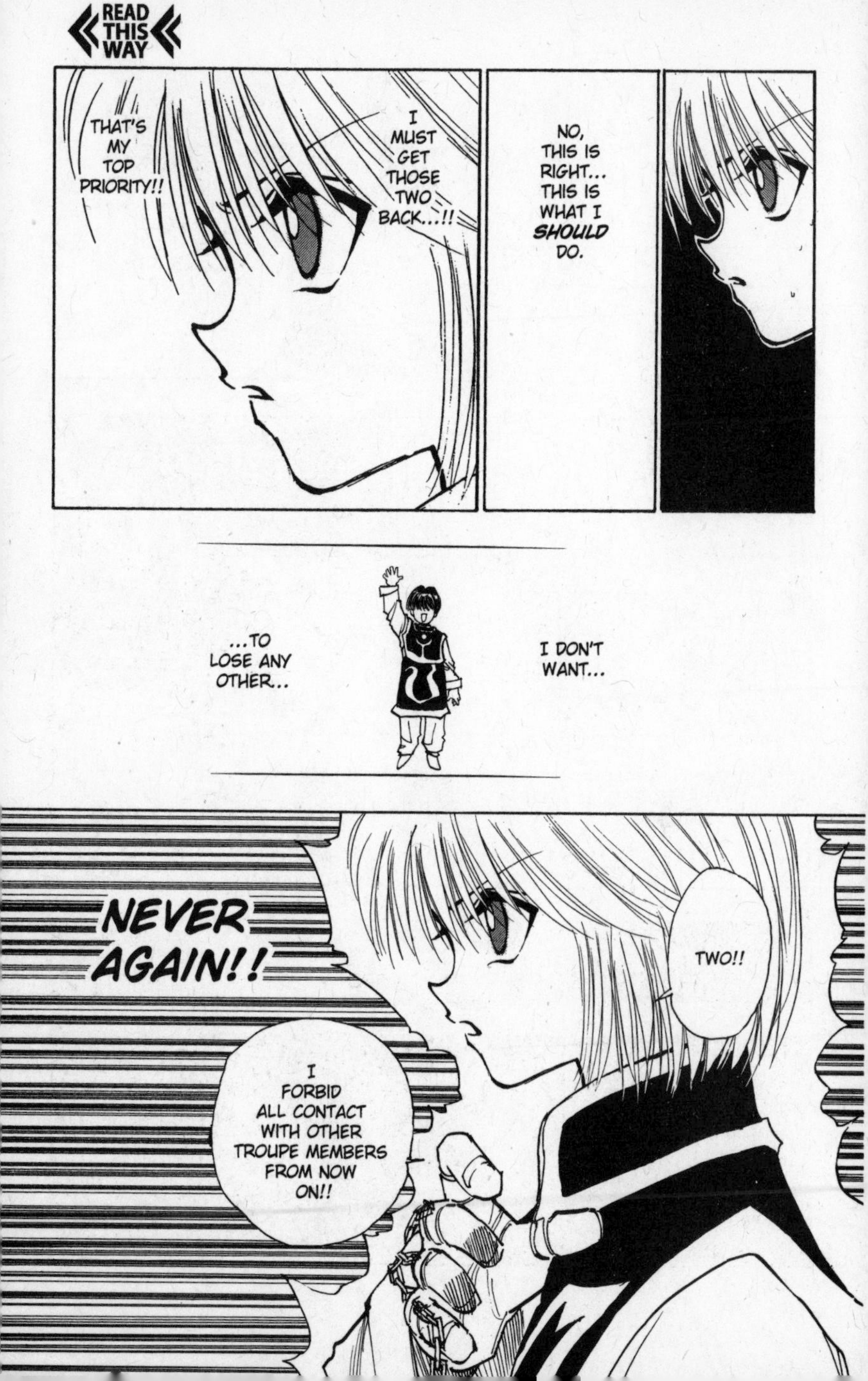
READ THIS WAY
NO, THIS IS RIGHT... THIS IS WHAT I SHOULD DO.
I MUST GET THOSE TWO BACK...!!
THAT'S MY TOP PRIORITY!!
I DON'T WANT...
...TO LOSE ANY OTHER...
TWO!!
NEVER AGAIN!!
I FORBID ALL CONTACT WITH OTHER TROUPE MEMBERS FROM NOW ON!!

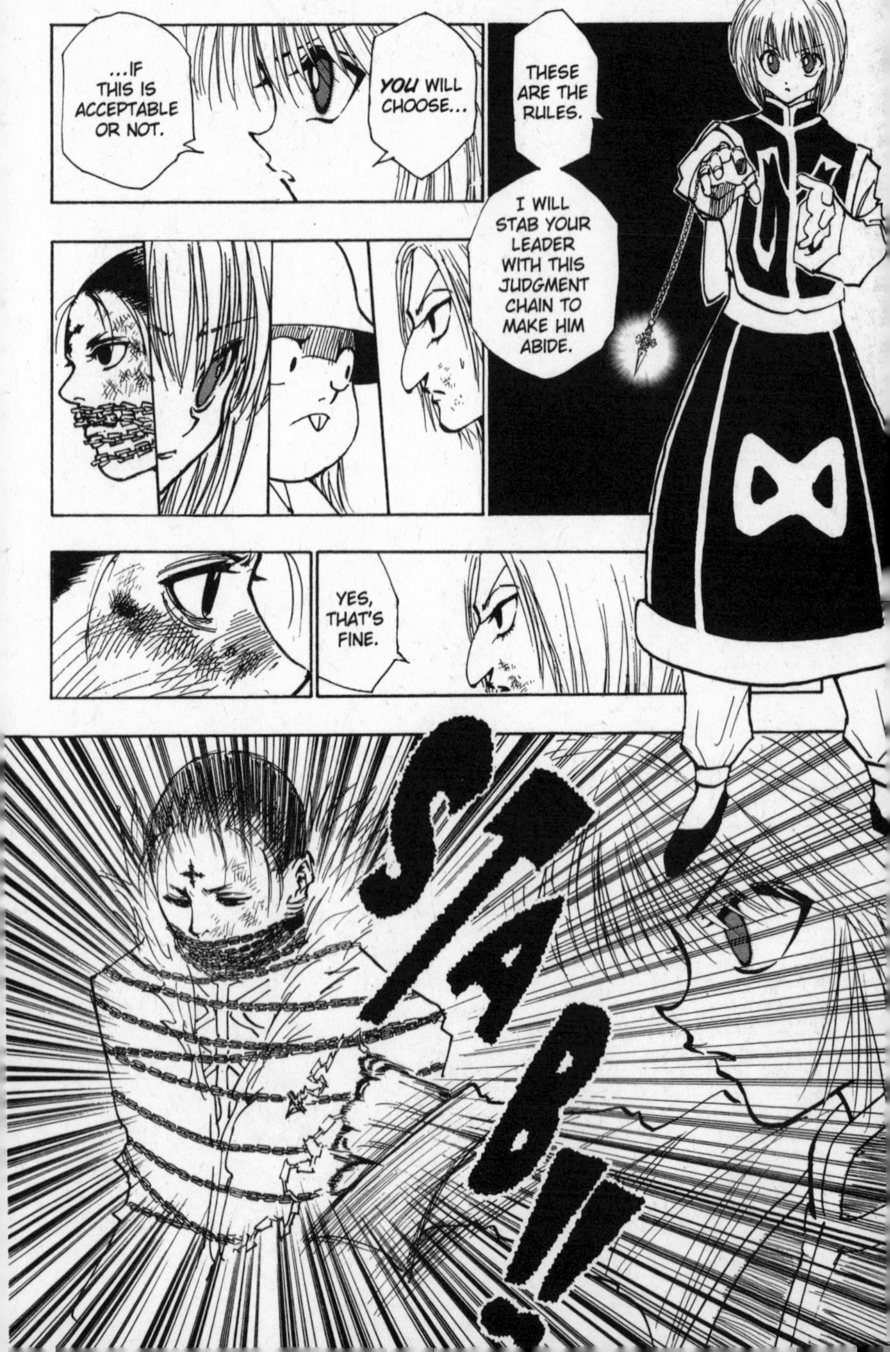
THESE ARE THE RULES.
I WILL STAB YOUR LEADER WITH THIS JUDGMENT CHAIN TO MAKE HIM ABIDE.
YOU WILL CHOOSE...
...IF THIS IS ACCEPTABLE OR NOT.
YES, THAT'S FINE.
STAB!!

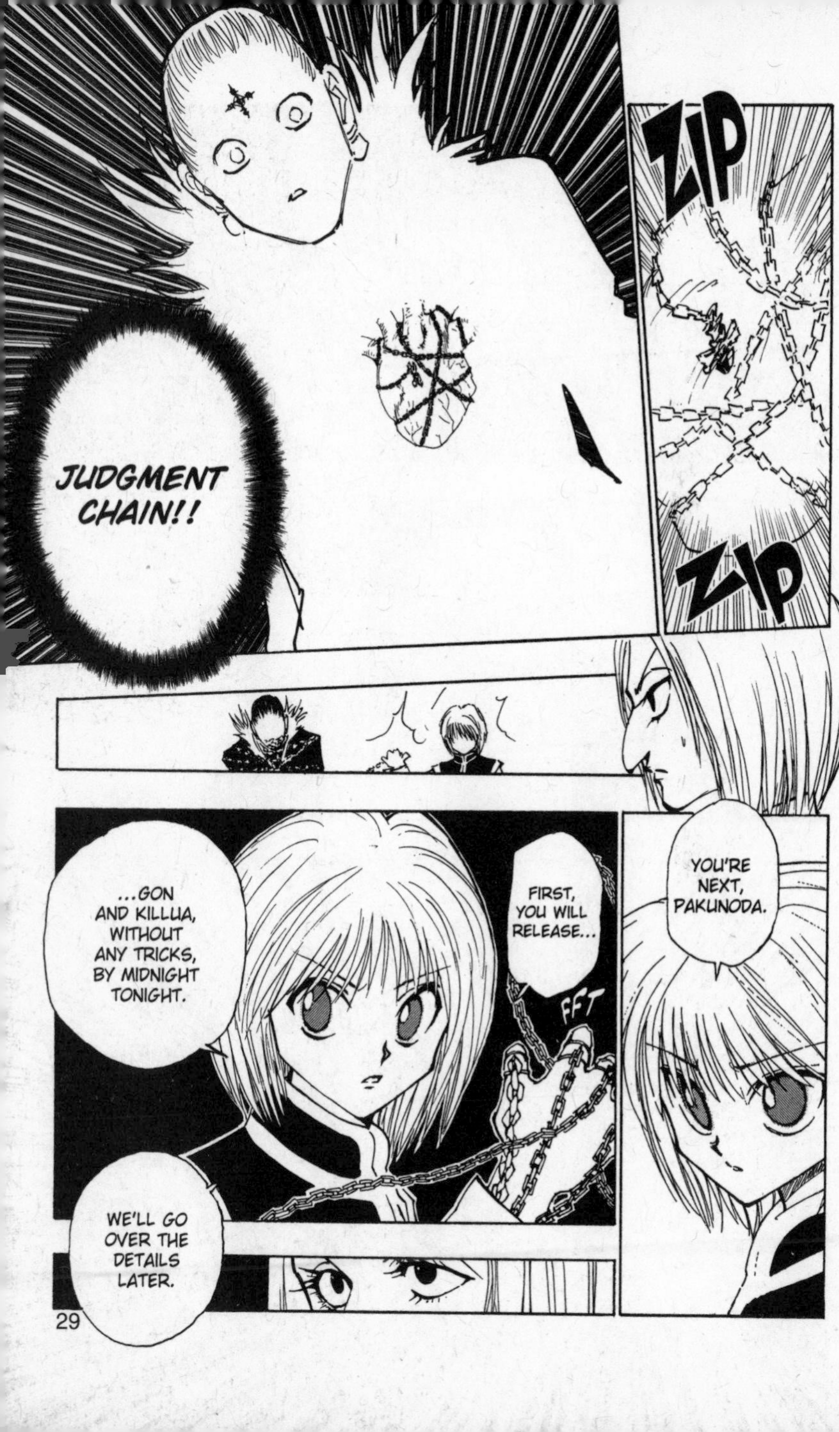
ZIP
ZIP
JUDGMENT CHAIN!!
YOU'RE NEXT, PAKUNODA.
FIRST, YOU WILL RELEASE...
...GON AND KILLUA, WITHOUT ANY TRICKS, BY MIDNIGHT TONIGHT.
FFT
WE'LL GO OVER THE DETAILS LATER.

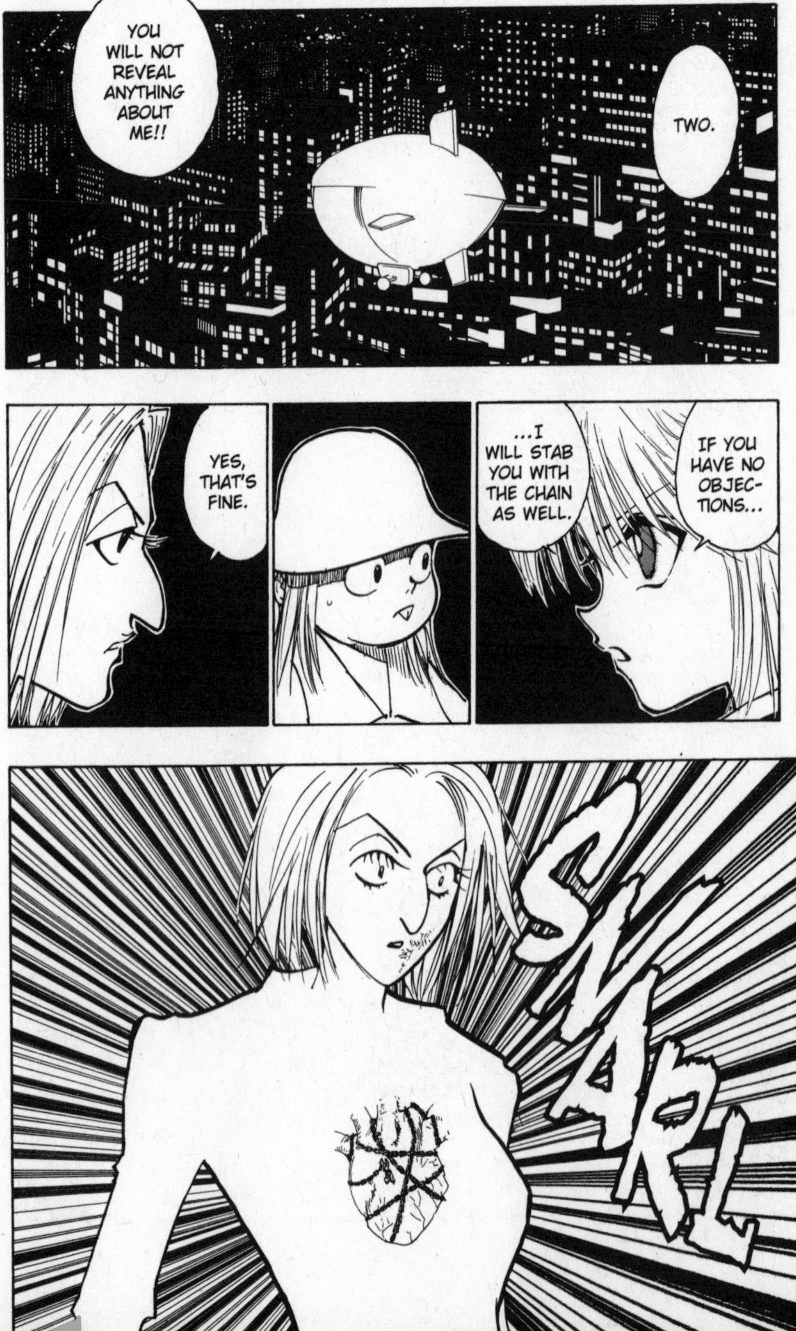
TWO.
YOU WILL NOT REVEAL ANYTHING ABOUT ME!!
IF YOU HAVE NO OBJEC-TIONS...
...I WILL STAB YOU WITH THE CHAIN AS WELL.
YES, THAT'S FINE.
SNARL

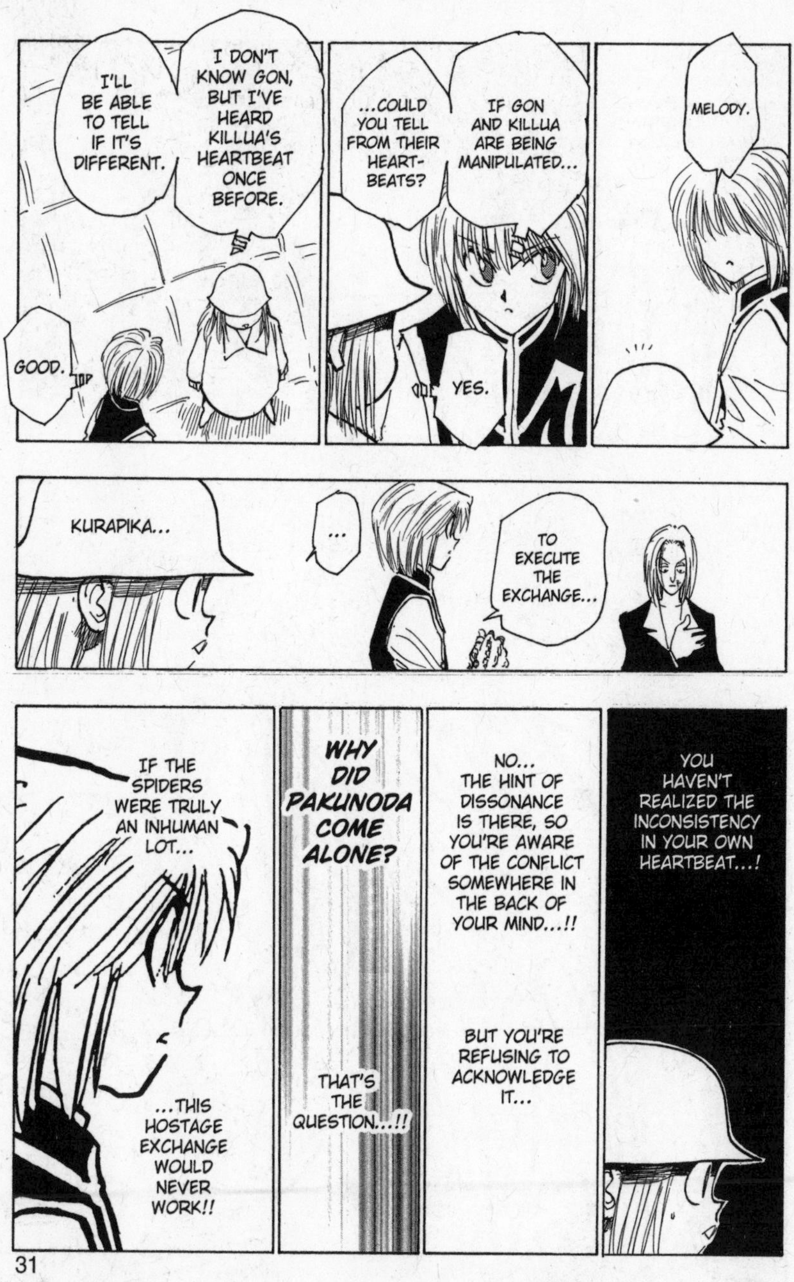
MELODY.
IF GON AND KILLUA ARE BEING MANIPULATED...
...COULD YOU TELL FROM THEIR HEART-BEATS?
YES.
I DON'T KNOW GON, BUT I'VE HEARD KILLUA'S HEARTBEAT ONCE BEFORE.
I'LL BE ABLE TO TELL IF IT'S DIFFERENT.
GOOD.
TO EXECUTE THE EXCHANGE...
...
KURAPIKA...
YOU HAVEN'T REALIZED THE INCONSISTENCY IN YOUR OWN HEARTBEAT...!
NO... THE HINT OF DISSONANCE IS THERE, SO YOU'RE AWARE OF THE CONFLICT SOMEWHERE IN THE BACK OF YOUR MIND...!!
BUT YOU'RE REFUSING TO ACKNOWLEDGE IT...
WHY DID PAKUNODA COME ALONE?
THAT'S THE QUESTION...!!
IF THE SPIDERS WERE TRULY AN INHUMAN LOT...
...THIS HOSTAGE EXCHANGE WOULD NEVER WORK!!

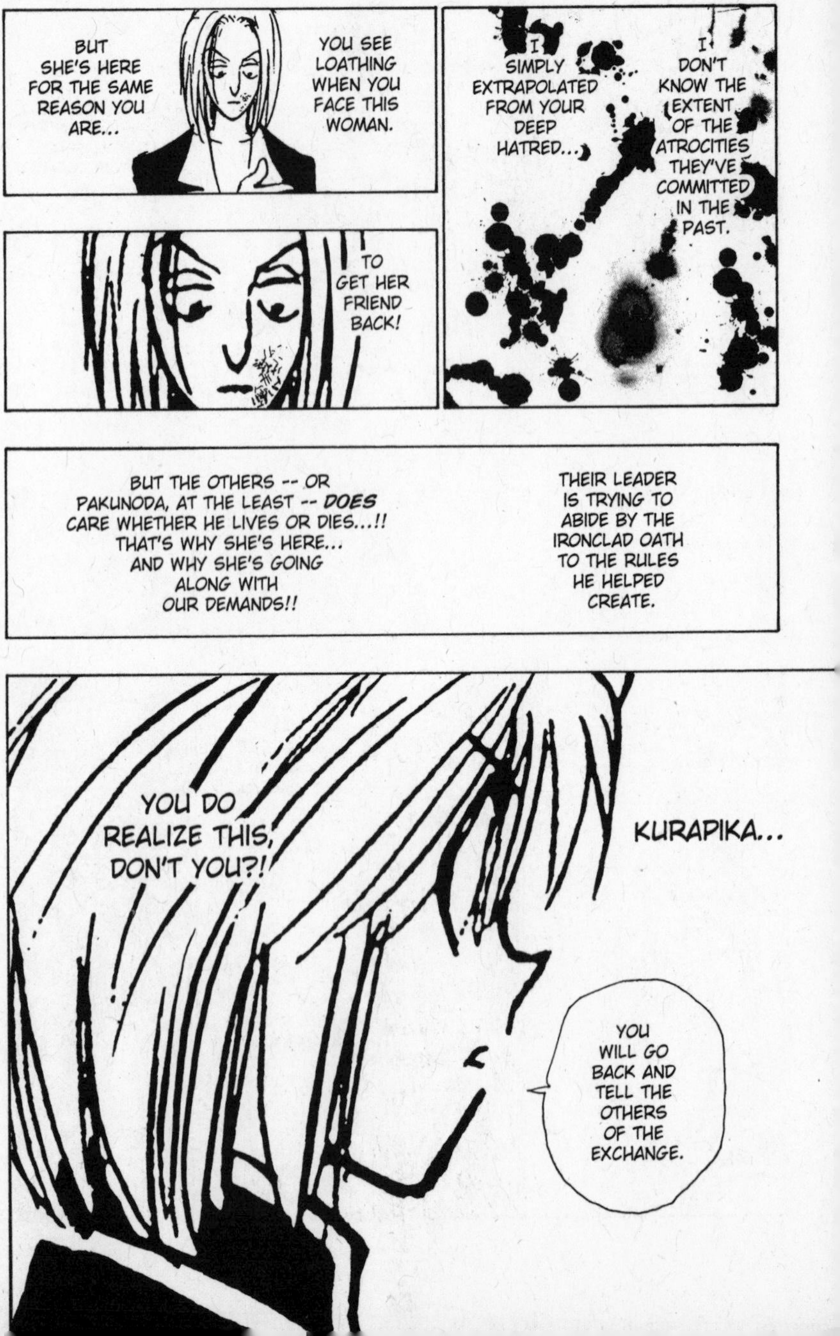
I DON'T KNOW THE EXTENT OF THE ATROCITIES THEY'VE COMMITTED IN THE PAST.
I SIMPLY EXTRAPOLATED FROM YOUR DEEP HATRED...
YOU SEE LOATHING WHEN YOU FACE THIS WOMAN.
BUT SHE'S HERE FOR THE SAME REASON YOU ARE...
TO GET HER FRIEND BACK!
THEIR LEADER IS TRYING TO ABIDE BY THE IRONCLAD OATH TO THE RULES HE HELPED CREATE.
BUT THE OTHERS -- OR PAKUNODA, AT THE LEAST -- *DOES* CARE WHETHER HE LIVES OR DIES...!! THAT'S WHY SHE'S HERE... AND WHY SHE'S GOING ALONG WITH OUR DEMANDS!!
KURAPIKA...
YOU DO REALIZE THIS, DON'T YOU?!
YOU WILL GO BACK AND TELL THE OTHERS OF THE EXCHANGE.

READ THIS WAY

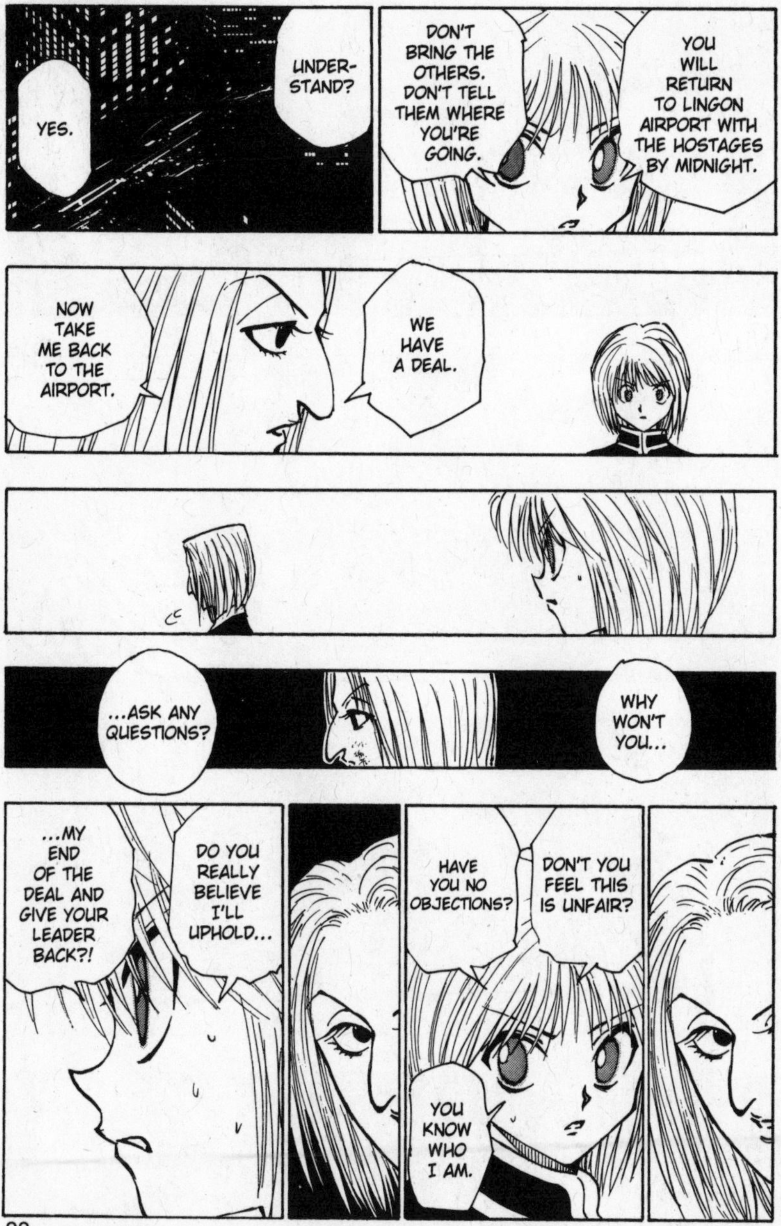
YOU WILL RETURN TO LINGON AIRPORT WITH THE HOSTAGES BY MIDNIGHT.
DON'T BRING THE OTHERS. DON'T TELL THEM WHERE YOU'RE GOING.
UNDER-STAND?
YES.
WE HAVE A DEAL.
NOW TAKE ME BACK TO THE AIRPORT.
WHY WON'T YOU...
...ASK ANY QUESTIONS?
DON'T YOU FEEL THIS IS UNFAIR?
HAVE YOU NO OBJECTIONS?
YOU KNOW WHO I AM.
DO YOU REALLY BELIEVE I'LL UPHOLD...
...MY END OF THE DEAL AND GIVE YOUR LEADER BACK?!

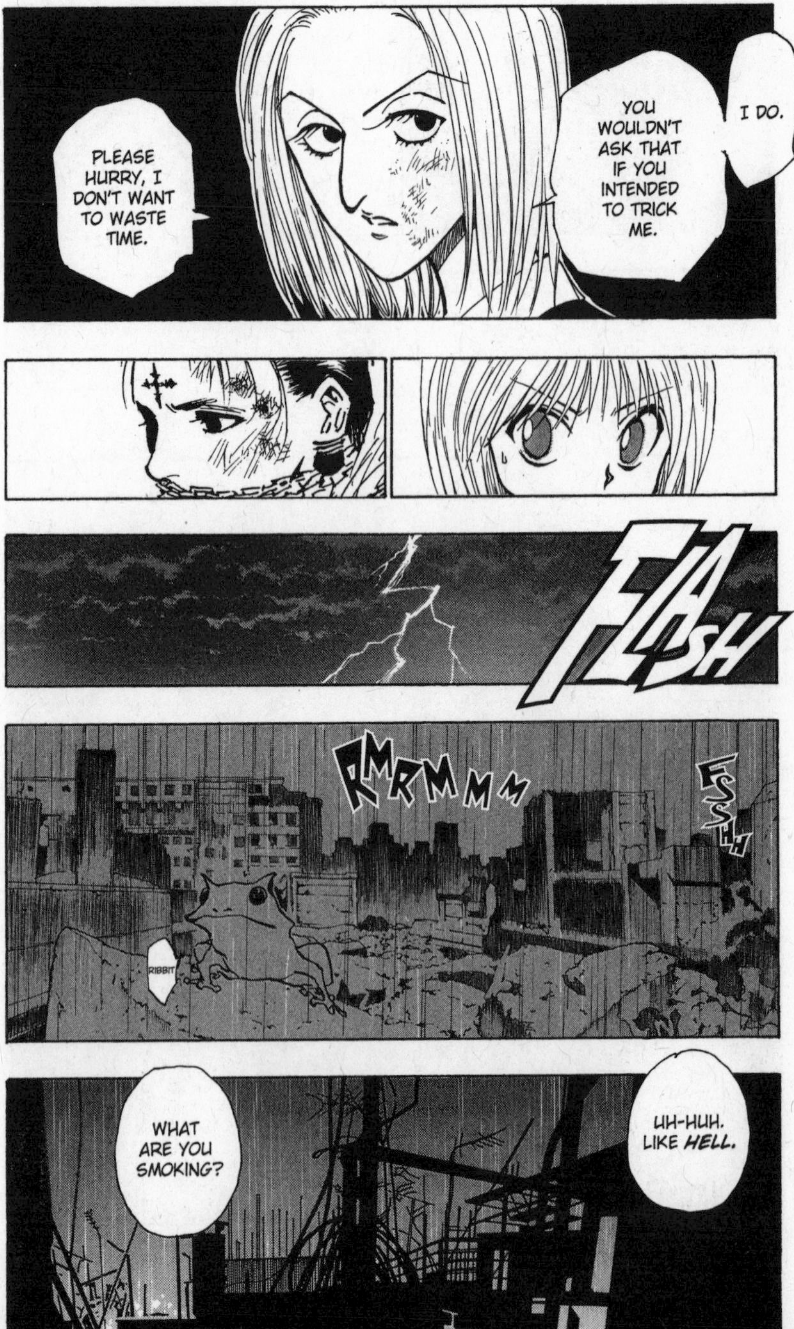
I DO.
YOU WOULDN'T ASK THAT IF YOU INTENDED TO TRICK ME.
PLEASE HURRY, I DON'T WANT TO WASTE TIME.
FLASH
FSSHH
RMRMMMM
RIBBIT
UH-HUH. LIKE *HELL.*
WHAT ARE YOU SMOKING?

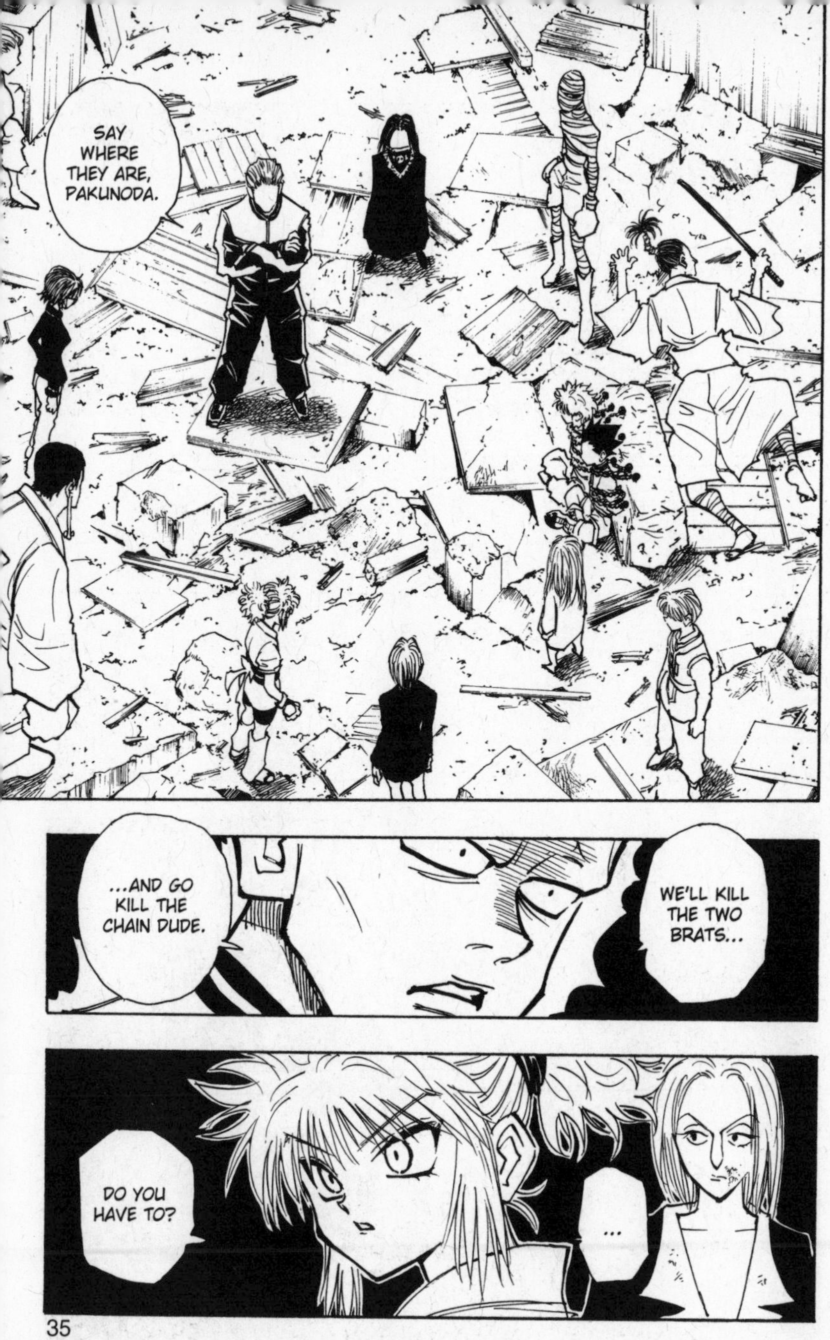
SAY WHERE THEY ARE, PAKUNODA.
WE'LL KILL THE TWO BRATS...
...AND GO KILL THE CHAIN DUDE.
...
DO YOU HAVE TO?

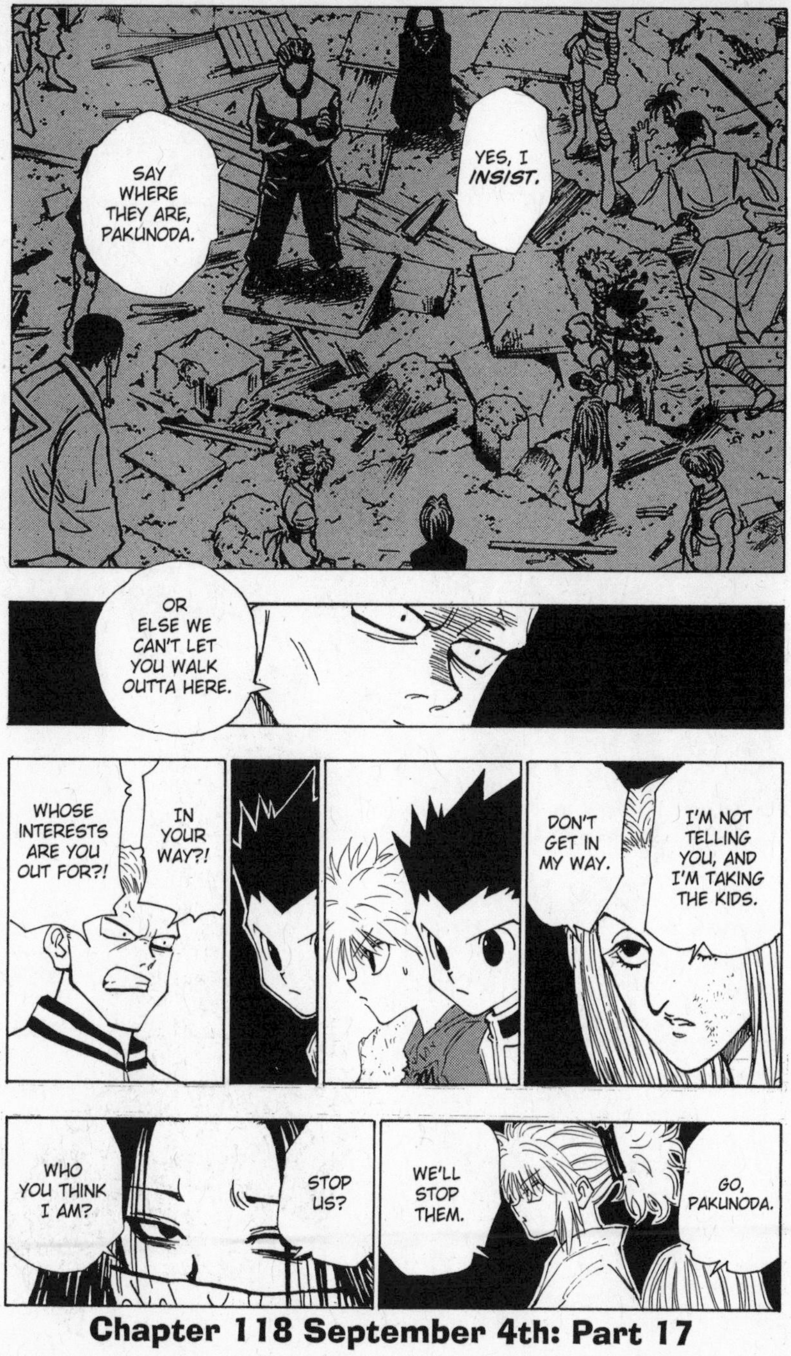
YES, I *INSIST.*
SAY WHERE THEY ARE, PAKUNODA.
OR ELSE WE CAN'T LET YOU WALK OUTTA HERE.
I'M NOT TELLING YOU, AND I'M TAKING THE KIDS.
DON'T GET IN MY WAY.
IN YOUR WAY?!
WHOSE INTERESTS ARE YOU OUT FOR?!
GO, PAKUNODA.
WE'LL STOP THEM.
STOP US?
WHO YOU THINK I AM?

Chapter 118 September 4th: Part 17

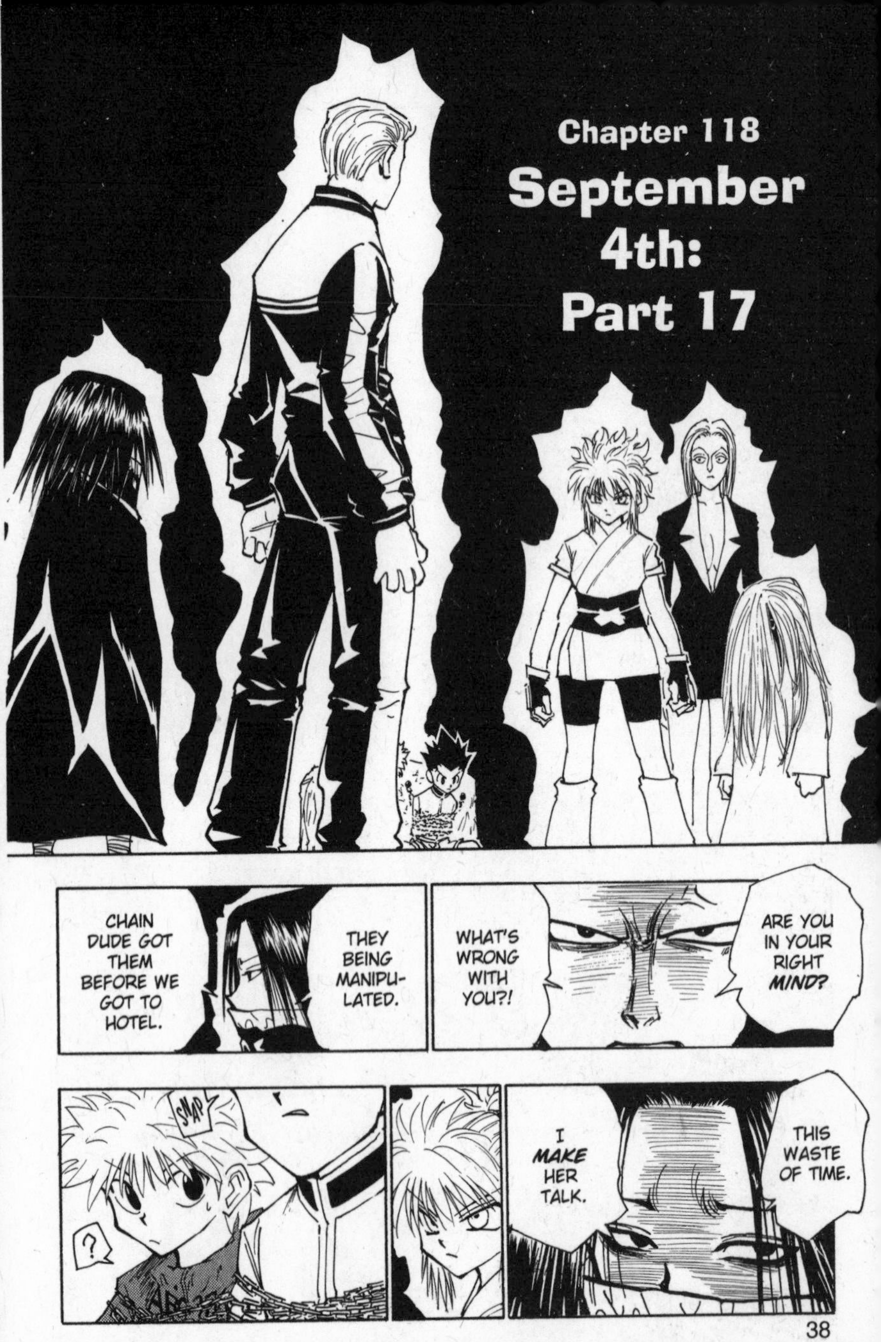
Chapter 118
September 4th: Part 17
ARE YOU IN YOUR RIGHT MIND?
WHAT'S WRONG WITH YOU?!
THEY BEING MANIPULATED.
CHAIN DUDE GOT THEM BEFORE WE GOT TO HOTEL.
THIS WASTE OF TIME.
I MAKE HER TALK.
SNAP
?

READ THIS WAY

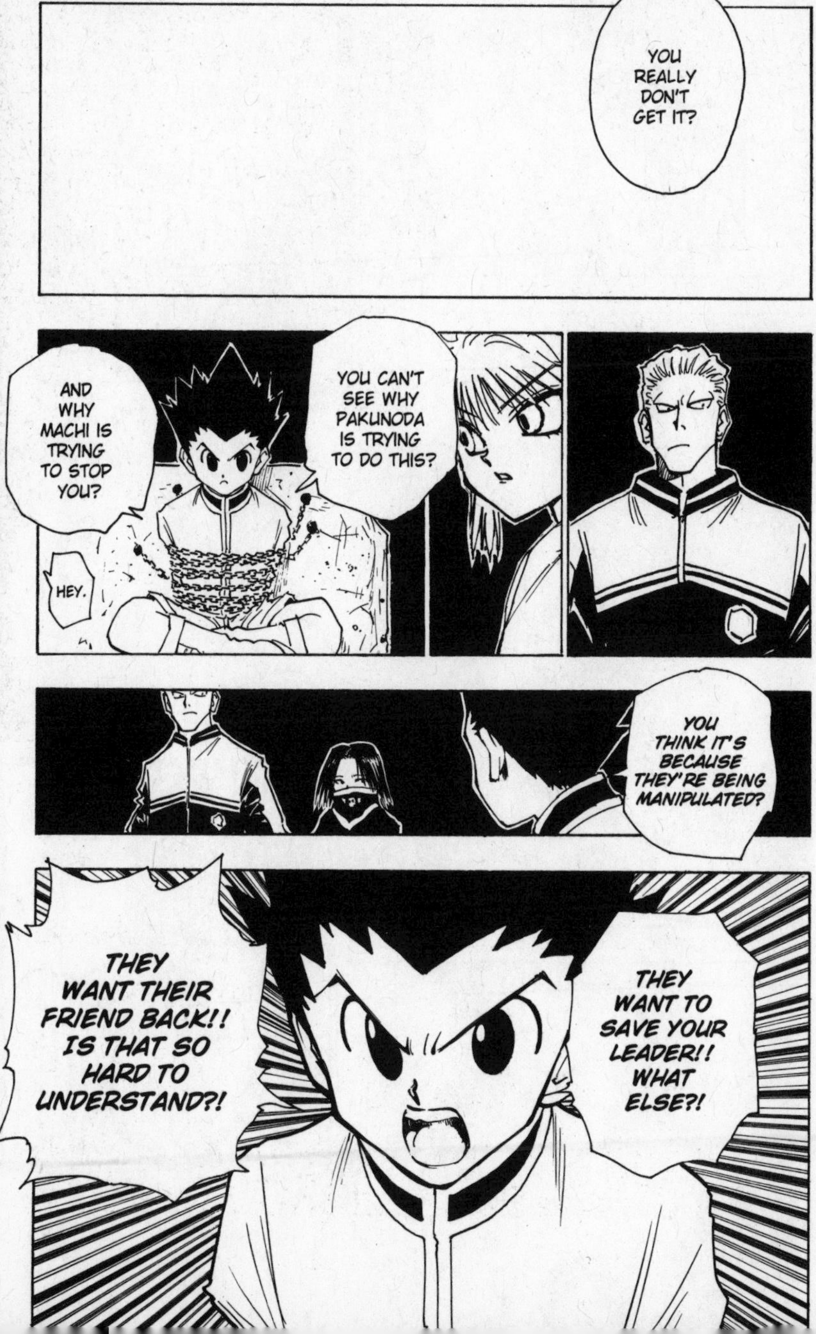
YOU REALLY DON'T GET IT?
YOU CAN'T SEE WHY PAKUNODA IS TRYING TO DO THIS?
AND WHY MACHI IS TRYING TO STOP YOU?
HEY.
YOU THINK IT'S BECAUSE THEY'RE BEING MANIPULATED?
THEY WANT TO SAVE YOUR LEADER!! WHAT ELSE?!
THEY WANT THEIR FRIEND BACK!! IS THAT SO HARD TO UNDERSTAND?!

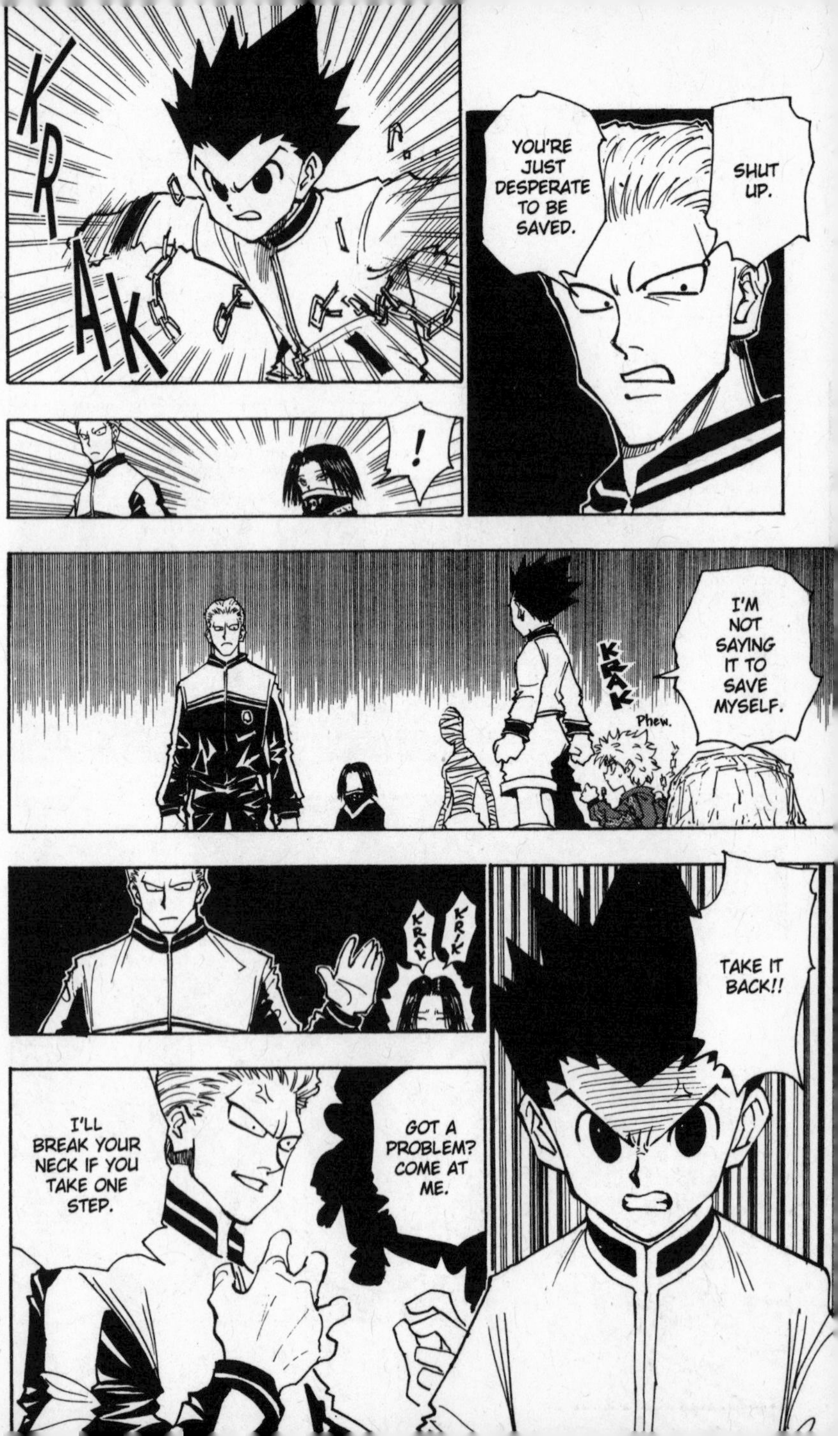
SHUT UP.
YOU'RE JUST DESPERATE TO BE SAVED.
KRAK
!
I'M NOT SAYING IT TO SAVE MYSELF.
KRAK
Phew.
TAKE IT BACK!!
KRIK
KRAK
GOT A PROBLEM? COME AT ME.
I'LL BREAK YOUR NECK IF YOU TAKE ONE STEP.

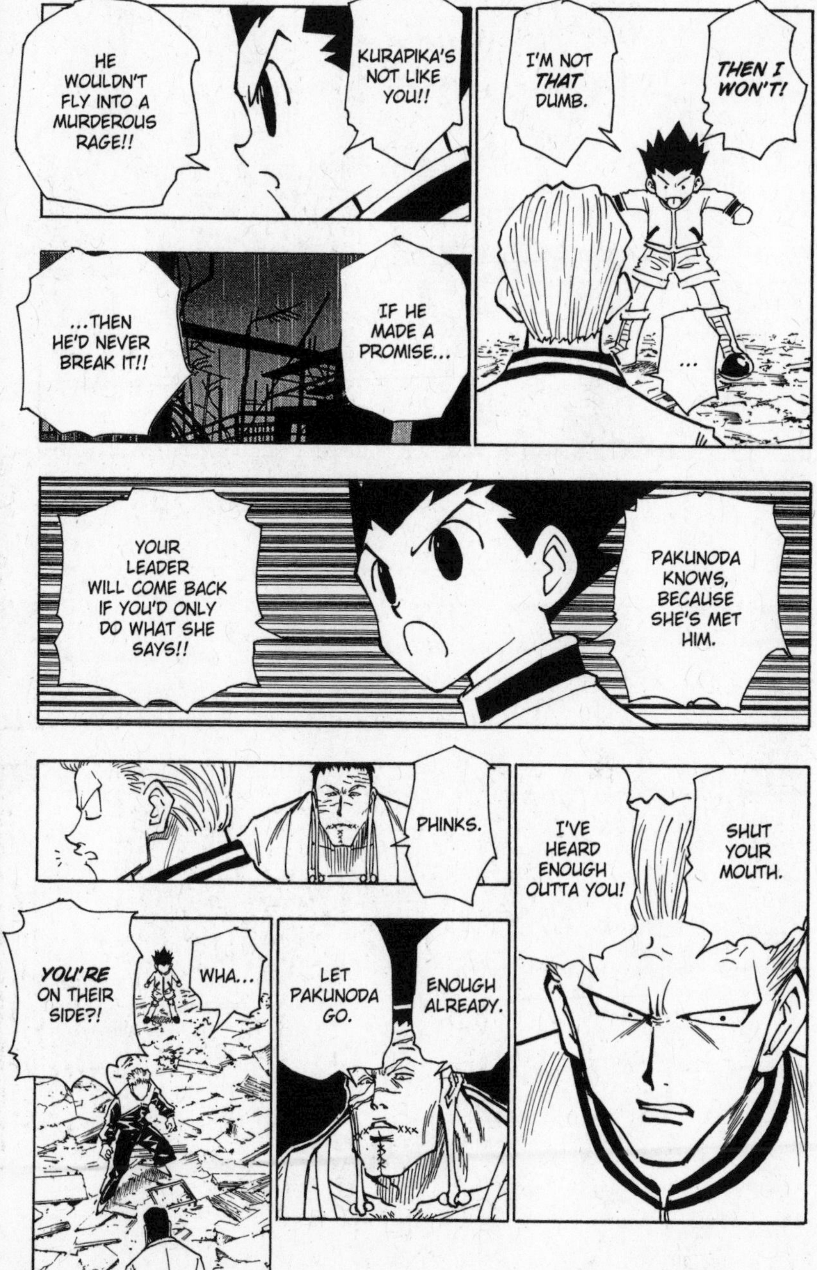

THEN I WON'T!
I'M NOT *THAT* DUMB.
...
KURAPIKA'S NOT LIKE YOU!!
HE WOULDN'T FLY INTO A MURDEROUS RAGE!!
IF HE MADE A PROMISE...
...THEN HE'D NEVER BREAK IT!!
PAKUNODA KNOWS, BECAUSE SHE'S MET HIM.
YOUR LEADER WILL COME BACK IF YOU'D ONLY DO WHAT SHE SAYS!!
SHUT YOUR MOUTH.
I'VE HEARD ENOUGH OUTTA YOU!
PHINKS.
ENOUGH ALREADY.
LET PAKUNODA GO.
WHA...
YOU'RE ON THEIR SIDE?!

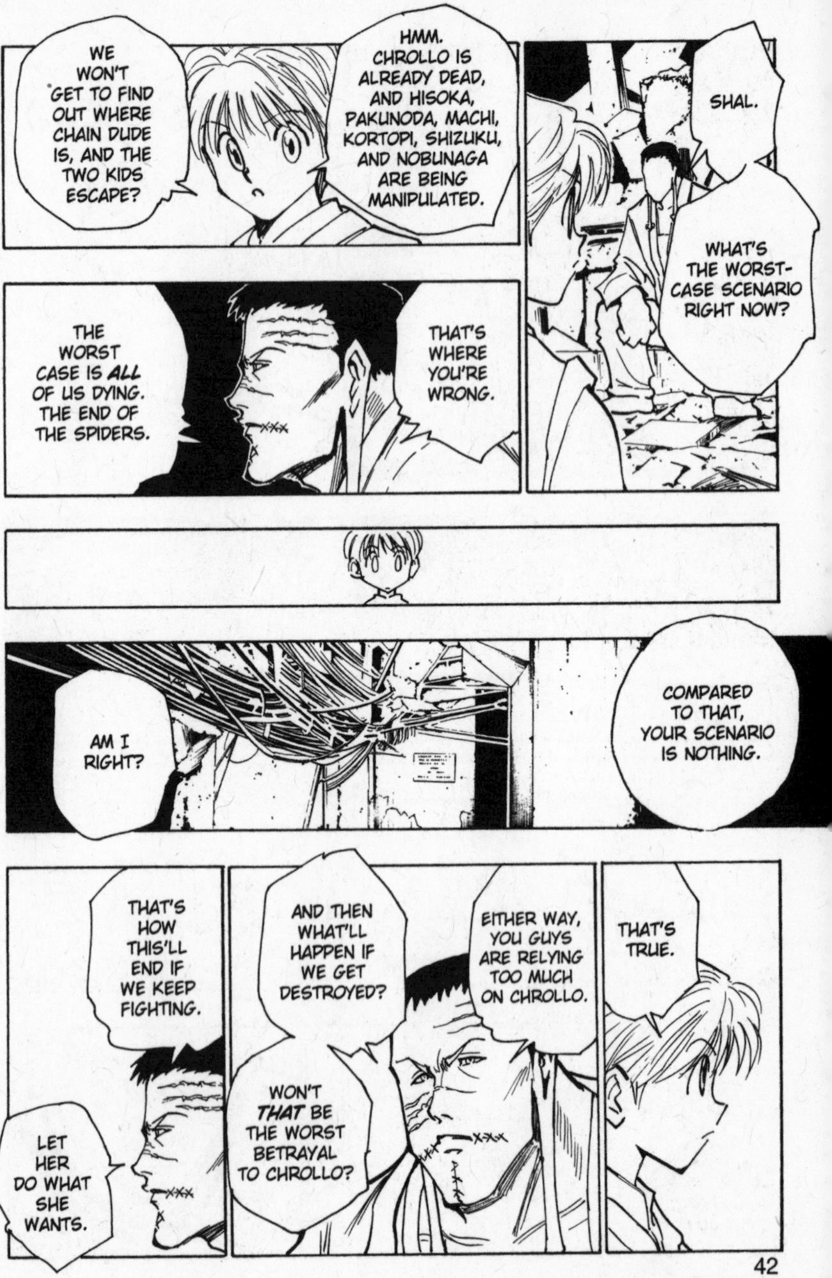
SHAL.
WHAT'S THE WORST-CASE SCENARIO RIGHT NOW?
HMM. CHROLLO IS ALREADY DEAD, AND HISOKA, PAKUNODA, MACHI, KORTOPI, SHIZUKU, AND NOBUNAGA ARE BEING MANIPULATED.
WE WON'T GET TO FIND OUT WHERE CHAIN DUDE IS, AND THE TWO KIDS ESCAPE?
THAT'S WHERE YOU'RE WRONG.
THE WORST CASE IS *ALL* OF US DYING. THE END OF THE SPIDERS.
COMPARED TO THAT, YOUR SCENARIO IS NOTHING.
AM I RIGHT?
THAT'S TRUE.
EITHER WAY, YOU GUYS ARE RELYING TOO MUCH ON CHROLLO.
AND THEN WHAT'LL HAPPEN IF WE GET DESTROYED?
WON'T *THAT* BE THE WORST BETRAYAL TO CHROLLO?
THAT'S HOW THIS'LL END IF WE KEEP FIGHTING.
LET HER DO WHAT SHE WANTS.

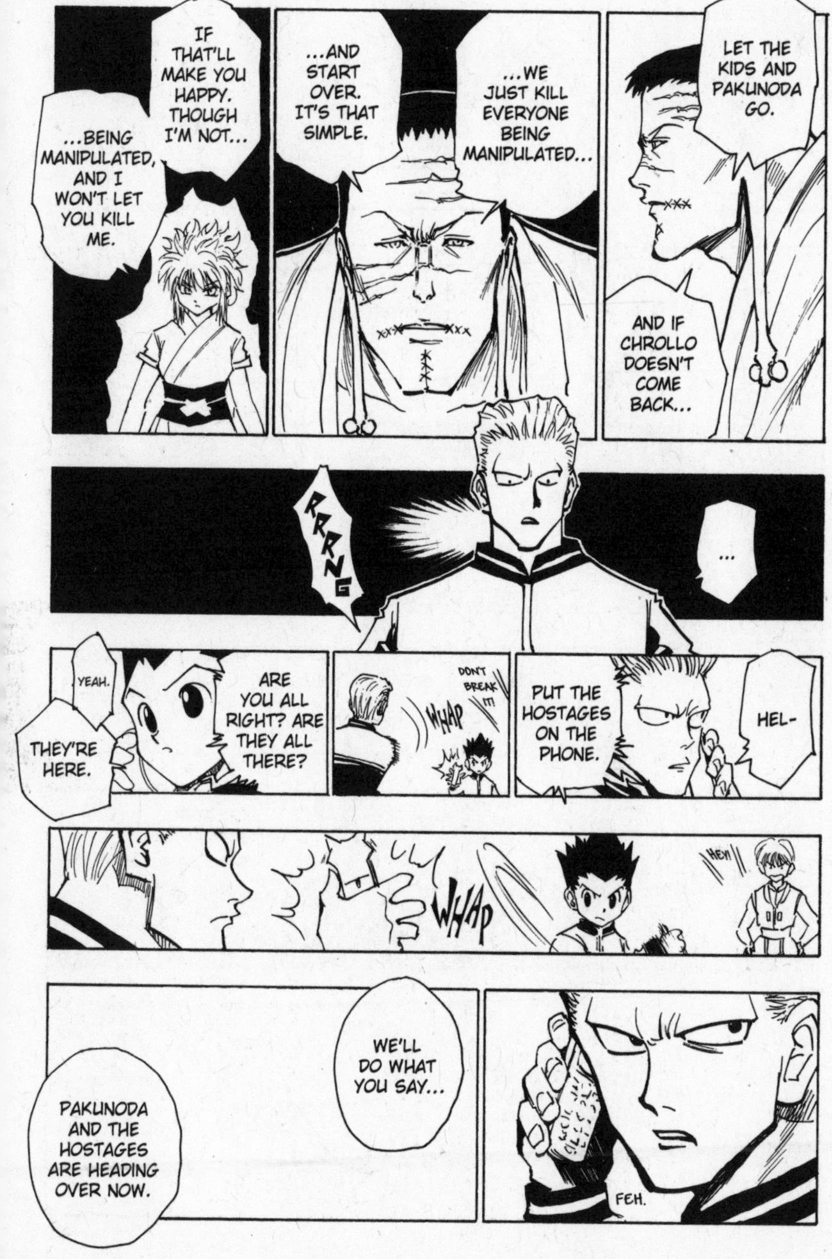
LET THE KIDS AND PAKUNODA GO.
AND IF CHROLLO DOESN'T COME BACK...
...WE JUST KILL EVERYONE BEING MANIPULATED...
...AND START OVER. IT'S THAT SIMPLE.
IF THAT'LL MAKE YOU HAPPY. THOUGH I'M NOT...
...BEING MANIPULATED, AND I WON'T LET YOU KILL ME.
...
RRRNG
HEL-
PUT THE HOSTAGES ON THE PHONE.
DON'T BREAK IT!
WHAP
ARE YOU ALL RIGHT? ARE THEY ALL THERE?
YEAH.
THEY'RE HERE.
HEY!
WHAP
FEH.
WE'LL DO WHAT YOU SAY...
PAKUNODA AND THE HOSTAGES ARE HEADING OVER NOW.

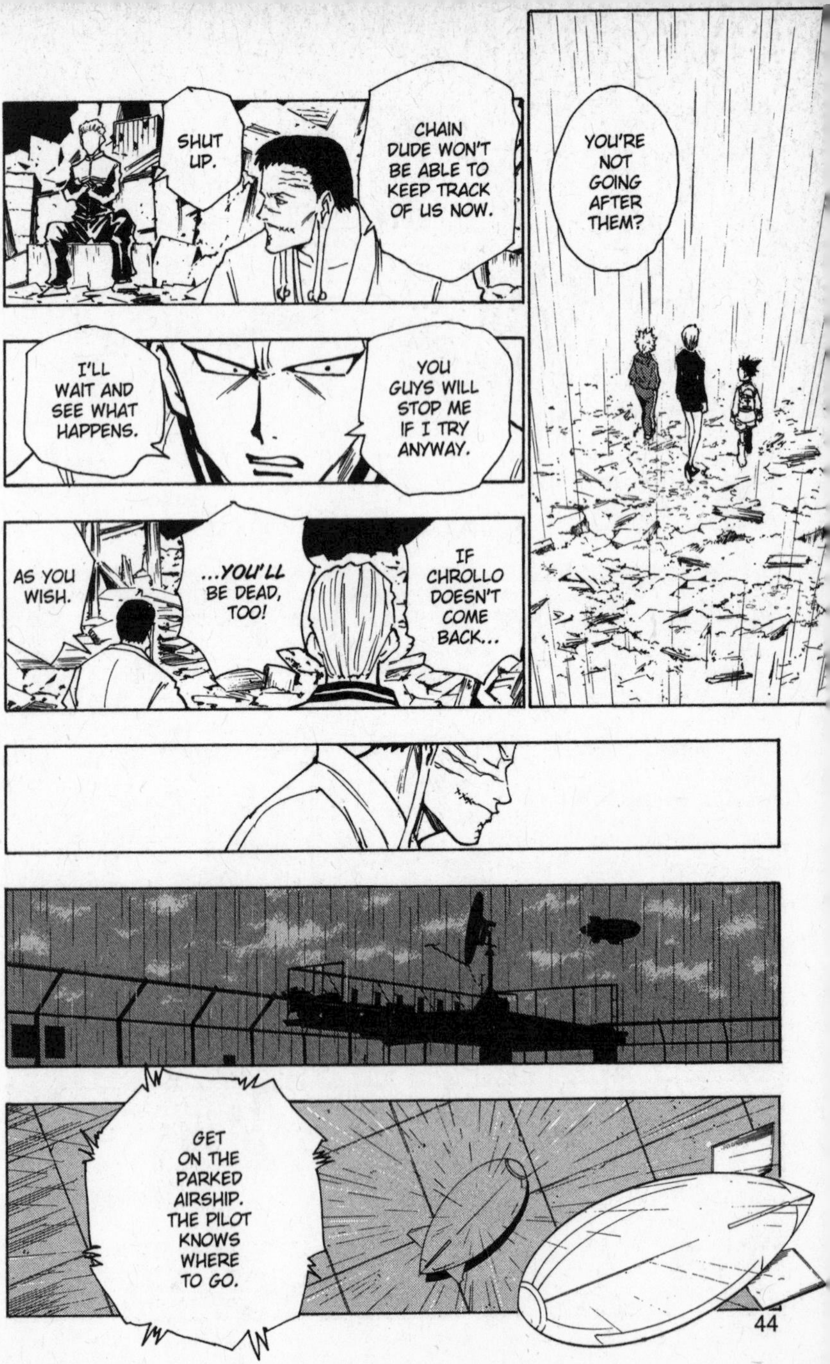
YOU'RE NOT GOING AFTER THEM?
CHAIN DUDE WON'T BE ABLE TO KEEP TRACK OF US NOW.
SHUT UP.
YOU GUYS WILL STOP ME IF I TRY ANYWAY.
I'LL WAIT AND SEE WHAT HAPPENS.
IF CHROLLO DOESN'T COME BACK...
...*YOU'LL* BE DEAD, TOO!
AS YOU WISH.
GET ON THE PARKED AIRSHIP. THE PILOT KNOWS WHERE TO GO.

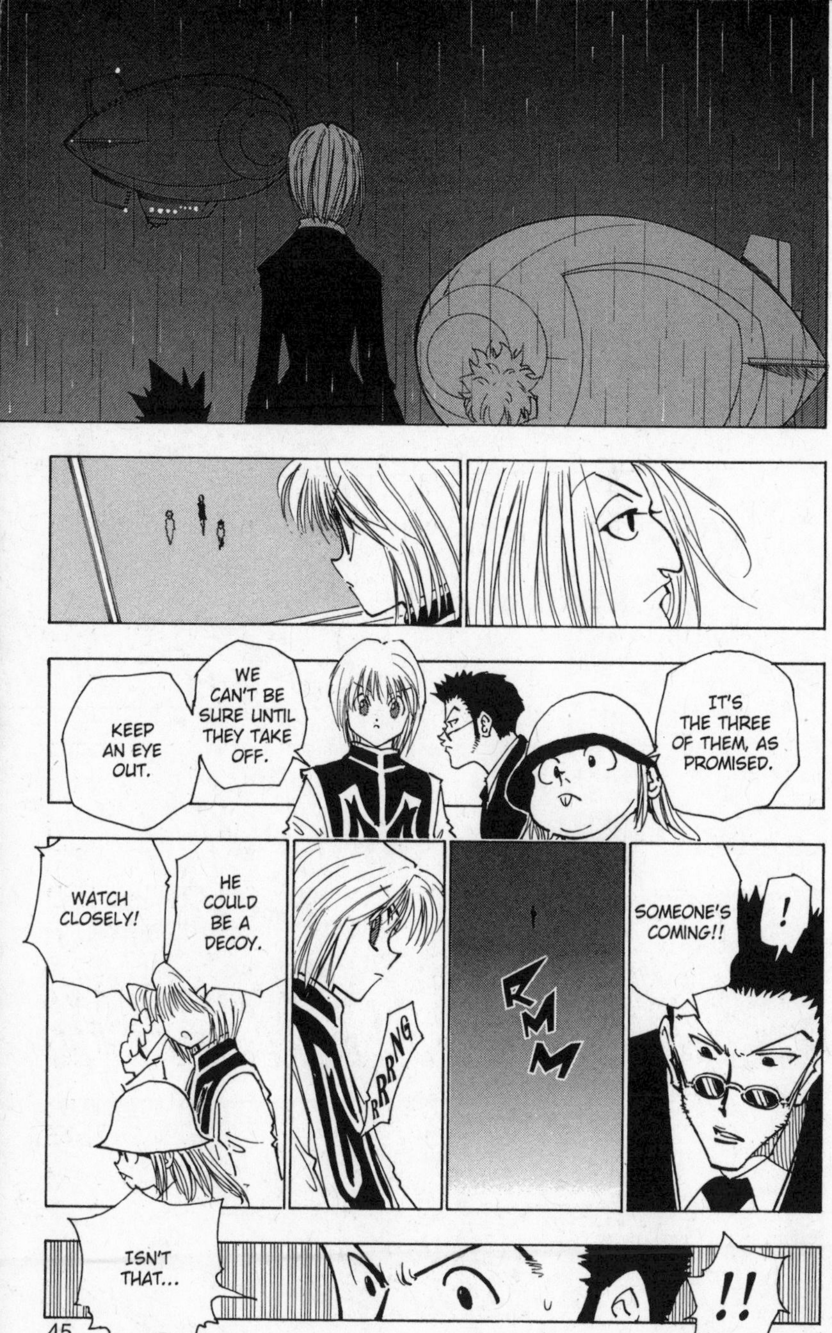
IT'S THE THREE OF THEM, AS PROMISED.
WE CAN'T BE SURE UNTIL THEY TAKE OFF.
KEEP AN EYE OUT.
!
SOMEONE'S COMING!!
RMM
RRRNG
HE COULD BE A DECOY.
WATCH CLOSELY!
!!
ISN'T THAT...

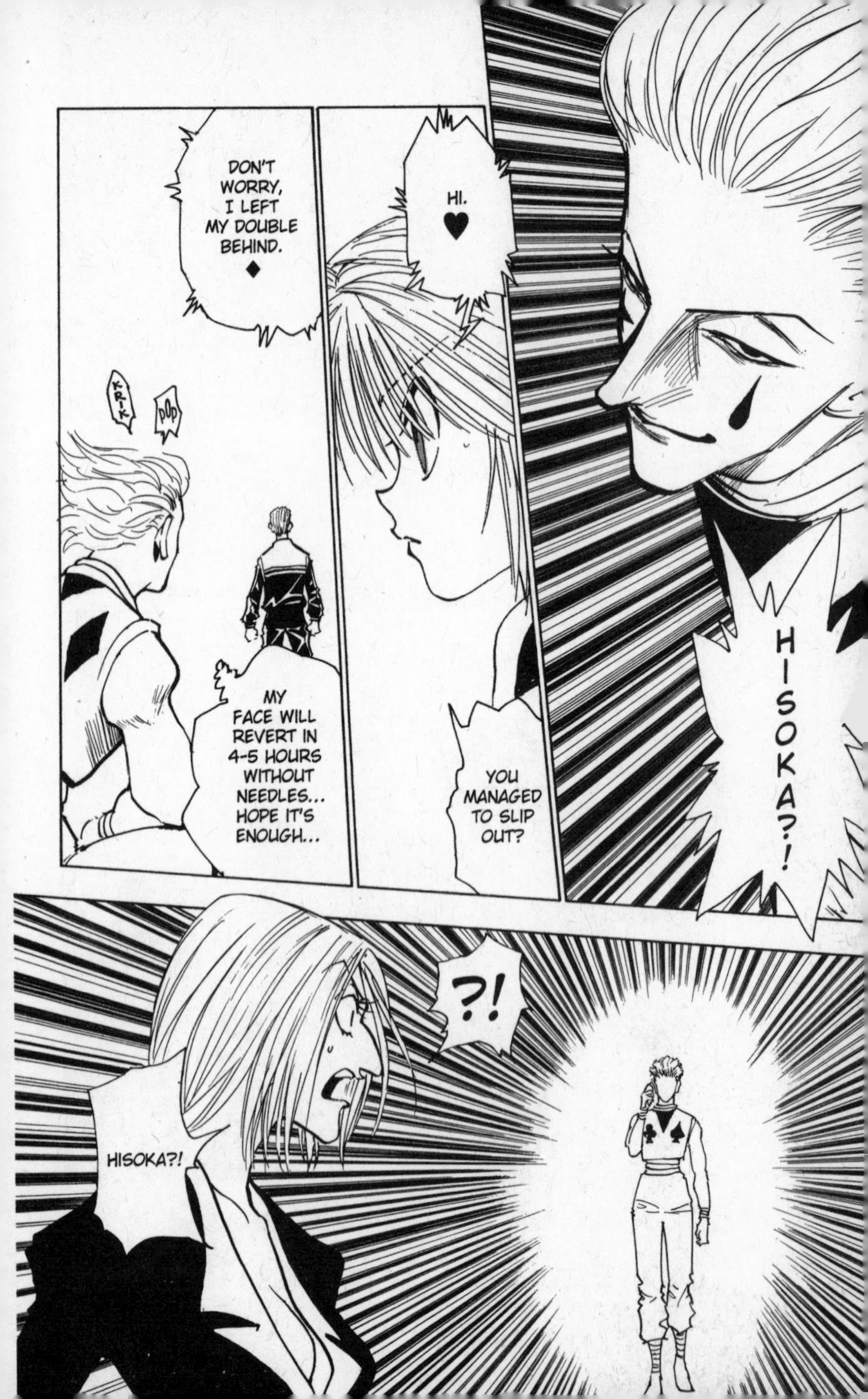
HISOKA?!
HI. ♥
YOU MANAGED TO SLIP OUT?
DON'T WORRY, I LEFT MY DOUBLE BEHIND. ♦
KRIK
POP
MY FACE WILL REVERT IN 4-5 HOURS WITHOUT NEEDLES... HOPE IT'S ENOUGH...
?!
HISOKA?!

READ THIS WAY

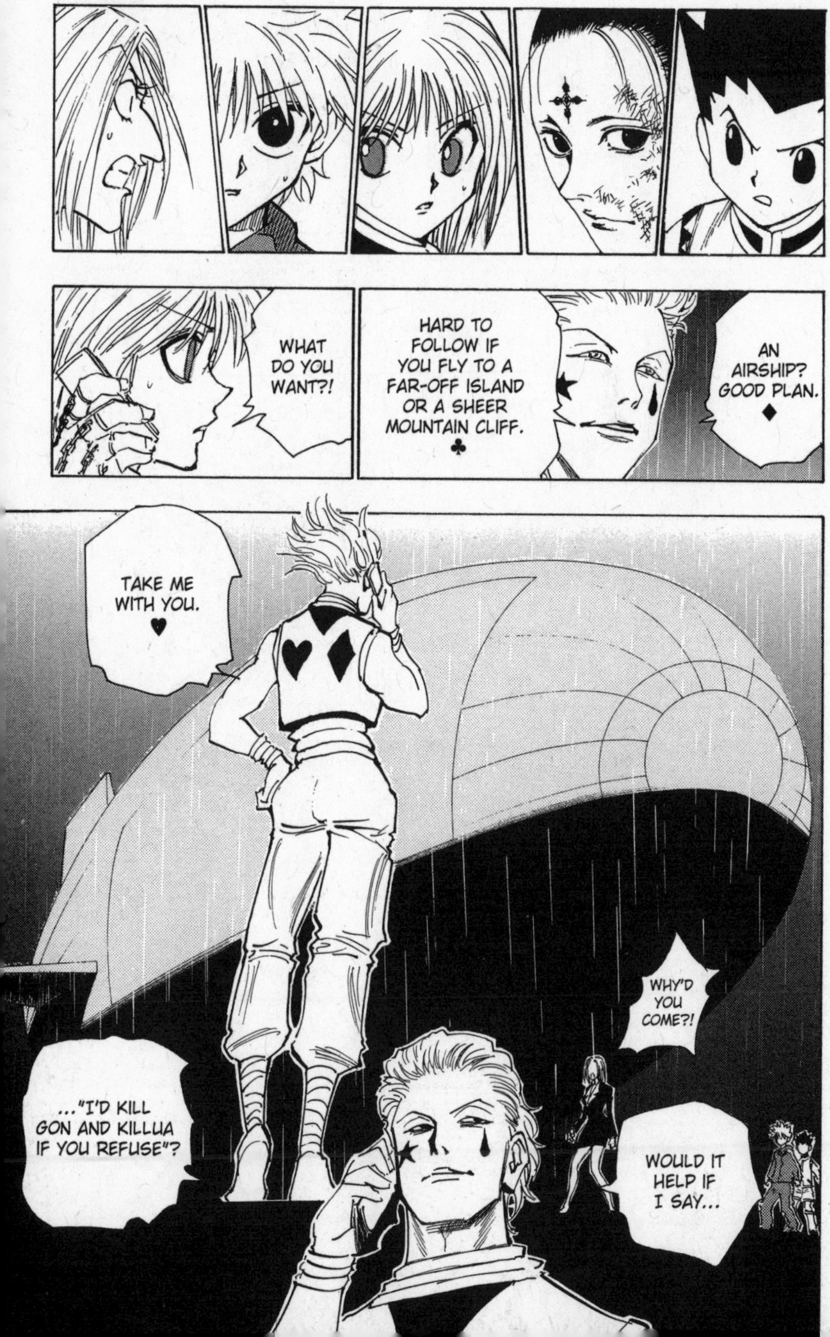
AN AIRSHIP? GOOD PLAN. ♦
HARD TO FOLLOW IF YOU FLY TO A FAR-OFF ISLAND OR A SHEER MOUNTAIN CLIFF. ♣
WHAT DO YOU WANT?!
TAKE ME WITH YOU. ♥
WHY'D YOU COME?!
WOULD IT HELP IF I SAY...
..."I'D KILL GON AND KILLUA IF YOU REFUSE"?

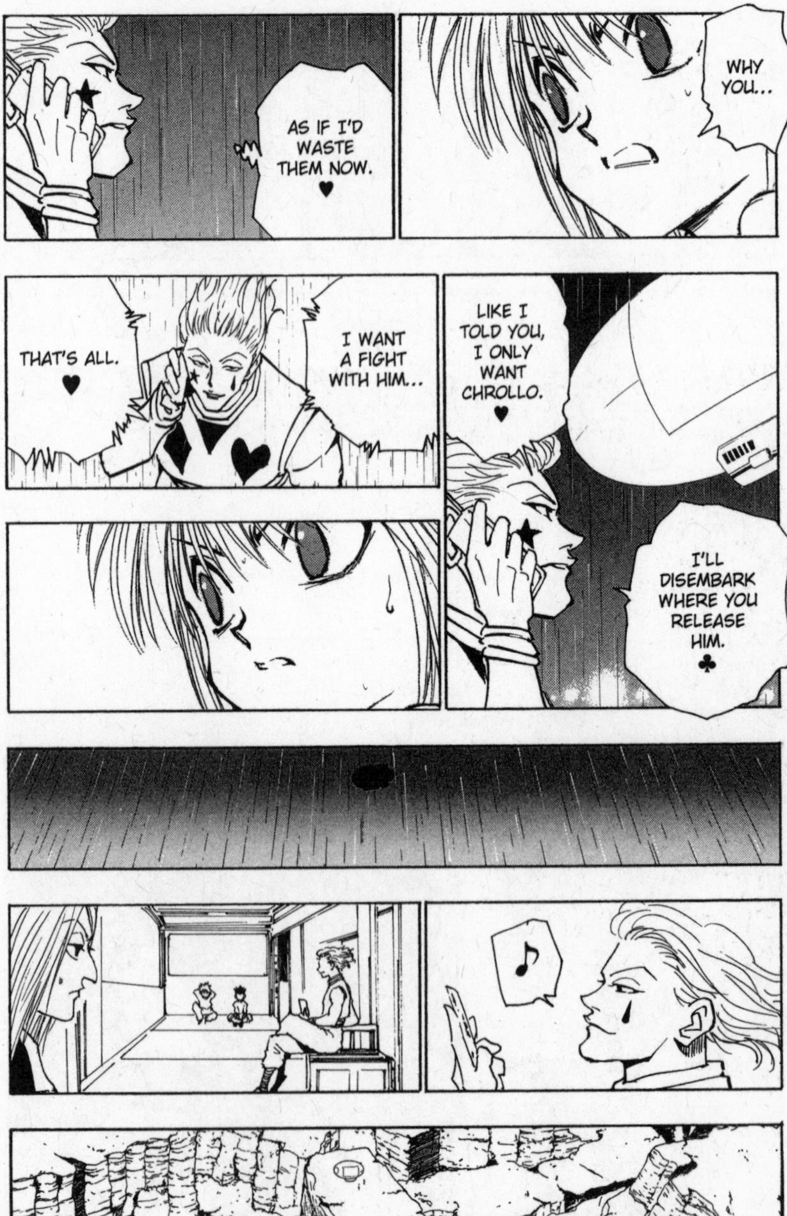
WHY YOU...
AS IF I'D WASTE THEM NOW. ♥
LIKE I TOLD YOU, I ONLY WANT CHROLLO. ♥
I'LL DISEMBARK WHERE YOU RELEASE HIM. ♣
I WANT A FIGHT WITH HIM...
THAT'S ALL. ♥
♪

READ THIS WAY

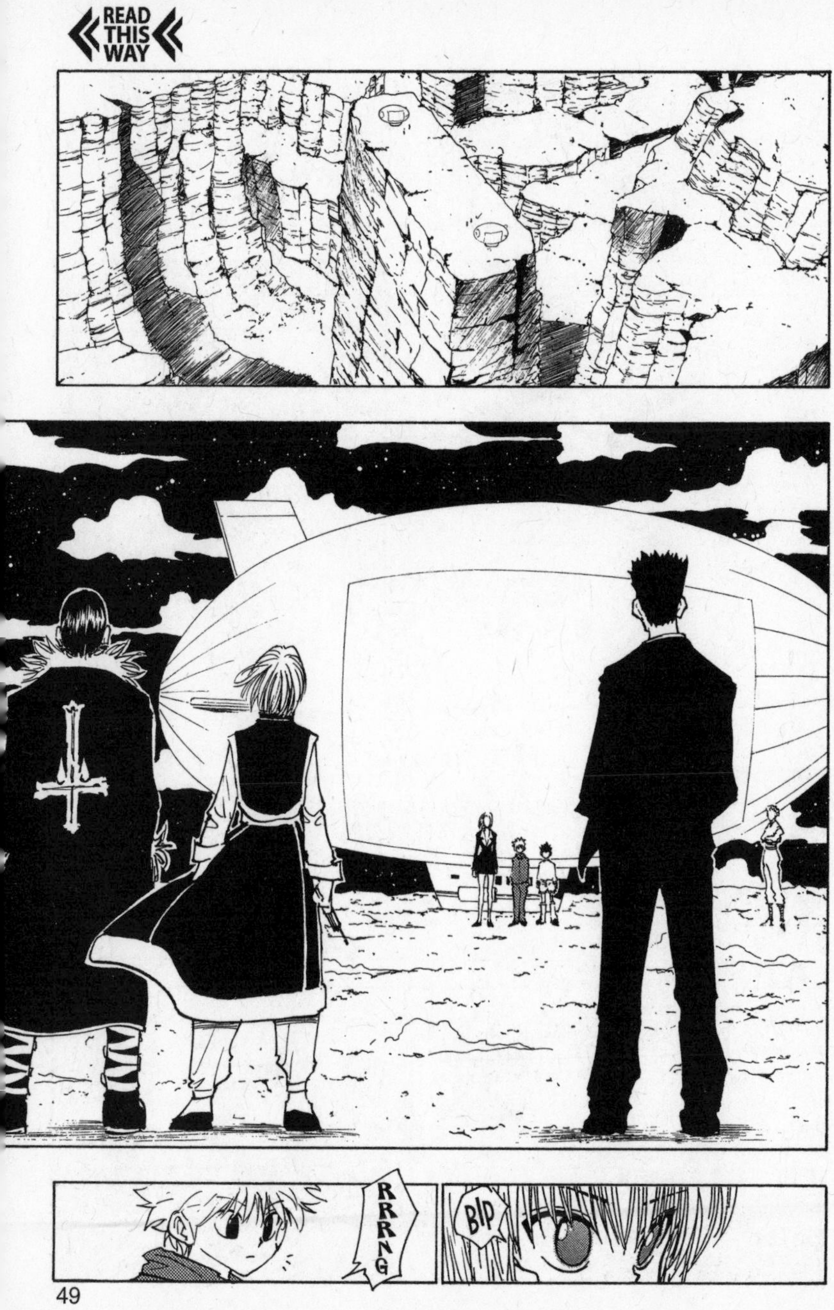
BIP
RRRNG

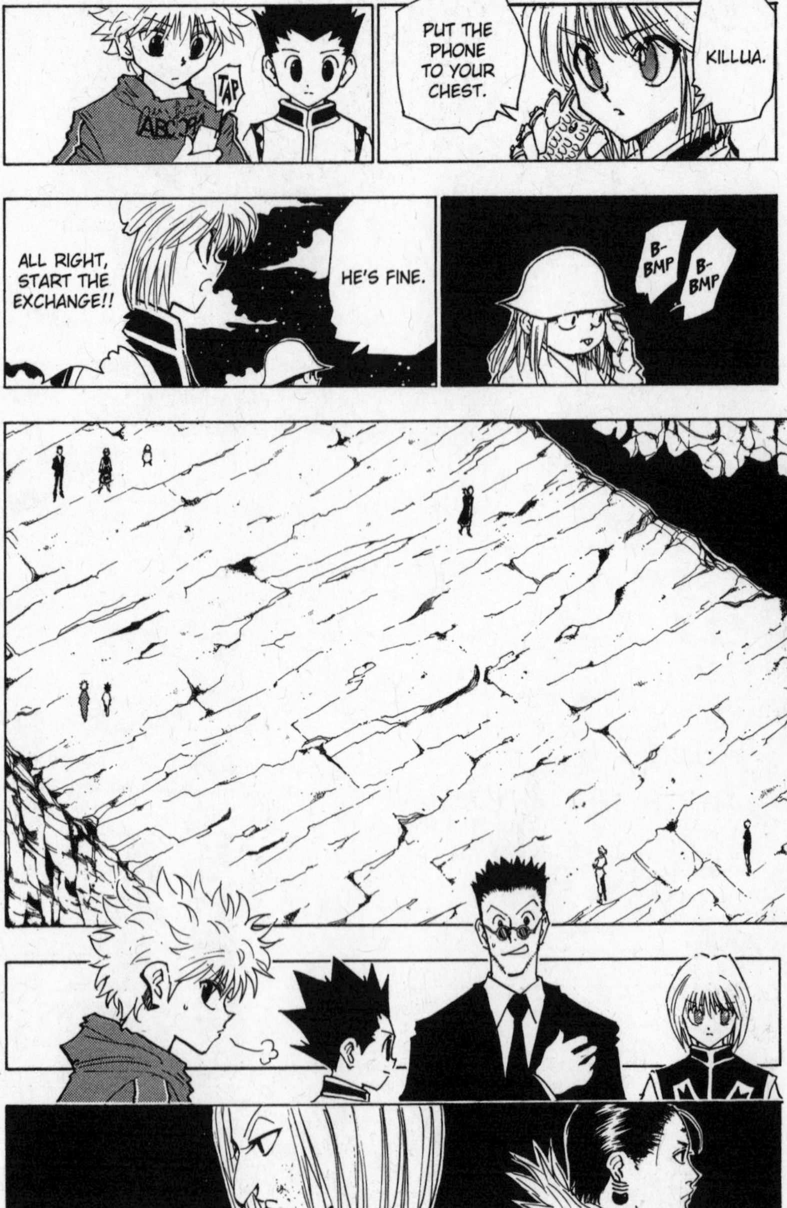
KILLUA.
PUT THE PHONE TO YOUR CHEST.
TAP
B-BMP
B-BMP
HE'S FINE.
ALL RIGHT, START THE EXCHANGE!!

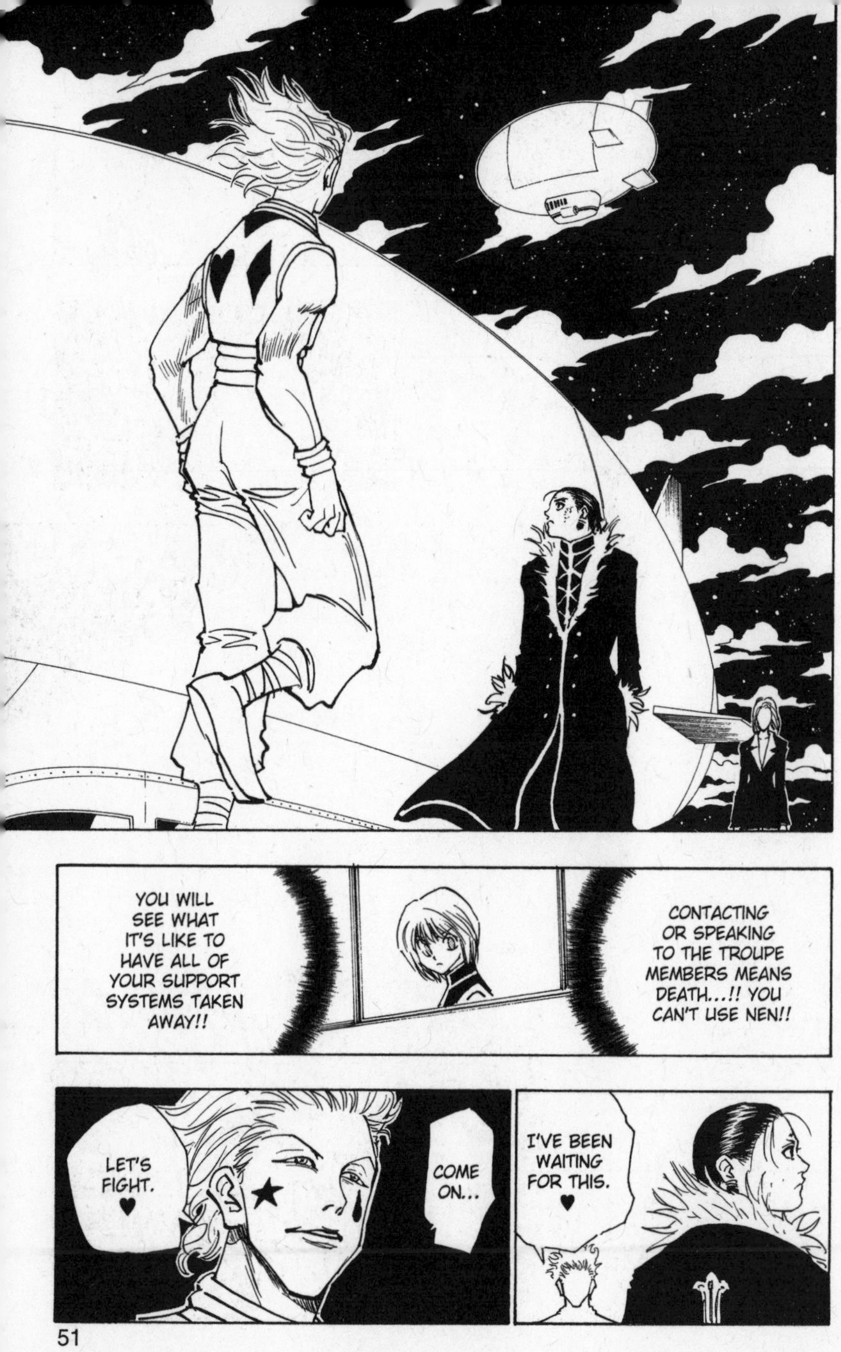
CONTACTING OR SPEAKING TO THE TROUPE MEMBERS MEANS DEATH...!! YOU CAN'T USE NEN!!
YOU WILL SEE WHAT IT'S LIKE TO HAVE ALL OF YOUR SUPPORT SYSTEMS TAKEN AWAY!!
I'VE BEEN WAITING FOR THIS. ♥
COME ON...
LET'S FIGHT. ♥

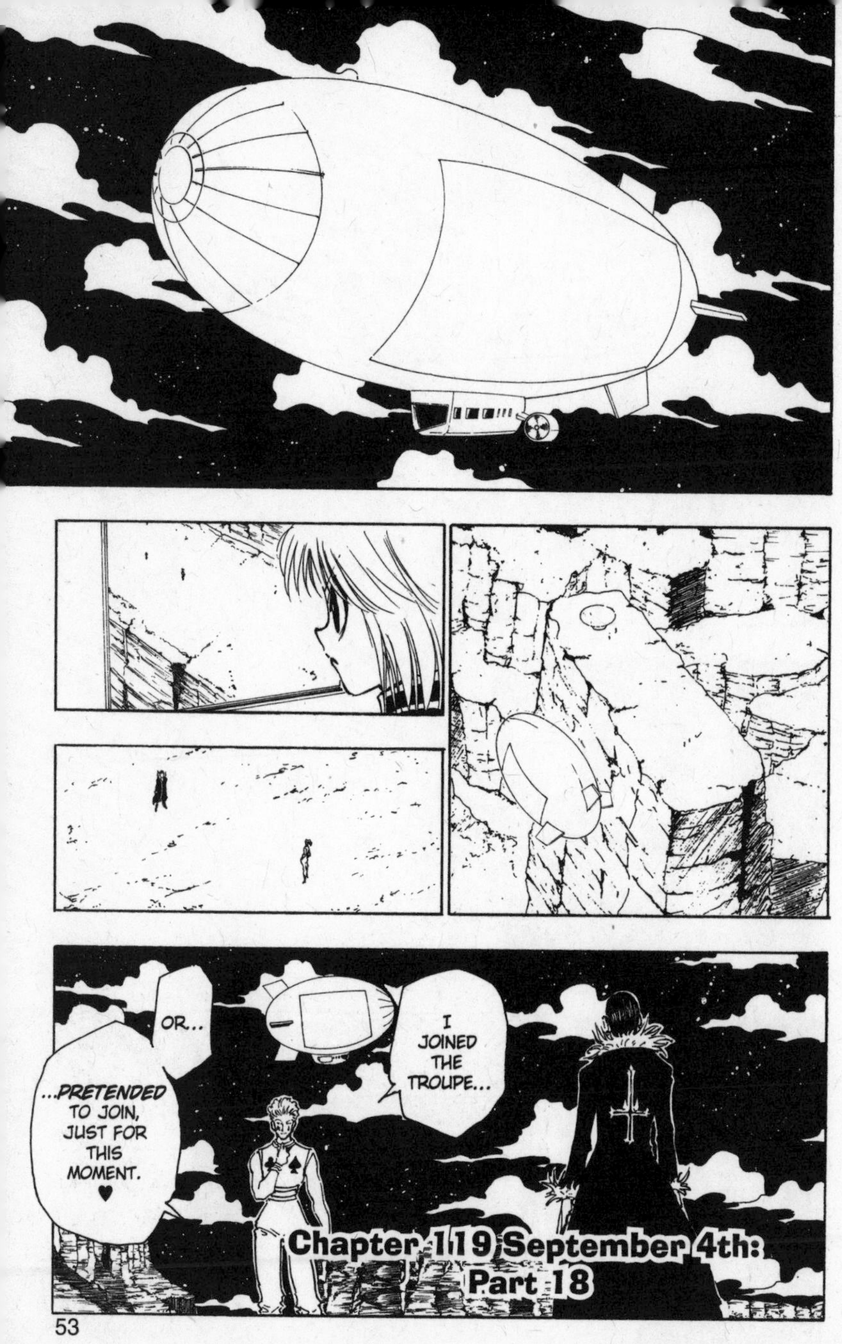
I JOINED THE TROUPE...
OR...
...PRETENDED TO JOIN, JUST FOR THIS MOMENT. ♥
Chapter 119 September 4th: Part 18

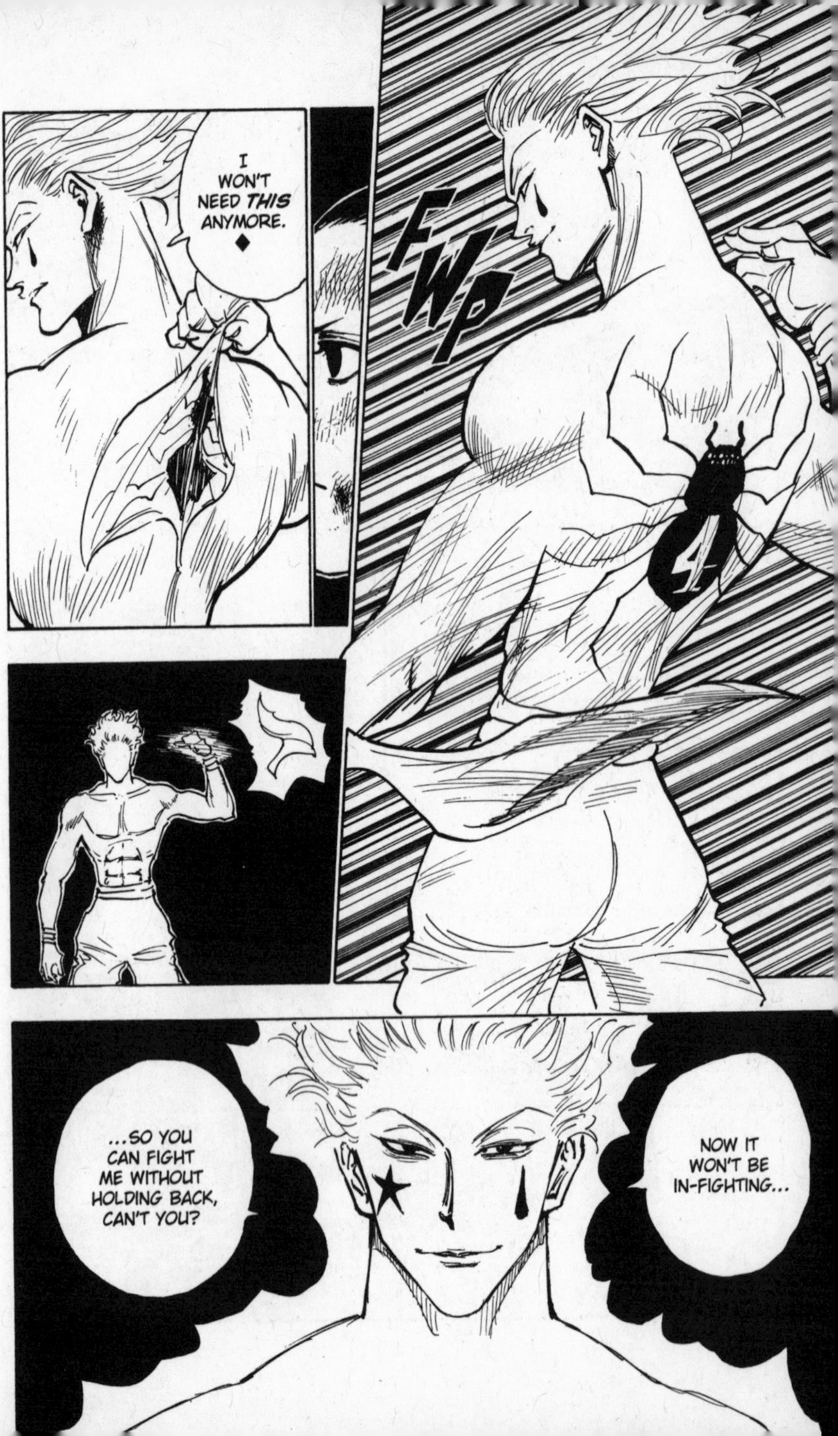
FWP
I WON'T NEED *THIS* ANYMORE. ◆
NOW IT WON'T BE IN-FIGHTING...
...SO YOU CAN FIGHT ME WITHOUT HOLDING BACK, CAN'T YOU?

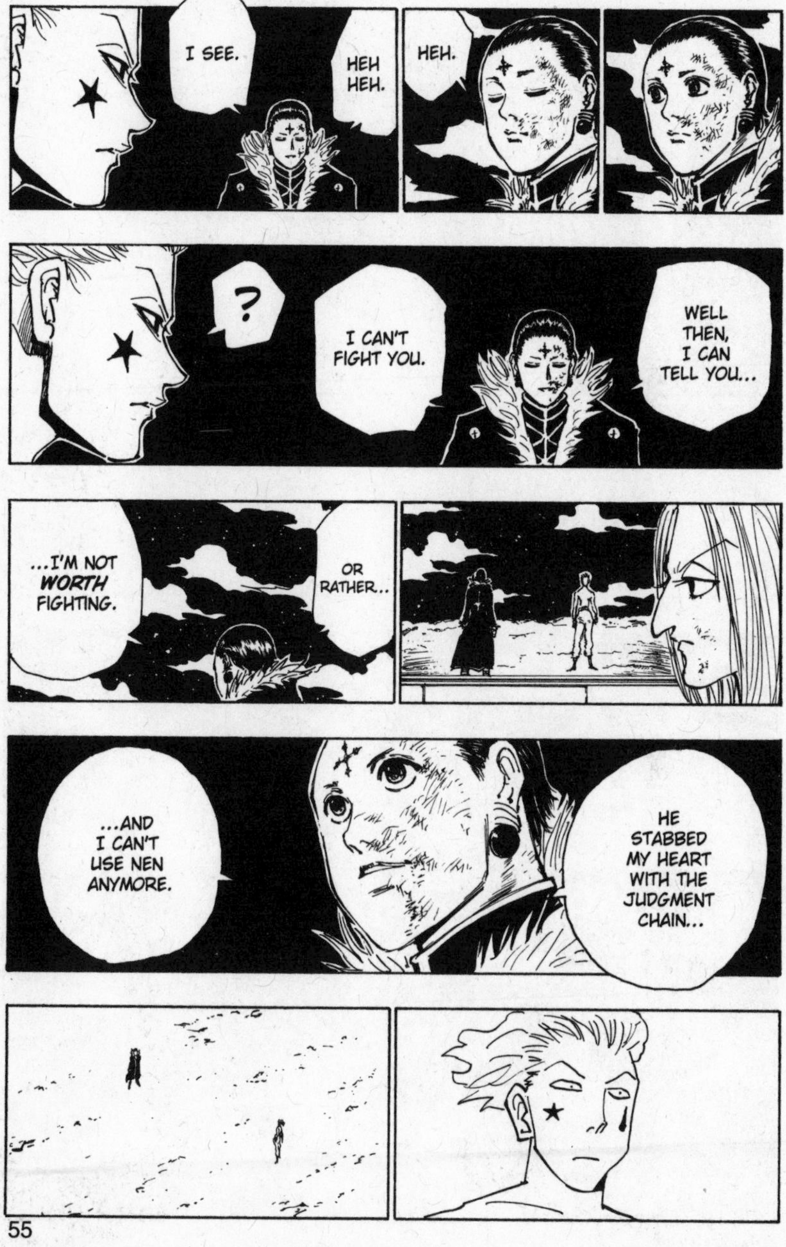
HEH.
HEH HEH.
I SEE.
WELL THEN, I CAN TELL YOU...
I CAN'T FIGHT YOU.
?
OR RATHER...
...I'M NOT *WORTH* FIGHTING.
HE STABBED MY HEART WITH THE JUDGMENT CHAIN...
...AND I CAN'T USE NEN ANYMORE.

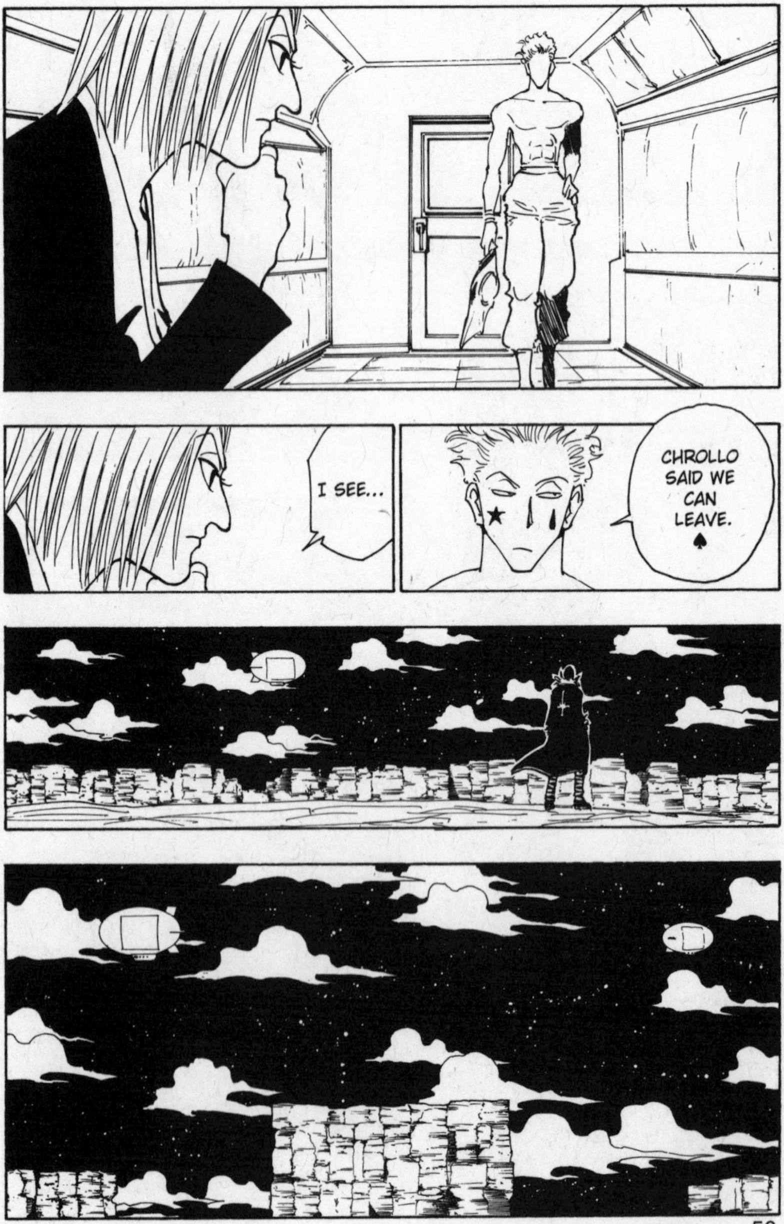
CHROLLO SAID WE CAN LEAVE.
I SEE...

READ THIS WAY

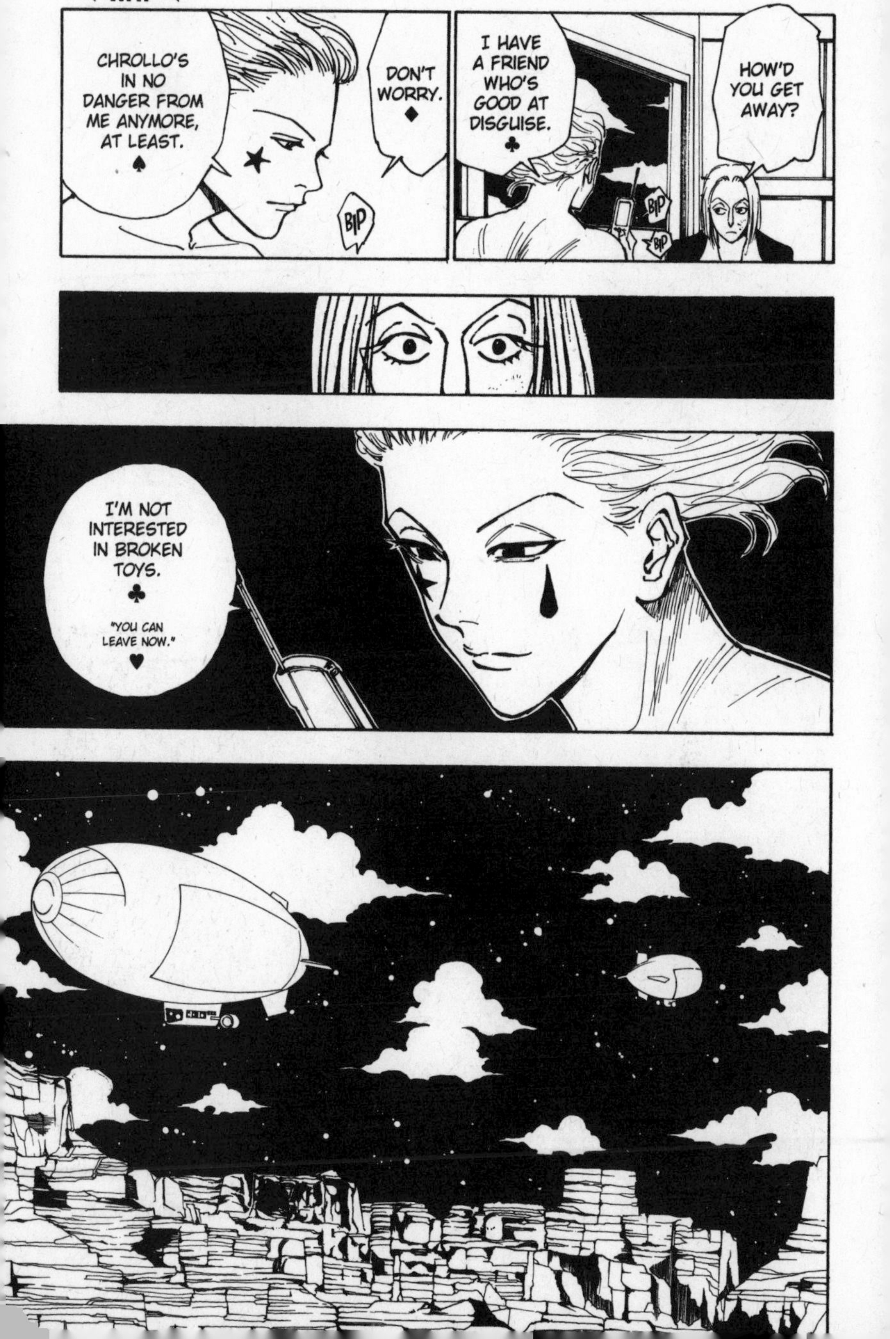
HOW'D YOU GET AWAY?
I HAVE A FRIEND WHO'S GOOD AT DISGUISE. ♣
BIP
BIP
DON'T WORRY. ♦
CHROLLO'S IN NO DANGER FROM ME ANYMORE, AT LEAST. ♠
BIP
I'M NOT INTERESTED IN BROKEN TOYS. ♣
"YOU CAN LEAVE NOW." ♥

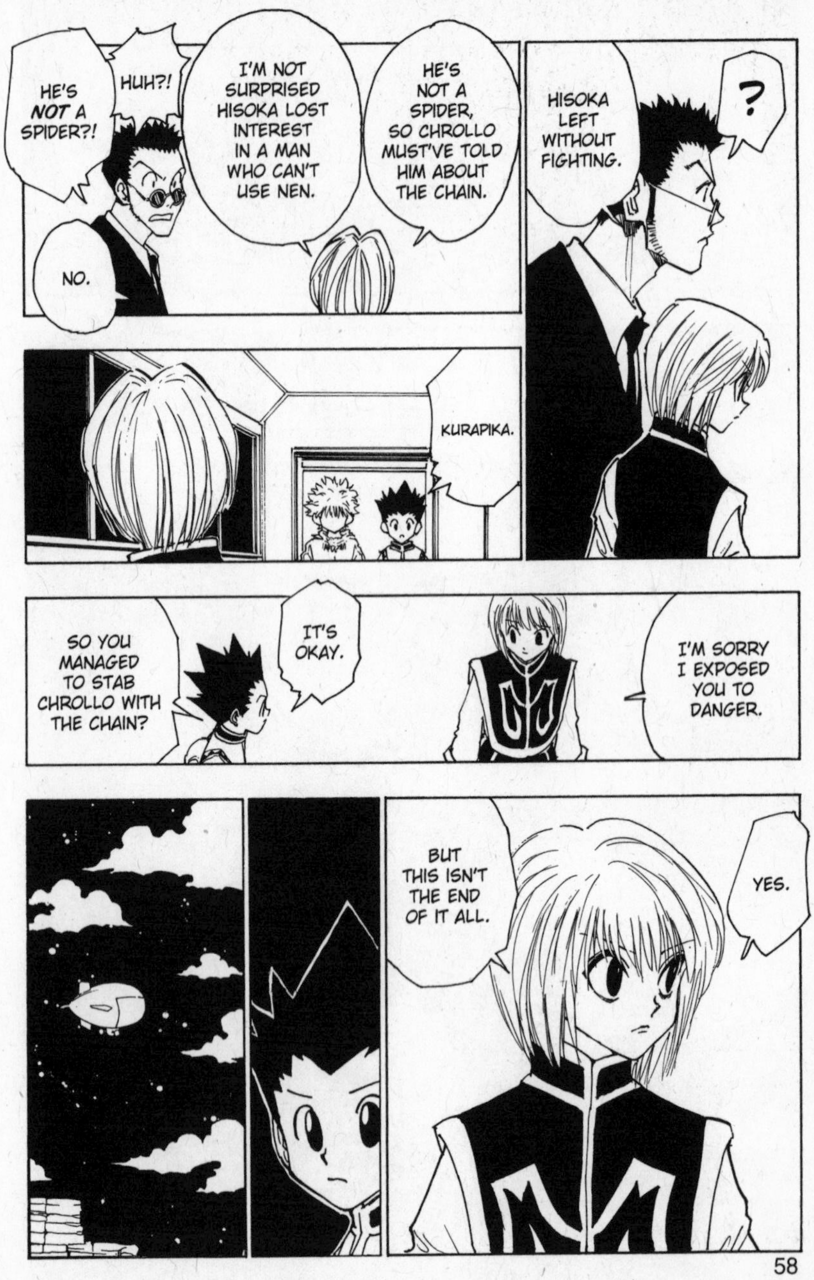
?
HISOKA LEFT WITHOUT FIGHTING.
HE'S NOT A SPIDER, SO CHROLLO MUST'VE TOLD HIM ABOUT THE CHAIN.
I'M NOT SURPRISED HISOKA LOST INTEREST IN A MAN WHO CAN'T USE NEN.
HUH?!
HE'S *NOT* A SPIDER?!
NO.
KURAPIKA.
I'M SORRY I EXPOSED YOU TO DANGER.
IT'S OKAY.
SO YOU MANAGED TO STAB CHROLLO WITH THE CHAIN?
YES.
BUT THIS ISN'T THE END OF IT ALL.

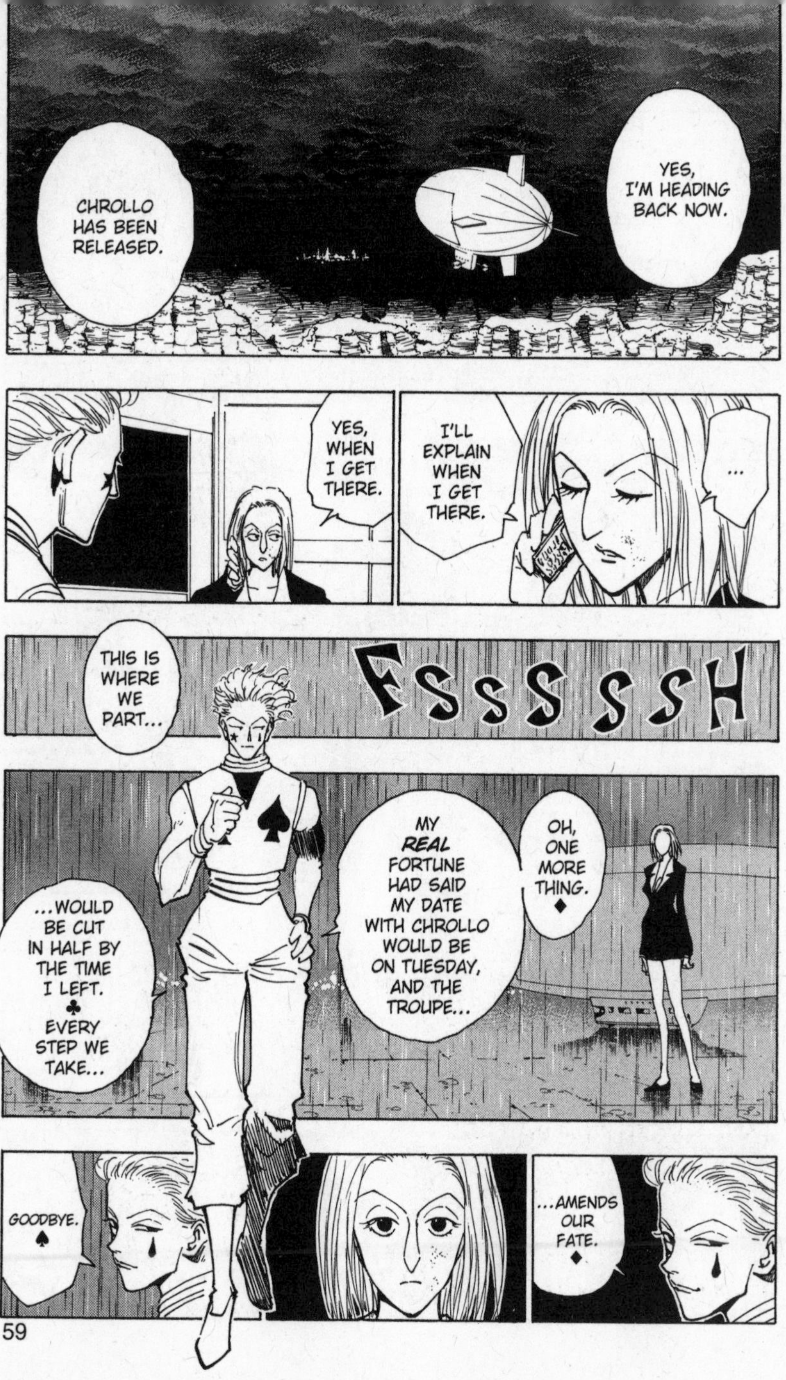
YES, I'M HEADING BACK NOW.
CHROLLO HAS BEEN RELEASED.
...
I'LL EXPLAIN WHEN I GET THERE.
YES, WHEN I GET THERE.
FSSSSSH
THIS IS WHERE WE PART...
OH, ONE MORE THING. ♦
MY *REAL* FORTUNE HAD SAID MY DATE WITH CHROLLO WOULD BE ON TUESDAY, AND THE TROUPE...
...WOULD BE CUT IN HALF BY THE TIME I LEFT. ♣ EVERY STEP WE TAKE...
...AMENDS OUR FATE. ♦
GOODBYE. ♠

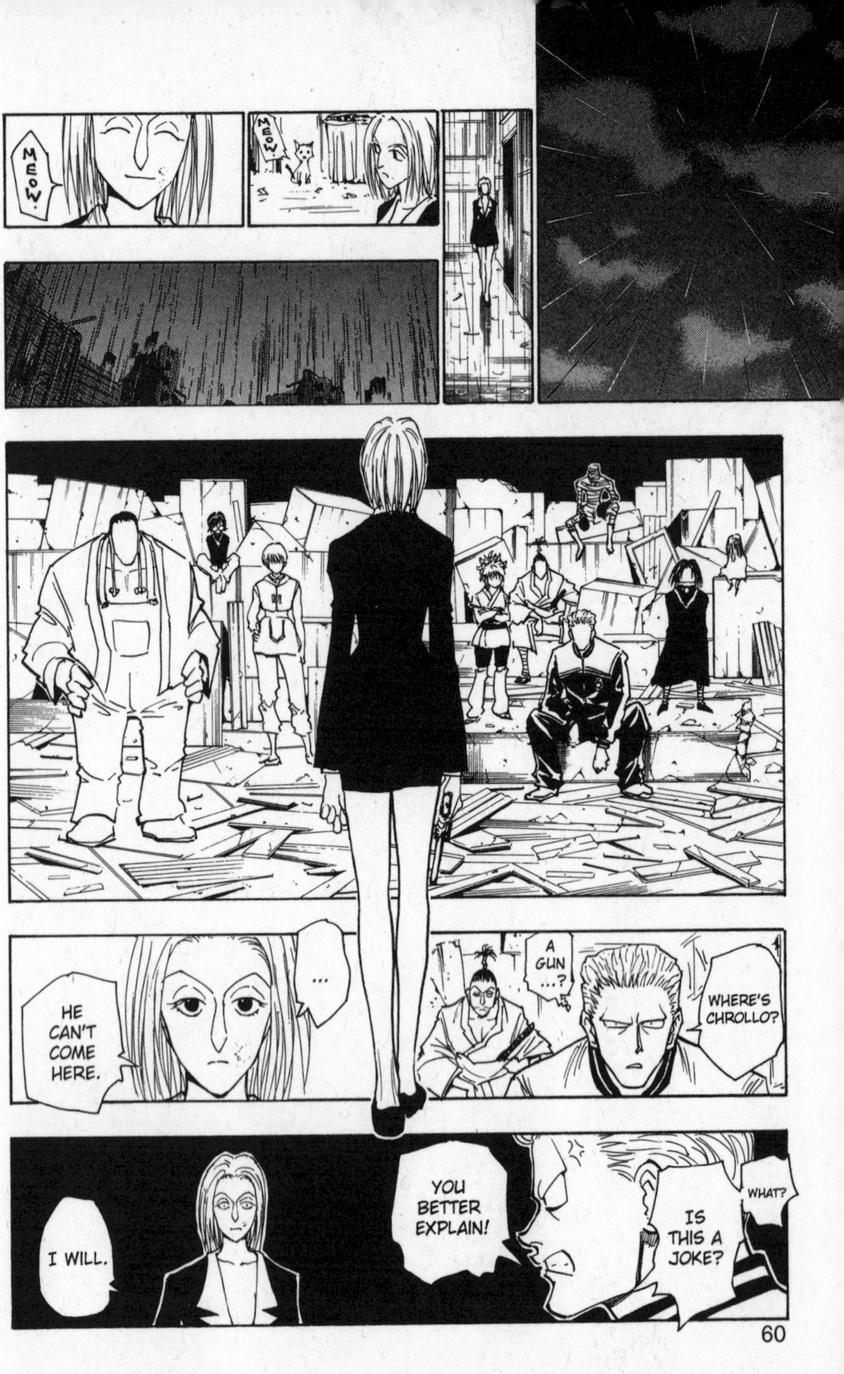
MEOW.
MEOW.
WHERE'S CHROLLO?
A GUN ...?
...
HE CAN'T COME HERE.
WHAT?
IS THIS A JOKE?
YOU BETTER EXPLAIN!
I WILL.

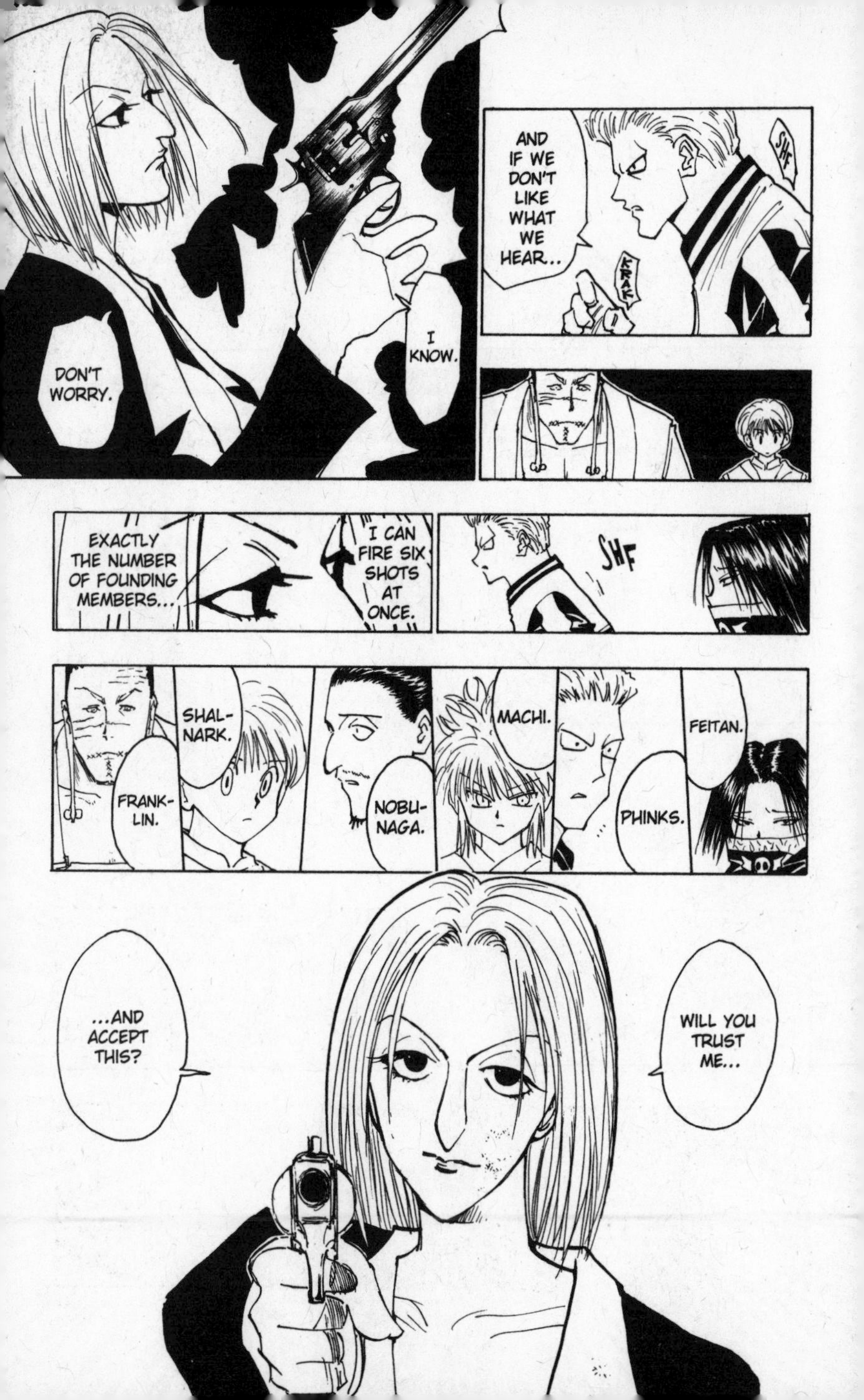
AND IF WE DON'T LIKE WHAT WE HEAR...
SHF
KRAK
I KNOW.
DON'T WORRY.
SHF
I CAN FIRE SIX SHOTS AT ONCE.
EXACTLY THE NUMBER OF FOUNDING MEMBERS...
FEITAN.
PHINKS.
MACHI.
NOBU-NAGA.
SHAL-NARK.
FRANK-LIN.
WILL YOU TRUST ME...
...AND ACCEPT THIS?

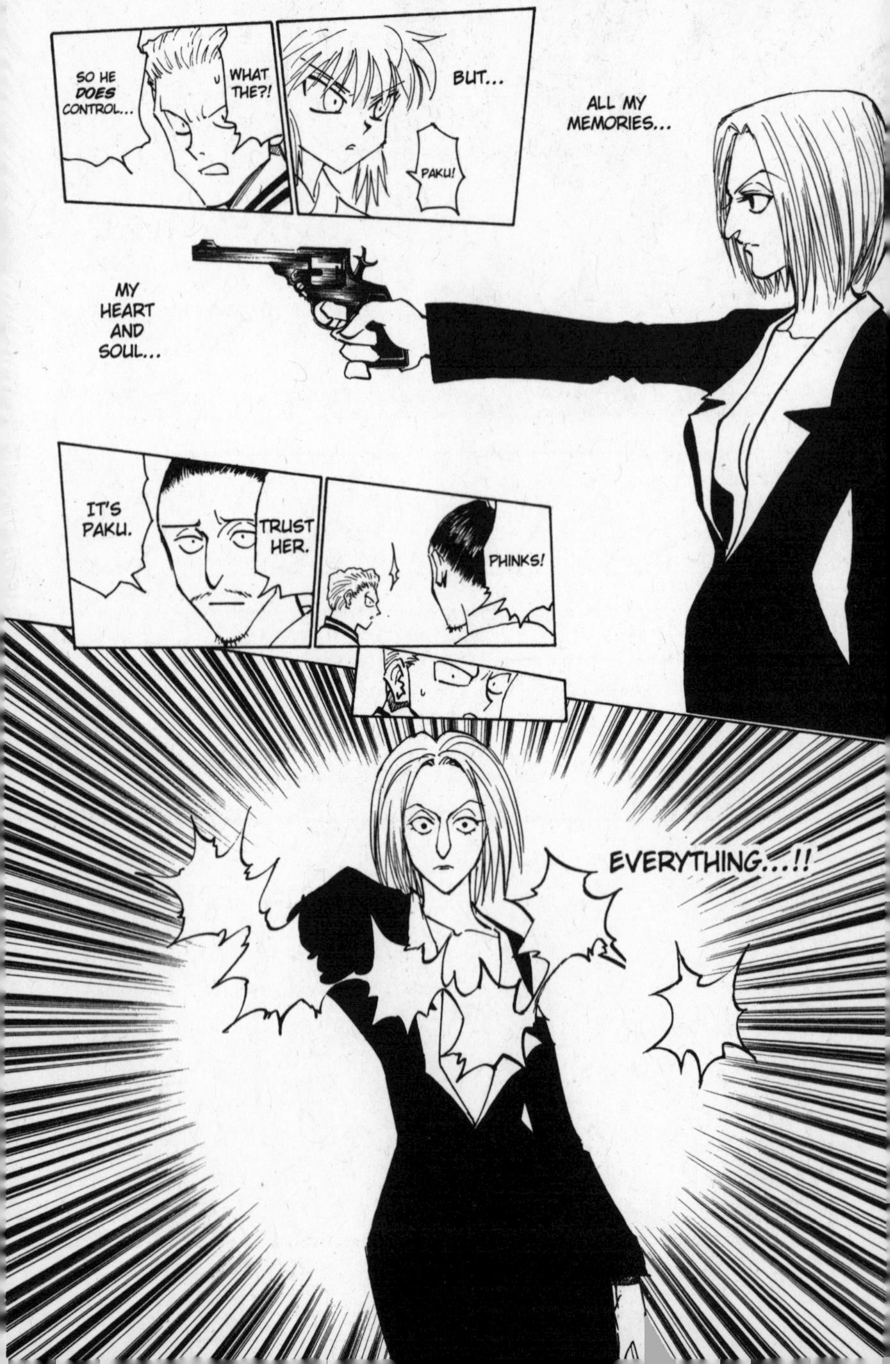
ALL MY MEMORIES...
MY HEART AND SOUL...
BUT...
PAKU!
WHAT THE?!
SO HE DOES CONTROL...
PHINKS!
TRUST HER.
IT'S PAKU.
EVERYTHING...!!

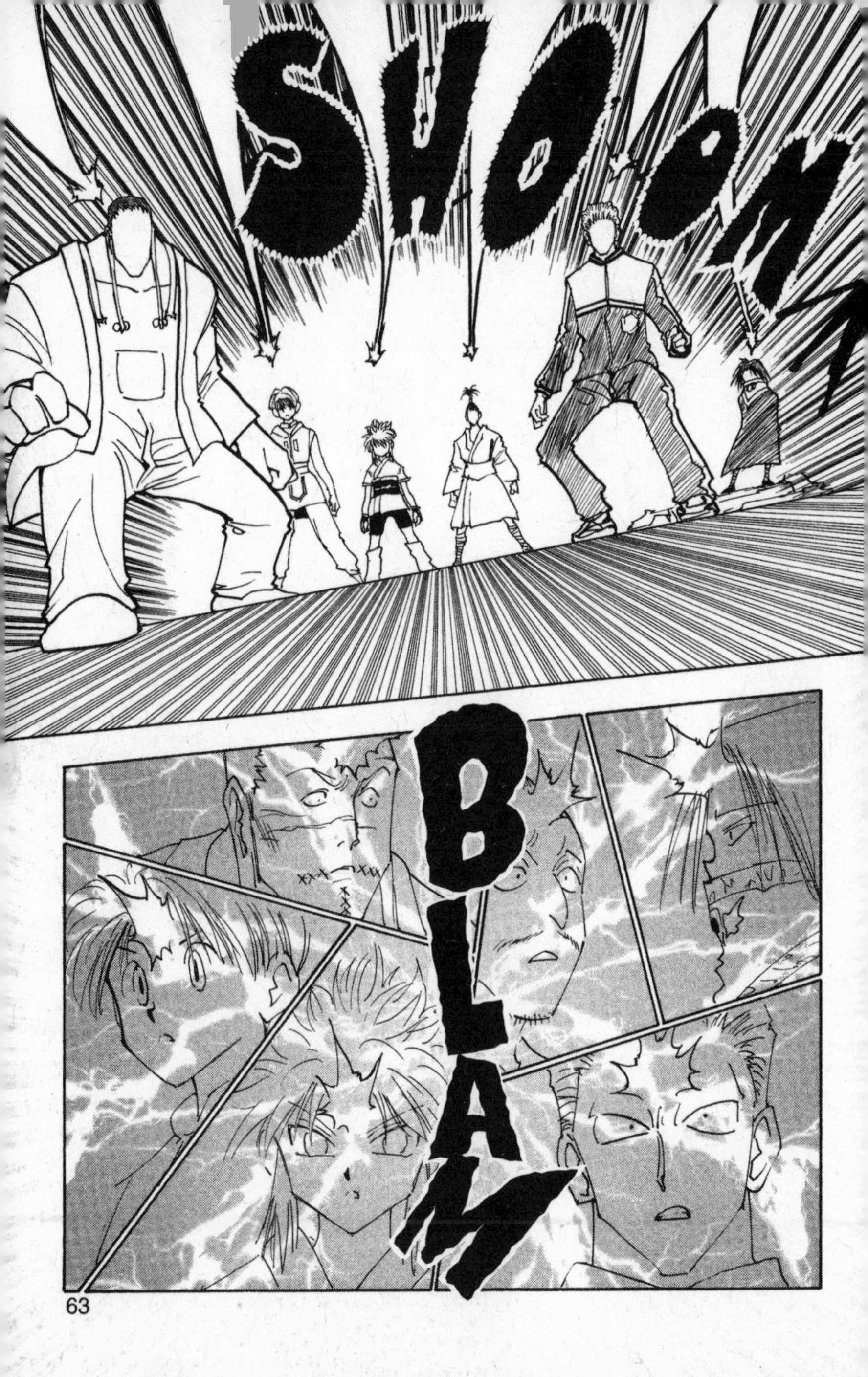
SHOOM
BLAM

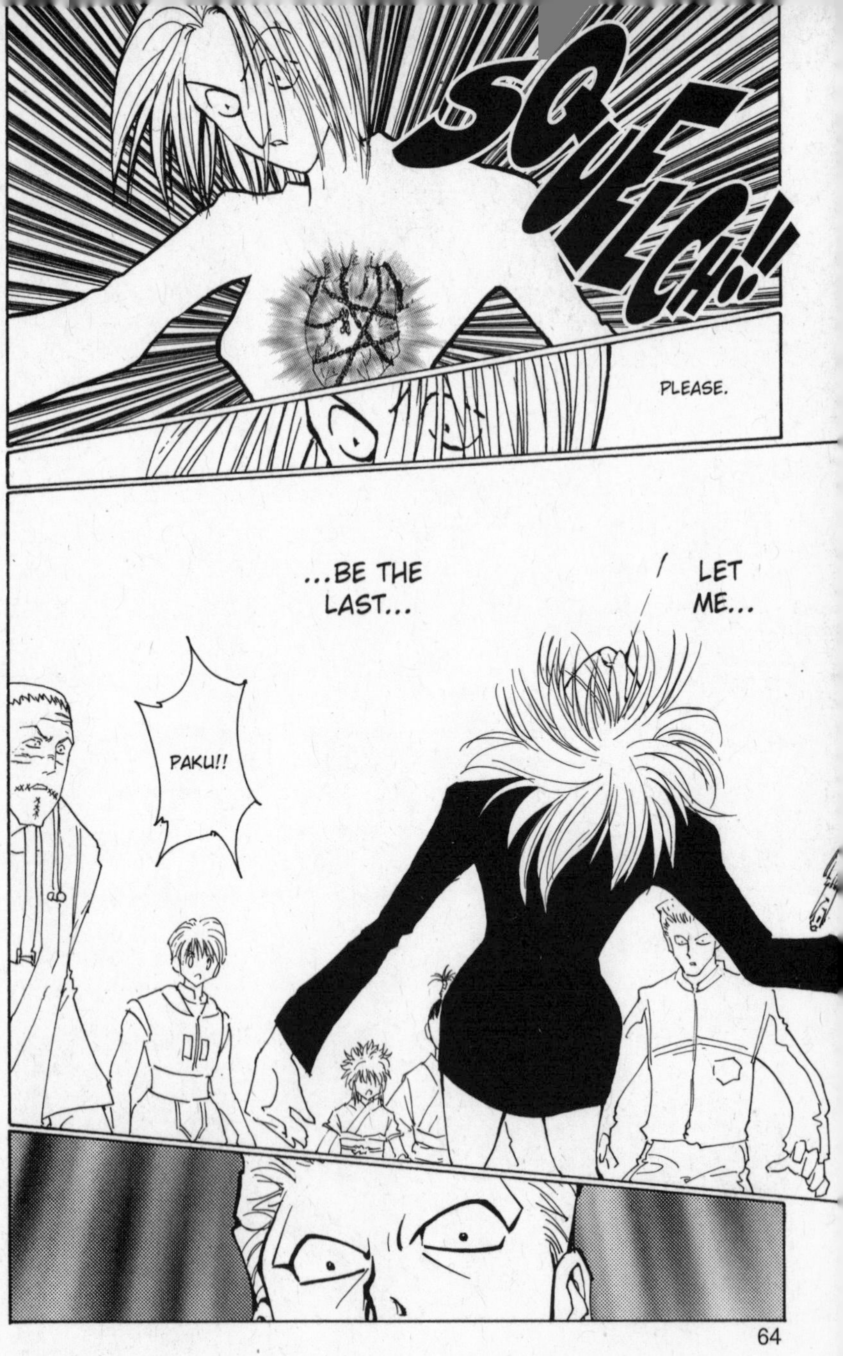
SQUELCH..!!
PLEASE.
LET ME...
...BE THE LAST...
PAKU!!

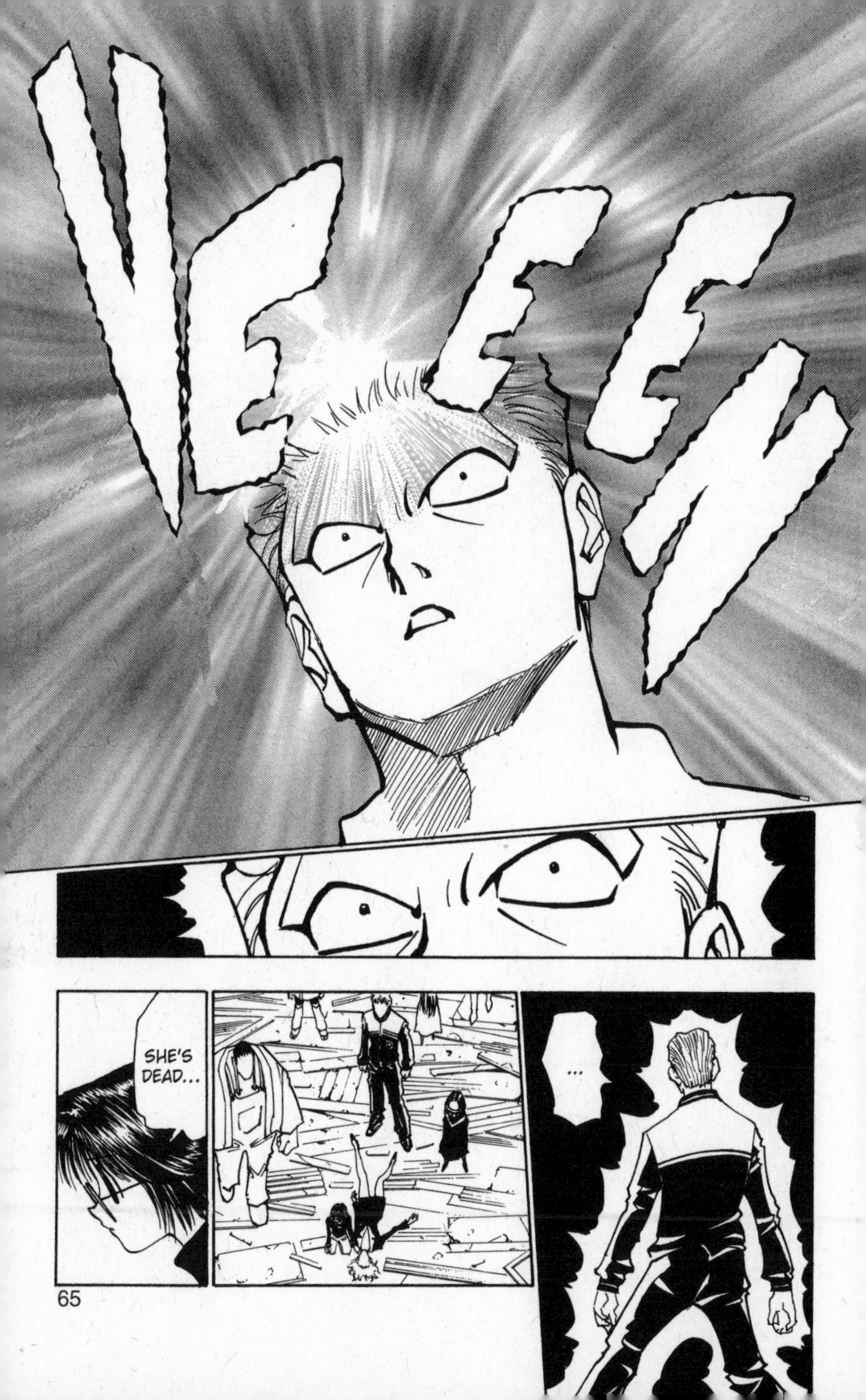
VEEEN
...
SHE'S DEAD...

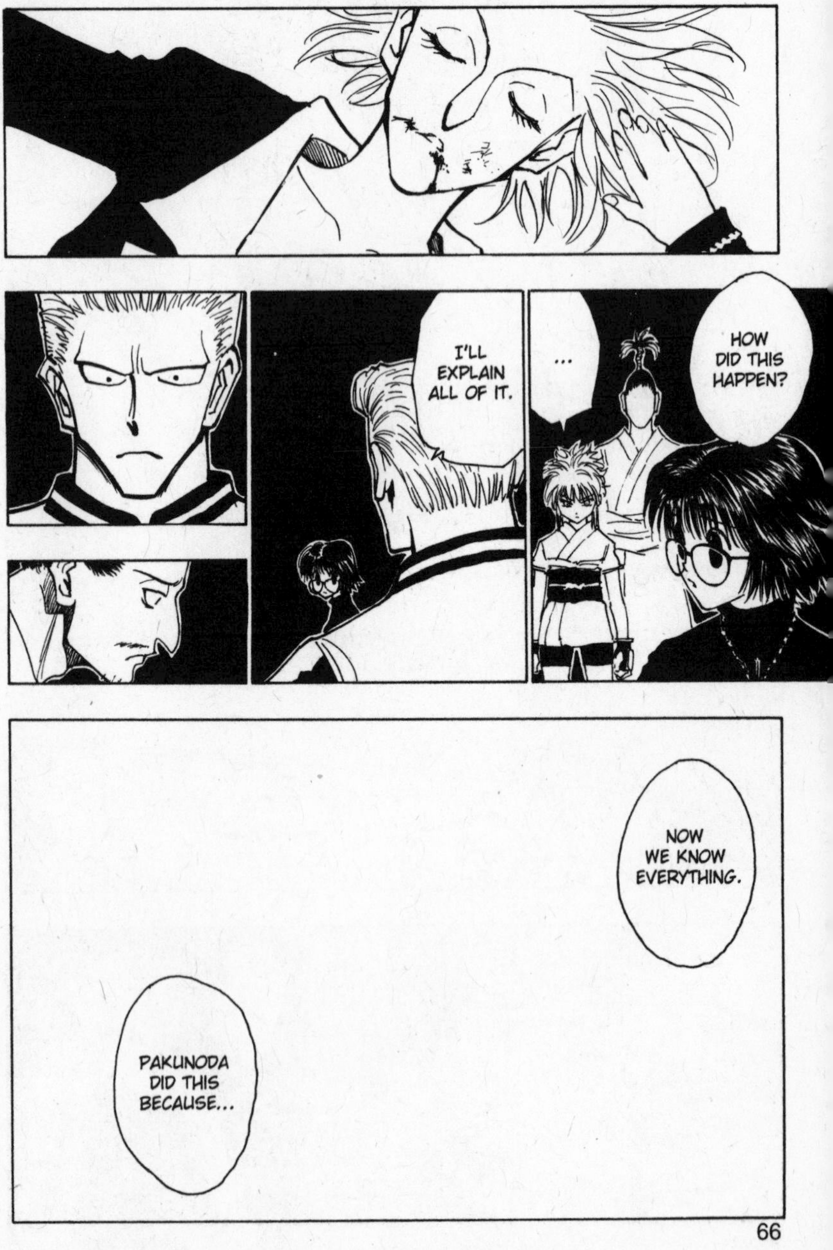
HOW DID THIS HAPPEN?
...
I'LL EXPLAIN ALL OF IT.
NOW WE KNOW EVERYTHING.
PAKUNODA DID THIS BECAUSE...

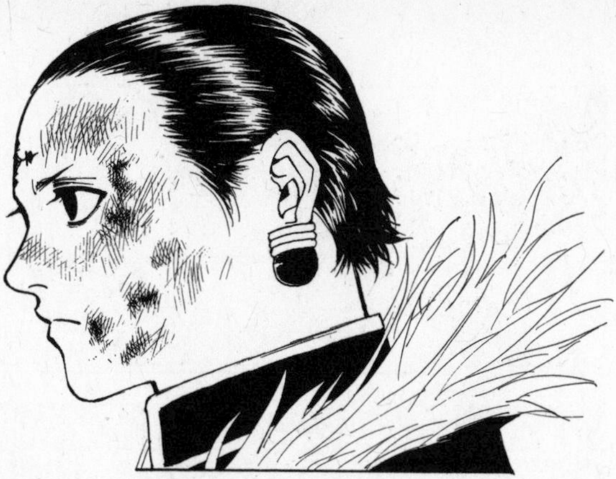

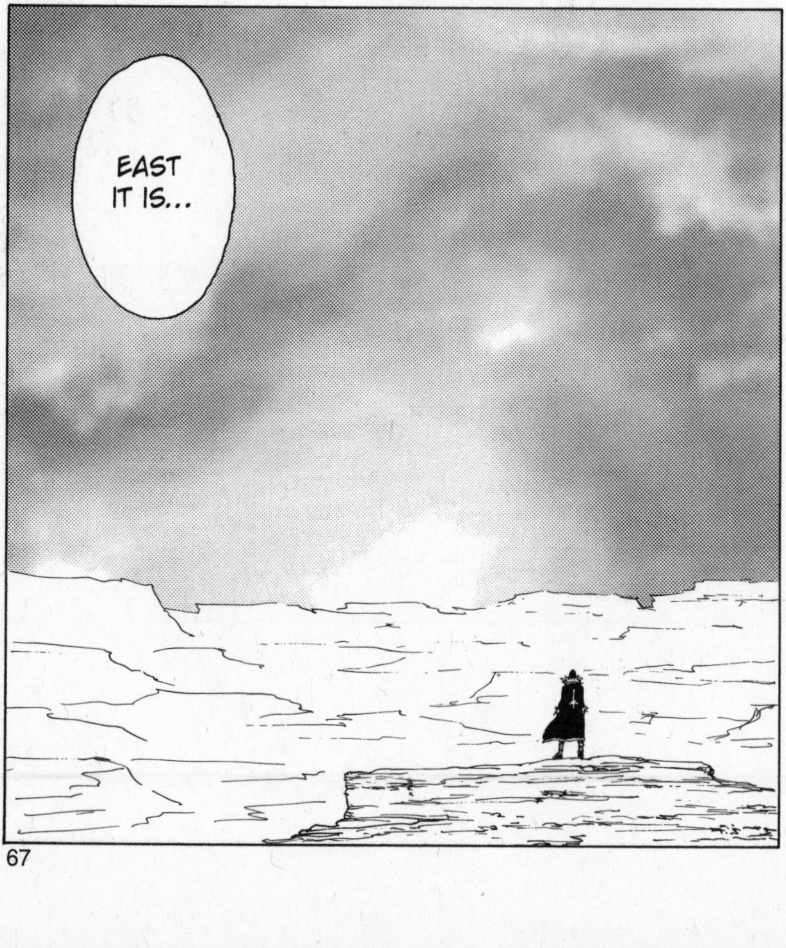
EAST IT IS...

Chapter 120
September 6th: Part 1

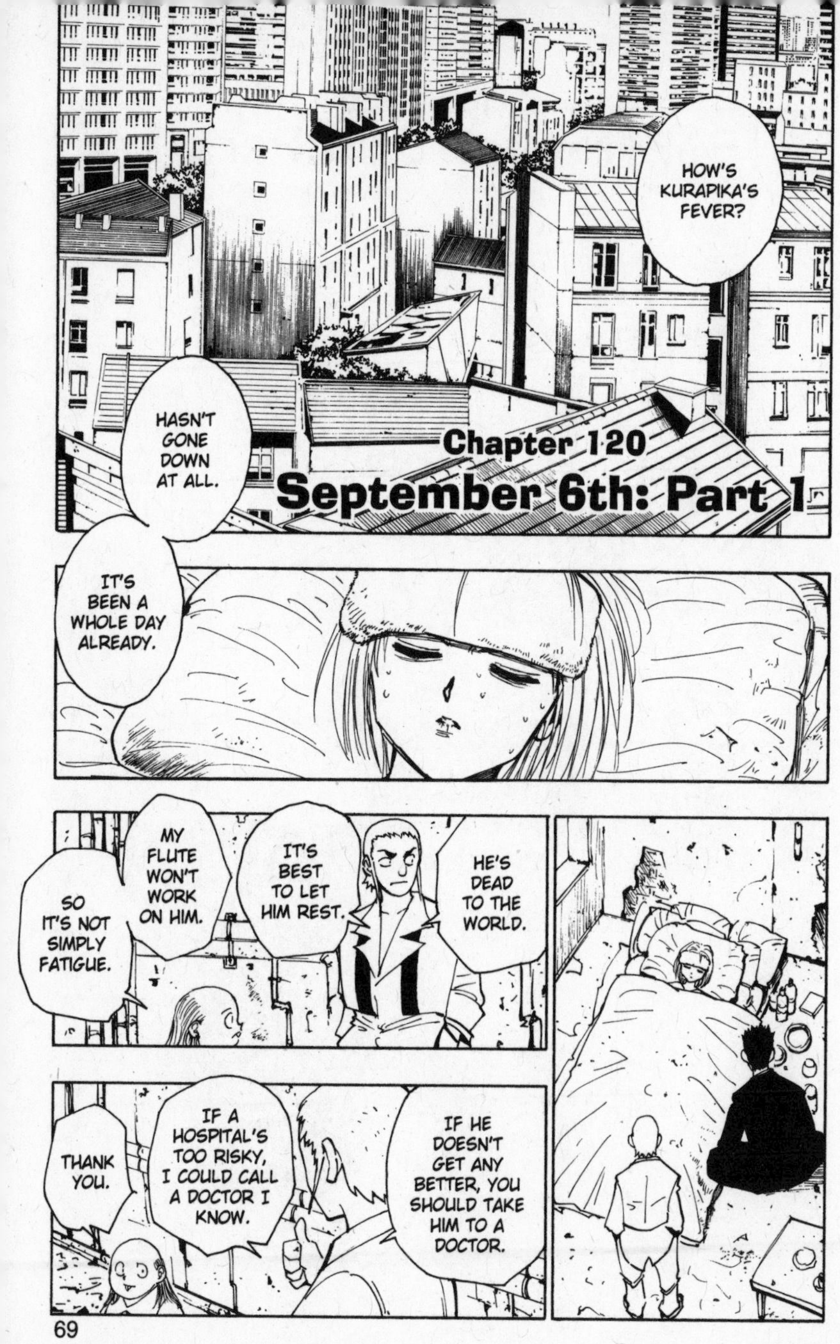
HOW'S KURAPIKA'S FEVER?
HASN'T GONE DOWN AT ALL.
IT'S BEEN A WHOLE DAY ALREADY.
HE'S DEAD TO THE WORLD.
IT'S BEST TO LET HIM REST.
MY FLUTE WON'T WORK ON HIM.
SO IT'S NOT SIMPLY FATIGUE.
IF HE DOESN'T GET ANY BETTER, YOU SHOULD TAKE HIM TO A DOCTOR.
IF A HOSPITAL'S TOO RISKY, I COULD CALL A DOCTOR I KNOW.
THANK YOU.

Chapter 120
September 6th: Part 1

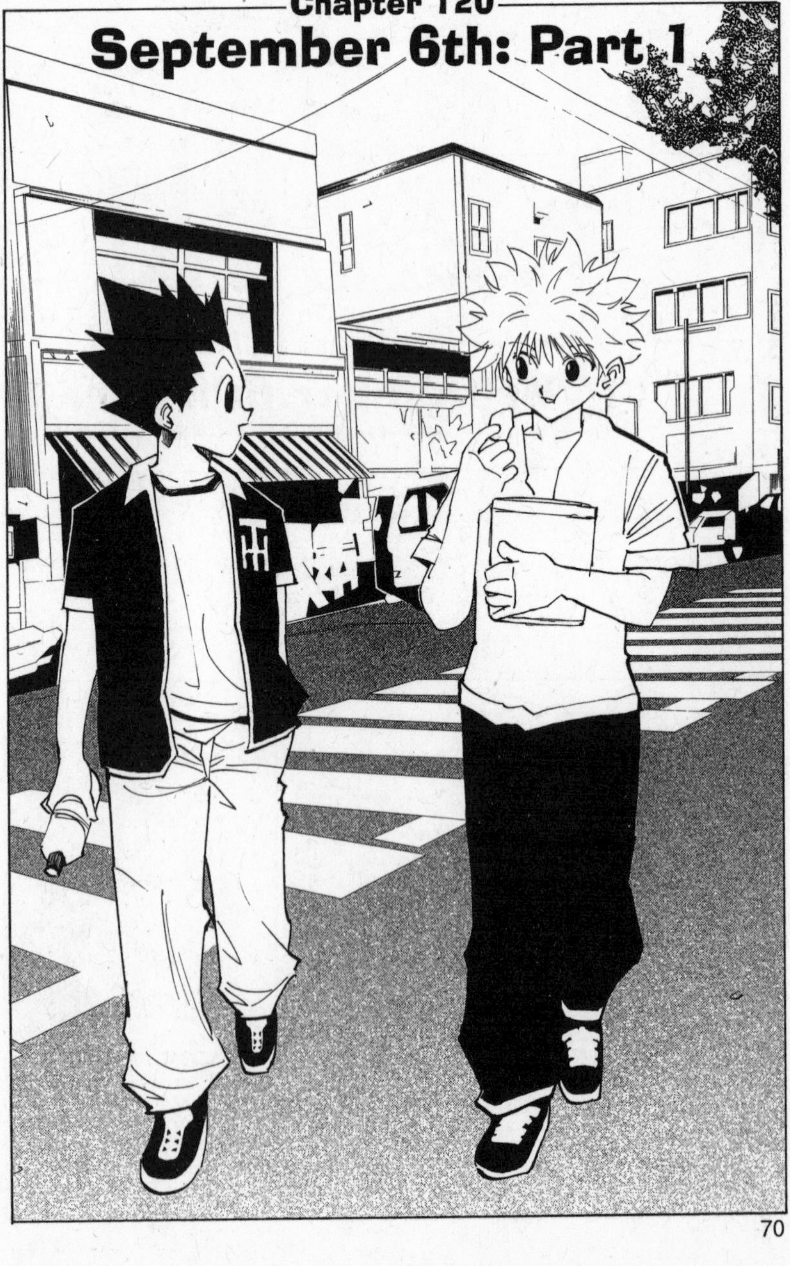

READ THIS WAY

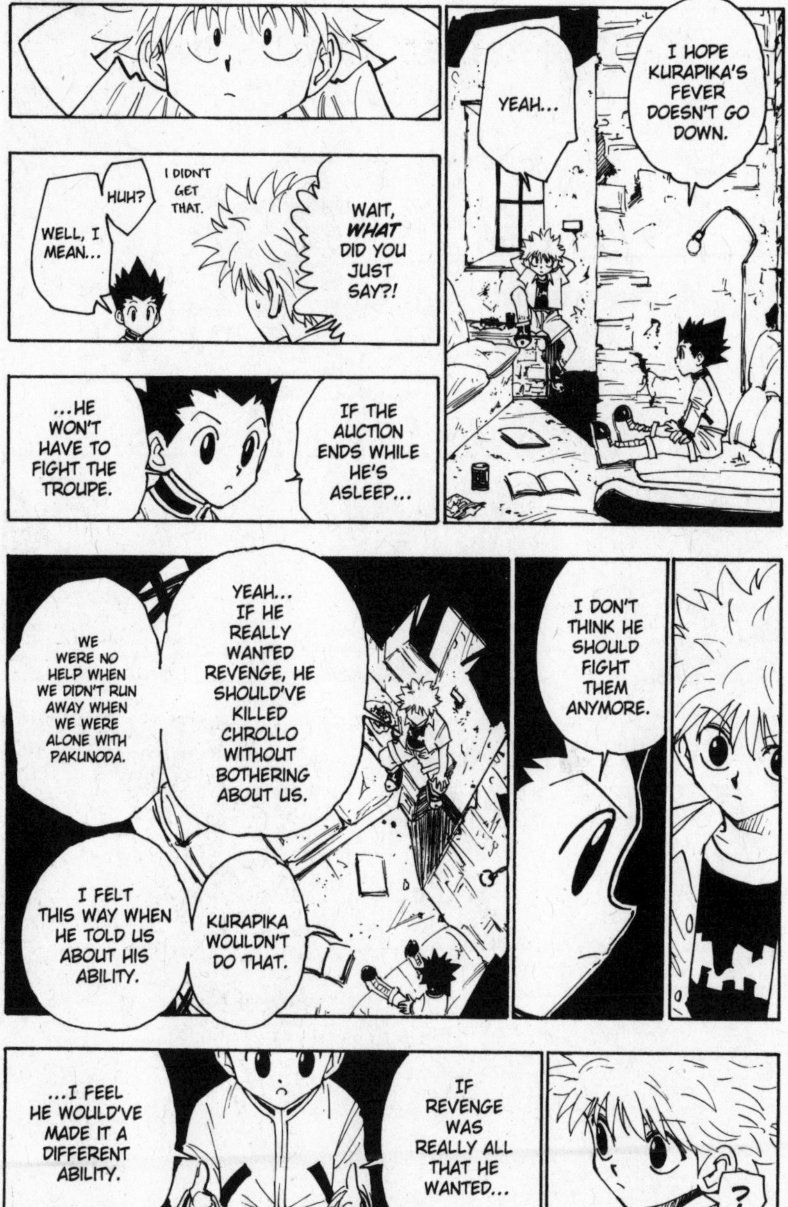
I HOPE KURAPIKA'S FEVER DOESN'T GO DOWN.
YEAH...
WAIT, *WHAT* DID YOU JUST SAY?!
I DIDN'T GET THAT.
HUH?
WELL, I MEAN...
IF THE AUCTION ENDS WHILE HE'S ASLEEP...
...HE WON'T HAVE TO FIGHT THE TROUPE.
I DON'T THINK HE SHOULD FIGHT THEM ANYMORE.
YEAH... IF HE REALLY WANTED REVENGE, HE SHOULD'VE KILLED CHROLLO WITHOUT BOTHERING ABOUT US.
WE WERE NO HELP WHEN WE DIDN'T RUN AWAY WHEN WE WERE ALONE WITH PAKUNODA.
KURAPIKA WOULDN'T DO THAT.
I FELT THIS WAY WHEN HE TOLD US ABOUT HIS ABILITY.
?
IF REVENGE WAS REALLY ALL THAT HE WANTED...
...I FEEL HE WOULD'VE MADE IT A DIFFERENT ABILITY.

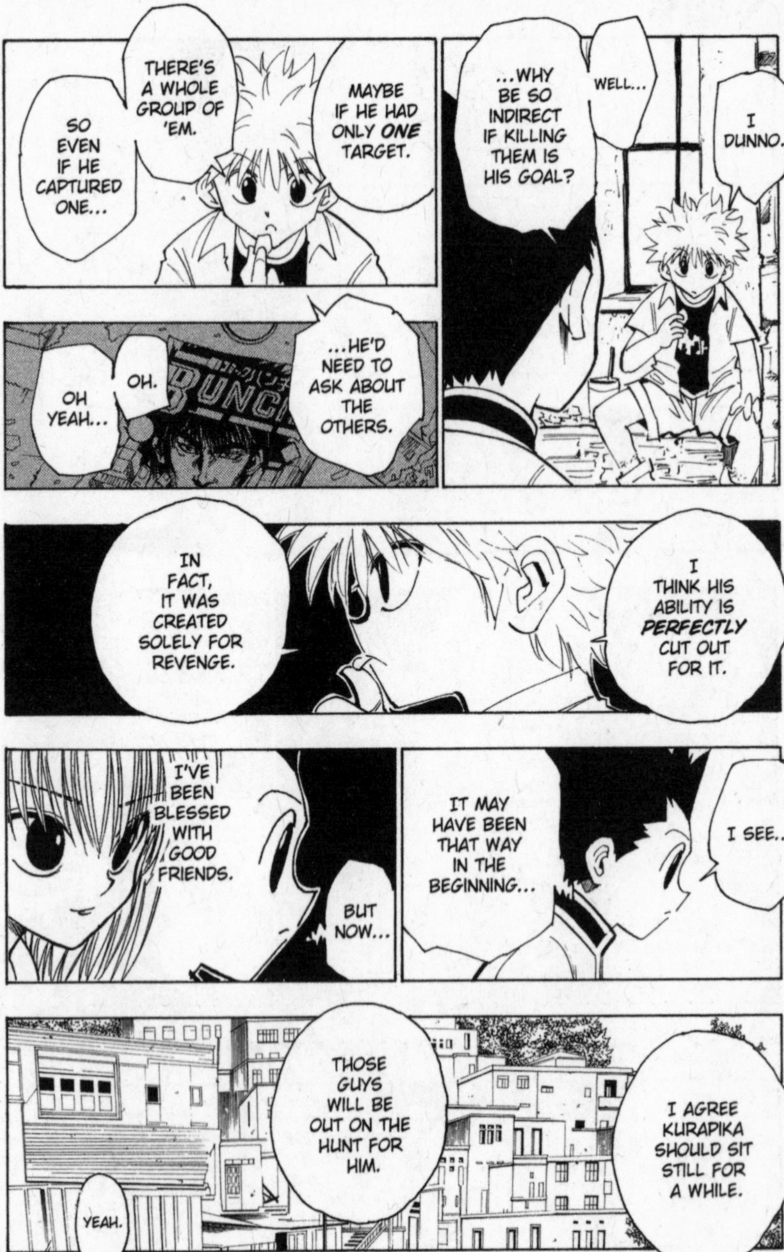
I DUNNO.
WELL...
...WHY BE SO INDIRECT IF KILLING THEM IS HIS GOAL?
MAYBE IF HE HAD ONLY *ONE* TARGET.
THERE'S A WHOLE GROUP OF 'EM.
SO EVEN IF HE CAPTURED ONE...
...HE'D NEED TO ASK ABOUT THE OTHERS.
OH.
OH YEAH...
I THINK HIS ABILITY IS *PERFECTLY* CUT OUT FOR IT.
IN FACT, IT WAS CREATED SOLELY FOR REVENGE.
I SEE...
IT MAY HAVE BEEN THAT WAY IN THE BEGINNING...
BUT NOW...
I'VE BEEN BLESSED WITH GOOD FRIENDS.
I AGREE KURAPIKA SHOULD SIT STILL FOR A WHILE.
THOSE GUYS WILL BE OUT ON THE HUNT FOR HIM.
YEAH.

READ THIS WAY

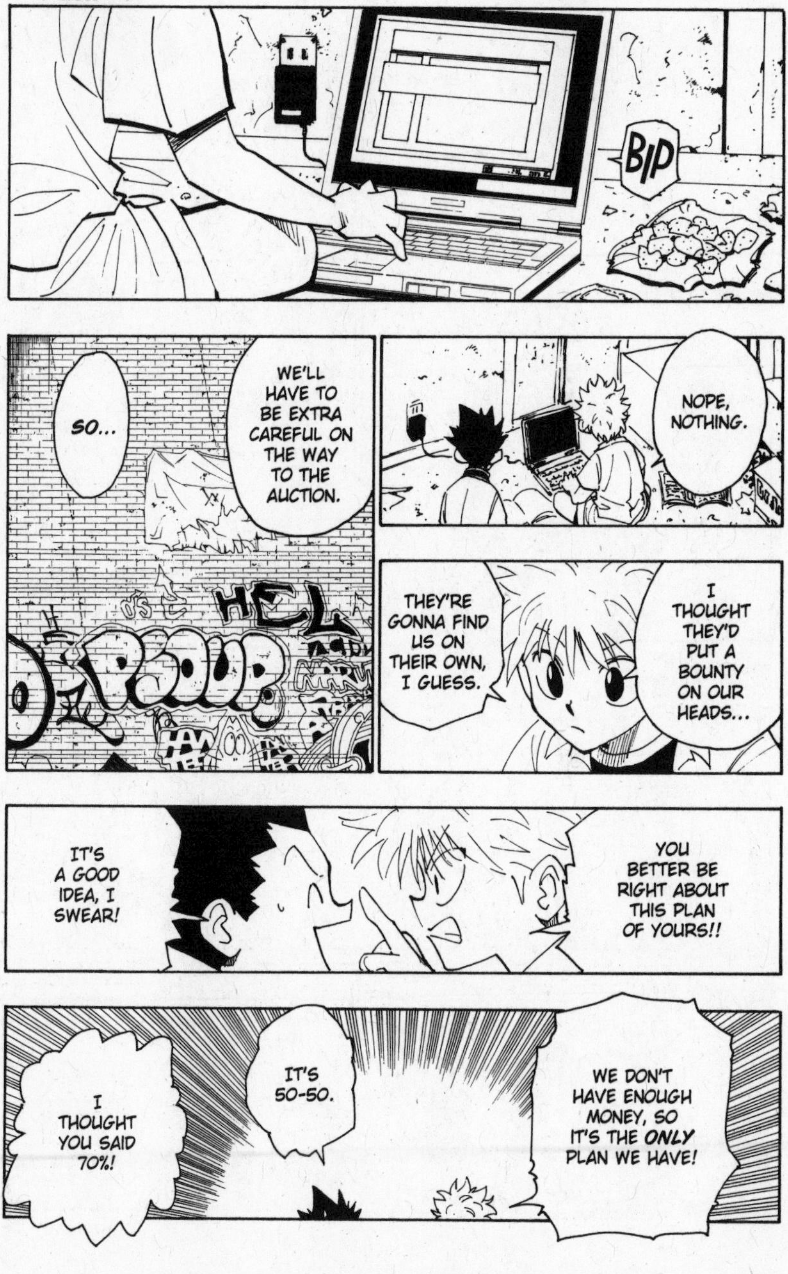
BIP
NOPE, NOTHING.
I THOUGHT THEY'D PUT A BOUNTY ON OUR HEADS...
THEY'RE GONNA FIND US ON THEIR OWN, I GUESS.
WE'LL HAVE TO BE EXTRA CAREFUL ON THE WAY TO THE AUCTION.
SO...
HEL
YOU BETTER BE RIGHT ABOUT THIS PLAN OF YOURS!!
IT'S A GOOD IDEA, I SWEAR!
WE DON'T HAVE ENOUGH MONEY, SO IT'S THE *ONLY* PLAN WE HAVE!
IT'S 50-50.
I THOUGHT YOU SAID 70%!

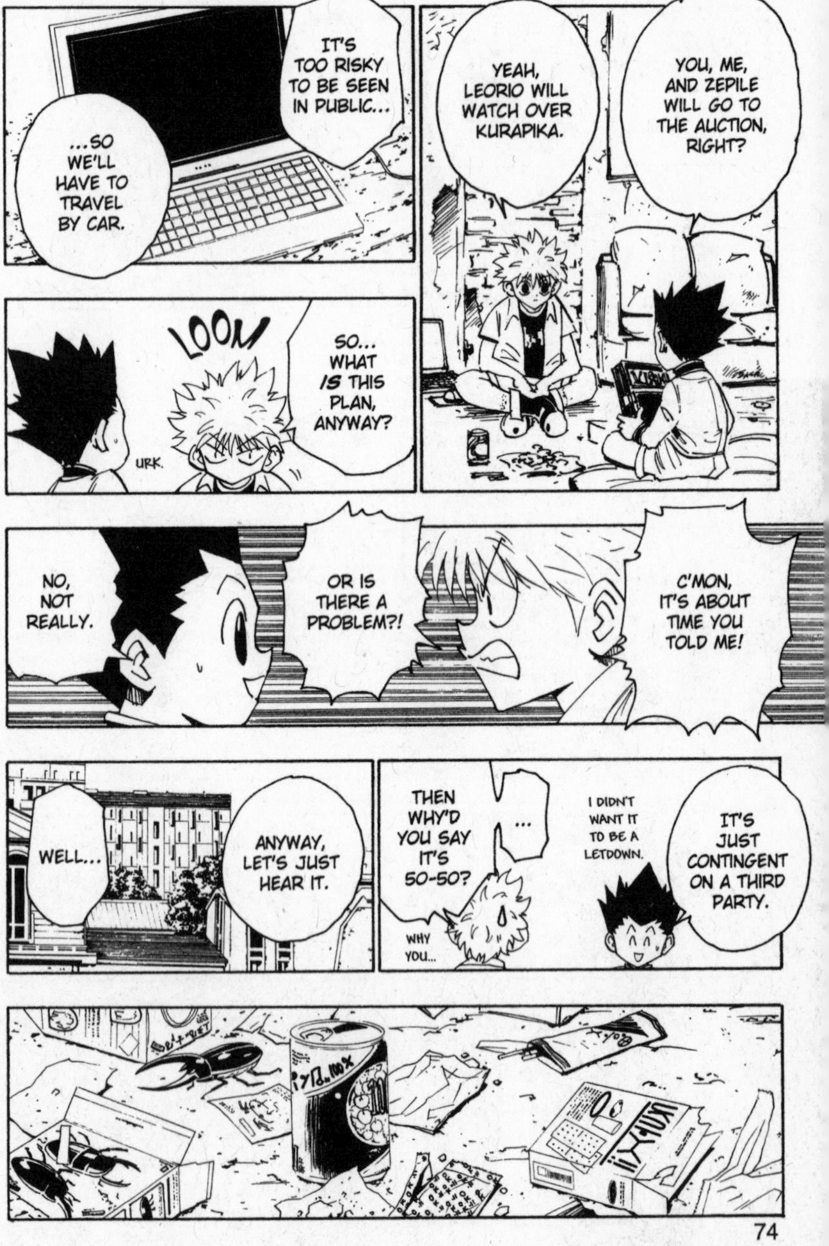
YOU, ME, AND ZEPILE WILL GO TO THE AUCTION, RIGHT?
YEAH, LEORIO WILL WATCH OVER KURAPIKA.
IT'S TOO RISKY TO BE SEEN IN PUBLIC...
...SO WE'LL HAVE TO TRAVEL BY CAR.
SO... WHAT *IS* THIS PLAN, ANYWAY?
LOOM
URK.
C'MON, IT'S ABOUT TIME YOU TOLD ME!
OR IS THERE A PROBLEM?!
NO, NOT REALLY.
IT'S JUST CONTINGENT ON A THIRD PARTY.
I DIDN'T WANT IT TO BE A LETDOWN.
...
THEN WHY'D YOU SAY IT'S 50-50?
WHY YOU...
ANYWAY, LET'S JUST HEAR IT.
WELL...

READ THIS WAY

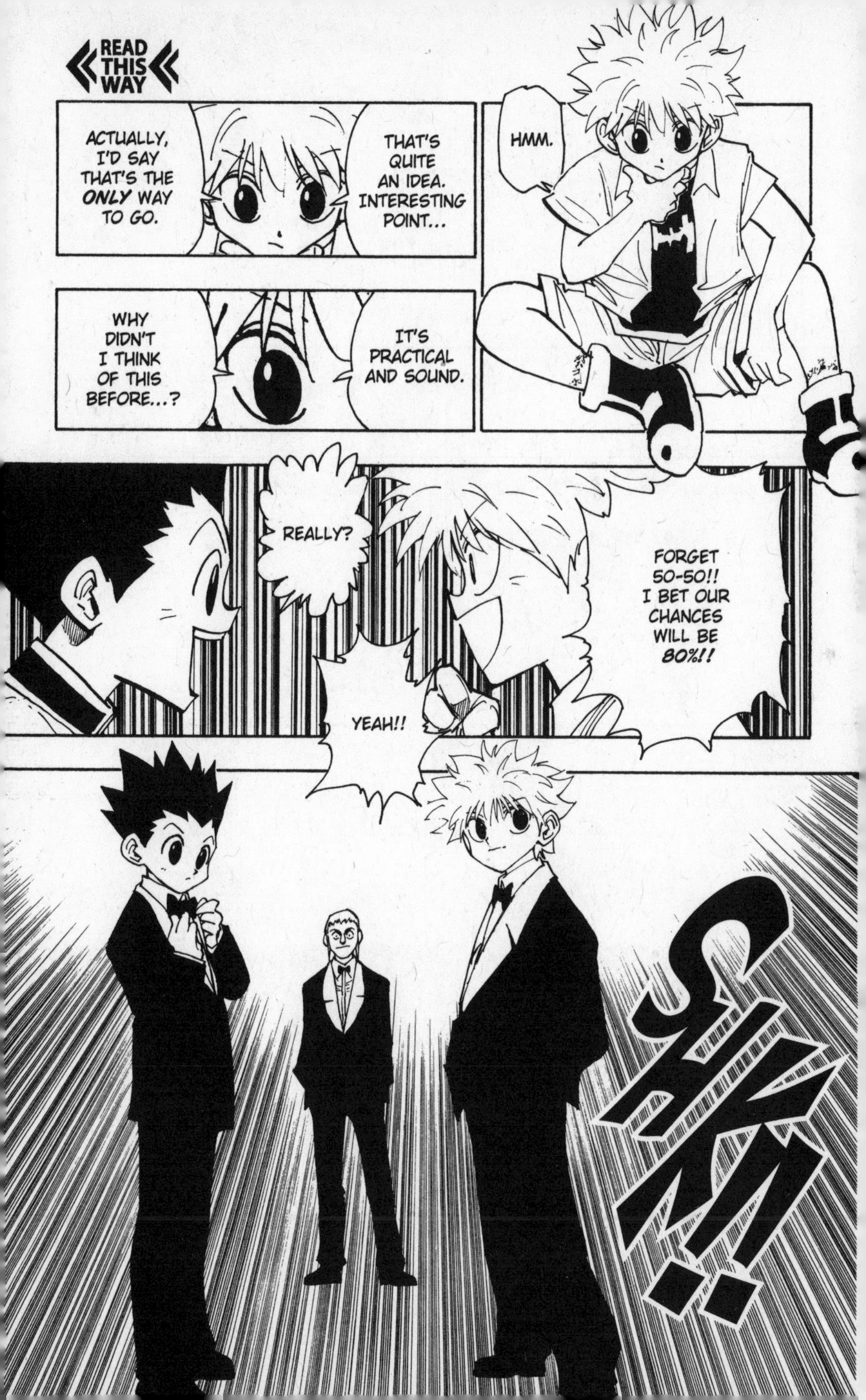
HMM.
THAT'S QUITE AN IDEA. INTERESTING POINT...
ACTUALLY, I'D SAY THAT'S THE *ONLY* WAY TO GO.
IT'S PRACTICAL AND SOUND.
WHY DIDN'T I THINK OF THIS BEFORE...?
FORGET 50-50!! I BET OUR CHANCES WILL BE 80%!!
REALLY?
YEAH!!

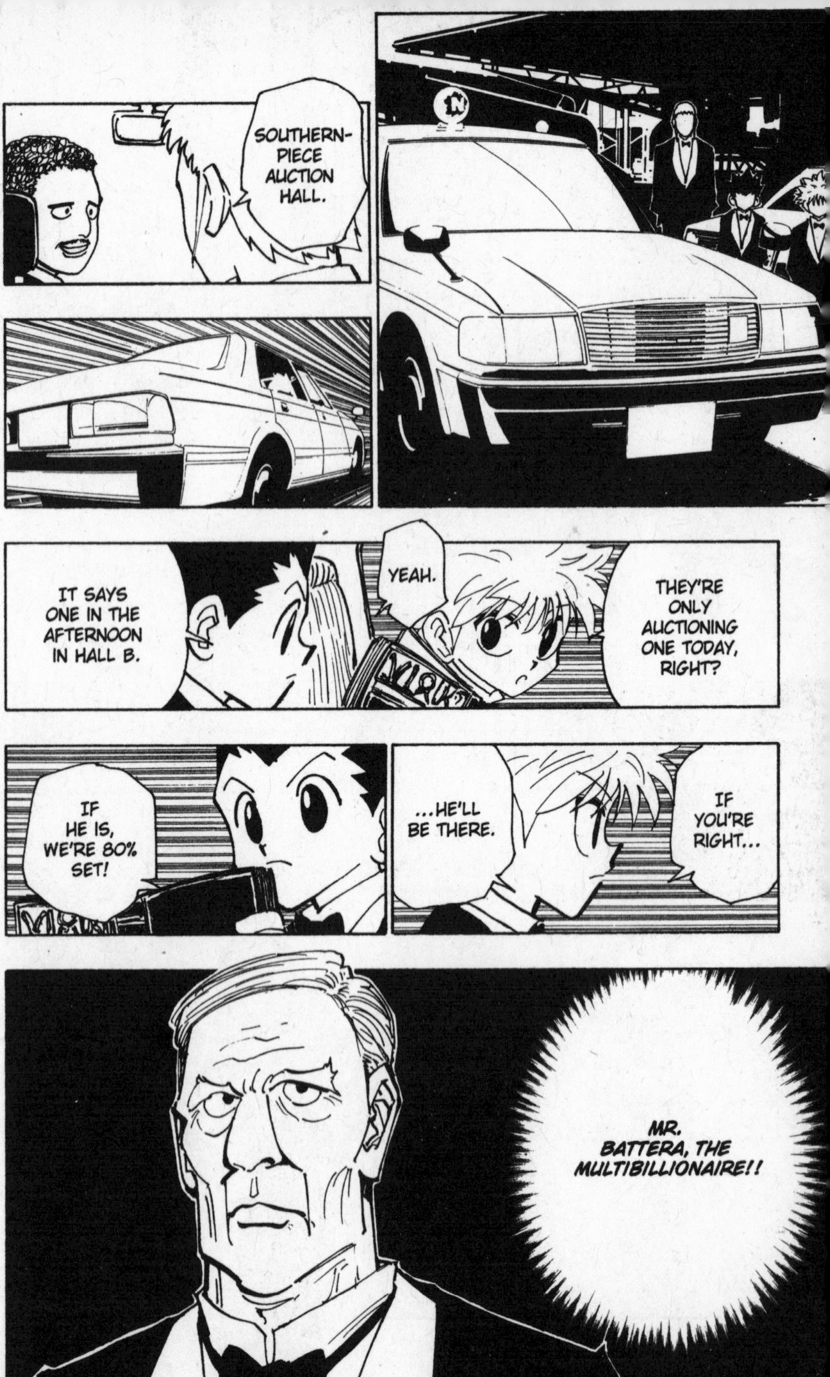
SOUTHERN-PIECE AUCTION HALL.
THEY'RE ONLY AUCTIONING ONE TODAY, RIGHT?
YEAH.
IT SAYS ONE IN THE AFTERNOON IN HALL B.
IF YOU'RE RIGHT...
...HE'LL BE THERE.
IF HE IS, WE'RE 80% SET!
MR. BATTERA, THE MULTIBILLIONAIRE!!

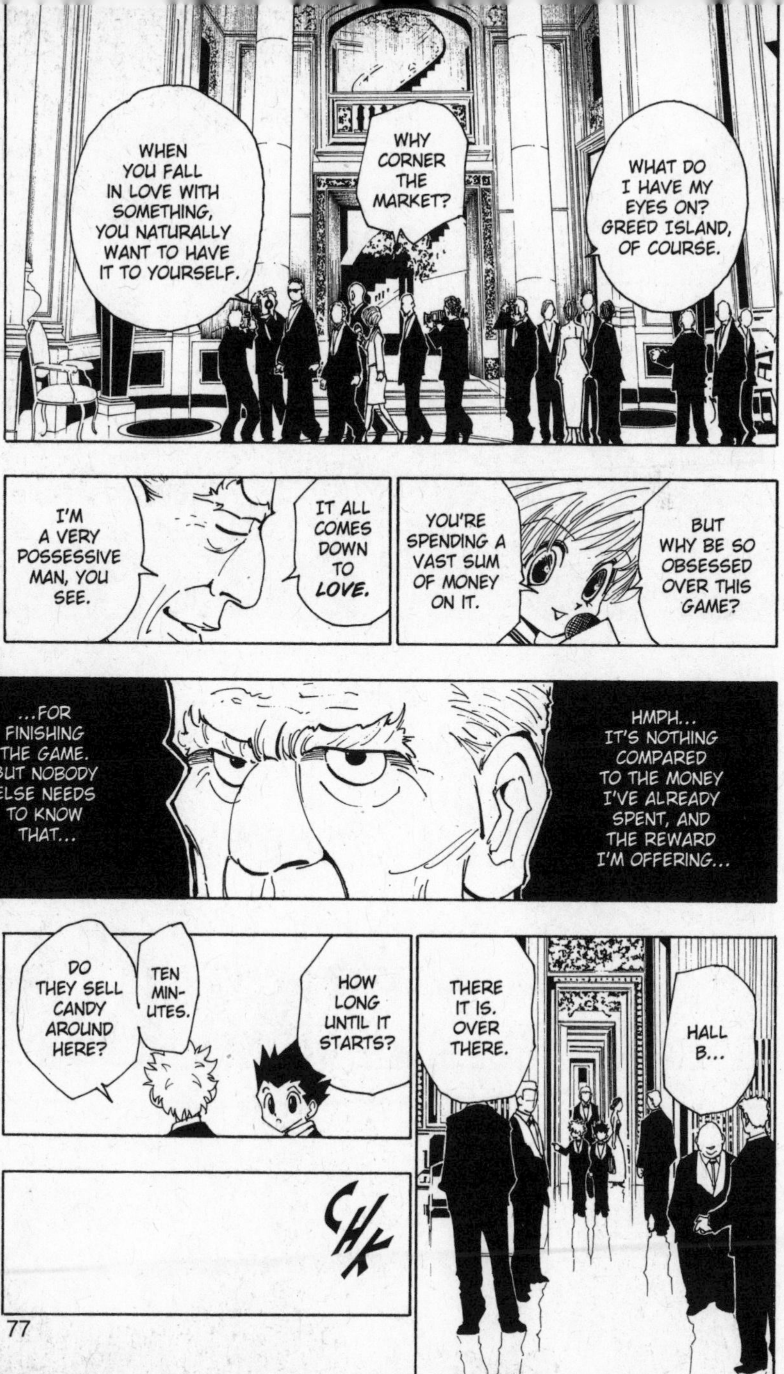
WHAT DO I HAVE MY EYES ON? GREED ISLAND, OF COURSE.
WHY CORNER THE MARKET?
WHEN YOU FALL IN LOVE WITH SOMETHING, YOU NATURALLY WANT TO HAVE IT TO YOURSELF.
BUT WHY BE SO OBSESSED OVER THIS GAME?
YOU'RE SPENDING A VAST SUM OF MONEY ON IT.
IT ALL COMES DOWN TO *LOVE.*
I'M A VERY POSSESSIVE MAN, YOU SEE.
HMPH... IT'S NOTHING COMPARED TO THE MONEY I'VE ALREADY SPENT, AND THE REWARD I'M OFFERING...
...FOR FINISHING THE GAME. BUT NOBODY ELSE NEEDS TO KNOW THAT...
HALL B...
THERE IT IS. OVER THERE.
HOW LONG UNTIL IT STARTS?
TEN MIN-UTES.
DO THEY SELL CANDY AROUND HERE?
CHK

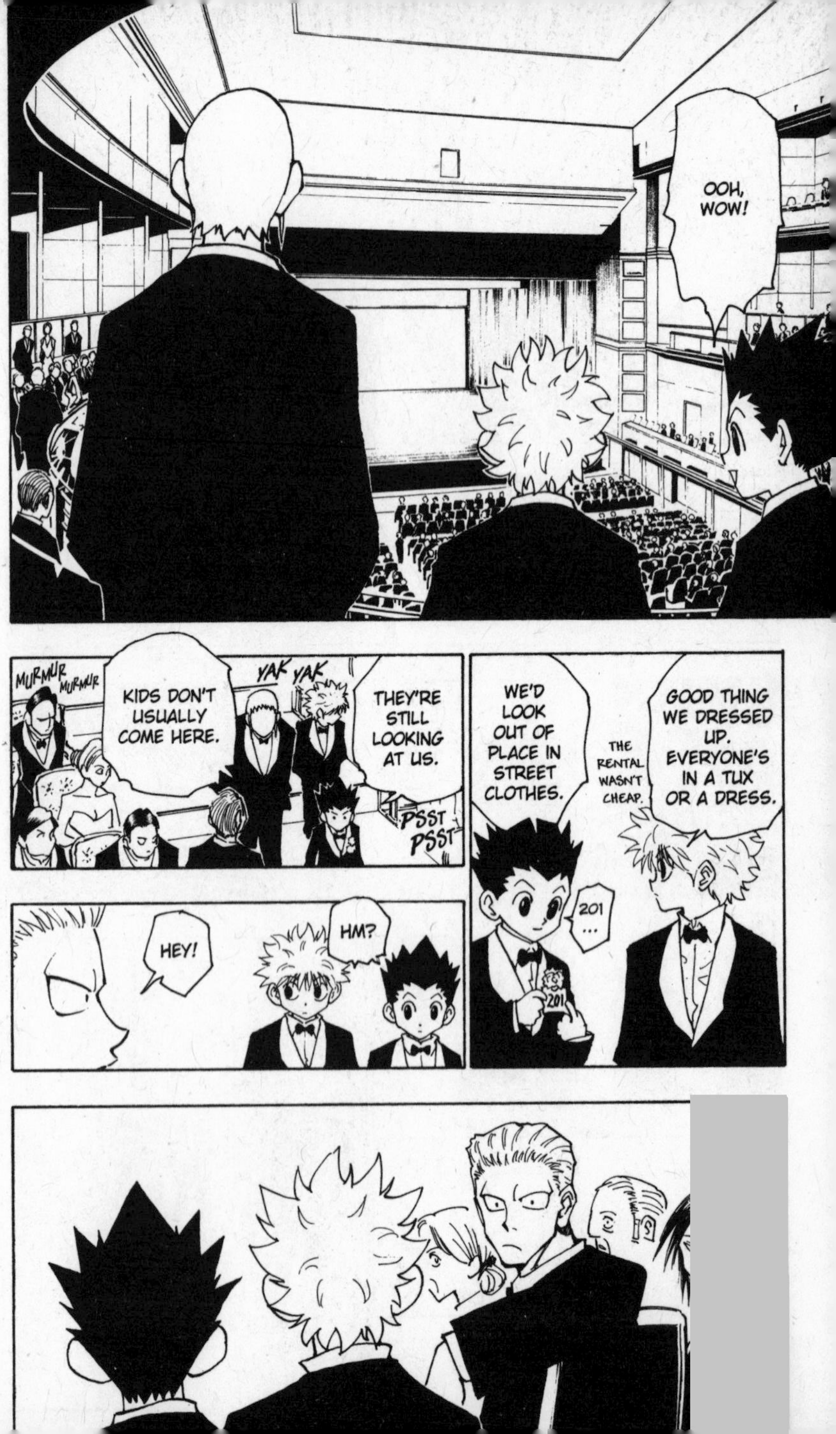
OOH, WOW!
GOOD THING WE DRESSED UP. EVERYONE'S IN A TUX OR A DRESS.
THE RENTAL WASN'T CHEAP.
WE'D LOOK OUT OF PLACE IN STREET CLOTHES.
201 ...
201
YAK YAK
THEY'RE STILL LOOKING AT US.
PSST PSST
KIDS DON'T USUALLY COME HERE.
MURMUR MURMUR
HEY!
HM?

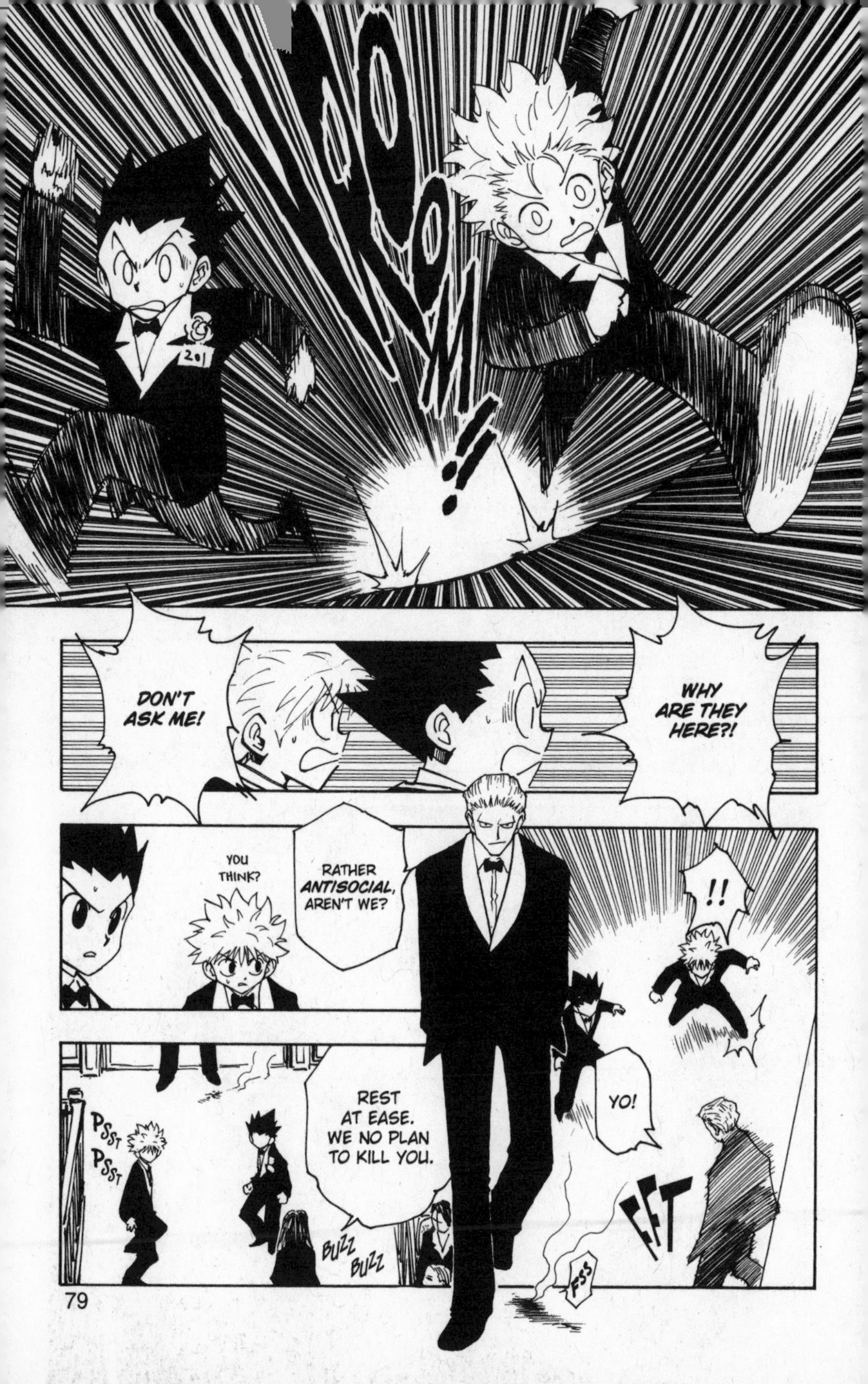
!!
WHY ARE THEY HERE?!
DON'T ASK ME!
!!
RATHER ANTISOCIAL, AREN'T WE?
YOU THINK?
YO!
FSS
FFT
REST AT EASE. WE NO PLAN TO KILL YOU.
BUZZ BUZZ
PSST PSST

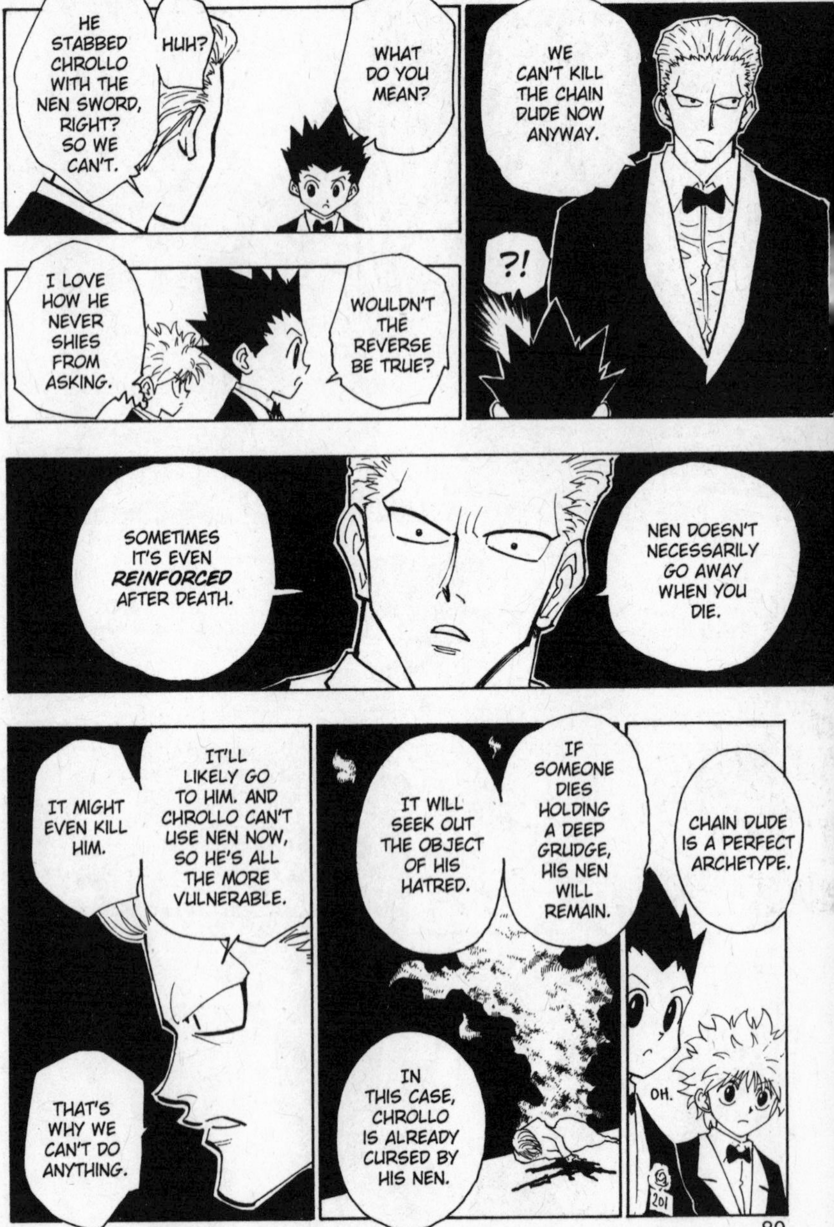
WE CAN'T KILL THE CHAIN DUDE NOW ANYWAY.
?!
WHAT DO YOU MEAN?
HUH?
HE STABBED CHROLLO WITH THE NEN SWORD, RIGHT? SO WE CAN'T.
WOULDN'T THE REVERSE BE TRUE?
I LOVE HOW HE NEVER SHIES FROM ASKING.
NEN DOESN'T NECESSARILY GO AWAY WHEN YOU DIE.
SOMETIMES IT'S EVEN *REINFORCED* AFTER DEATH.
CHAIN DUDE IS A PERFECT ARCHETYPE.
OH.
IF SOMEONE DIES HOLDING A DEEP GRUDGE, HIS NEN WILL REMAIN.
IT WILL SEEK OUT THE OBJECT OF HIS HATRED.
IN THIS CASE, CHROLLO IS ALREADY CURSED BY HIS NEN.
IT'LL LIKELY GO TO HIM. AND CHROLLO CAN'T USE NEN NOW, SO HE'S ALL THE MORE VULNERABLE.
IT MIGHT EVEN KILL HIM.
THAT'S WHY WE CAN'T DO ANYTHING.

READ THIS WAY

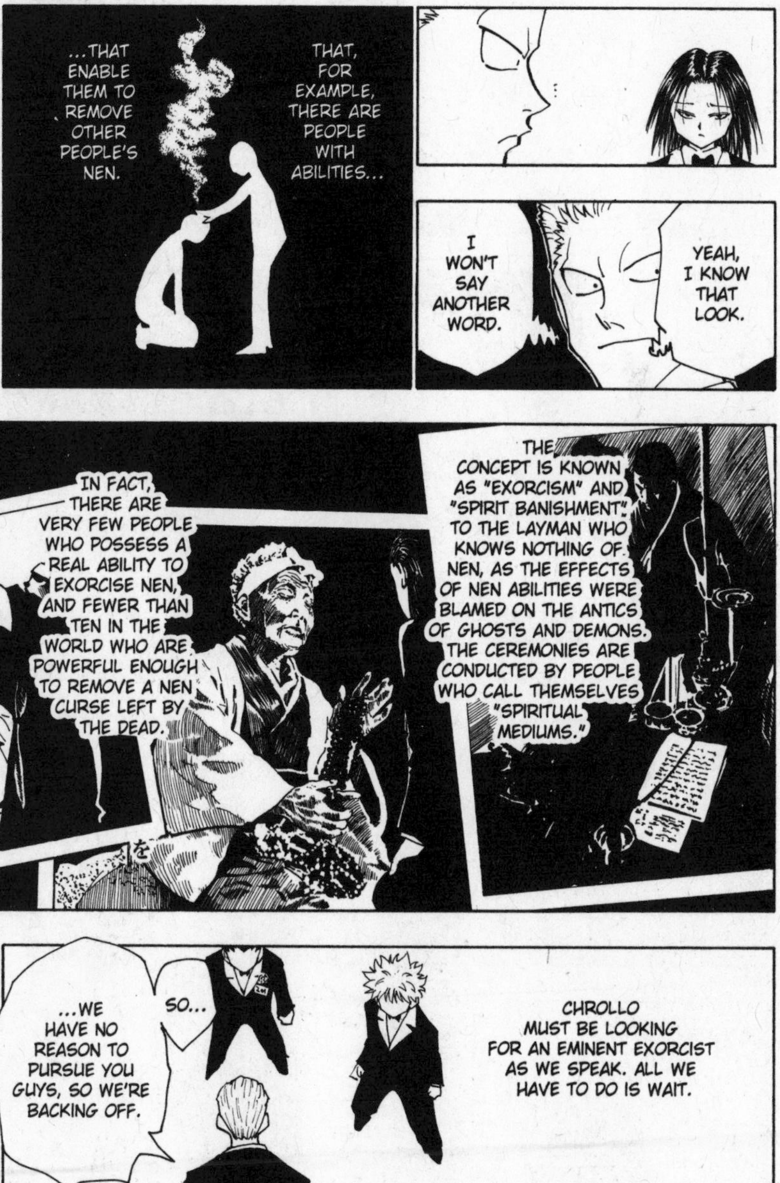
YEAH, I KNOW THAT LOOK.
I WON'T SAY ANOTHER WORD.
THAT, FOR EXAMPLE, THERE ARE PEOPLE WITH ABILITIES...
...THAT ENABLE THEM TO REMOVE OTHER PEOPLE'S NEN.
THE CONCEPT IS KNOWN AS "EXORCISM" AND "SPIRIT BANISHMENT" TO THE LAYMAN WHO KNOWS NOTHING OF NEN, AS THE EFFECTS OF NEN ABILITIES WERE BLAMED ON THE ANTICS OF GHOSTS AND DEMONS. THE CEREMONIES ARE CONDUCTED BY PEOPLE WHO CALL THEMSELVES "SPIRITUAL MEDIUMS."
IN FACT, THERE ARE VERY FEW PEOPLE WHO POSSESS A REAL ABILITY TO EXORCISE NEN, AND FEWER THAN TEN IN THE WORLD WHO ARE POWERFUL ENOUGH TO REMOVE A NEN CURSE LEFT BY THE DEAD.
CHROLLO MUST BE LOOKING FOR AN EMINENT EXORCIST AS WE SPEAK. ALL WE HAVE TO DO IS WAIT.
SO...
...WE HAVE NO REASON TO PURSUE YOU GUYS, SO WE'RE BACKING OFF.

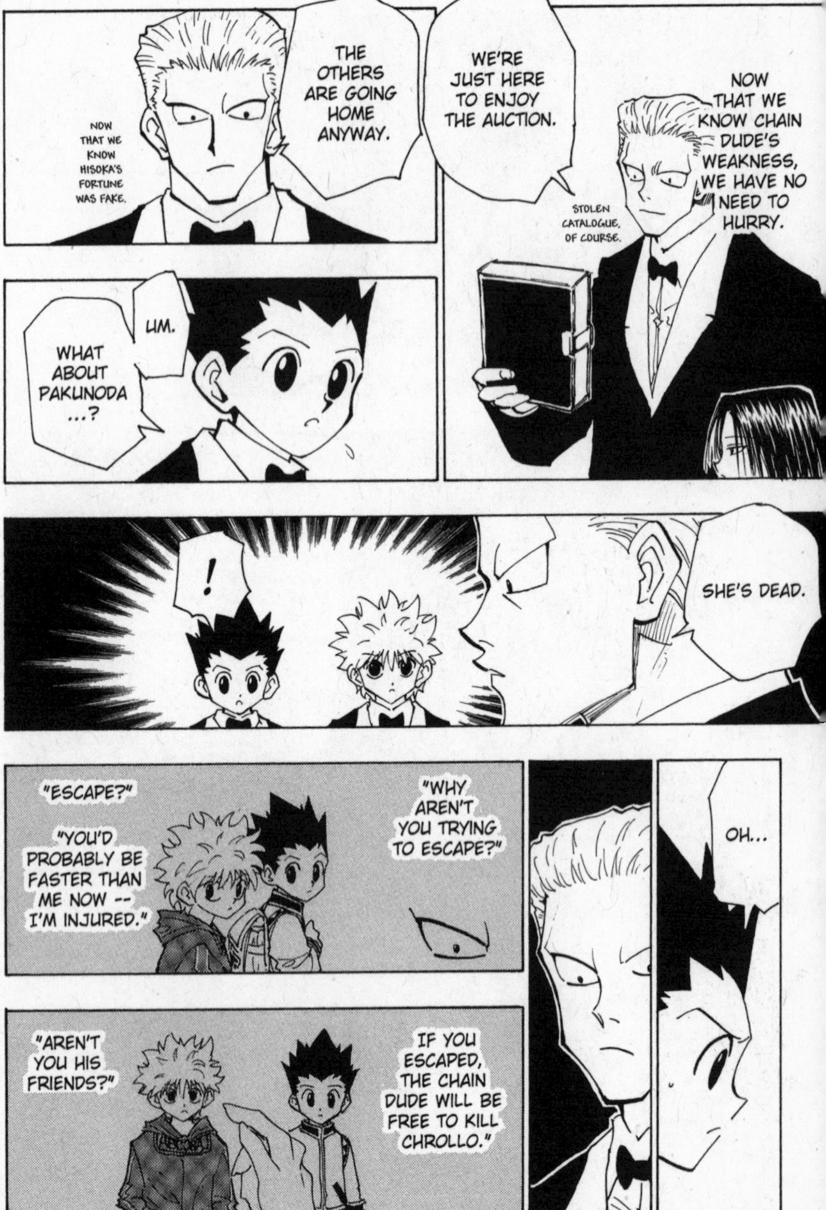
NOW THAT WE KNOW CHAIN DUDE'S WEAKNESS, WE HAVE NO NEED TO HURRY.
WE'RE JUST HERE TO ENJOY THE AUCTION.
STOLEN CATALOGUE, OF COURSE.
THE OTHERS ARE GOING HOME ANYWAY.
NOW THAT WE KNOW HISOKA'S FORTUNE WAS FAKE.
UM.
WHAT ABOUT PAKUNODA ...?
SHE'S DEAD.
!
OH...
"WHY AREN'T YOU TRYING TO ESCAPE?"
"ESCAPE?"
"YOU'D PROBABLY BE FASTER THAN ME NOW -- I'M INJURED."
IF YOU ESCAPED, THE CHAIN DUDE WILL BE FREE TO KILL CHROLLO."
"AREN'T YOU HIS FRIENDS?"

READ THIS WAY

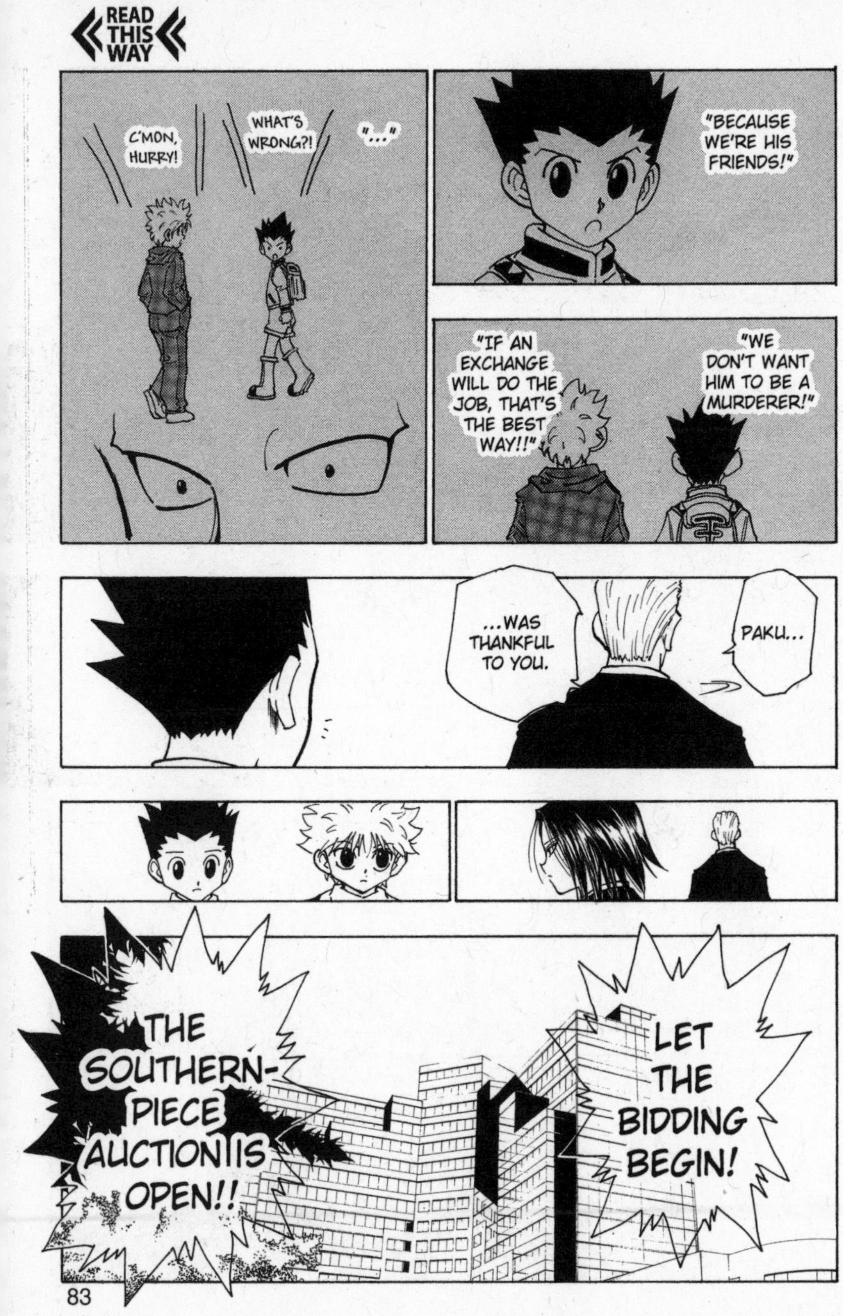

"BECAUSE WE'RE HIS FRIENDS!"
"WE DON'T WANT HIM TO BE A MURDERER!"
"IF AN EXCHANGE WILL DO THE JOB, THAT'S THE BEST WAY!!"
"..."
WHAT'S WRONG?!
C'MON, HURRY!
PAKU...
...WAS THANKFUL TO YOU.
LET THE BIDDING BEGIN!
THE SOUTHERN-PIECE AUCTION IS OPEN!!

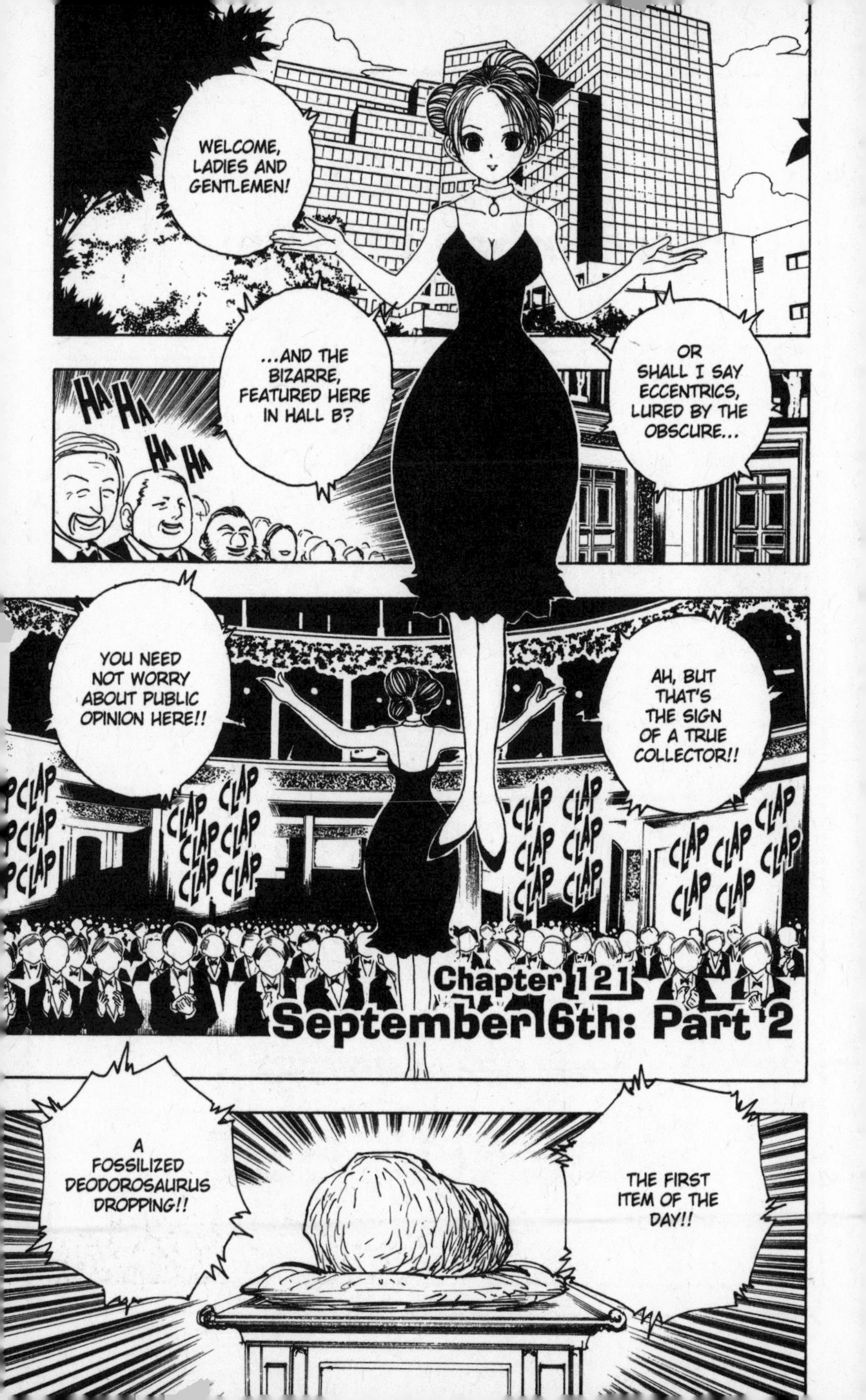
WELCOME, LADIES AND GENTLEMEN!
OR SHALL I SAY ECCENTRICS, LURED BY THE OBSCURE...
...AND THE BIZARRE, FEATURED HERE IN HALL B?
HA HA HA HA
AH, BUT THAT'S THE SIGN OF A TRUE COLLECTOR!!
YOU NEED NOT WORRY ABOUT PUBLIC OPINION HERE!!
CLAP CLAP CLAP CLAP CLAP CLAP CLAP CLAP CLAP CLAP CLAP CLAP
Chapter 121
September 16th: Part 2
THE FIRST ITEM OF THE DAY!!
A FOSSILIZED DEODOROSAURUS DROPPING!!

Chapter 121

September 6th: Part 2

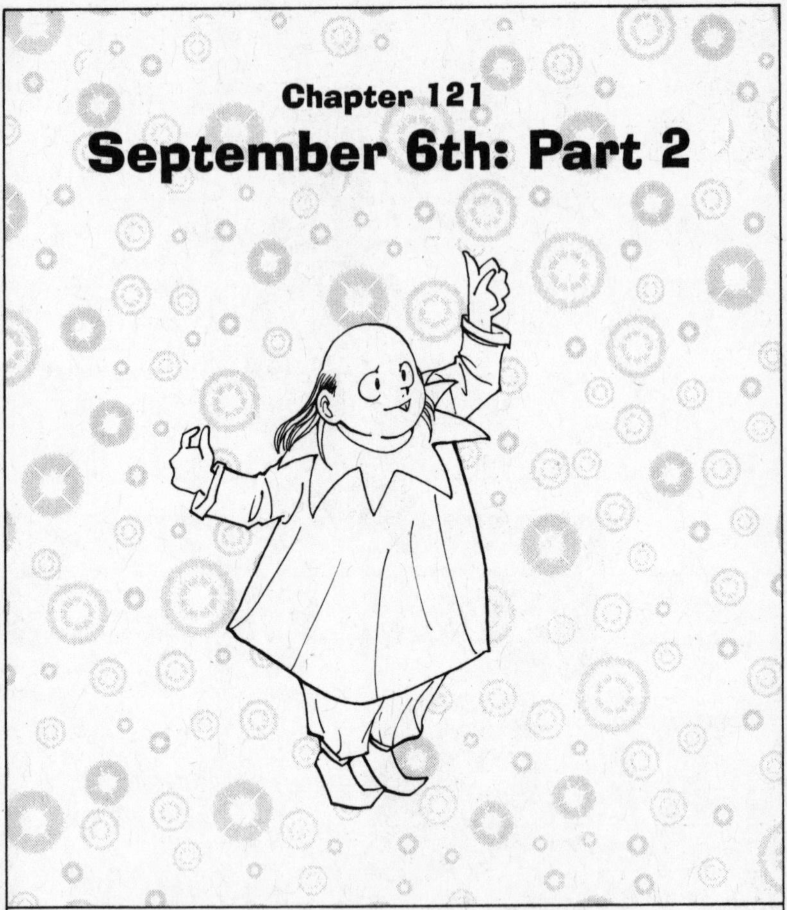

MELODY (EMITTER)

SHE EMITS HER AURA ALONG WITH THE MUSIC SHE PLAYS TO EASE OTHERS' FATIGUE. SHE HAS EXCEPTIONAL HEARING, AND CAN PERCEIVE A PERSON'S PSYCHOLOGICAL STATE BY LISTENING TO THE RHYTHM OF HIS HEARTBEAT.

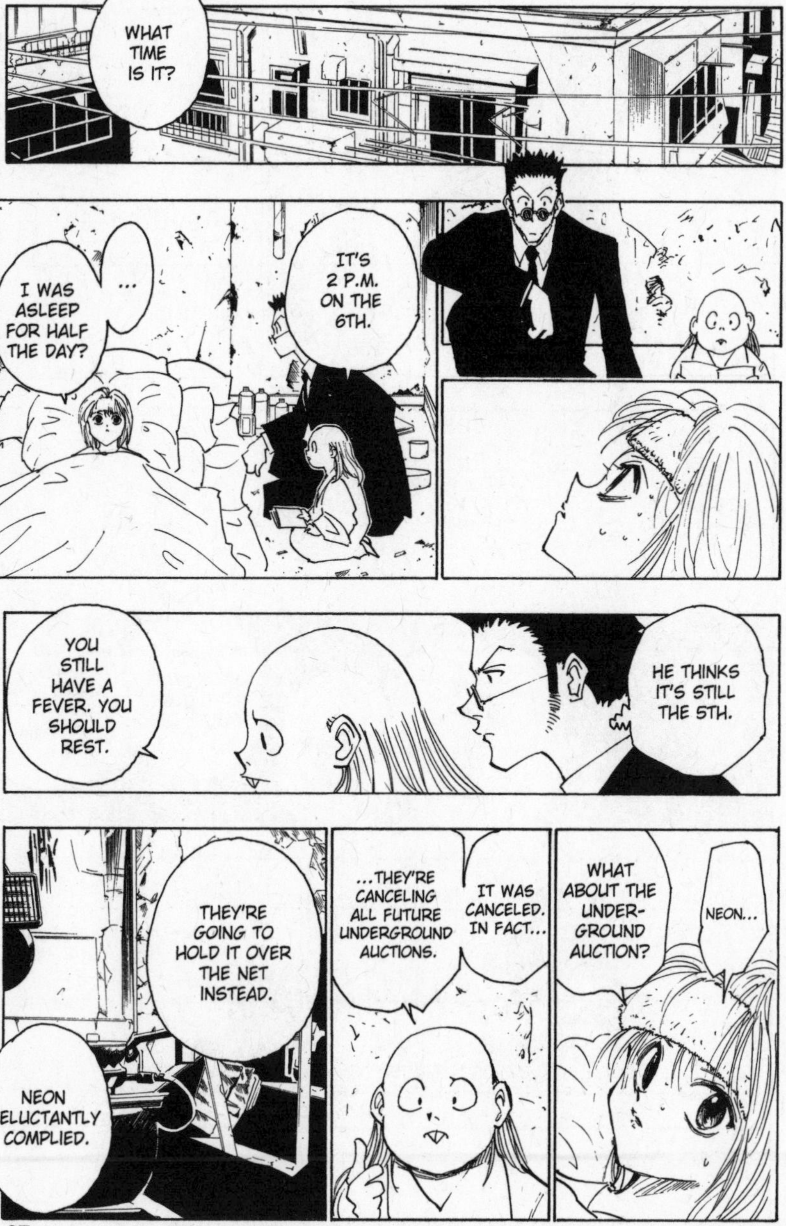
WHAT TIME IS IT?
IT'S 2 P.M. ON THE 6TH.
...
I WAS ASLEEP FOR HALF THE DAY?
HE THINKS IT'S STILL THE 5TH.
YOU STILL HAVE A FEVER. YOU SHOULD REST.
NEON...
WHAT ABOUT THE UNDER-GROUND AUCTION?
IT WAS CANCELED. IN FACT...
...THEY'RE CANCELING ALL FUTURE UNDERGROUND AUCTIONS.
THEY'RE GOING TO HOLD IT OVER THE NET INSTEAD.
NEON RELUCTANTLY COMPLIED.

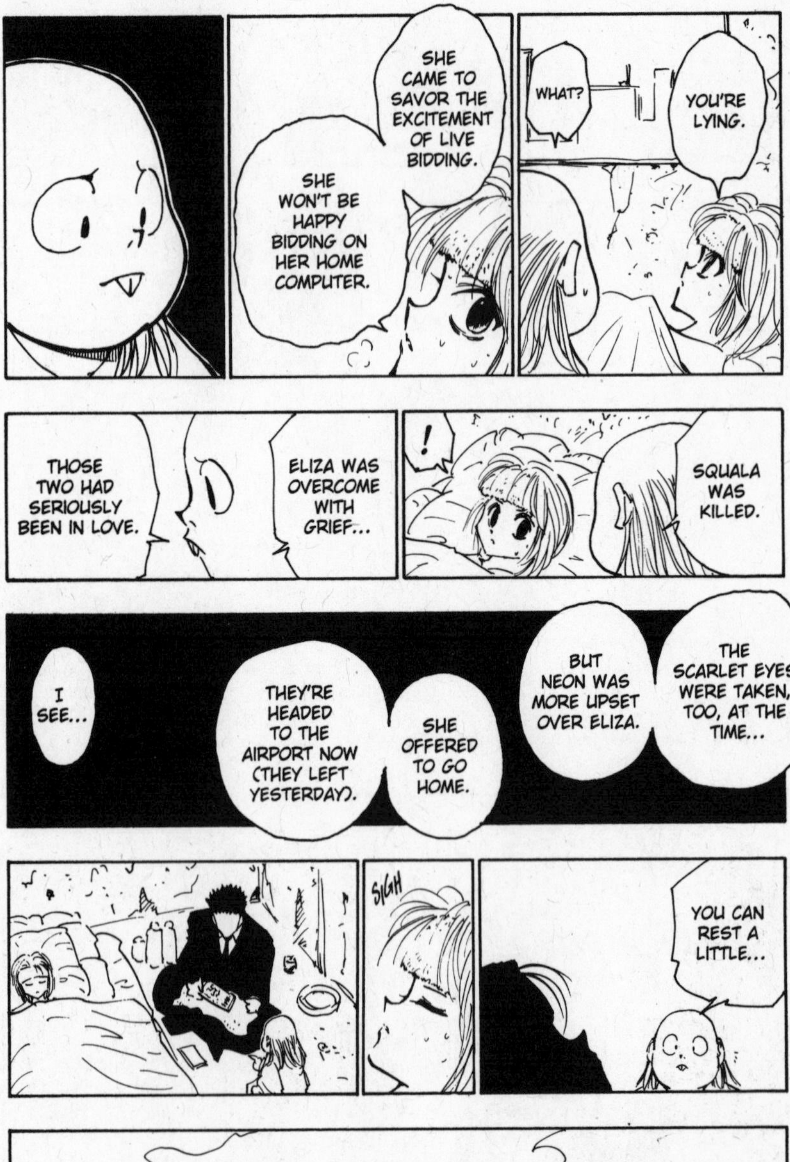
YOU'RE LYING.
WHAT?
SHE CAME TO SAVOR THE EXCITEMENT OF LIVE BIDDING.
SHE WON'T BE HAPPY BIDDING ON HER HOME COMPUTER.
SQUALA WAS KILLED.
!
ELIZA WAS OVERCOME WITH GRIEF...
THOSE TWO HAD SERIOUSLY BEEN IN LOVE.
THE SCARLET EYES WERE TAKEN, TOO, AT THE TIME...
BUT NEON WAS MORE UPSET OVER ELIZA.
SHE OFFERED TO GO HOME.
THEY'RE HEADED TO THE AIRPORT NOW (THEY LEFT YESTERDAY).
I SEE...
YOU CAN REST A LITTLE...
SIGH

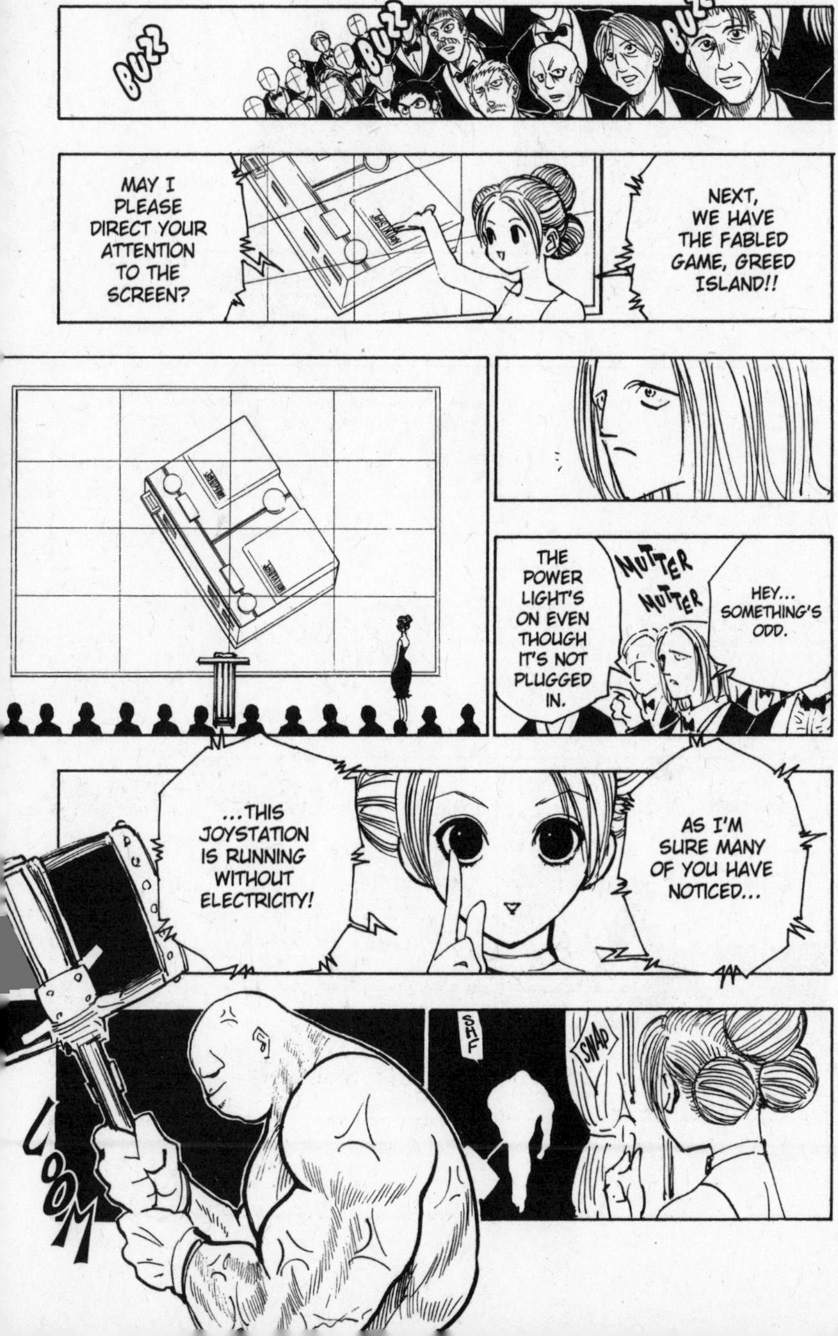
BUZZ
BUZZ
BUZZ
NEXT, WE HAVE THE FABLED GAME, GREED ISLAND!!
MAY I PLEASE DIRECT YOUR ATTENTION TO THE SCREEN?
HEY... SOMETHING'S ODD.
MUTTER MUTTER
THE POWER LIGHT'S ON EVEN THOUGH IT'S NOT PLUGGED IN.
AS I'M SURE MANY OF YOU HAVE NOTICED...
...THIS JOYSTATION IS RUNNING WITHOUT ELECTRICITY!
SNAP
SHF
VOOM

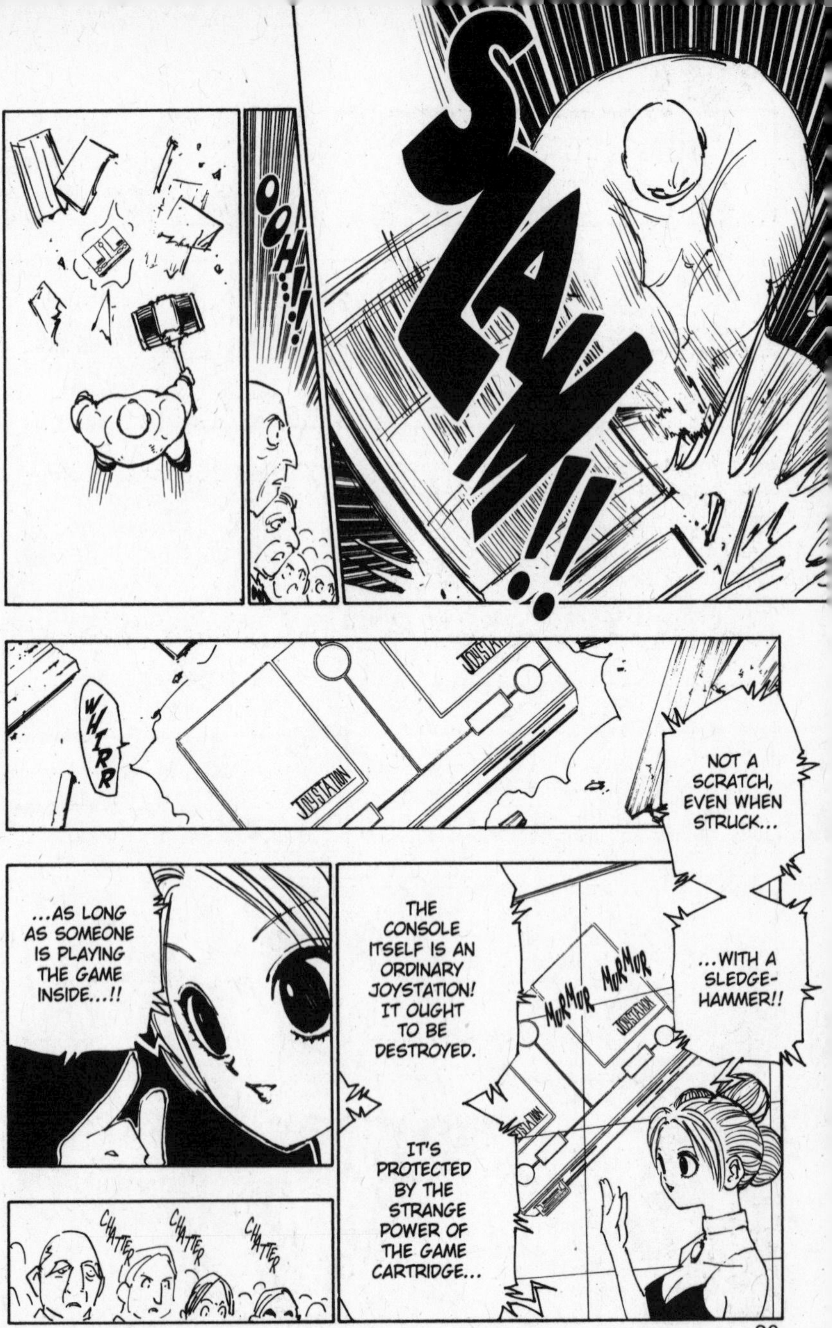
SLAM!!
OOH!!...
WHIRR
NOT A SCRATCH, EVEN WHEN STRUCK...
...WITH A SLEDGE-HAMMER!!
THE CONSOLE ITSELF IS AN ORDINARY JOYSTATION! IT OUGHT TO BE DESTROYED.
MURMUR MURMUR
IT'S PROTECTED BY THE STRANGE POWER OF THE GAME CARTRIDGE...
...AS LONG AS SOMEONE IS PLAYING THE GAME INSIDE...!!
CHATTER
CHATTER
CHATTER

READ THIS WAY

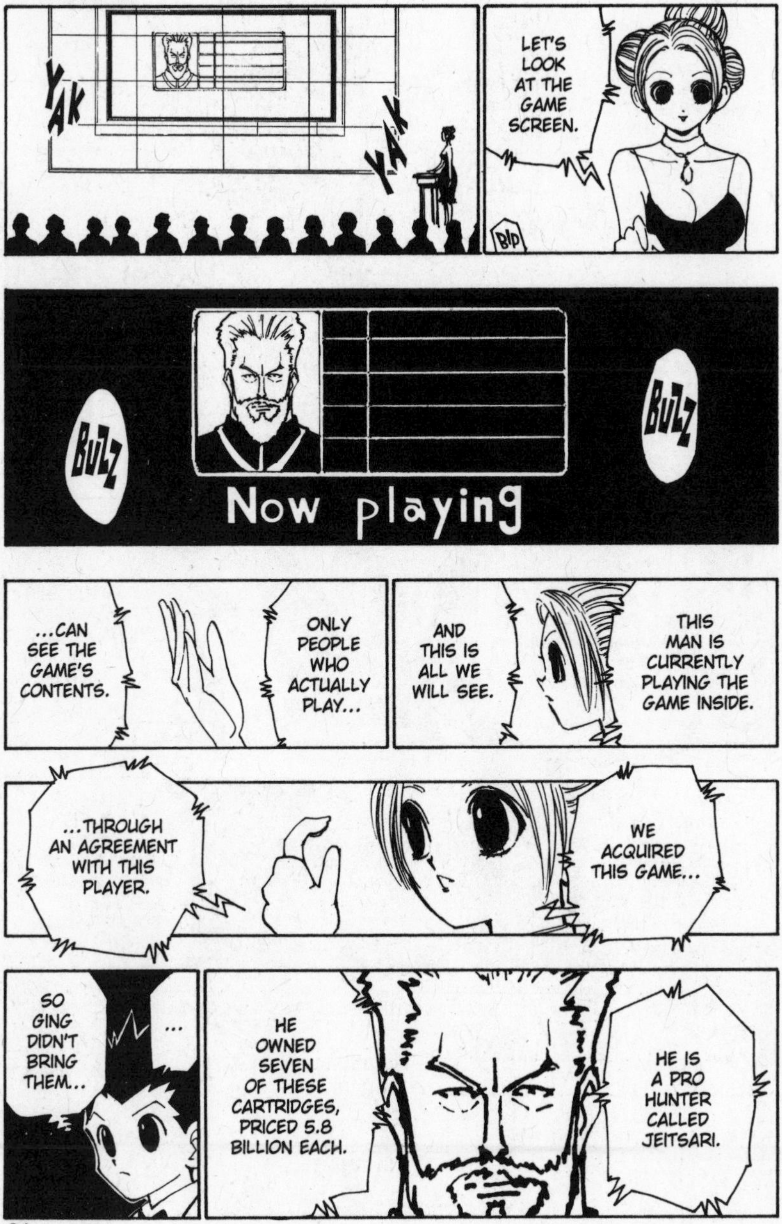

LET'S LOOK AT THE GAME SCREEN.
BIP
YAK
YAK
BUZZ
Now playing
BUZZ
THIS MAN IS CURRENTLY PLAYING THE GAME INSIDE.
AND THIS IS ALL WE WILL SEE.
ONLY PEOPLE WHO ACTUALLY PLAY...
...CAN SEE THE GAME'S CONTENTS.
WE ACQUIRED THIS GAME...
...THROUGH AN AGREEMENT WITH THIS PLAYER.
HE IS A PRO HUNTER CALLED JEITSARI.
HE OWNED SEVEN OF THESE CARTRIDGES, PRICED 5.8 BILLION EACH.
...
SO GING DIDN'T BRING THEM...

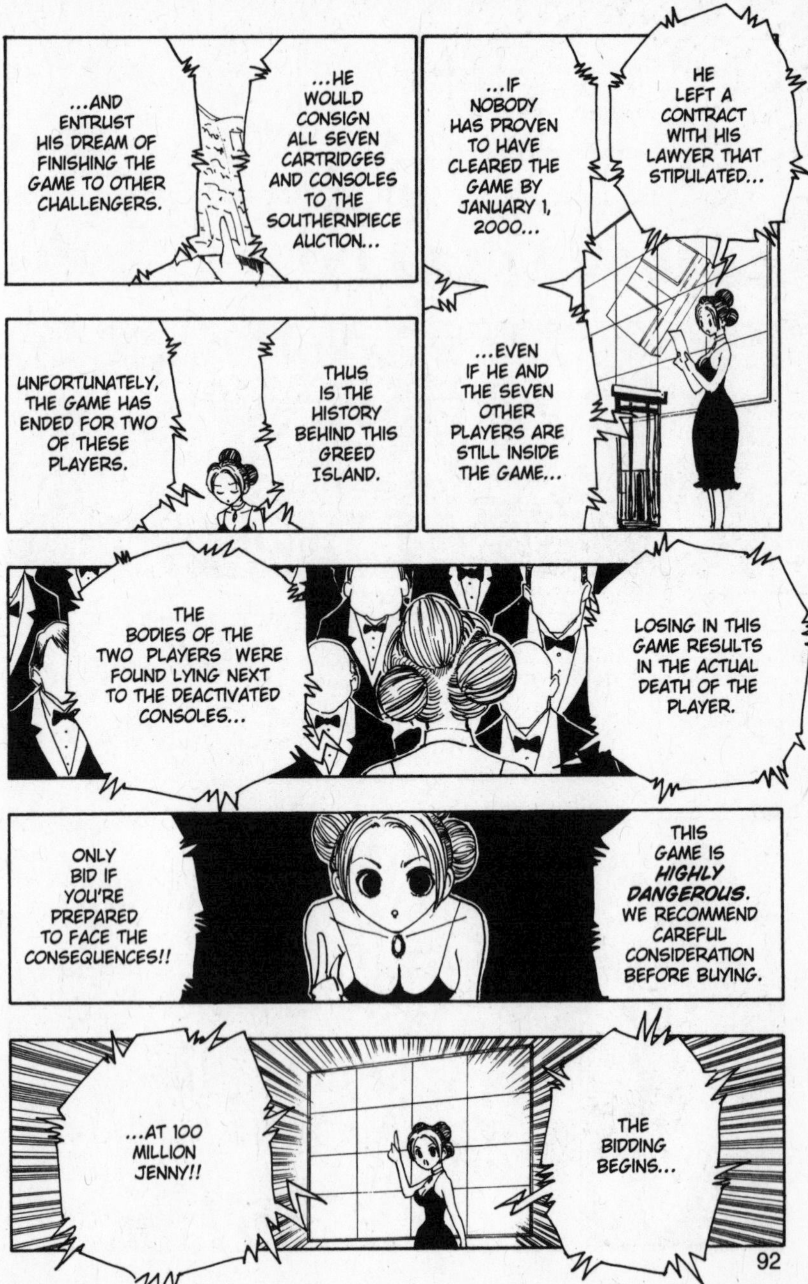
HE LEFT A CONTRACT WITH HIS LAWYER THAT STIPULATED...
...IF NOBODY HAS PROVEN TO HAVE CLEARED THE GAME BY JANUARY 1, 2000...
...EVEN IF HE AND THE SEVEN OTHER PLAYERS ARE STILL INSIDE THE GAME...
...HE WOULD CONSIGN ALL SEVEN CARTRIDGES AND CONSOLES TO THE SOUTHERNPIECE AUCTION...
...AND ENTRUST HIS DREAM OF FINISHING THE GAME TO OTHER CHALLENGERS.
THUS IS THE HISTORY BEHIND THIS GREED ISLAND.
UNFORTUNATELY, THE GAME HAS ENDED FOR TWO OF THESE PLAYERS.
LOSING IN THIS GAME RESULTS IN THE ACTUAL DEATH OF THE PLAYER.
THE BODIES OF THE TWO PLAYERS WERE FOUND LYING NEXT TO THE DEACTIVATED CONSOLES...
THIS GAME IS ***HIGHLY DANGEROUS***. WE RECOMMEND CAREFUL CONSIDERATION BEFORE BUYING.
ONLY BID IF YOU'RE PREPARED TO FACE THE CONSEQUENCES!!
THE BIDDING BEGINS...
...AT 100 MILLION JENNY!!

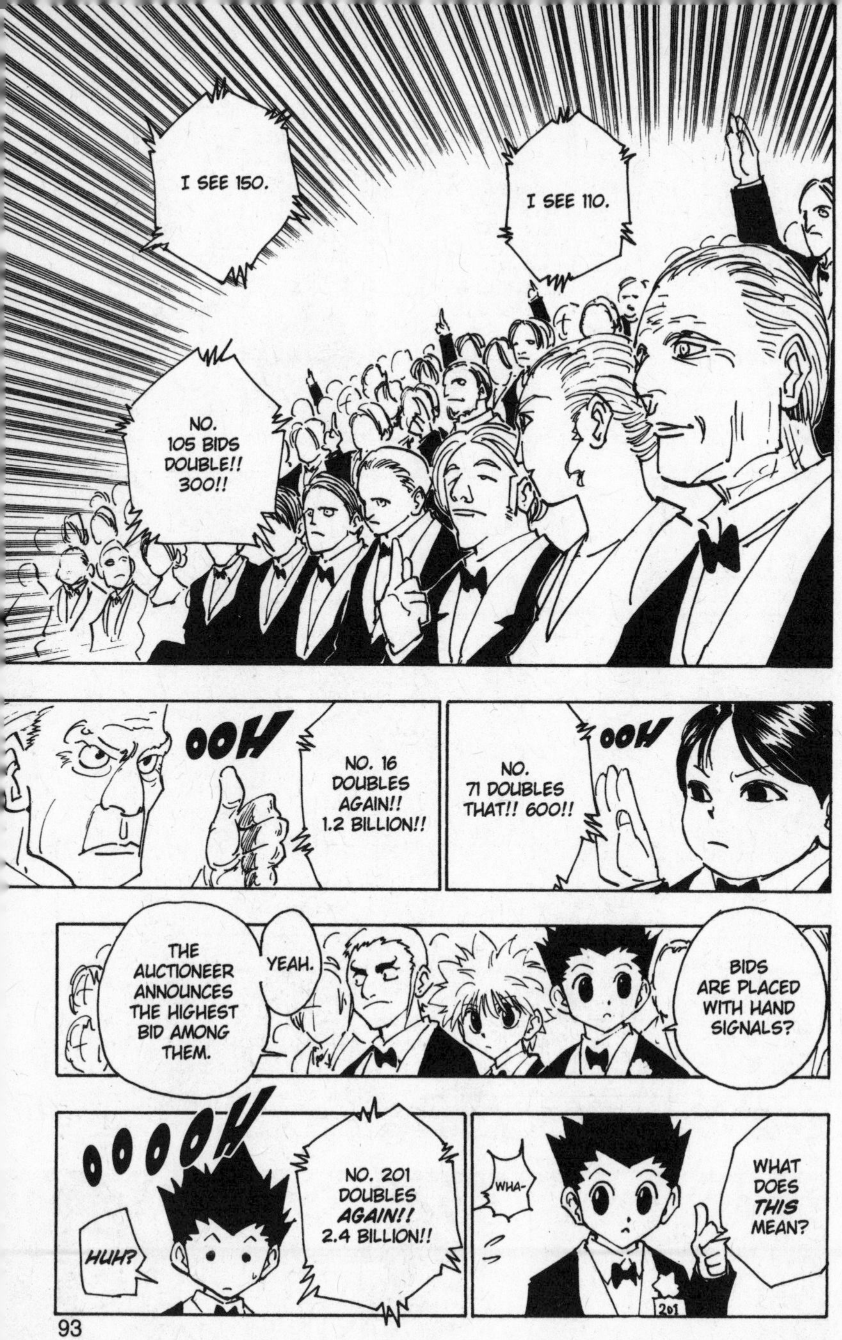
I SEE 110.
I SEE 150.
NO. 105 BIDS DOUBLE!! 300!!
OOH
NO. 71 DOUBLES THAT!! 600!!
OOH
NO. 16 DOUBLES AGAIN!! 1.2 BILLION!!
BIDS ARE PLACED WITH HAND SIGNALS?
YEAH.
THE AUCTIONEER ANNOUNCES THE HIGHEST BID AMONG THEM.
WHAT DOES *THIS* MEAN?
WHA-
201
OOOOH
NO. 201 DOUBLES *AGAIN!!* 2.4 BILLION!!
HUH?

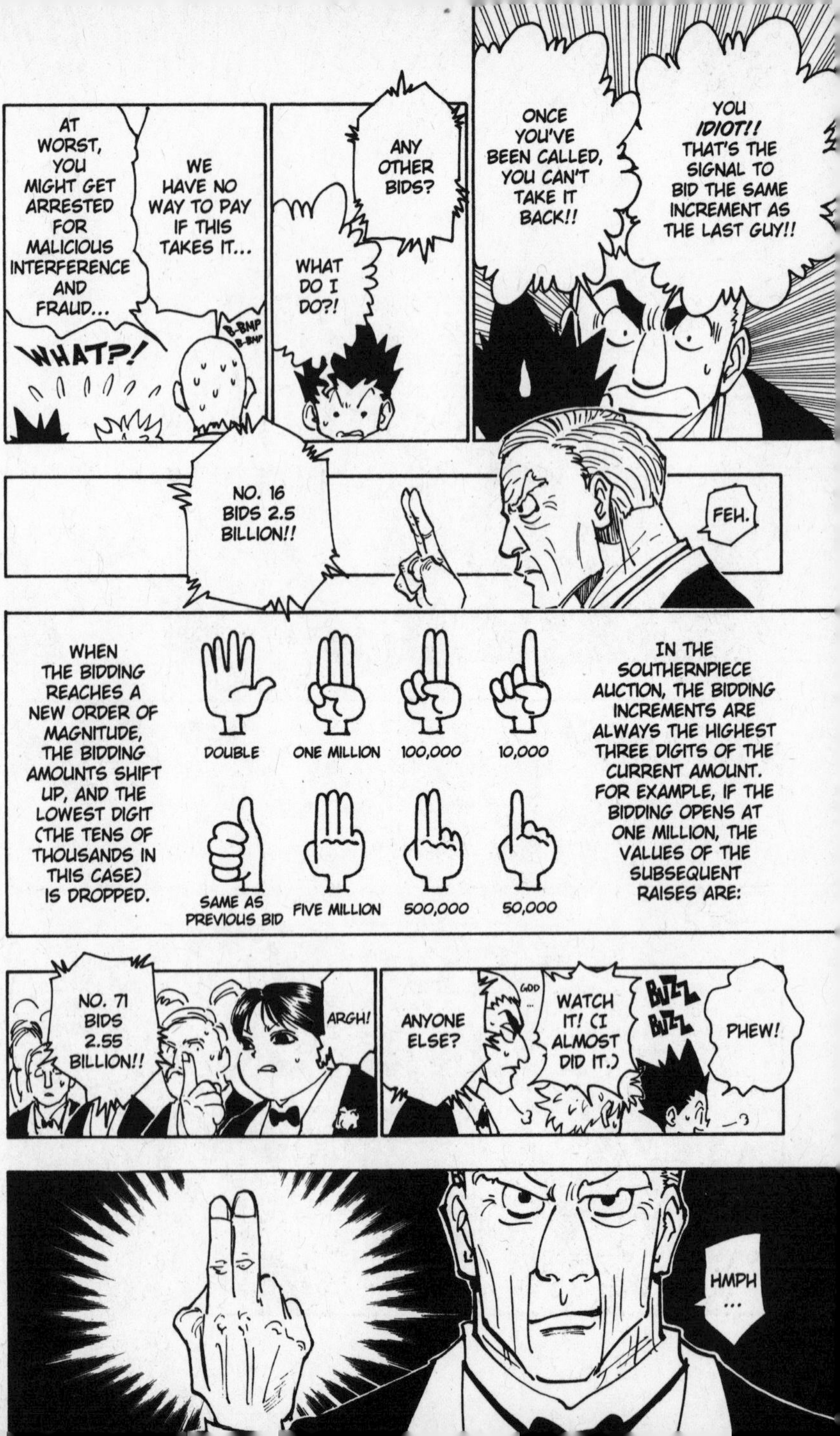
YOU IDIOT!! THAT'S THE SIGNAL TO BID THE SAME INCREMENT AS THE LAST GUY!!
ONCE YOU'VE BEEN CALLED, YOU CAN'T TAKE IT BACK!!
ANY OTHER BIDS?
WHAT DO I DO?!
WE HAVE NO WAY TO PAY IF THIS TAKES IT...
AT WORST, YOU MIGHT GET ARRESTED FOR MALICIOUS INTERFERENCE AND FRAUD...
B-BMP B-BMP
WHAT?!
FEH.
NO. 16 BIDS 2.5 BILLION!!
IN THE SOUTHERNPIECE AUCTION, THE BIDDING INCREMENTS ARE ALWAYS THE HIGHEST THREE DIGITS OF THE CURRENT AMOUNT. FOR EXAMPLE, IF THE BIDDING OPENS AT ONE MILLION, THE VALUES OF THE SUBSEQUENT RAISES ARE:
10,000
100,000
ONE MILLION
DOUBLE
50,000
500,000
FIVE MILLION
SAME AS PREVIOUS BID
WHEN THE BIDDING REACHES A NEW ORDER OF MAGNITUDE, THE BIDDING AMOUNTS SHIFT UP, AND THE LOWEST DIGIT (THE TENS OF THOUSANDS IN THIS CASE) IS DROPPED.
PHEW!
BUZZ BUZZ
WATCH IT! (I ALMOST DID IT.)
ANYONE ELSE?
ARGH!
NO. 71 BIDS 2.55 BILLION!!
HMPH ...

READ THIS WAY

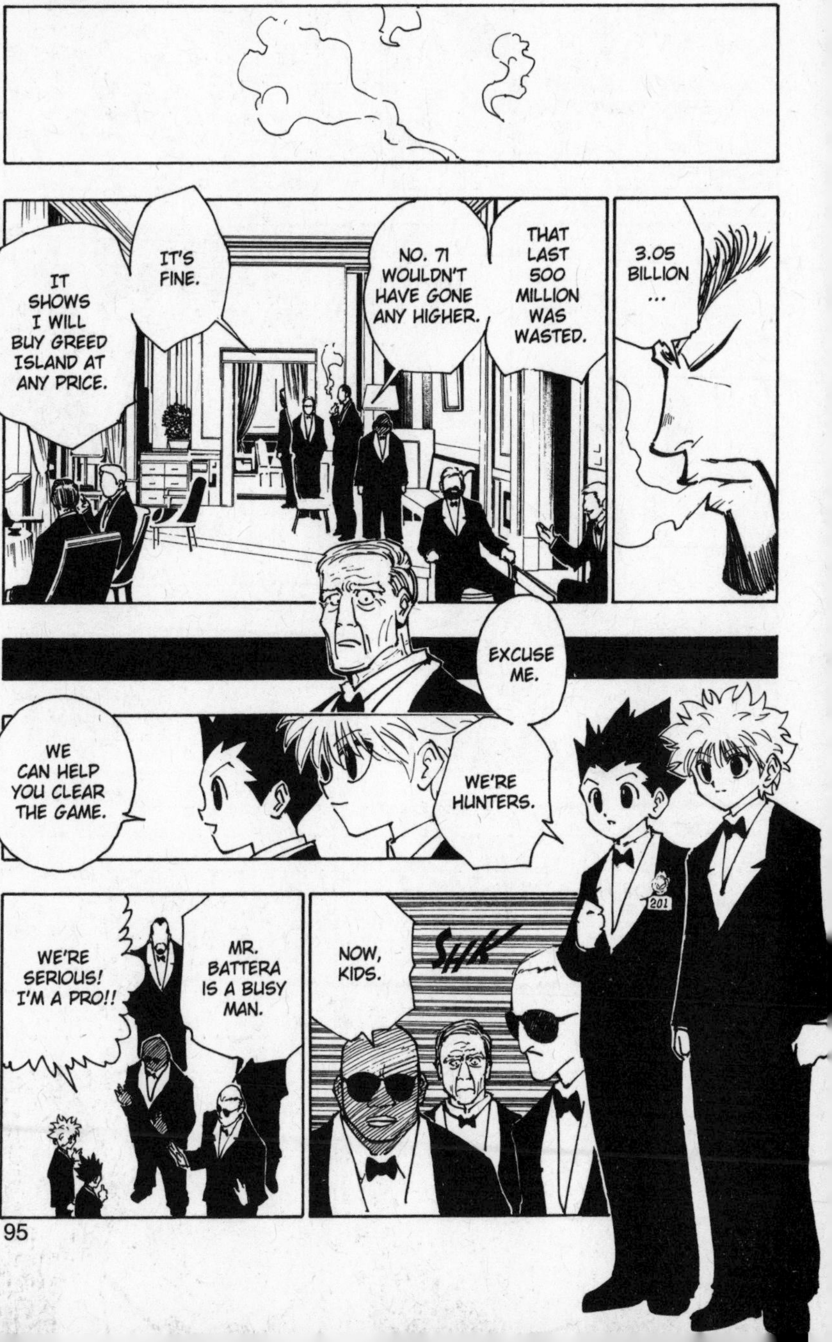
3.05 BILLION ...
THAT LAST 500 MILLION WAS WASTED.
NO. 71 WOULDN'T HAVE GONE ANY HIGHER.
IT'S FINE.
IT SHOWS I WILL BUY GREED ISLAND AT ANY PRICE.
EXCUSE ME.
WE'RE HUNTERS.
WE CAN HELP YOU CLEAR THE GAME.
201
SHK
NOW, KIDS.
MR. BATTERA IS A BUSY MAN.
WE'RE SERIOUS! I'M A PRO!!

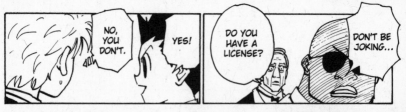

DON'T BE JOKING...
DO YOU HAVE A LICENSE?
YES!
NO, YOU DON'T.
IT'S STILL AT THE PAWNSHOP.
ACK!
UM, NOT NOW...
SEE, YOU'RE LYING!!
I'M *NOT!*
NOW, HOLD ON.
SIR?
THE FACT THAT YOU'RE HERE AT ALL SHOWS THAT YOU'RE NOT JUST ANY KIDS.
HOWEVER, WE CAN'T SIMPLY TAKE YOUR WORD AT FACE VALUE.
IT'S TRUE THAT I'M RECRUITING HUNTERS TO CLEAR THE GAME, BUT WE GO THROUGH A CAREFUL SCREENING PROCESS.
THERE'S A LIMIT TO THE NUMBER...
...OF PLAYERS. I'M AFRAID WE CAN'T HIRE YOU ON THE SPOT.
DID WE FAIL...?!
I THOUGHT IT WAS A GOOD PLAN.
I DON'T THINK WE EVEN NEED TO BUY THE GAME. WE DON'T NEED THE CARTRIDGE -- JUST THE INFORMATION INSIDE.
WE READ THAT A MR. BATTERA IS OFFERING A REWARD FOR CLEAR DATA.
I BET HE'D COME TO THE AUCTION... AND I ALSO BET HE'S LOOKING FOR PEOPLE TO PLAY THE GAME, TOO.

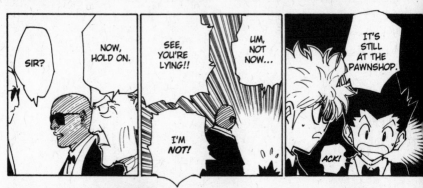

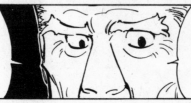

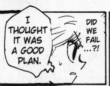

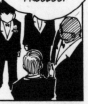

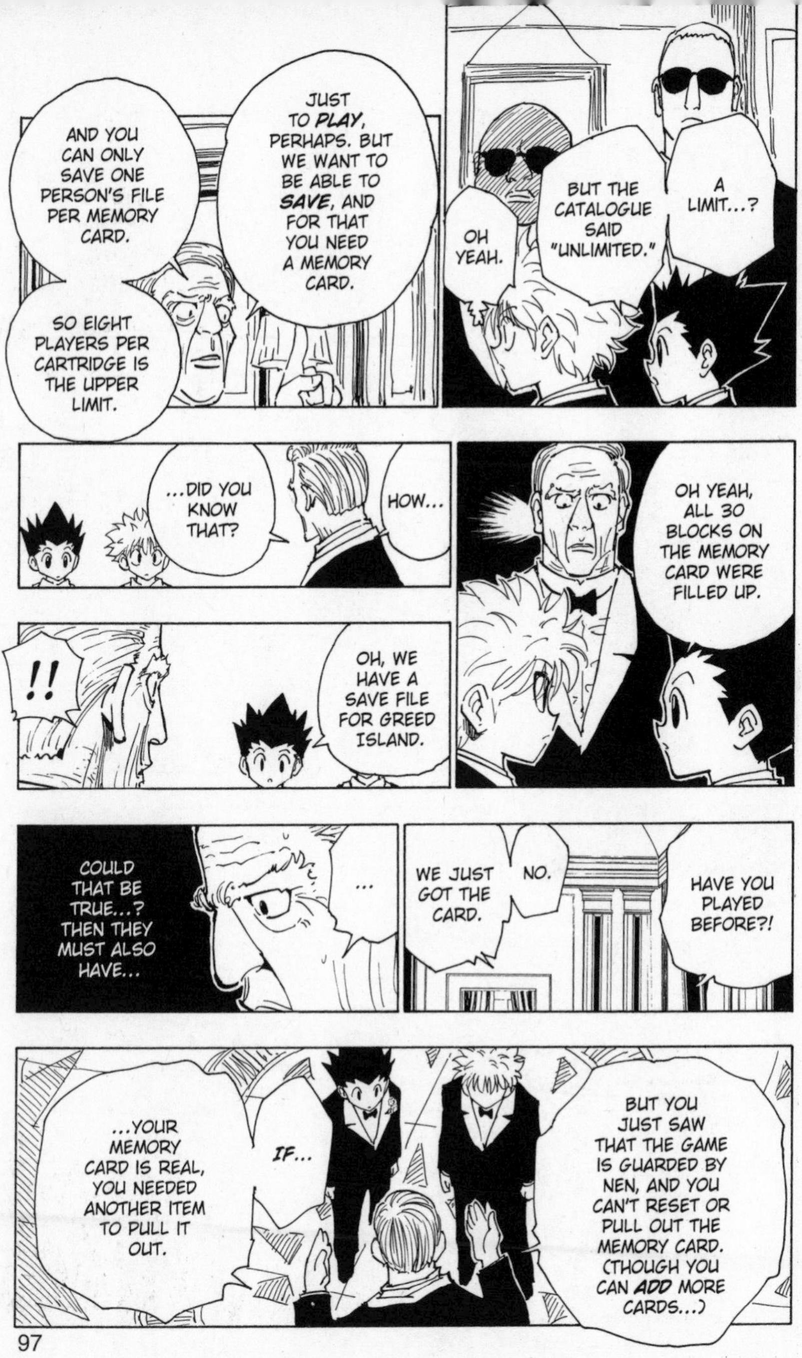
A LIMIT...?
BUT THE CATALOGUE SAID "UNLIMITED."
OH YEAH.
JUST TO PLAY, PERHAPS. BUT WE WANT TO BE ABLE TO SAVE, AND FOR THAT YOU NEED A MEMORY CARD.
AND YOU CAN ONLY SAVE ONE PERSON'S FILE PER MEMORY CARD.
SO EIGHT PLAYERS PER CARTRIDGE IS THE UPPER LIMIT.
OH YEAH, ALL 30 BLOCKS ON THE MEMORY CARD WERE FILLED UP.
HOW...
...DID YOU KNOW THAT?
OH, WE HAVE A SAVE FILE FOR GREED ISLAND.
!!
HAVE YOU PLAYED BEFORE?!
NO.
WE JUST GOT THE CARD.
...
COULD THAT BE TRUE...? THEN THEY MUST ALSO HAVE...
BUT YOU JUST SAW THAT THE GAME IS GUARDED BY NEN, AND YOU CAN'T RESET OR PULL OUT THE MEMORY CARD. (THOUGH YOU CAN ADD MORE CARDS...)
IF...
...YOUR MEMORY CARD IS REAL, YOU NEEDED ANOTHER ITEM TO PULL IT OUT.

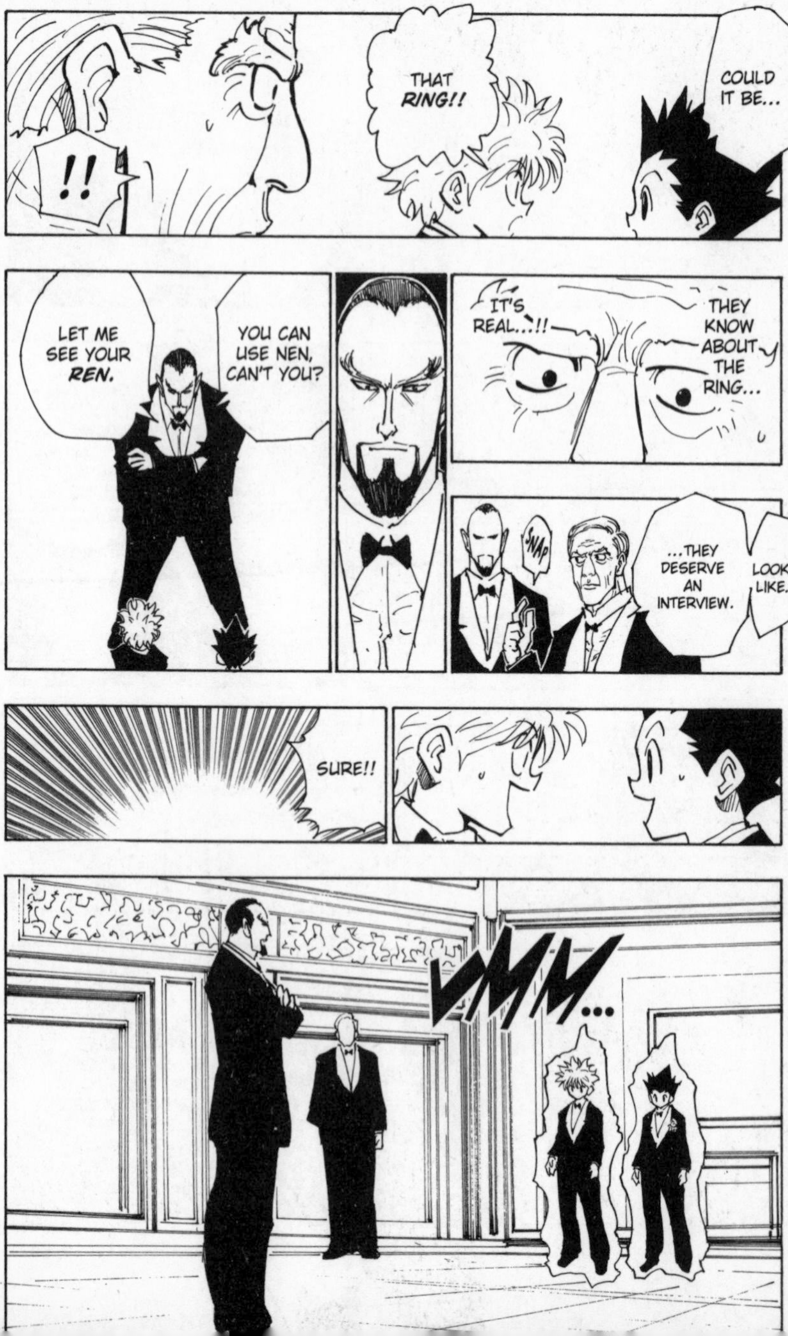
COULD IT BE...
THAT *RING!!*
!!
THEY KNOW ABOUT THE RING...
IT'S REAL...!!
LOOKS LIKE...
...THEY DESERVE AN INTERVIEW.
SNAP
YOU CAN USE NEN, CAN'T YOU?
LET ME SEE YOUR ***REN.***
SURE!!
VMM...

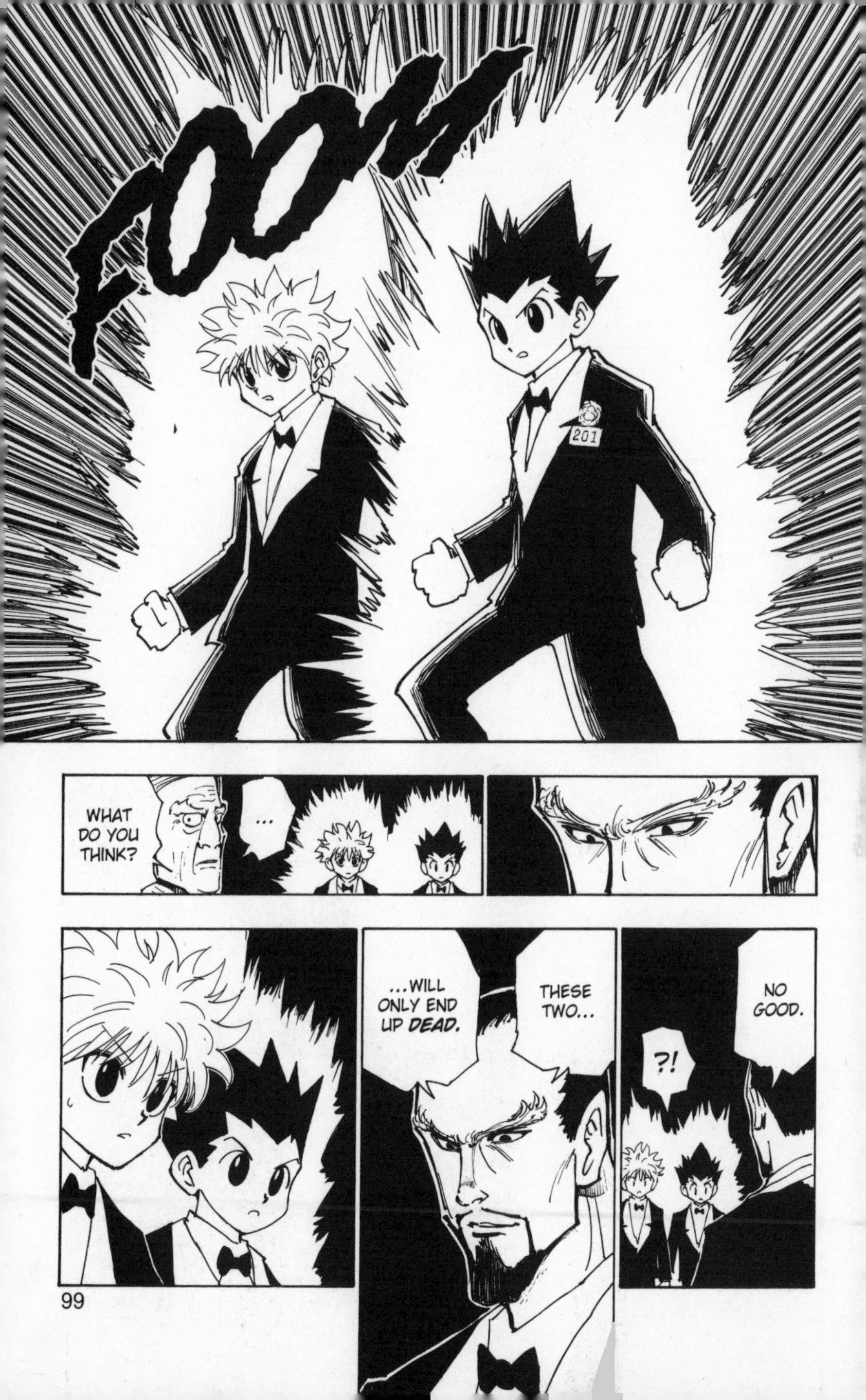
FOOM
...
WHAT DO YOU THINK?
NO GOOD.
?!
THESE TWO...
...WILL ONLY END UP DEAD.

Chapter 122
September 6th: Part 3

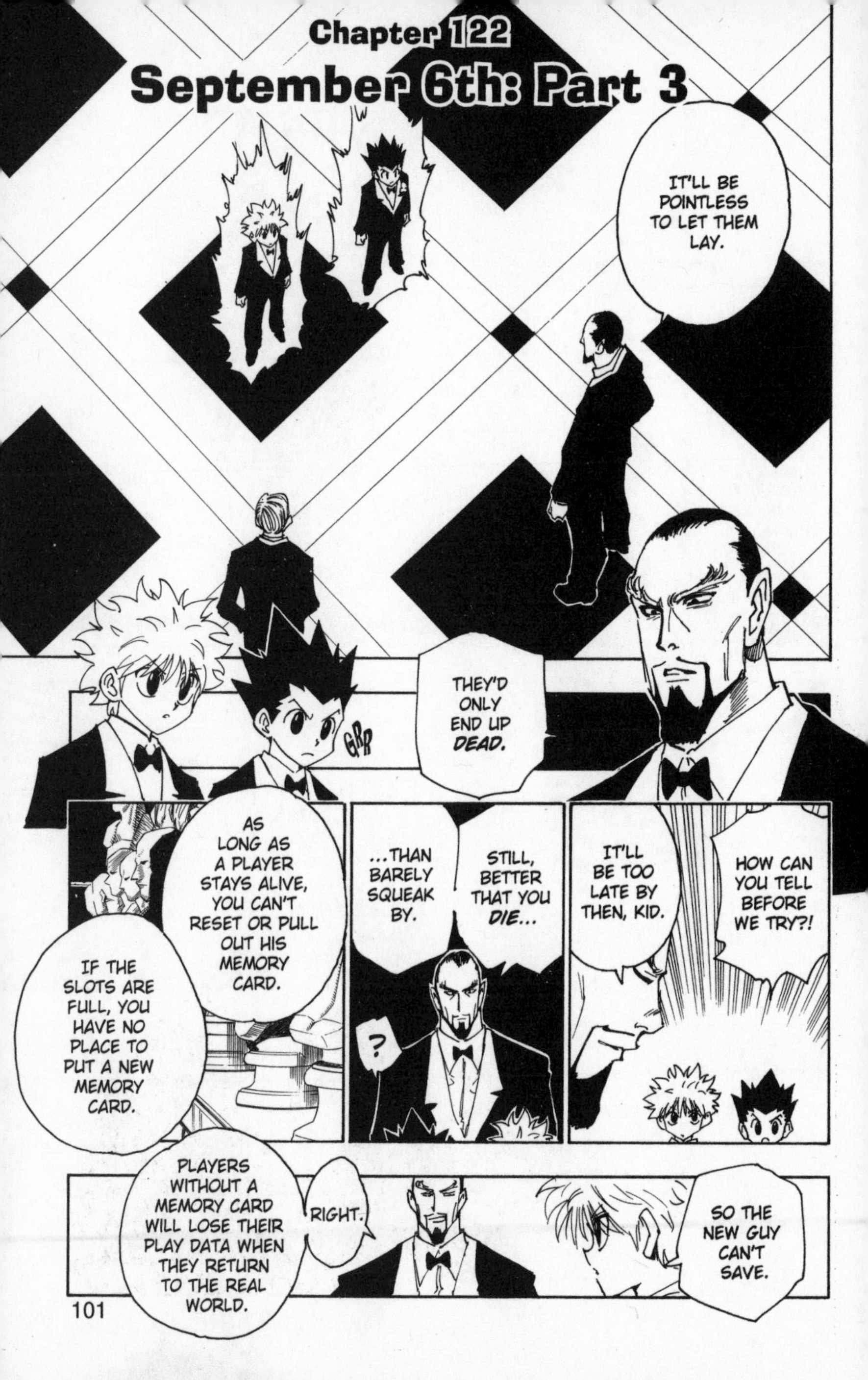
IT'LL BE POINTLESS TO LET THEM LAY.
THEY'D ONLY END UP *DEAD.*
GRR
HOW CAN YOU TELL BEFORE WE TRY?!
IT'LL BE TOO LATE BY THEN, KID.
STILL, BETTER THAT YOU *DIE...*
...THAN BARELY SQUEAK BY.
?
AS LONG AS A PLAYER STAYS ALIVE, YOU CAN'T RESET OR PULL OUT HIS MEMORY CARD.
IF THE SLOTS ARE FULL, YOU HAVE NO PLACE TO PUT A NEW MEMORY CARD.
SO THE NEW GUY CAN'T SAVE.
RIGHT.
PLAYERS WITHOUT A MEMORY CARD WILL LOSE THEIR PLAY DATA WHEN THEY RETURN TO THE REAL WORLD.

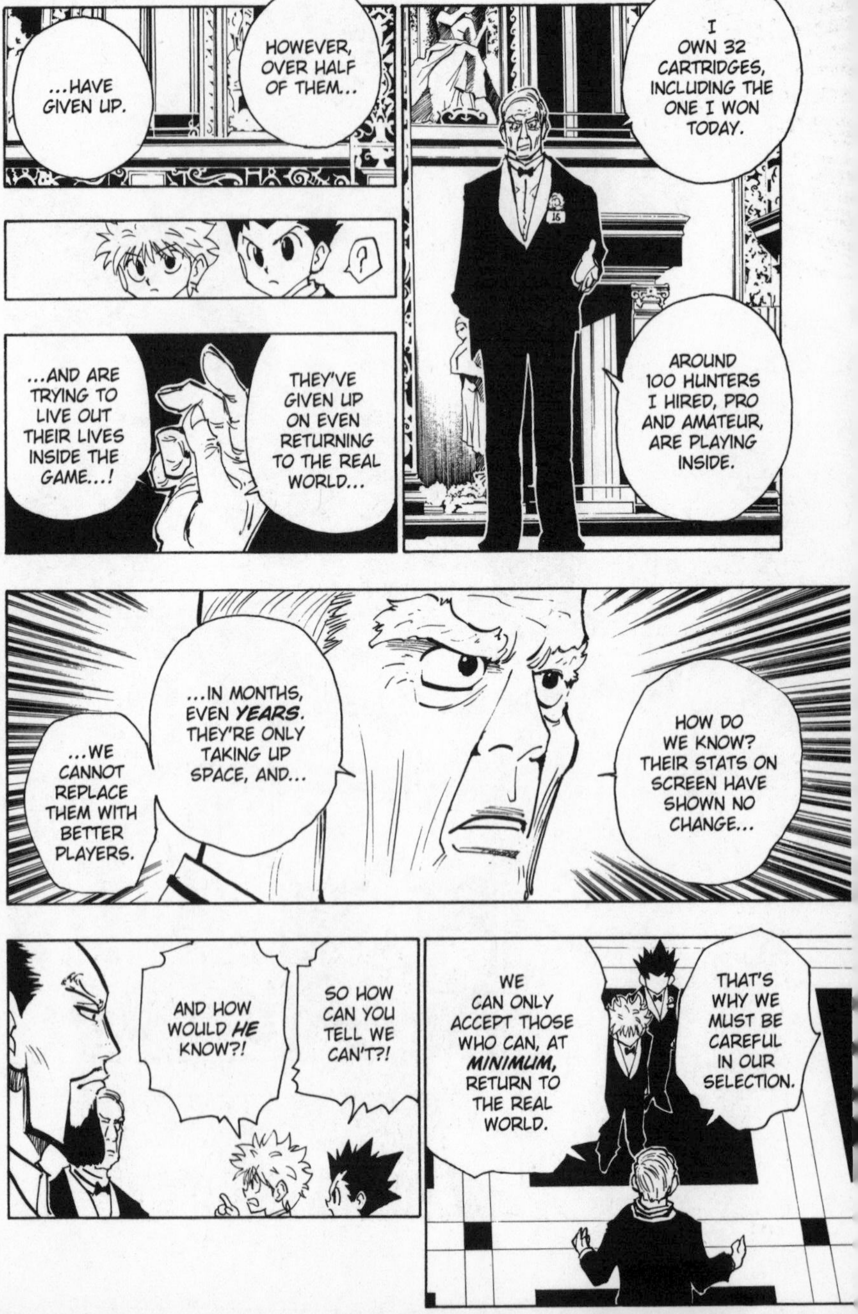
I OWN 32 CARTRIDGES, INCLUDING THE ONE I WON TODAY.
AROUND 100 HUNTERS I HIRED, PRO AND AMATEUR, ARE PLAYING INSIDE.
HOWEVER, OVER HALF OF THEM...
...HAVE GIVEN UP.
?
THEY'VE GIVEN UP ON EVEN RETURNING TO THE REAL WORLD...
...AND ARE TRYING TO LIVE OUT THEIR LIVES INSIDE THE GAME...!
HOW DO WE KNOW? THEIR STATS ON SCREEN HAVE SHOWN NO CHANGE...
...IN MONTHS, EVEN *YEARS*. THEY'RE ONLY TAKING UP SPACE, AND...
...WE CANNOT REPLACE THEM WITH BETTER PLAYERS.
THAT'S WHY WE MUST BE CAREFUL IN OUR SELECTION.
WE CAN ONLY ACCEPT THOSE WHO CAN, AT *MINIMUM*, RETURN TO THE REAL WORLD.
SO HOW CAN YOU TELL WE CAN'T?!
AND HOW WOULD *HE* KNOW?!

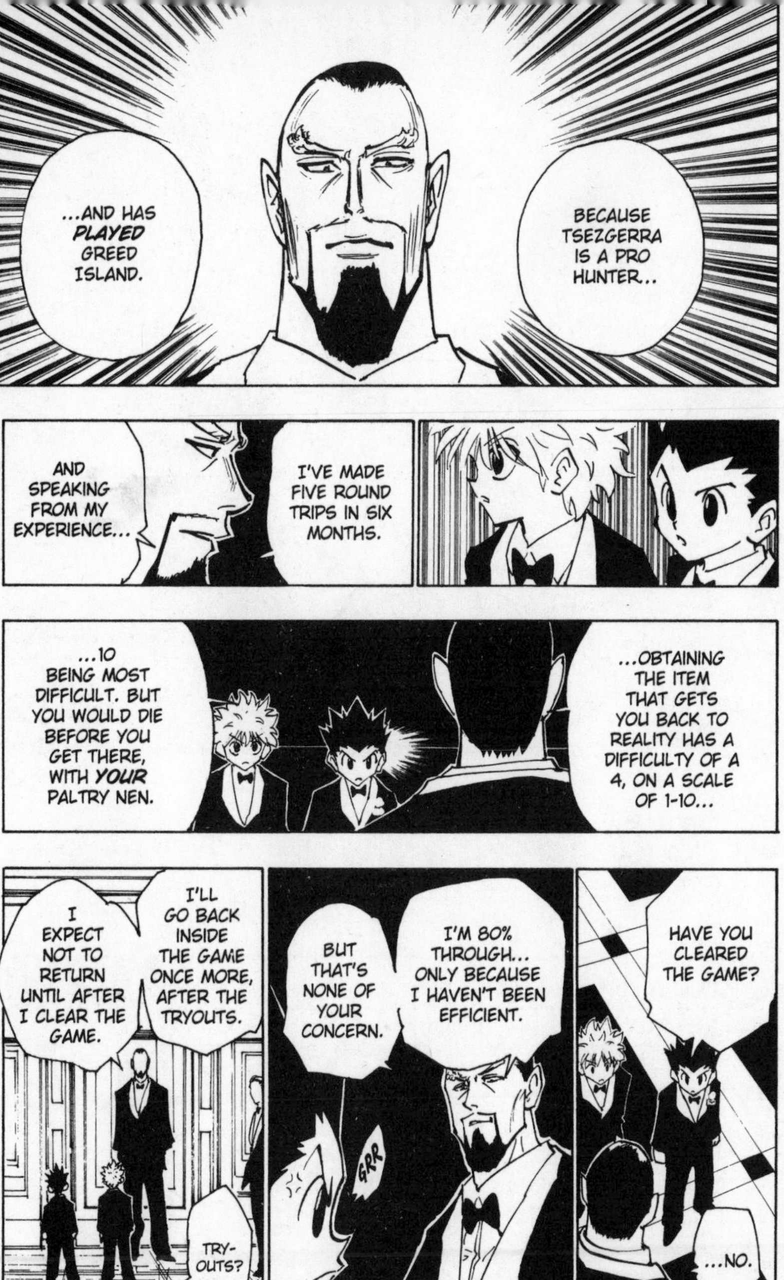
BECAUSE TSEZGERRA IS A PRO HUNTER...
...AND HAS *PLAYED* GREED ISLAND.
I'VE MADE FIVE ROUND TRIPS IN SIX MONTHS.
AND SPEAKING FROM MY EXPERIENCE...
...OBTAINING THE ITEM THAT GETS YOU BACK TO REALITY HAS A DIFFICULTY OF A 4, ON A SCALE OF 1-10...
...10 BEING MOST DIFFICULT. BUT YOU WOULD DIE BEFORE YOU GET THERE, WITH *YOUR* PALTRY NEN.
HAVE YOU CLEARED THE GAME?
...NO.
I'M 80% THROUGH... ONLY BECAUSE I HAVEN'T BEEN EFFICIENT.
BUT THAT'S NONE OF YOUR CONCERN.
GRR
I'LL GO BACK INSIDE THE GAME ONCE MORE, AFTER THE TRYOUTS.
I EXPECT NOT TO RETURN UNTIL AFTER I CLEAR THE GAME.
TRY-OUTS?

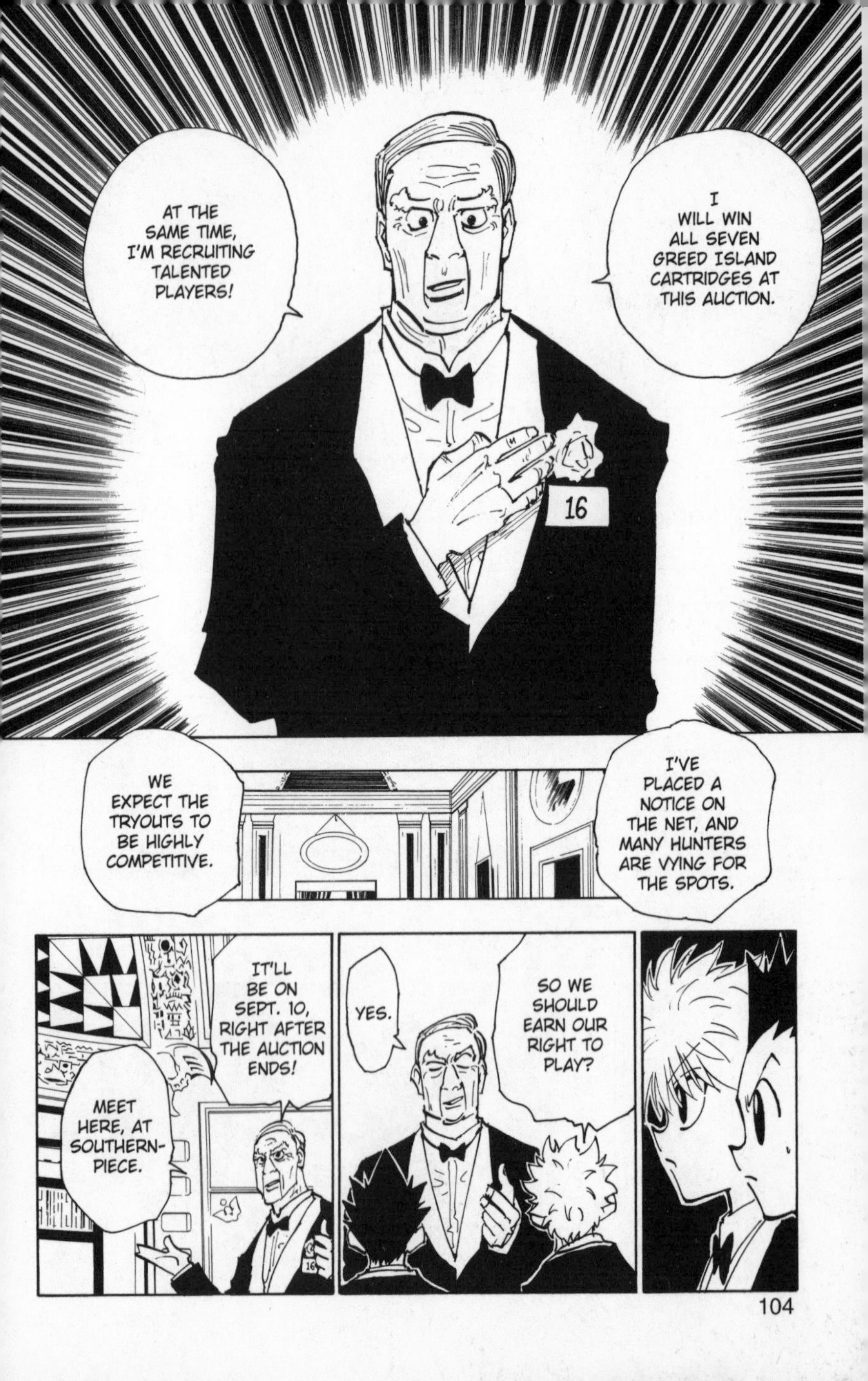
I WILL WIN ALL SEVEN GREED ISLAND CARTRIDGES AT THIS AUCTION.
AT THE SAME TIME, I'M RECRUITING TALENTED PLAYERS!
16
I'VE PLACED A NOTICE ON THE NET, AND MANY HUNTERS ARE VYING FOR THE SPOTS.
WE EXPECT THE TRYOUTS TO BE HIGHLY COMPETITIVE.
SO WE SHOULD EARN OUR RIGHT TO PLAY?
YES.
IT'LL BE ON SEPT. 10, RIGHT AFTER THE AUCTION ENDS!
MEET HERE, AT SOUTHERN-PIECE.
16

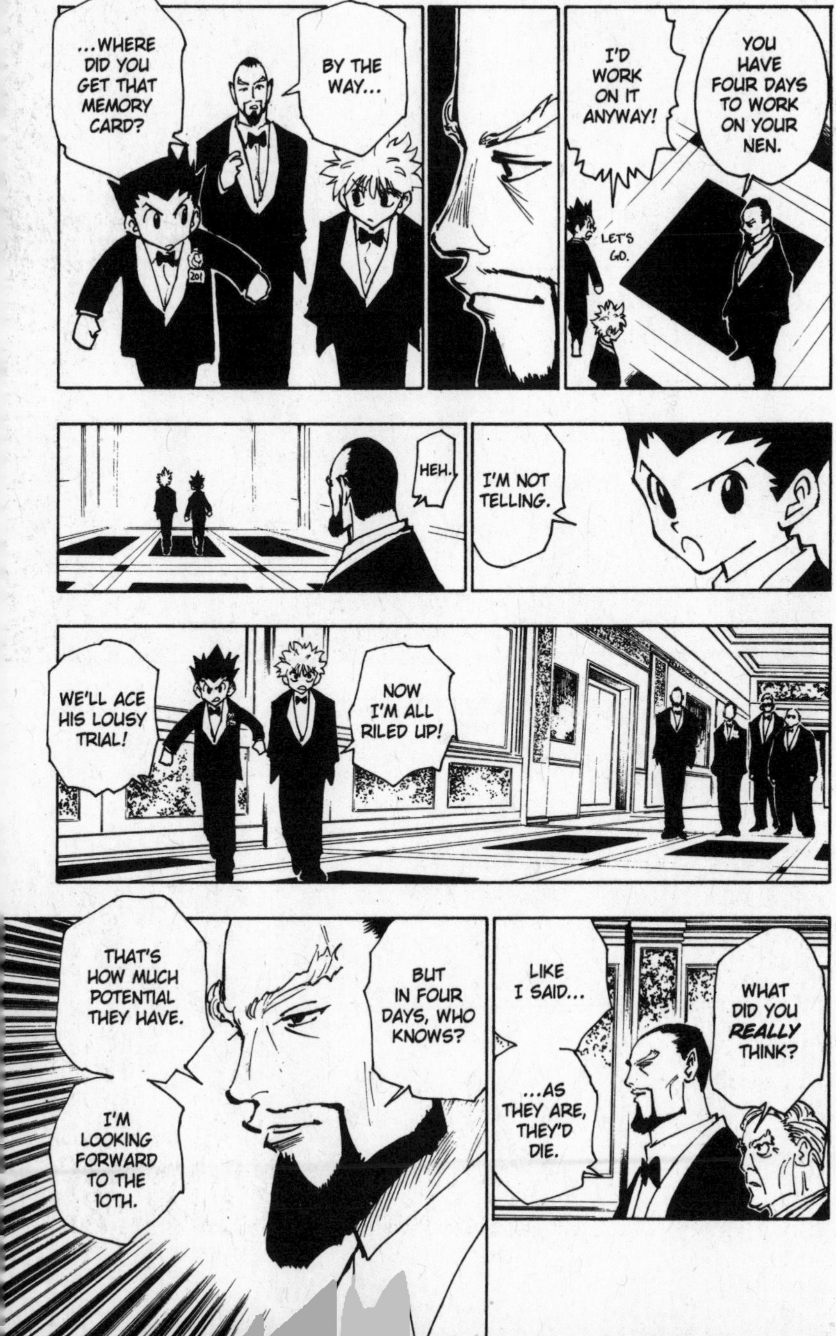
YOU HAVE FOUR DAYS TO WORK ON YOUR NEN.
I'D WORK ON IT ANYWAY!
LET'S GO.
BY THE WAY...
...WHERE DID YOU GET THAT MEMORY CARD?
I'M NOT TELLING.
HEH.
NOW I'M ALL RILED UP!
WE'LL ACE HIS LOUSY TRIAL!
WHAT DID YOU *REALLY* THINK?
LIKE I SAID...
...AS THEY ARE, THEY'D DIE.
BUT IN FOUR DAYS, WHO KNOWS?
THAT'S HOW MUCH POTENTIAL THEY HAVE.
I'M LOOKING FORWARD TO THE 10TH.

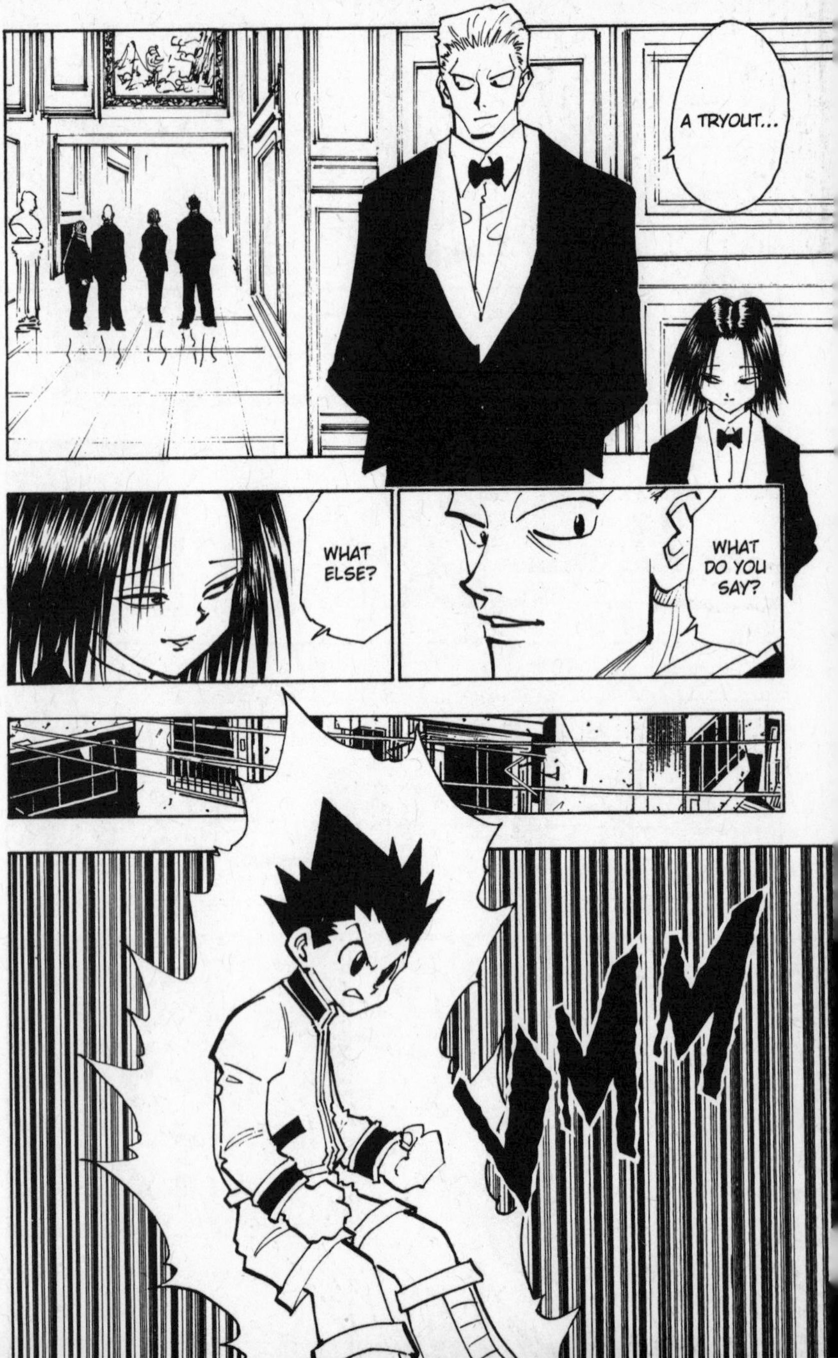
A TRYOUT...
WHAT DO YOU SAY?
WHAT ELSE?
VMM

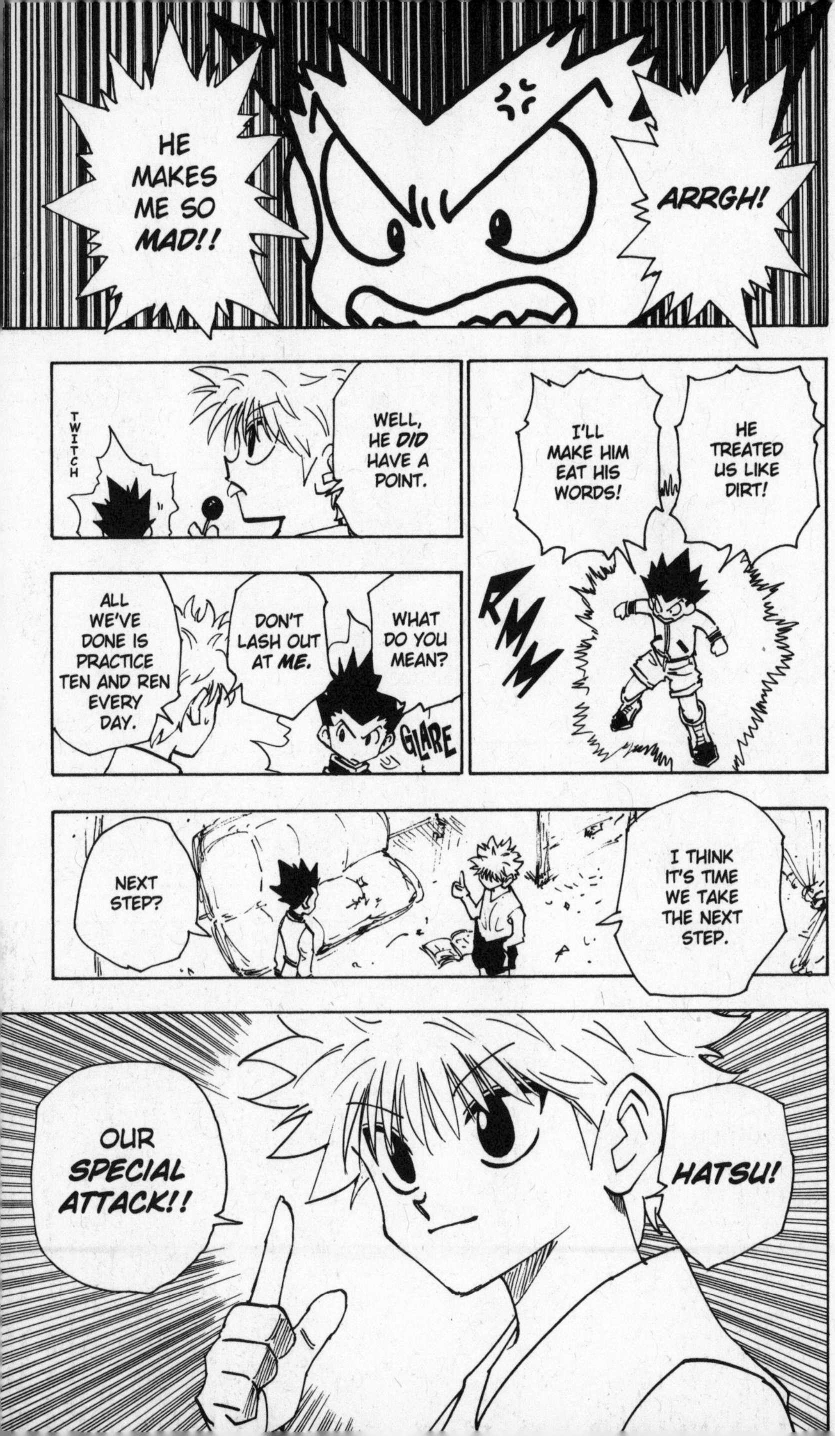
ARRGH!
HE MAKES ME SO MAD!!
HE TREATED US LIKE DIRT!
I'LL MAKE HIM EAT HIS WORDS!
RMM
WELL, HE DID HAVE A POINT.
TWITCH
WHAT DO YOU MEAN?
DON'T LASH OUT AT ME.
GLARE
ALL WE'VE DONE IS PRACTICE TEN AND REN EVERY DAY.
I THINK IT'S TIME WE TAKE THE NEXT STEP.
NEXT STEP?
HATSU!
OUR SPECIAL ATTACK!!

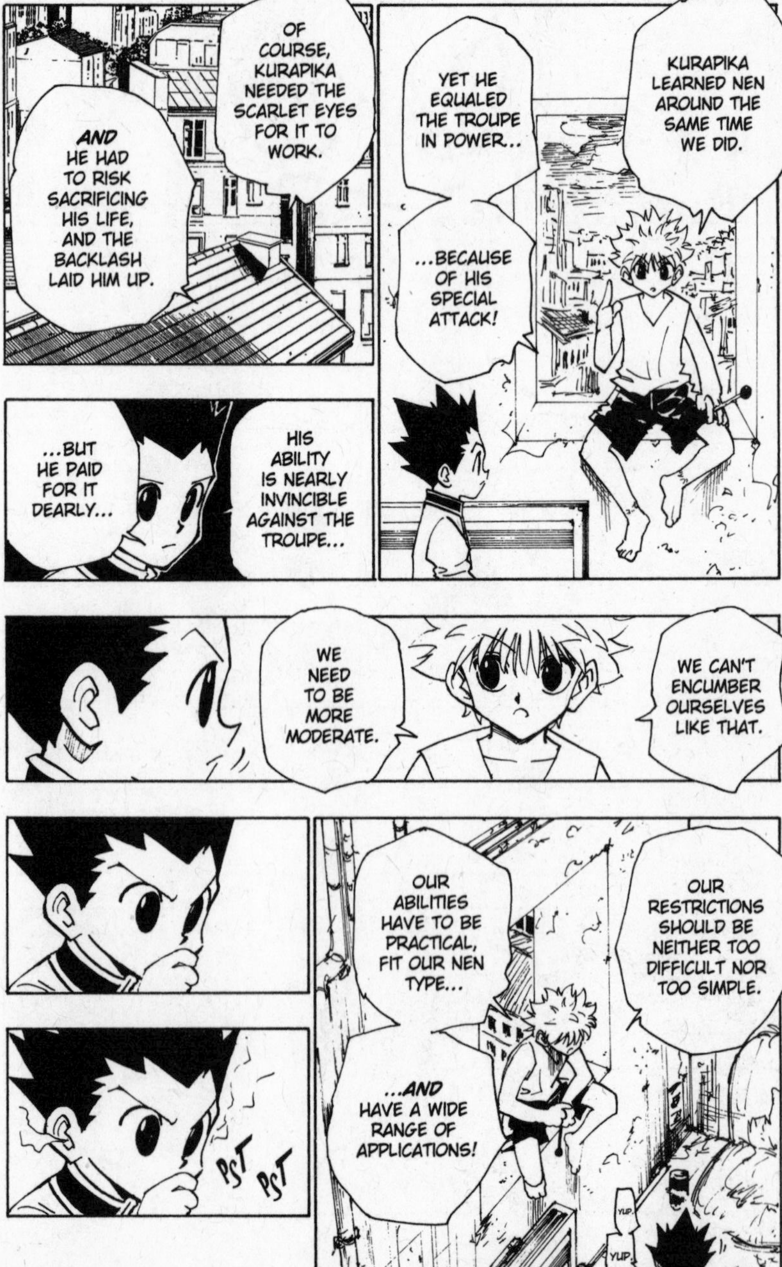
KURAPIKA LEARNED NEN AROUND THE SAME TIME WE DID.
YET HE EQUALED THE TROUPE IN POWER...
...BECAUSE OF HIS SPECIAL ATTACK!
OF COURSE, KURAPIKA NEEDED THE SCARLET EYES FOR IT TO WORK.
AND HE HAD TO RISK SACRIFICING HIS LIFE, AND THE BACKLASH LAID HIM UP.
HIS ABILITY IS NEARLY INVINCIBLE AGAINST THE TROUPE...
...BUT HE PAID FOR IT DEARLY...
WE CAN'T ENCUMBER OURSELVES LIKE THAT.
WE NEED TO BE MORE MODERATE.
OUR RESTRICTIONS SHOULD BE NEITHER TOO DIFFICULT NOR TOO SIMPLE.
OUR ABILITIES HAVE TO BE PRACTICAL, FIT OUR NEN TYPE...
...*AND* HAVE A WIDE RANGE OF APPLICATIONS!
YUP.
YUP.
PST
PST

READ THIS WAY

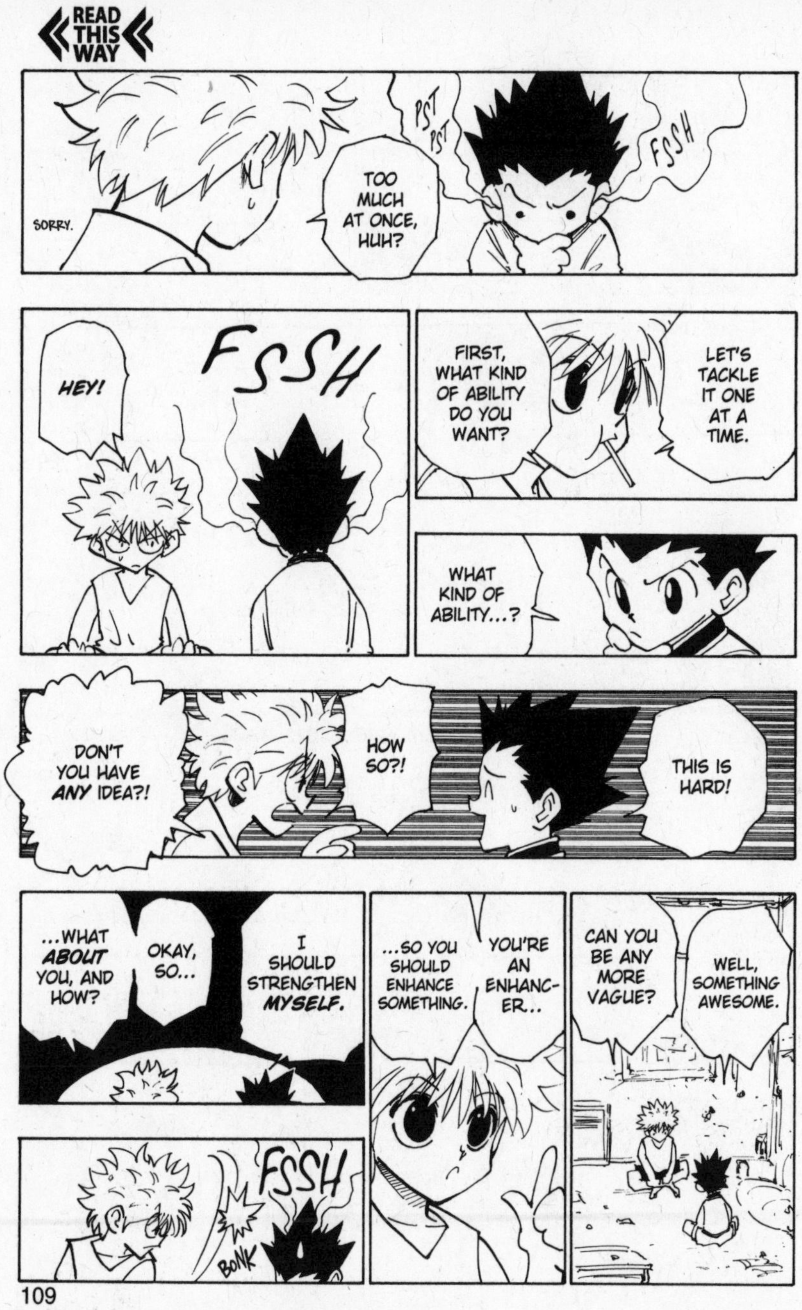
FSSH
PST PST
TOO MUCH AT ONCE, HUH?
SORRY.
LET'S TACKLE IT ONE AT A TIME.
FIRST, WHAT KIND OF ABILITY DO YOU WANT?
WHAT KIND OF ABILITY...?
FSSH
HEY!
THIS IS HARD!
HOW SO?!
DON'T YOU HAVE ANY IDEA?!
WELL, SOMETHING AWESOME.
CAN YOU BE ANY MORE VAGUE?
YOU'RE AN ENHANCER...
...SO YOU SHOULD ENHANCE SOMETHING.
I SHOULD STRENGTHEN MYSELF.
OKAY, SO...
...WHAT ABOUT YOU, AND HOW?
FSSH
BONK

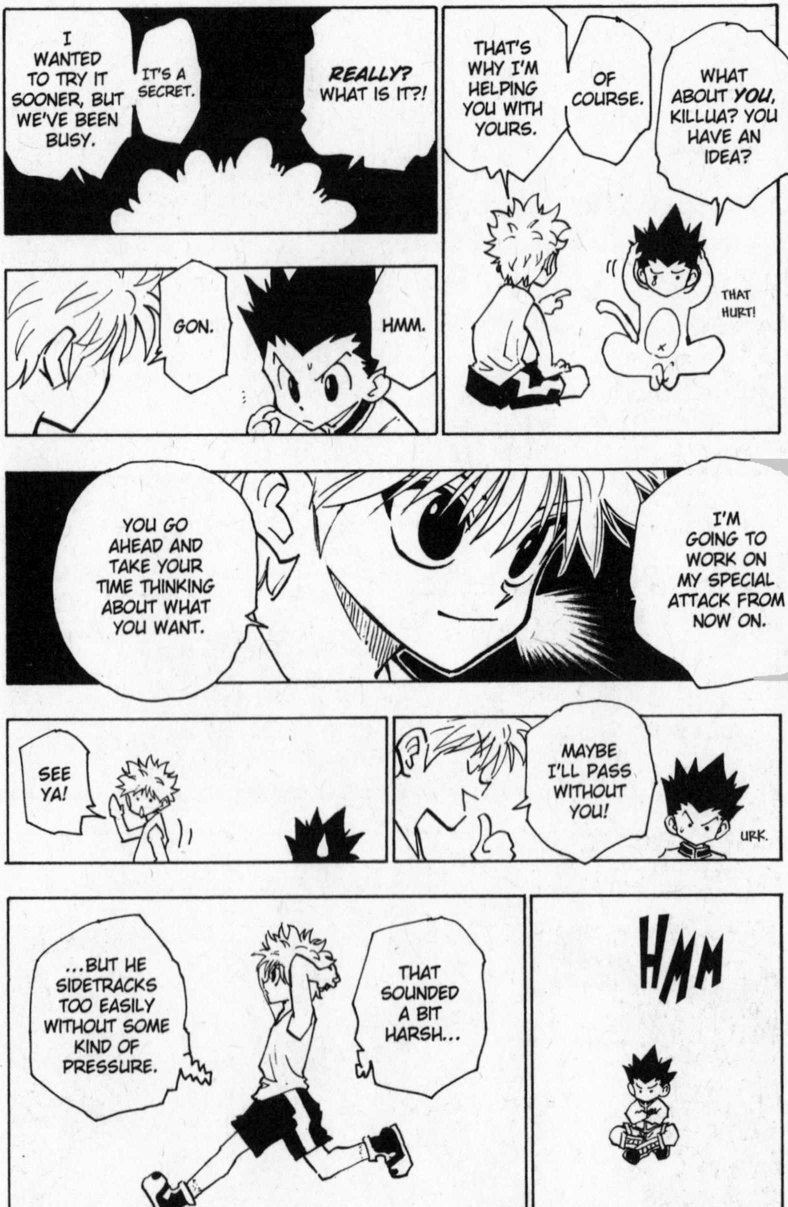

WHAT ABOUT YOU, KILLUA? YOU HAVE AN IDEA?
OF COURSE.
THAT'S WHY I'M HELPING YOU WITH YOURS.
THAT HURT!
REALLY? WHAT IS IT?!
IT'S A SECRET.
I WANTED TO TRY IT SOONER, BUT WE'VE BEEN BUSY.
HMM.
GON.
I'M GOING TO WORK ON MY SPECIAL ATTACK FROM NOW ON.
YOU GO AHEAD AND TAKE YOUR TIME THINKING ABOUT WHAT YOU WANT.
MAYBE I'LL PASS WITHOUT YOU!
URK.
SEE YA!
HMM
THAT SOUNDED A BIT HARSH...
...BUT HE SIDETRACKS TOO EASILY WITHOUT SOME KIND OF PRESSURE.

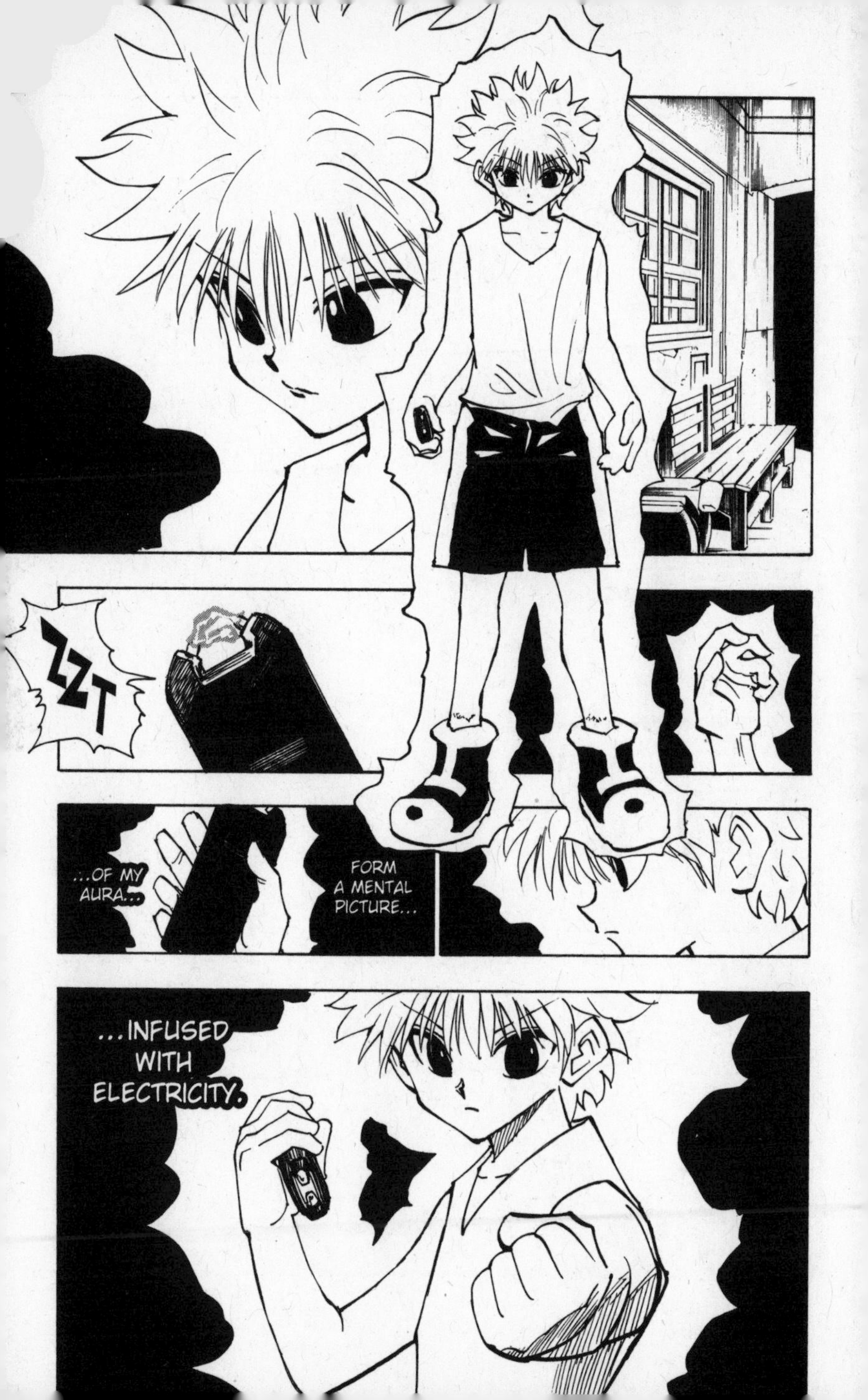
ZZT
FORM A MENTAL PICTURE...
...OF MY AURA...
...INFUSED WITH ELECTRICITY.

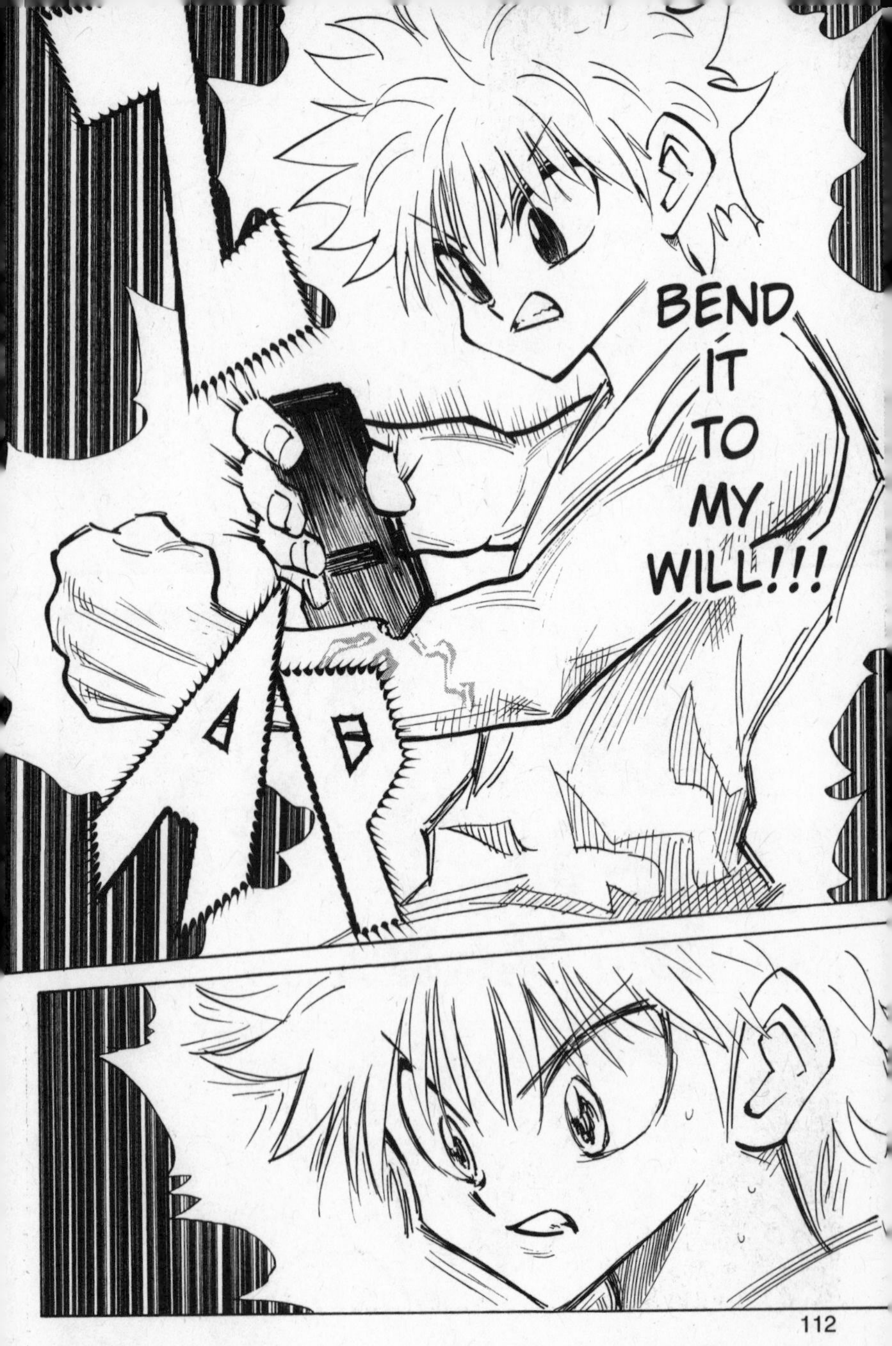
BEND IT TO MY WILL!!!

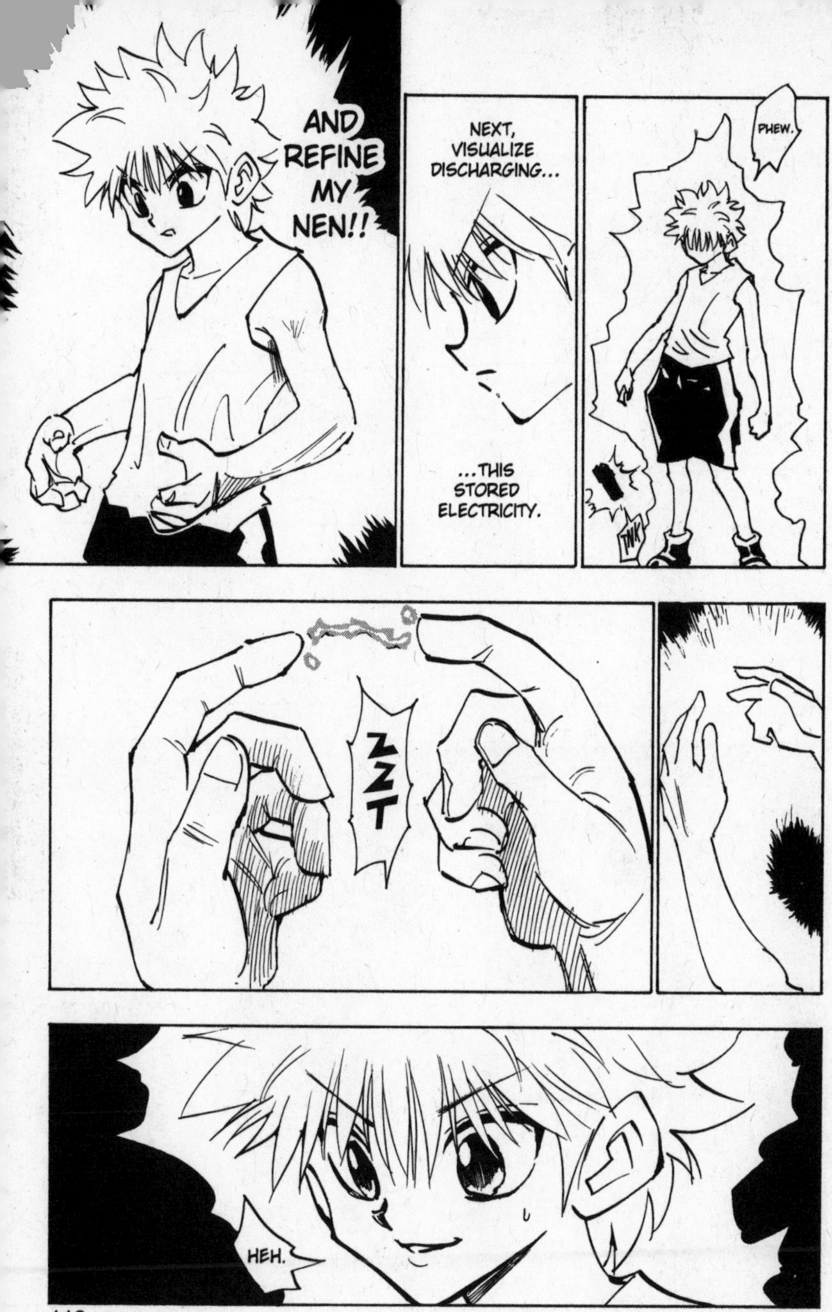
PHEW.
TINK
NEXT, VISUALIZE DISCHARGING...
...THIS STORED ELECTRICITY.
AND REFINE MY NEN!!
ZZT
HEH.

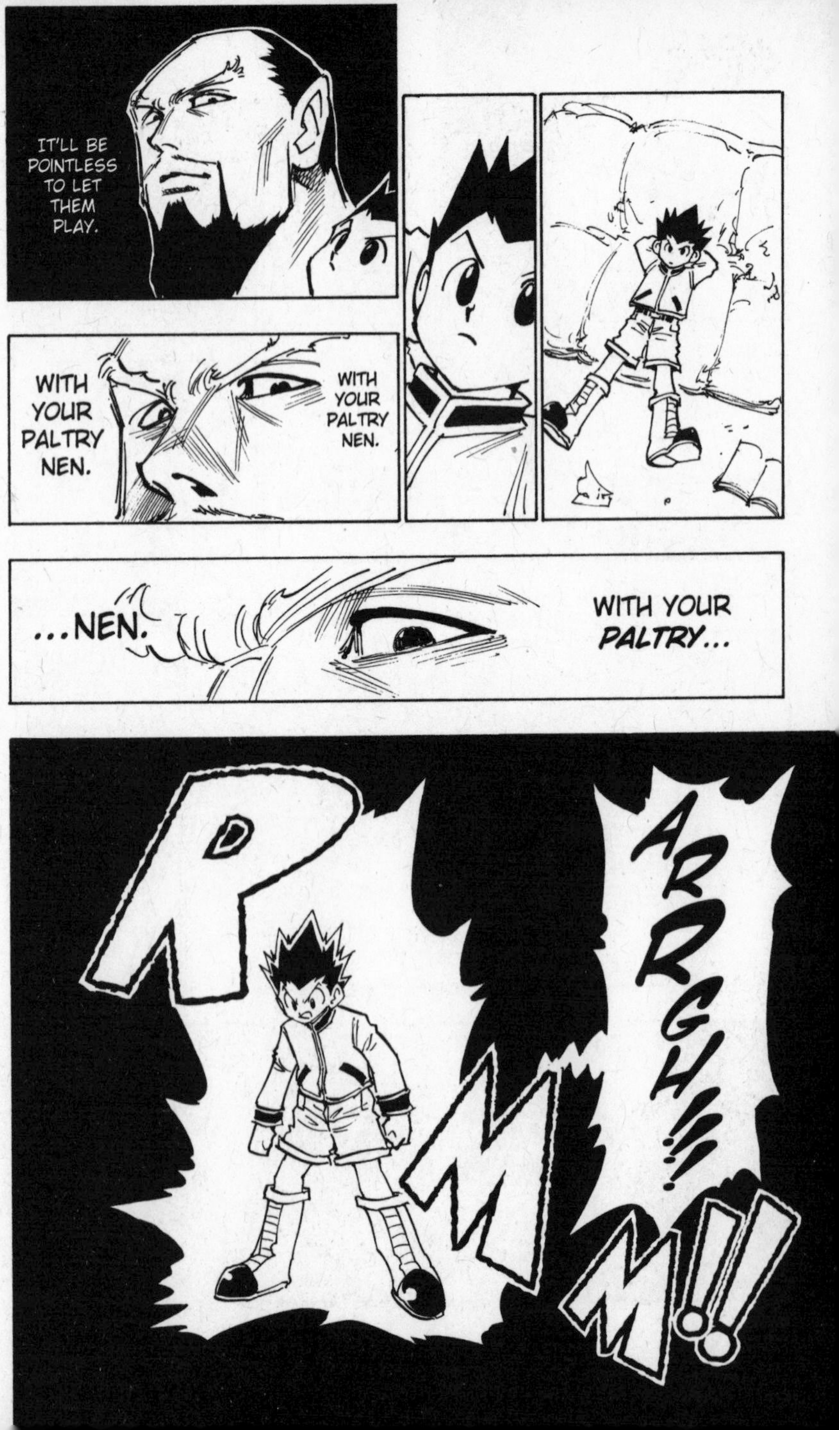
IT'LL BE POINTLESS TO LET THEM PLAY.
WITH YOUR PALTRY NEN.
WITH YOUR PALTRY NEN.
WITH YOUR PALTRY...
...NEN.
ARRGH!!!
RMM!!

READ THIS WAY

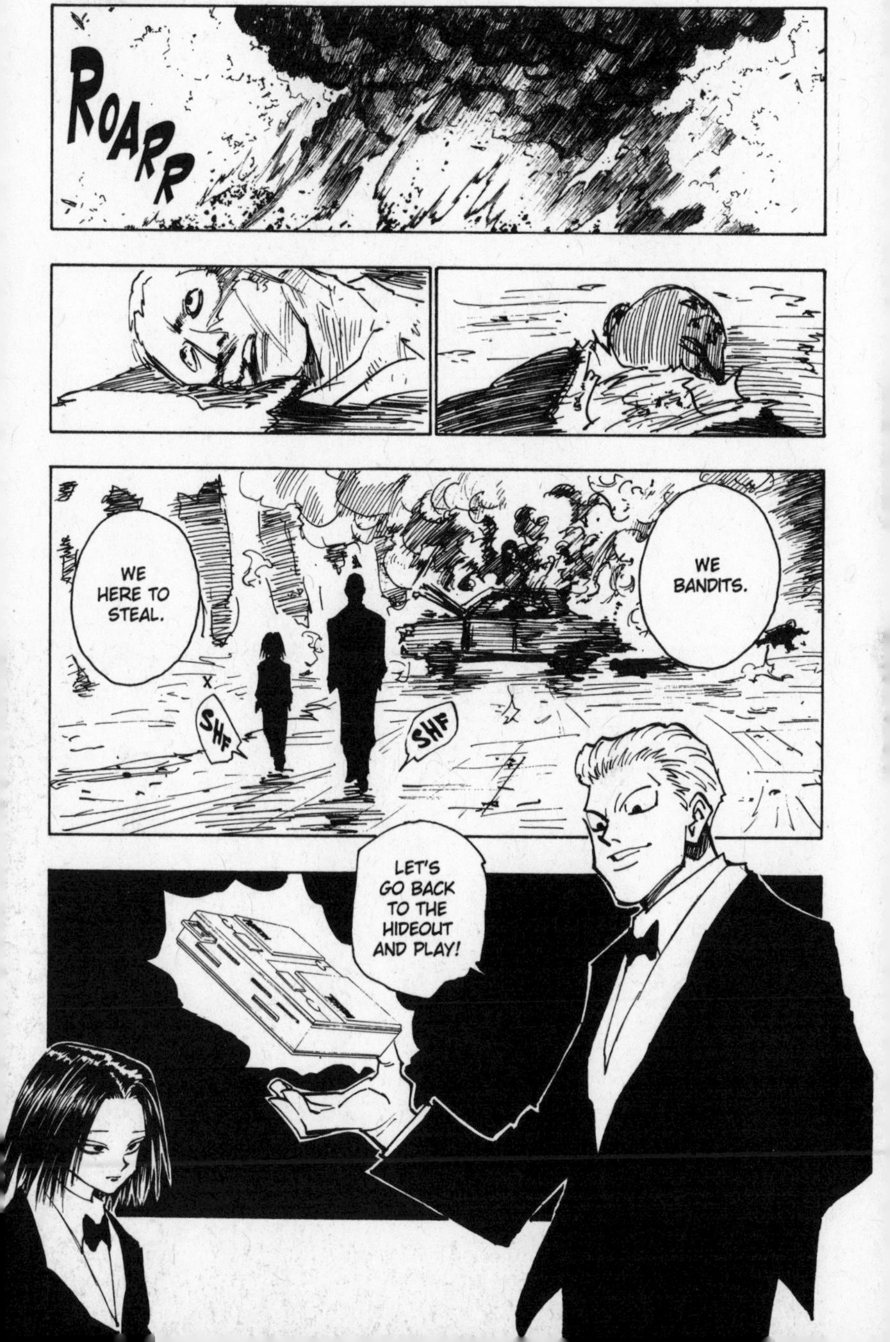
ROARR
WE BANDITS.
WE HERE TO STEAL.
SHF
SHF
LET'S GO BACK TO THE HIDEOUT AND PLAY!

Chapter 123 September 6th: Part 4

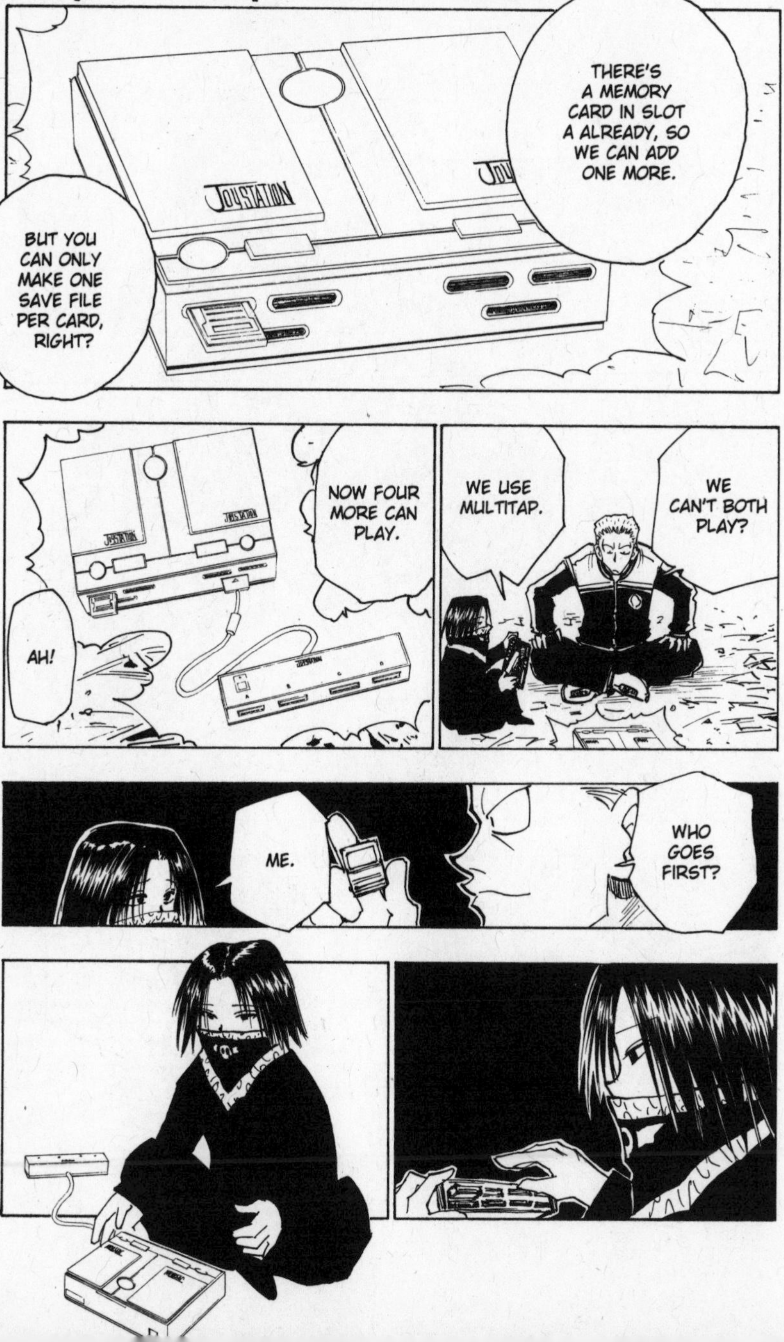
THERE'S A MEMORY CARD IN SLOT A ALREADY, SO WE CAN ADD ONE MORE.
BUT YOU CAN ONLY MAKE ONE SAVE FILE PER CARD, RIGHT?
WE CAN'T BOTH PLAY?
WE USE MULTITAP.
NOW FOUR MORE CAN PLAY.
AH!
WHO GOES FIRST?
ME.

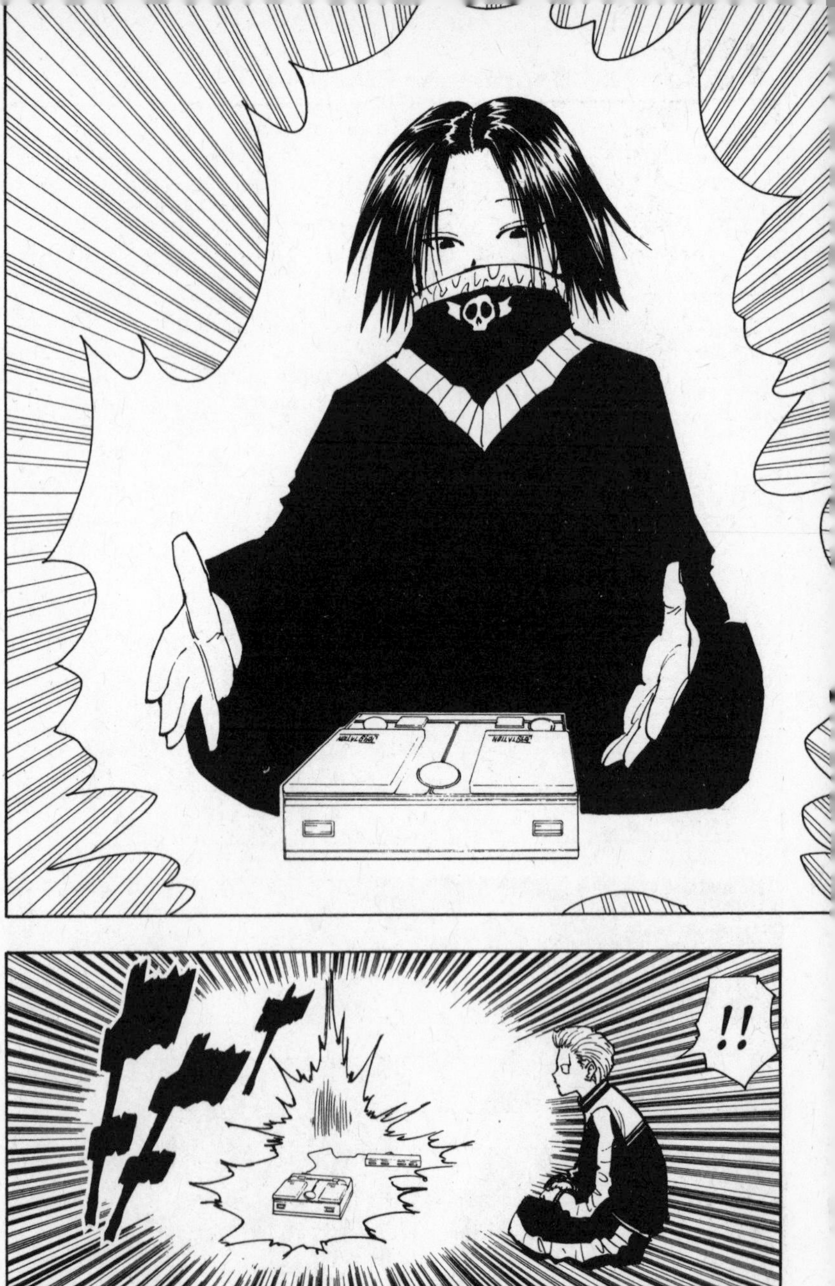

!!

READ THIS WAY

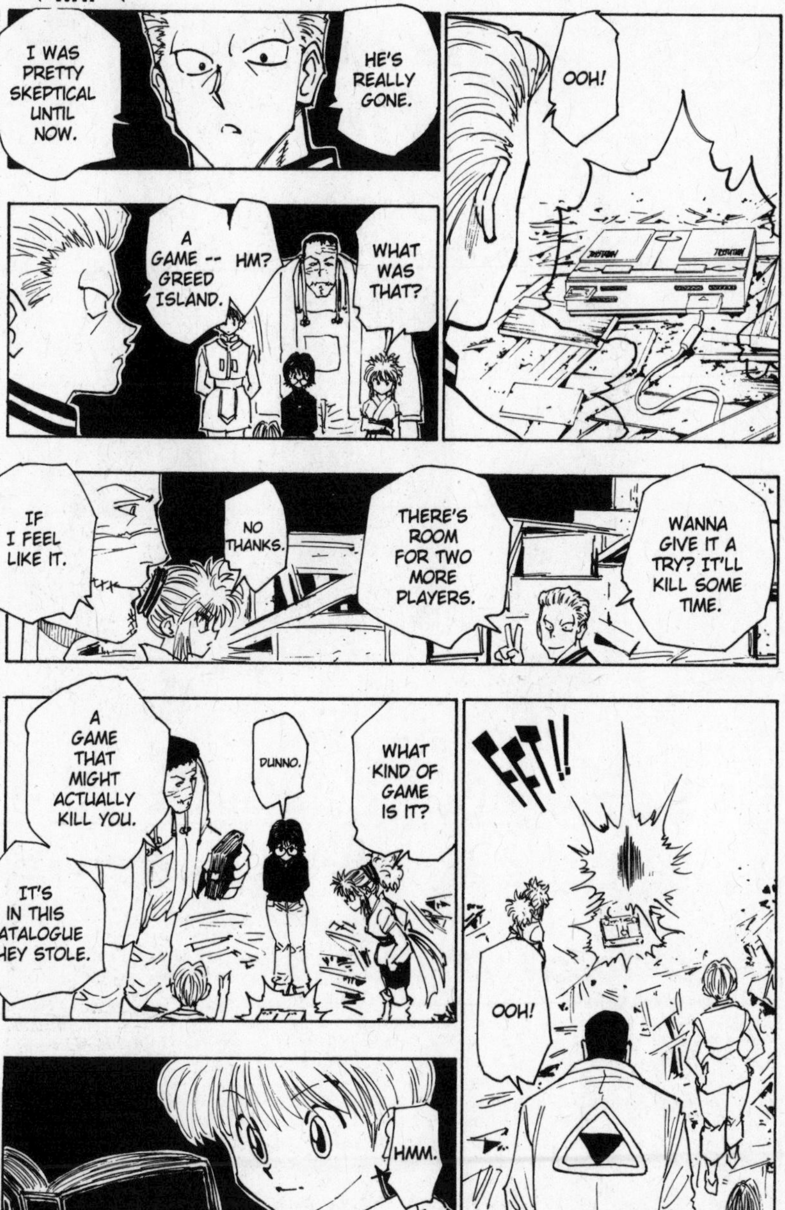
OOH!
HE'S REALLY GONE.
I WAS PRETTY SKEPTICAL UNTIL NOW.
WHAT WAS THAT?
HM?
A GAME -- GREED ISLAND.
WANNA GIVE IT A TRY? IT'LL KILL SOME TIME.
THERE'S ROOM FOR TWO MORE PLAYERS.
NO THANKS.
IF I FEEL LIKE IT.
FFT!!
OOH!
WHAT KIND OF GAME IS IT?
DUNNO.
A GAME THAT MIGHT ACTUALLY KILL YOU.
IT'S IN THIS CATALOGUE THEY STOLE.
HMM.

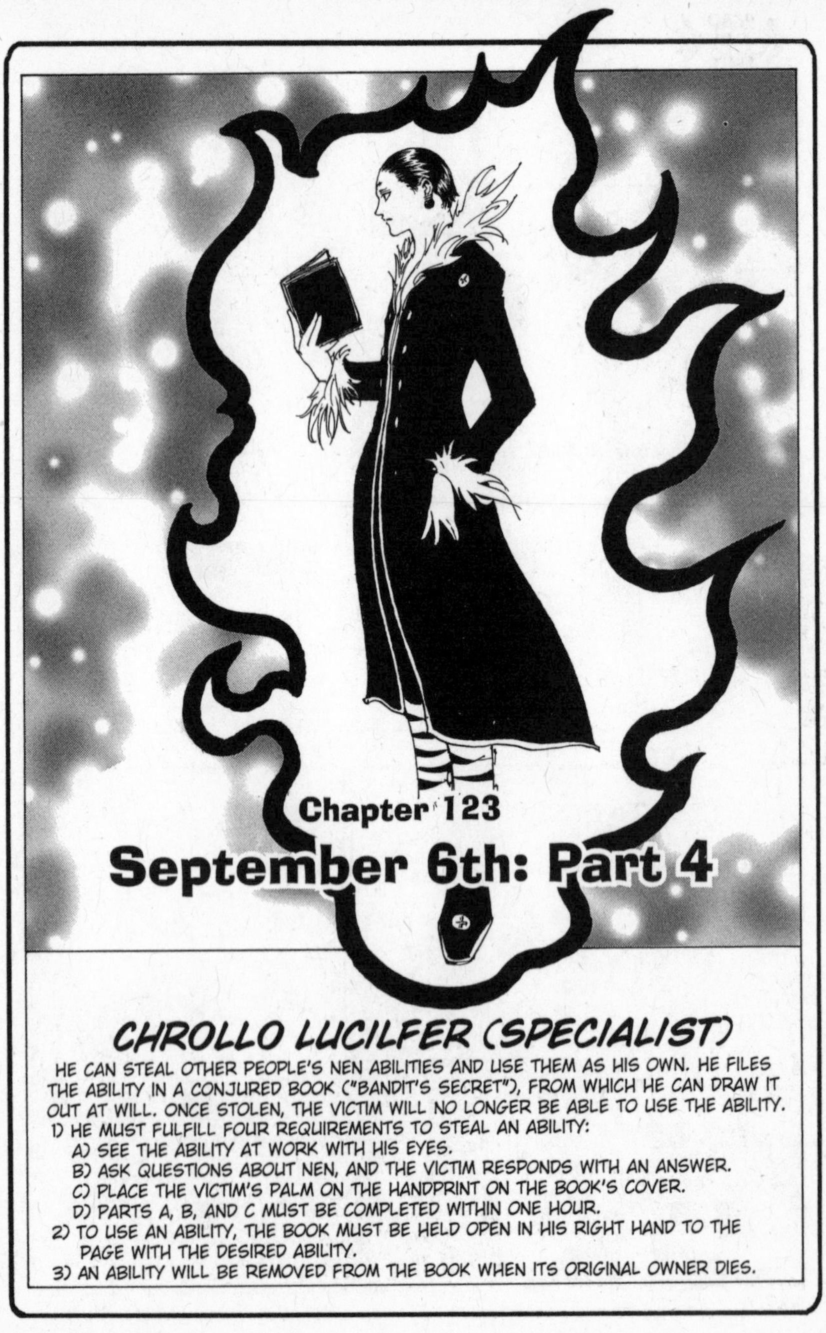

Chapter 123
September 6th: Part 4

CHROLLO LUCILFER (SPECIALIST)

HE CAN STEAL OTHER PEOPLE'S NEN ABILITIES AND USE THEM AS HIS OWN. HE FILES THE ABILITY IN A CONJURED BOOK ("BANDIT'S SECRET"), FROM WHICH HE CAN DRAW IT OUT AT WILL. ONCE STOLEN, THE VICTIM WILL NO LONGER BE ABLE TO USE THE ABILITY.

1) HE MUST FULFILL FOUR REQUIREMENTS TO STEAL AN ABILITY:
   A) SEE THE ABILITY AT WORK WITH HIS EYES.
   B) ASK QUESTIONS ABOUT NEN, AND THE VICTIM RESPONDS WITH AN ANSWER.
   C) PLACE THE VICTIM'S PALM ON THE HANDPRINT ON THE BOOK'S COVER.
   D) PARTS A, B, AND C MUST BE COMPLETED WITHIN ONE HOUR.
2) TO USE AN ABILITY, THE BOOK MUST BE HELD OPEN IN HIS RIGHT HAND TO THE PAGE WITH THE DESIRED ABILITY.
3) AN ABILITY WILL BE REMOVED FROM THE BOOK WHEN ITS ORIGINAL OWNER DIES.

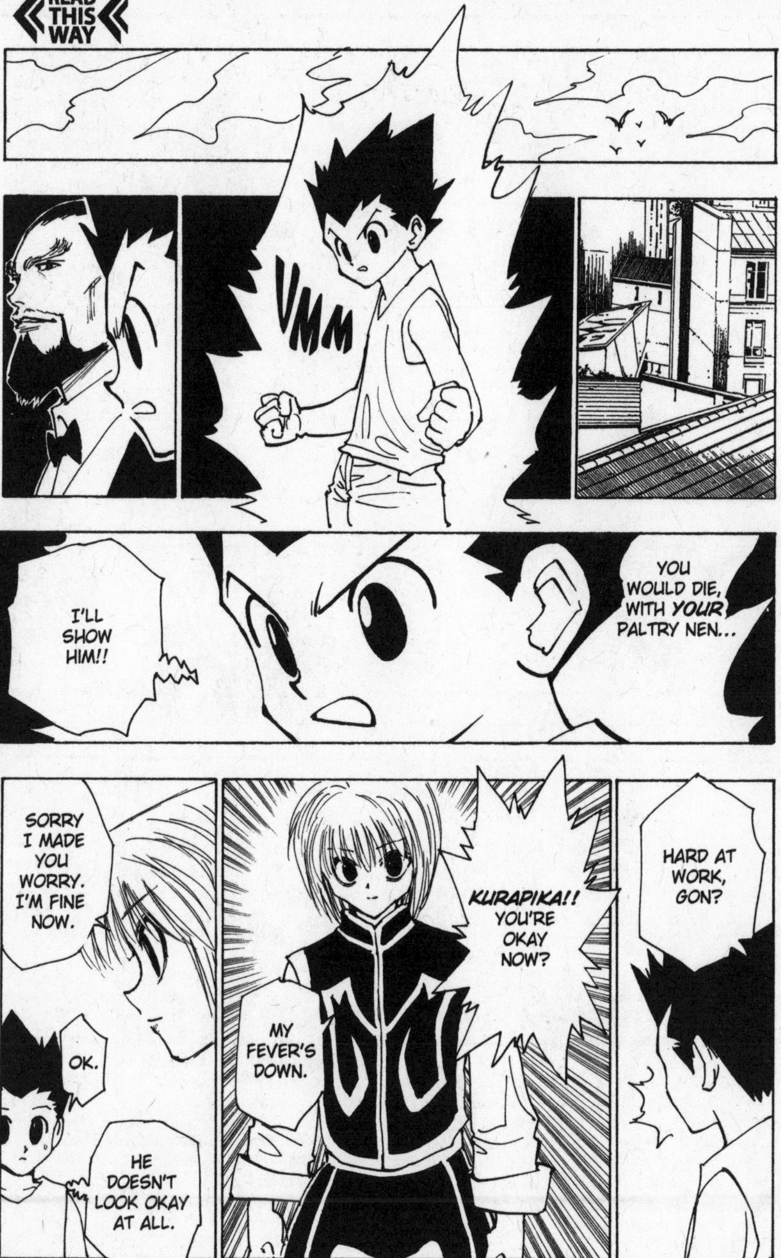
READ THIS WAY
VMM
YOU WOULD DIE, WITH *YOUR* PALTRY NEN...
I'LL SHOW HIM!!
HARD AT WORK, GON?
KURAPIKA!! YOU'RE OKAY NOW?
MY FEVER'S DOWN.
SORRY I MADE YOU WORRY. I'M FINE NOW.
OK.
HE DOESN'T LOOK OKAY AT ALL.

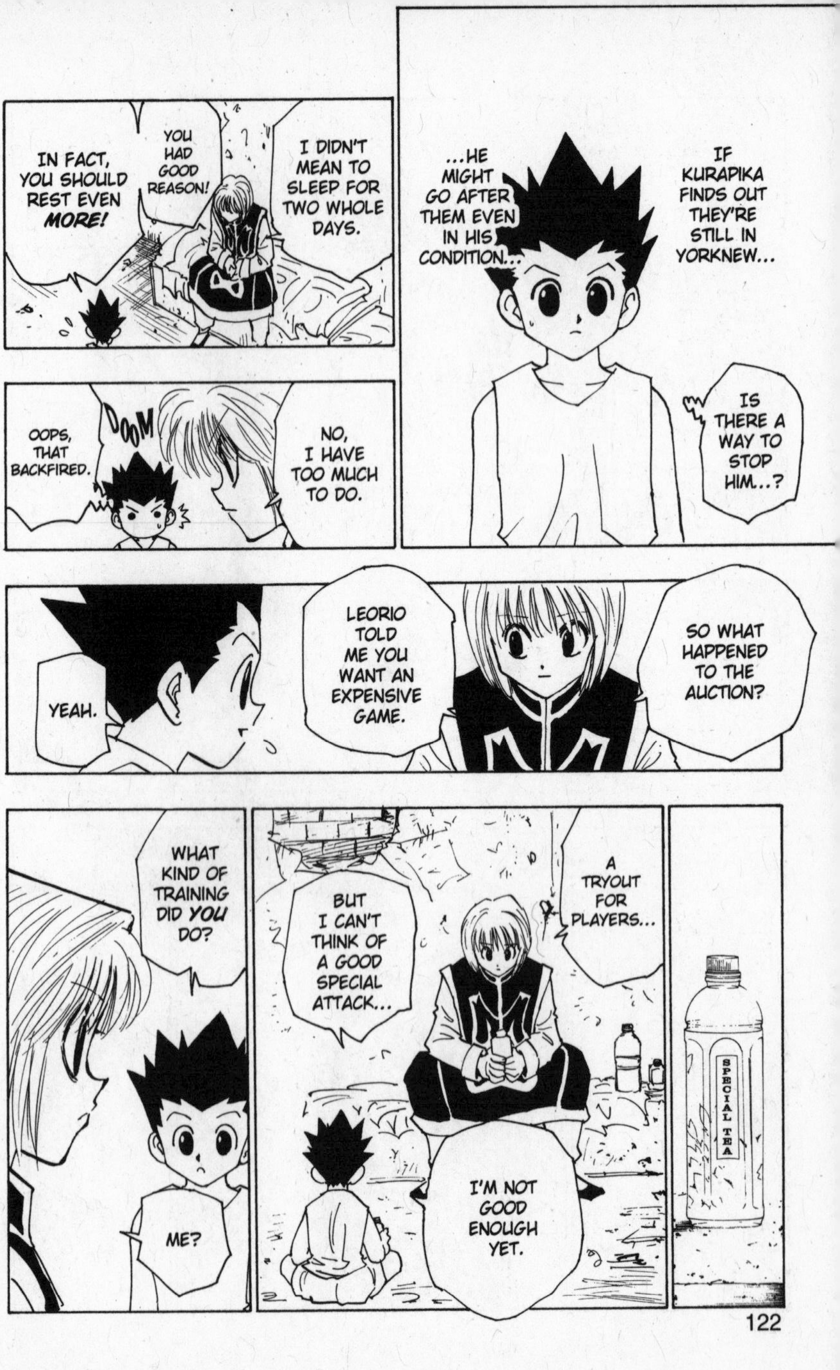
IF KURAPIKA FINDS OUT THEY'RE STILL IN YORKNEW...
...HE MIGHT GO AFTER THEM EVEN IN HIS CONDITION...
IS THERE A WAY TO STOP HIM...?
I DIDN'T MEAN TO SLEEP FOR TWO WHOLE DAYS.
YOU HAD GOOD REASON!
IN FACT, YOU SHOULD REST EVEN *MORE!*
NO, I HAVE TOO MUCH TO DO.
DOOM
OOPS, THAT BACKFIRED.
SO WHAT HAPPENED TO THE AUCTION?
LEORIO TOLD ME YOU WANT AN EXPENSIVE GAME.
YEAH.
SPECIAL TEA
A TRYOUT FOR PLAYERS...
BUT I CAN'T THINK OF A GOOD SPECIAL ATTACK...
I'M NOT GOOD ENOUGH YET.
WHAT KIND OF TRAINING DID *YOU* DO?
ME?

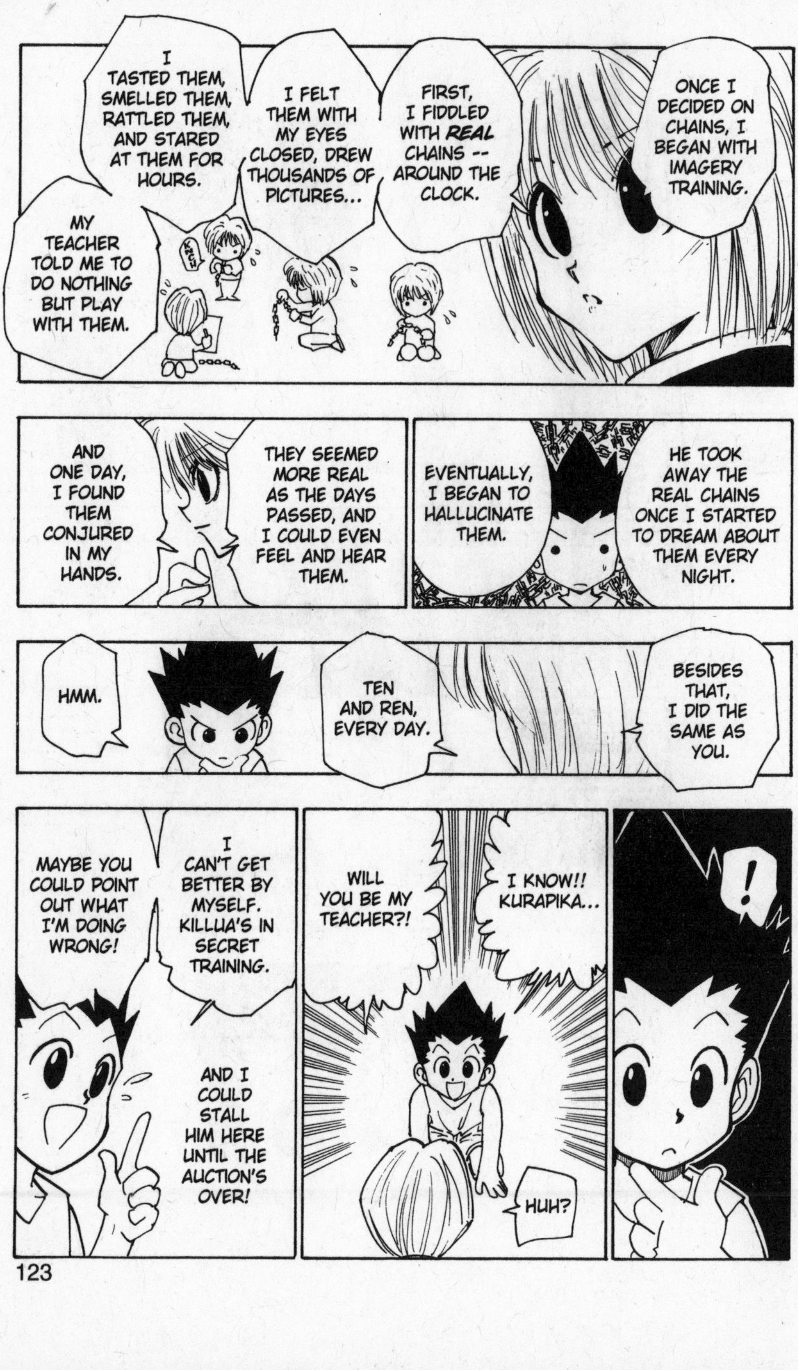
ONCE I DECIDED ON CHAINS, I BEGAN WITH IMAGERY TRAINING.
FIRST, I FIDDLED WITH *REAL* CHAINS -- AROUND THE CLOCK.
I FELT THEM WITH MY EYES CLOSED, DREW THOUSANDS OF PICTURES...
I TASTED THEM, SMELLED THEM, RATTLED THEM, AND STARED AT THEM FOR HOURS.
MY TEACHER TOLD ME TO DO NOTHING BUT PLAY WITH THEM.
HE TOOK AWAY THE REAL CHAINS ONCE I STARTED TO DREAM ABOUT THEM EVERY NIGHT.
EVENTUALLY, I BEGAN TO HALLUCINATE THEM.
THEY SEEMED MORE REAL AS THE DAYS PASSED, AND I COULD EVEN FEEL AND HEAR THEM.
AND ONE DAY, I FOUND THEM CONJURED IN MY HANDS.
BESIDES THAT, I DID THE SAME AS YOU.
TEN AND REN, EVERY DAY.
HMM.
!
I KNOW!! KURAPIKA...
WILL YOU BE MY TEACHER?!
HUH?
I CAN'T GET BETTER BY MYSELF. KILLUA'S IN SECRET TRAINING.
MAYBE YOU COULD POINT OUT WHAT I'M DOING WRONG!
AND I COULD STALL HIM HERE UNTIL THE AUCTION'S OVER!

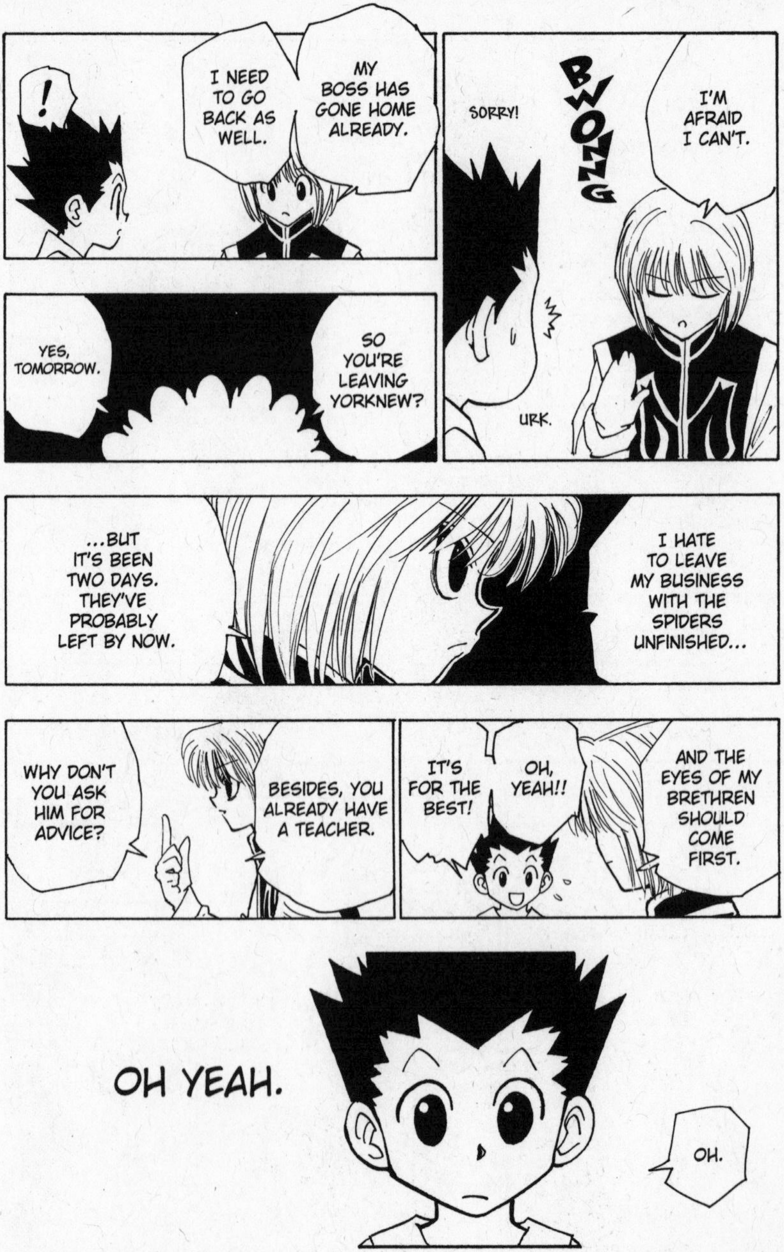
I'M AFRAID I CAN'T.
BWONG
SORRY!
URK.
MY BOSS HAS GONE HOME ALREADY.
I NEED TO GO BACK AS WELL.
!
SO YOU'RE LEAVING YORKNEW?
YES, TOMORROW.
I HATE TO LEAVE MY BUSINESS WITH THE SPIDERS UNFINISHED...
...BUT IT'S BEEN TWO DAYS. THEY'VE PROBABLY LEFT BY NOW.
AND THE EYES OF MY BRETHREN SHOULD COME FIRST.
OH, YEAH!!
IT'S FOR THE BEST!
BESIDES, YOU ALREADY HAVE A TEACHER.
WHY DON'T YOU ASK HIM FOR ADVICE?
OH.
OH YEAH.

READ THIS WAY

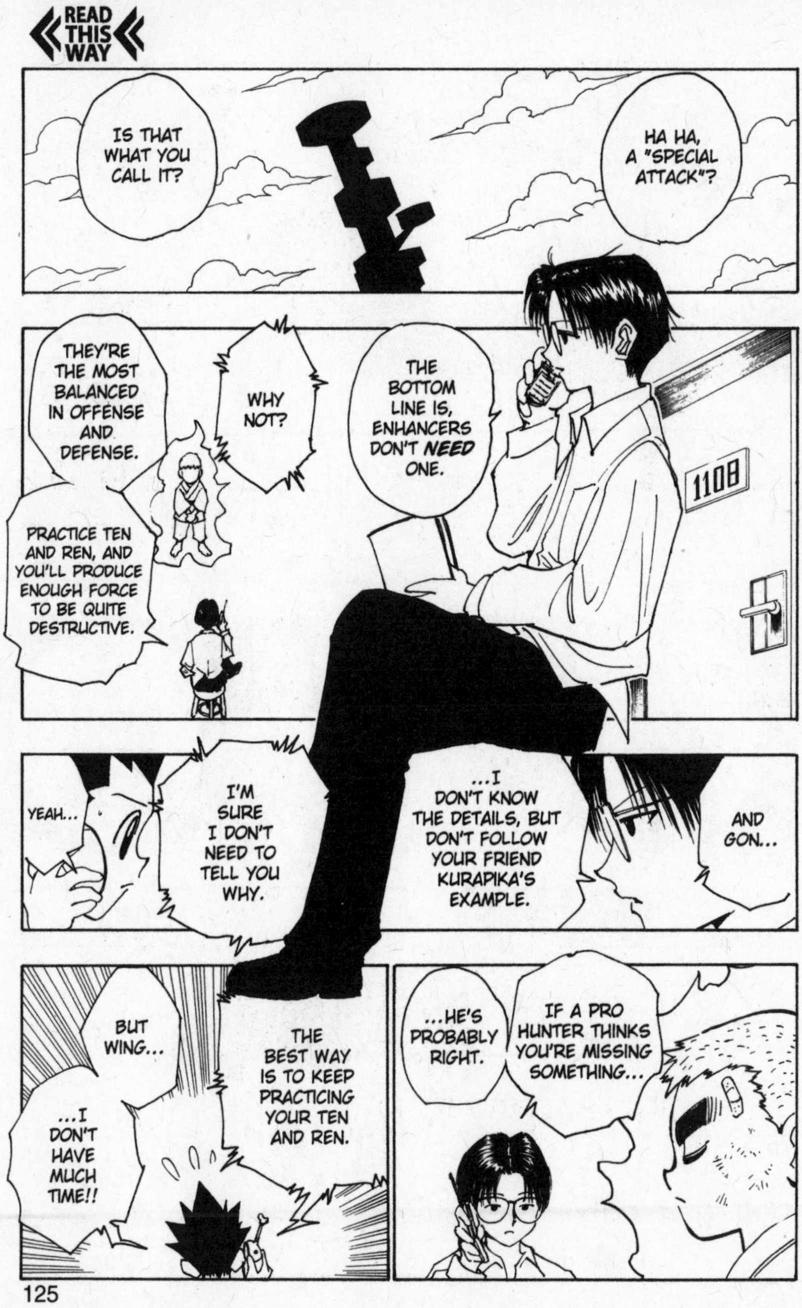
HA HA, A "SPECIAL ATTACK"?
IS THAT WHAT YOU CALL IT?
THE BOTTOM LINE IS, ENHANCERS DON'T *NEED* ONE.
WHY NOT?
THEY'RE THE MOST BALANCED IN OFFENSE AND DEFENSE.
PRACTICE TEN AND REN, AND YOU'LL PRODUCE ENOUGH FORCE TO BE QUITE DESTRUCTIVE.
1108
AND GON...
...I DON'T KNOW THE DETAILS, BUT DON'T FOLLOW YOUR FRIEND KURAPIKA'S EXAMPLE.
I'M SURE I DON'T NEED TO TELL YOU WHY.
YEAH...
IF A PRO HUNTER THINKS YOU'RE MISSING SOMETHING...
...HE'S PROBABLY RIGHT.
THE BEST WAY IS TO KEEP PRACTICING YOUR TEN AND REN.
BUT WING...
...I DON'T HAVE MUCH TIME!!

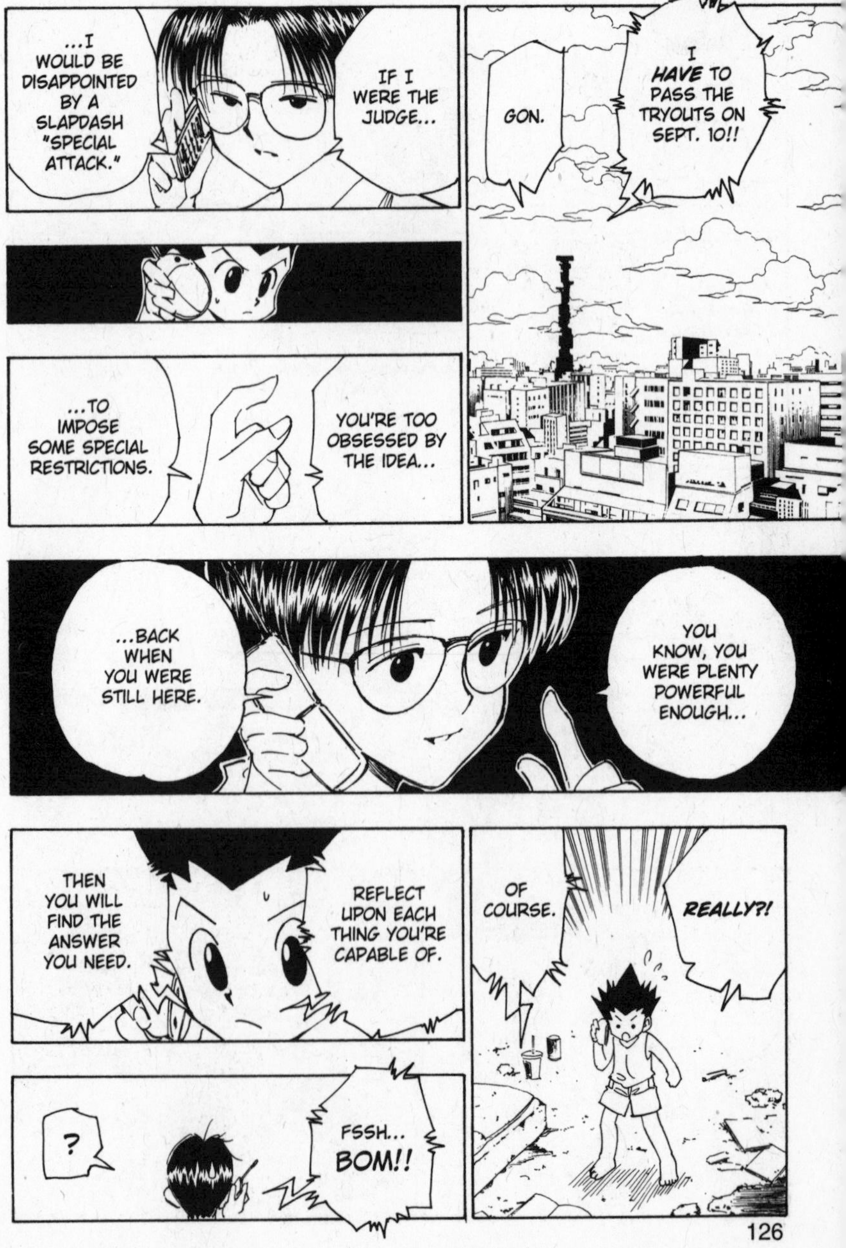
I ***HAVE*** TO PASS THE TRYOUTS ON SEPT. 10!!
GON.
IF I WERE THE JUDGE...
...I WOULD BE DISAPPOINTED BY A SLAPDASH "SPECIAL ATTACK."
YOU'RE TOO OBSESSED BY THE IDEA...
...TO IMPOSE SOME SPECIAL RESTRICTIONS.
YOU KNOW, YOU WERE PLENTY POWERFUL ENOUGH...
...BACK WHEN YOU WERE STILL HERE.
REALLY?!
OF COURSE.
REFLECT UPON EACH THING YOU'RE CAPABLE OF.
THEN YOU WILL FIND THE ANSWER YOU NEED.
FSSH... BOM!!
?

READ THIS WAY

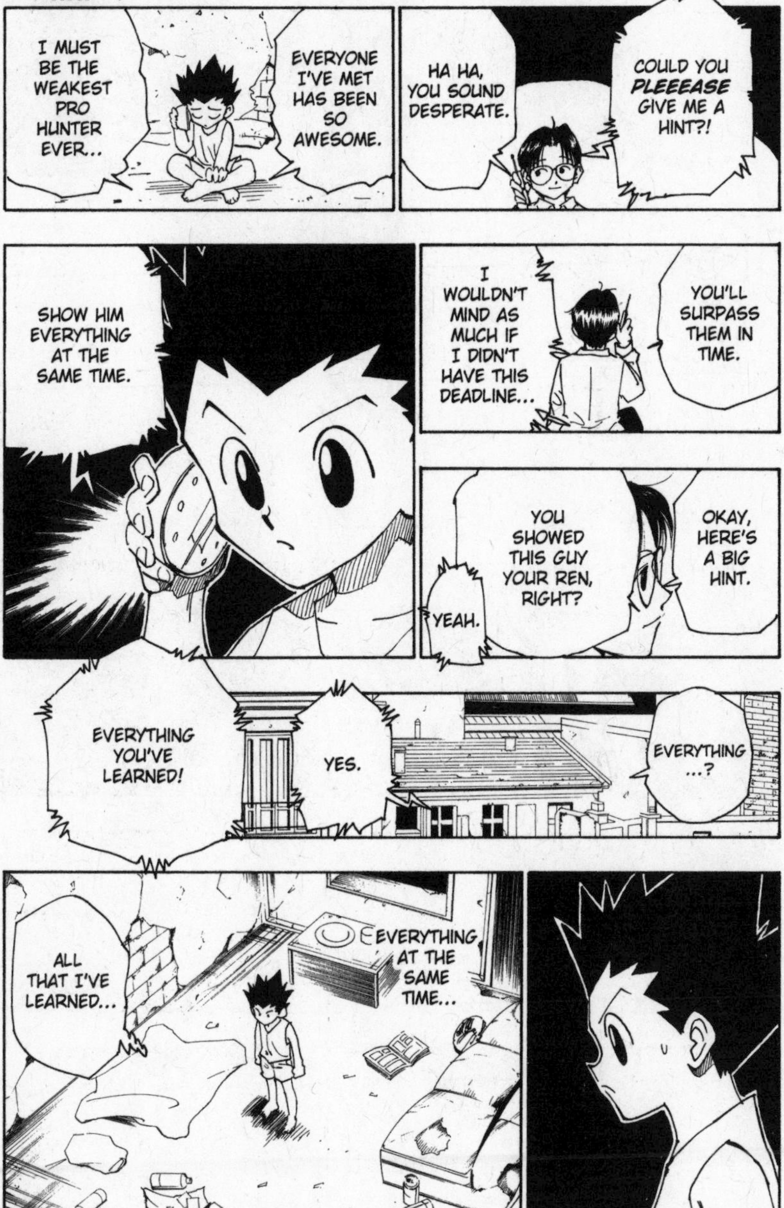
COULD YOU *PLEEEASE* GIVE ME A HINT?!
HA HA, YOU SOUND DESPERATE.
EVERYONE I'VE MET HAS BEEN SO AWESOME.
I MUST BE THE WEAKEST PRO HUNTER EVER...
YOU'LL SURPASS THEM IN TIME.
I WOULDN'T MIND AS MUCH IF I DIDN'T HAVE THIS DEADLINE...
OKAY, HERE'S A BIG HINT.
YOU SHOWED THIS GUY YOUR REN, RIGHT?
YEAH.
SHOW HIM EVERYTHING AT THE SAME TIME.
EVERYTHING ...?
YES.
EVERYTHING YOU'VE LEARNED!
EVERYTHING AT THE SAME TIME...
ALL THAT I'VE LEARNED...

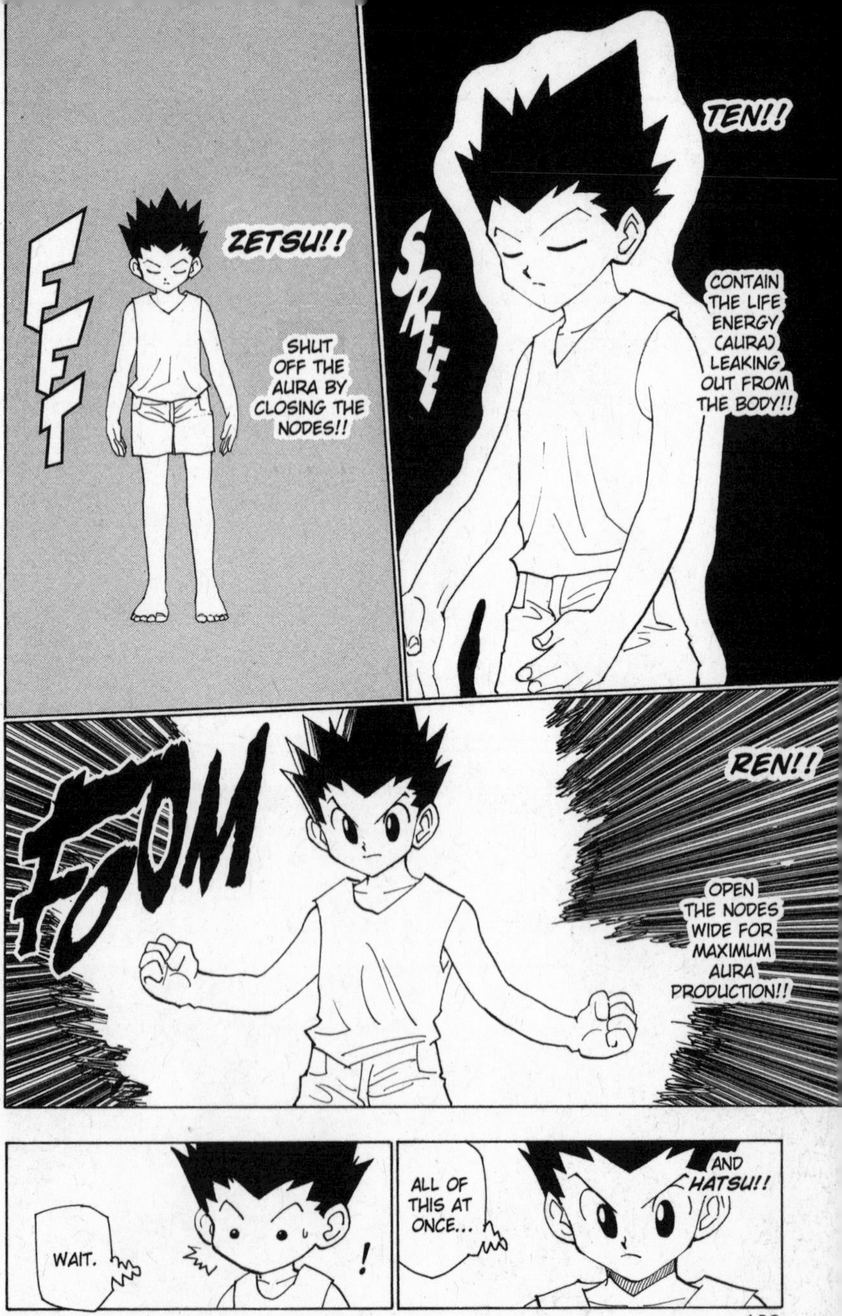
TEN!!
SREE
CONTAIN THE LIFE ENERGY (AURA) LEAKING OUT FROM THE BODY!!
ZETSU!!
FFFT
SHUT OFF THE AURA BY CLOSING THE NODES!!
REN!!
FOOM
OPEN THE NODES WIDE FOR MAXIMUM AURA PRODUCTION!!
AND HATSU!!
ALL OF THIS AT ONCE...
!
WAIT.

READ THIS WAY

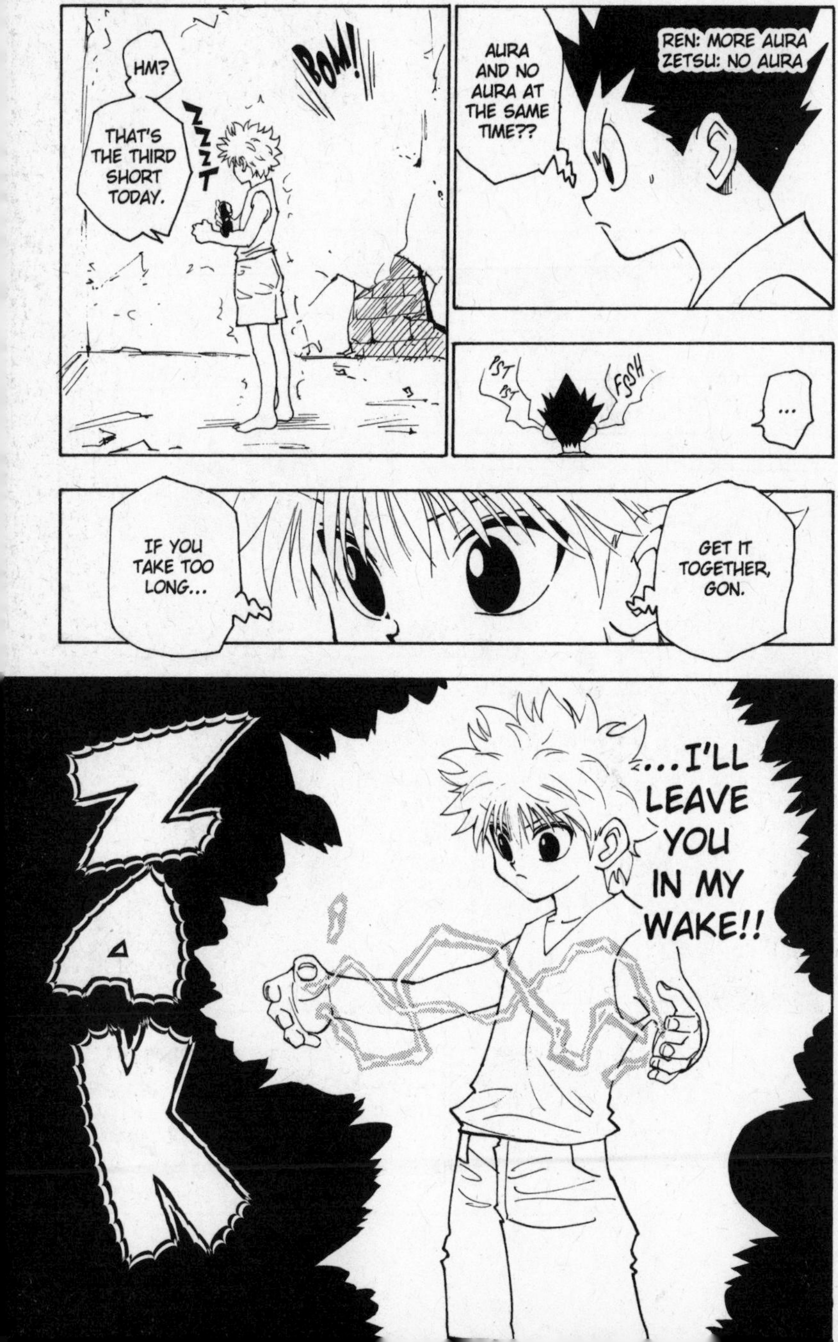
REN: MORE AURA
ZETSU: NO AURA
AURA AND NO AURA AT THE SAME TIME??
PST PST
FSSH
...
BOM!
HM?
THAT'S THE THIRD SHORT TODAY.
ZZZT
GET IT TOGETHER, GON.
IF YOU TAKE TOO LONG...
...I'LL LEAVE YOU IN MY WAKE!!
ZAK

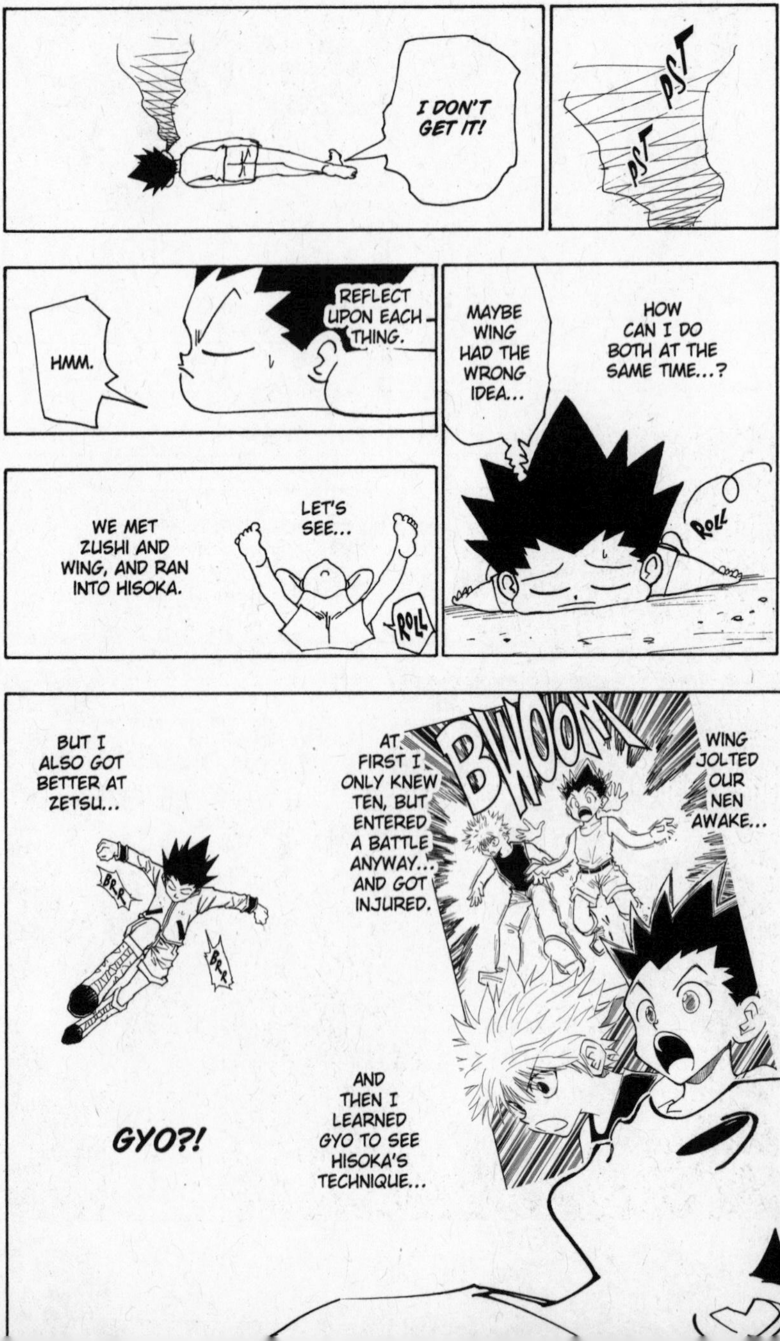
PST PST
I DON'T GET IT!
HOW CAN I DO BOTH AT THE SAME TIME...?
MAYBE WING HAD THE WRONG IDEA...
ROLL
REFLECT UPON EACH THING.
HMM.
LET'S SEE...
ROLL
WE MET ZUSHI AND WING, AND RAN INTO HISOKA.
WING JOLTED OUR NEN AWAKE...
BWOOM
AT FIRST I ONLY KNEW TEN, BUT ENTERED A BATTLE ANYWAY... AND GOT INJURED.
BUT I ALSO GOT BETTER AT ZETSU...
BRR
BRR
AND THEN I LEARNED GYO TO SEE HISOKA'S TECHNIQUE...
GYO?!

READ THIS WAY

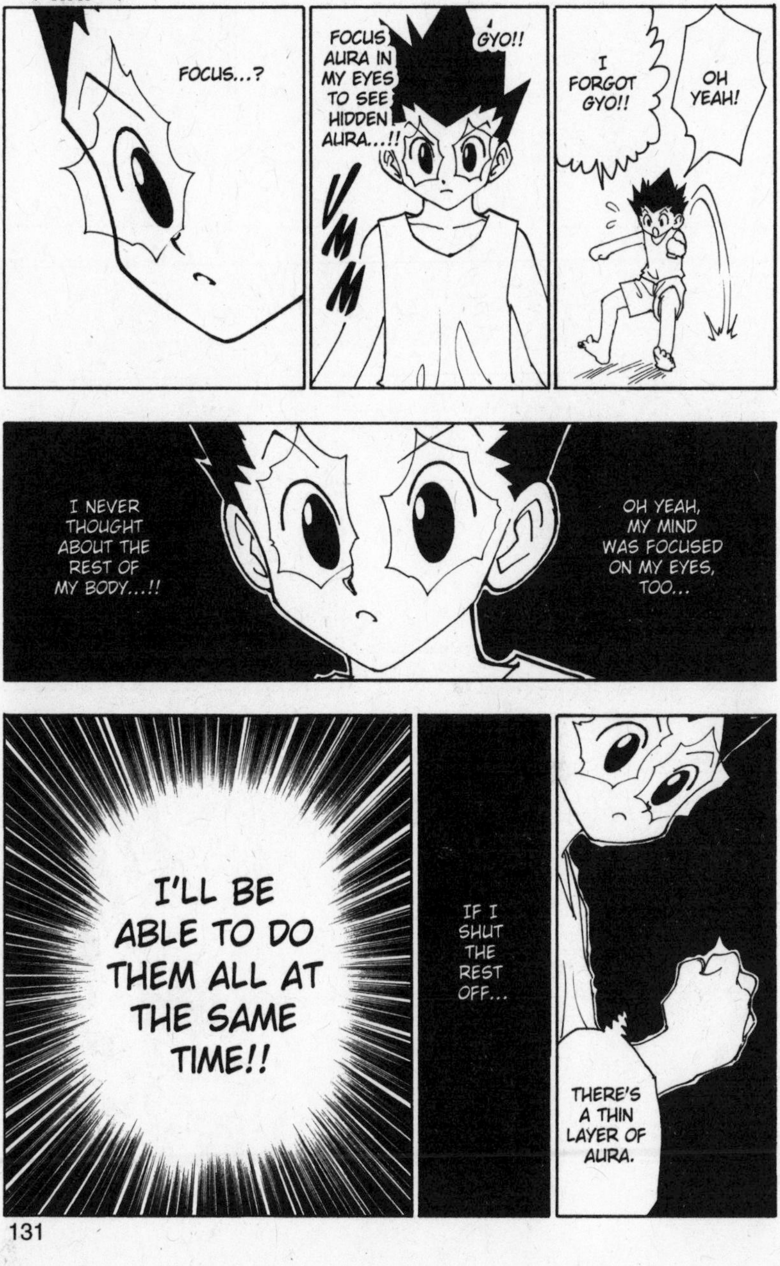
OH YEAH!
I FORGOT GYO!!
GYO!!
FOCUS AURA IN MY EYES TO SEE HIDDEN AURA...!!
VMM
FOCUS...?
OH YEAH, MY MIND WAS FOCUSED ON MY EYES, TOO...
I NEVER THOUGHT ABOUT THE REST OF MY BODY...!!
THERE'S A THIN LAYER OF AURA.
IF I SHUT THE REST OFF...
I'LL BE ABLE TO DO THEM ALL AT THE SAME TIME!!

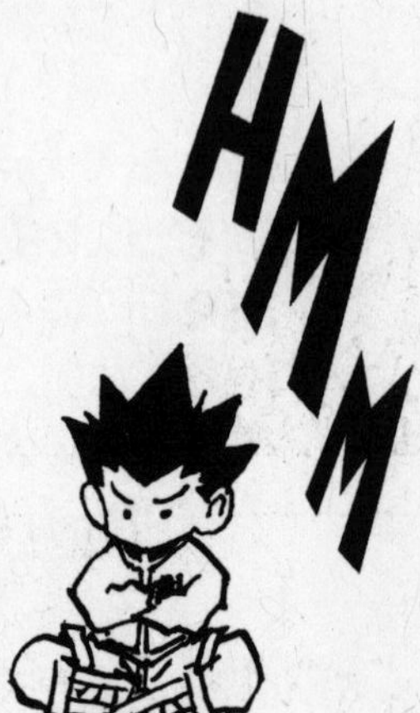
HMM

Chapter 124 September 7th-10th: Part 1

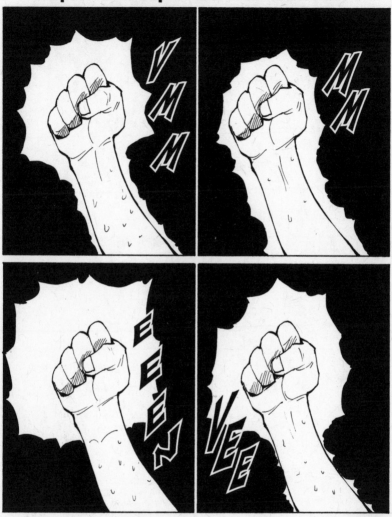

I DID IT!!

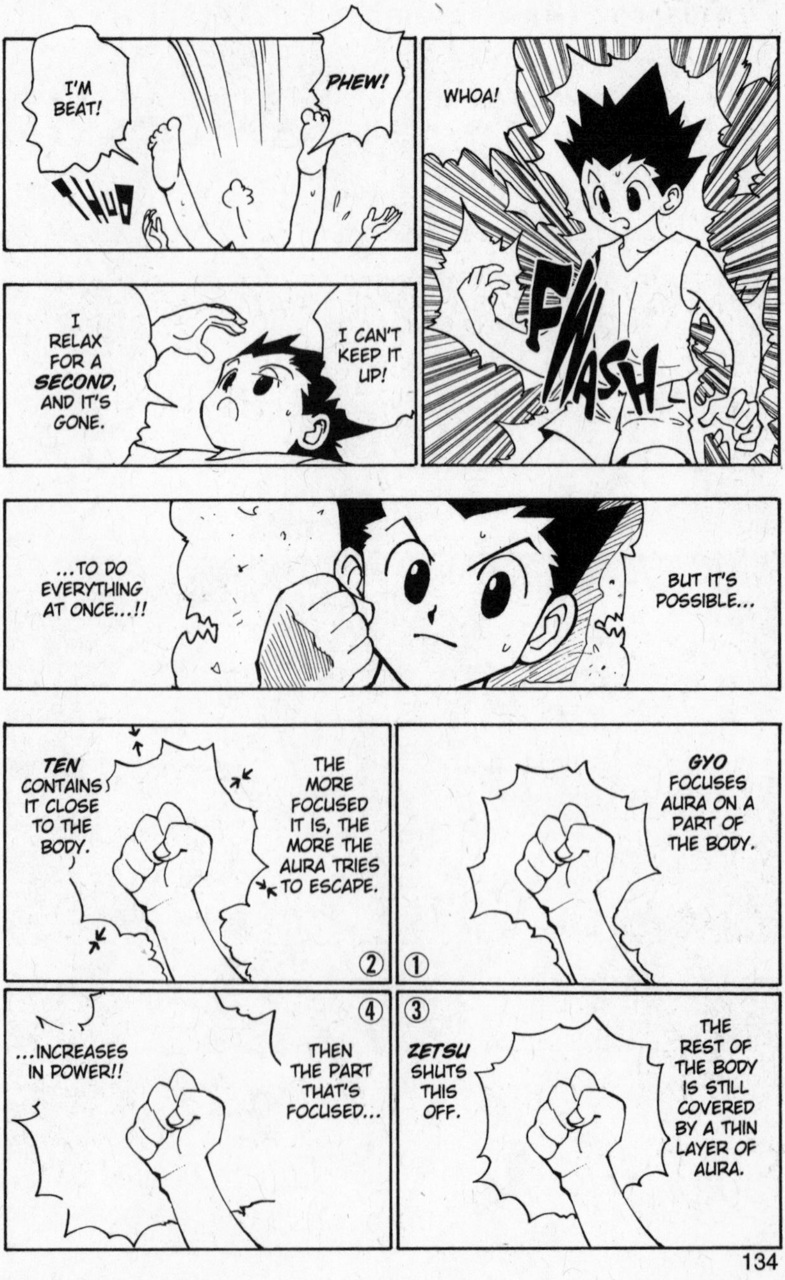
WHOA!
FWASH
PHEW!
I'M BEAT!
THUD
I CAN'T KEEP IT UP!
I RELAX FOR A *SECOND*, AND IT'S GONE.
BUT IT'S POSSIBLE...
...TO DO EVERYTHING AT ONCE...!!
①
GYO FOCUSES AURA ON A PART OF THE BODY.
②
TEN CONTAINS IT CLOSE TO THE BODY.
THE MORE FOCUSED IT IS, THE MORE THE AURA TRIES TO ESCAPE.
③
THE REST OF THE BODY IS STILL COVERED BY A THIN LAYER OF AURA.
ZETSU SHUTS THIS OFF.
④
THEN THE PART THAT'S FOCUSED...
...INCREASES IN POWER!!

READ THIS WAY

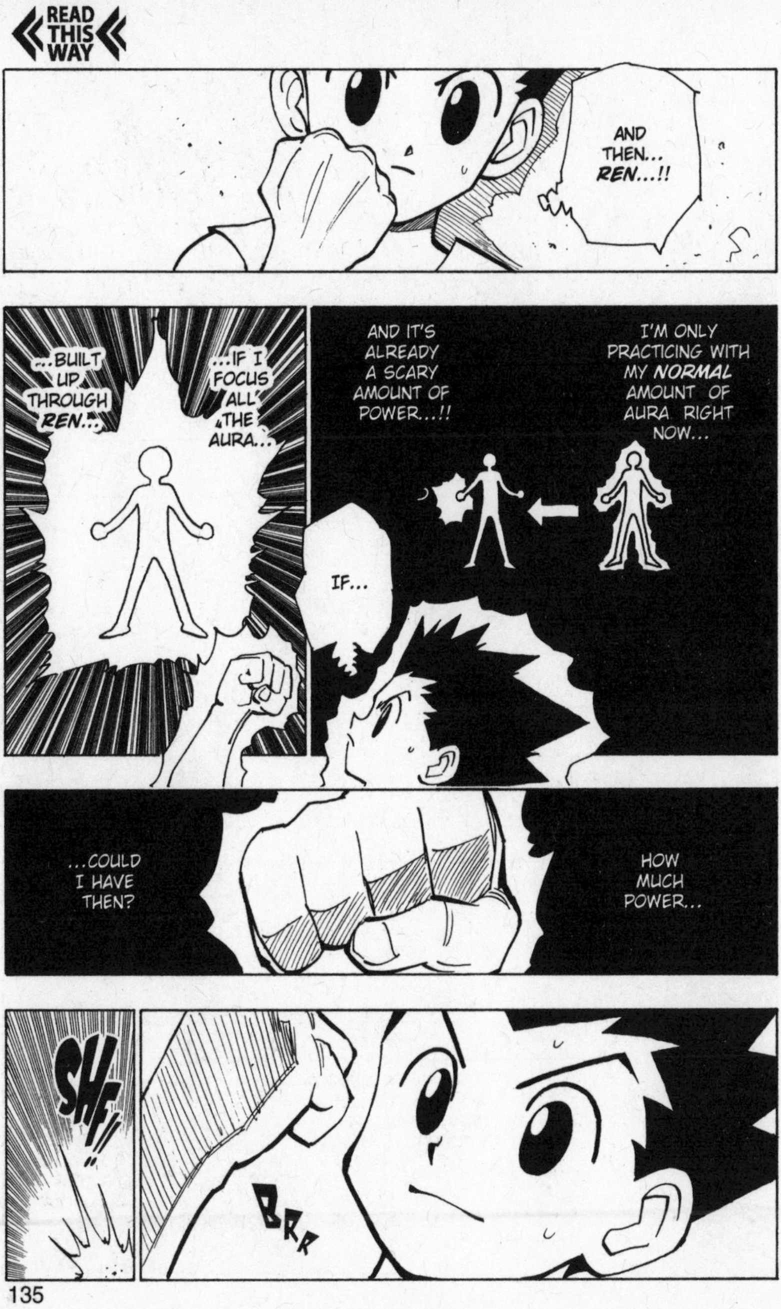
AND THEN... REN...!!
I'M ONLY PRACTICING WITH MY NORMAL AMOUNT OF AURA RIGHT NOW...
AND IT'S ALREADY A SCARY AMOUNT OF POWER...!!
IF...
...IF I FOCUS ALL THE AURA...
...BUILT UP THROUGH REN...
HOW MUCH POWER...
...COULD I HAVE THEN?
BRR
SHF!!

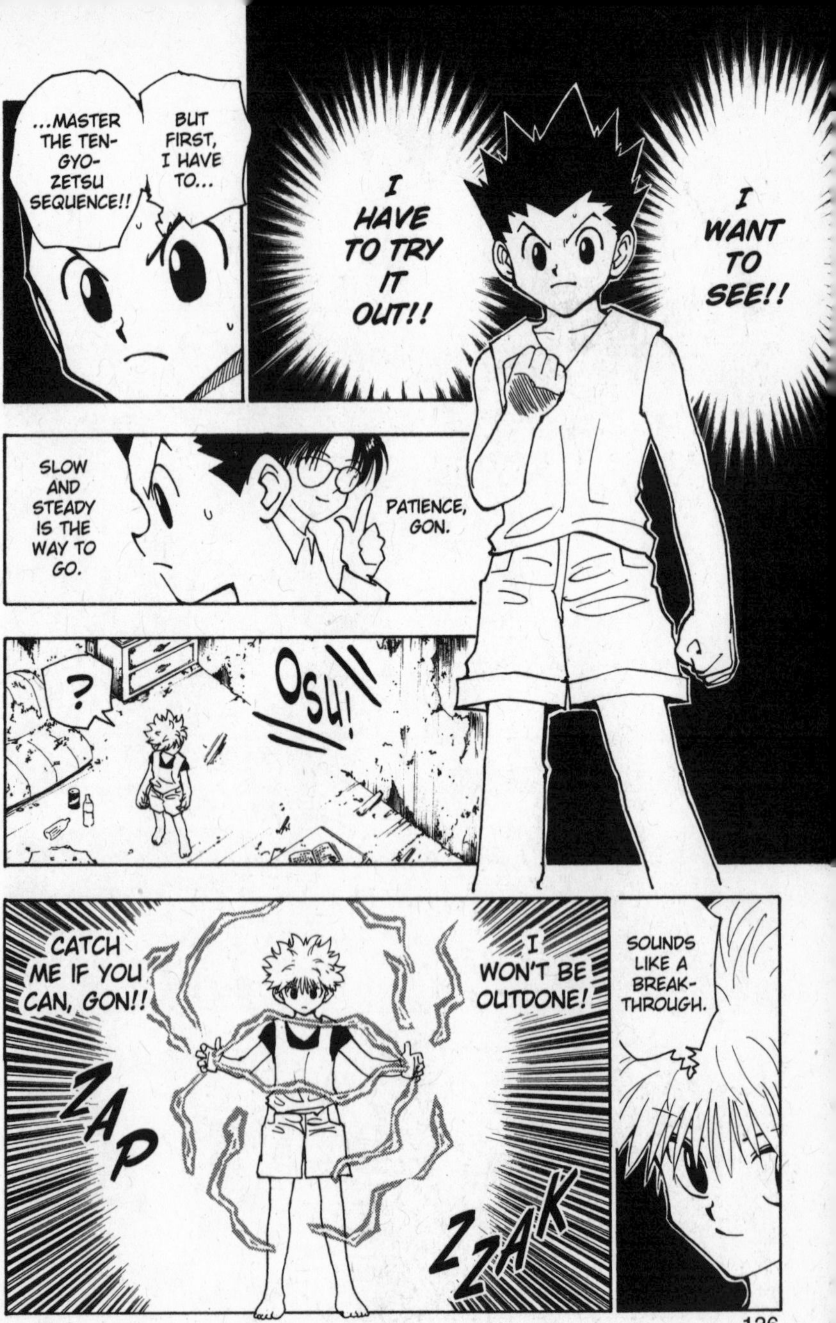
I WANT TO SEE!!
I HAVE TO TRY IT OUT!!
BUT FIRST, I HAVE TO...
...MASTER THE TEN-GYO-ZETSU SEQUENCE!!
PATIENCE, GON.
SLOW AND STEADY IS THE WAY TO GO.
OSU!
?
SOUNDS LIKE A BREAK-THROUGH.
I WON'T BE OUTDONE!
CATCH ME IF YOU CAN, GON!!
ZZAK
ZAP

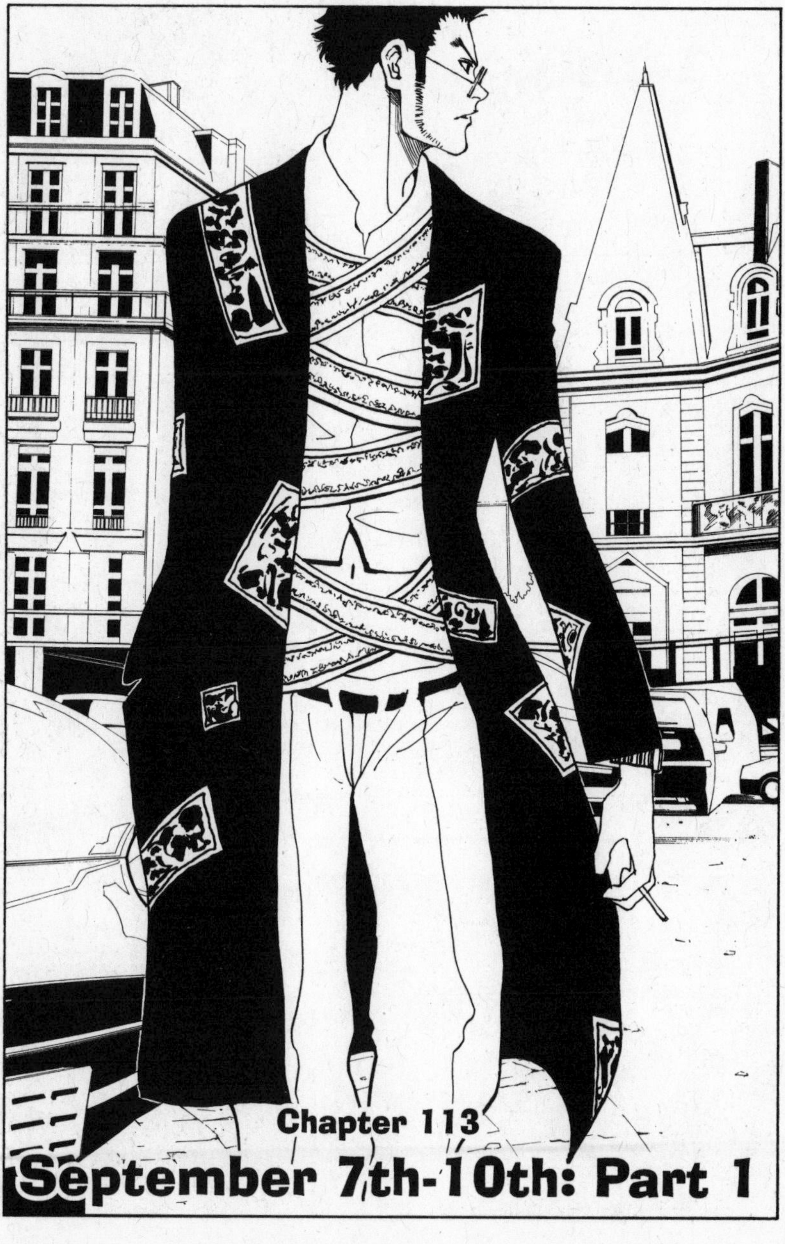

Chapter 113

September 7th-10th: Part 1

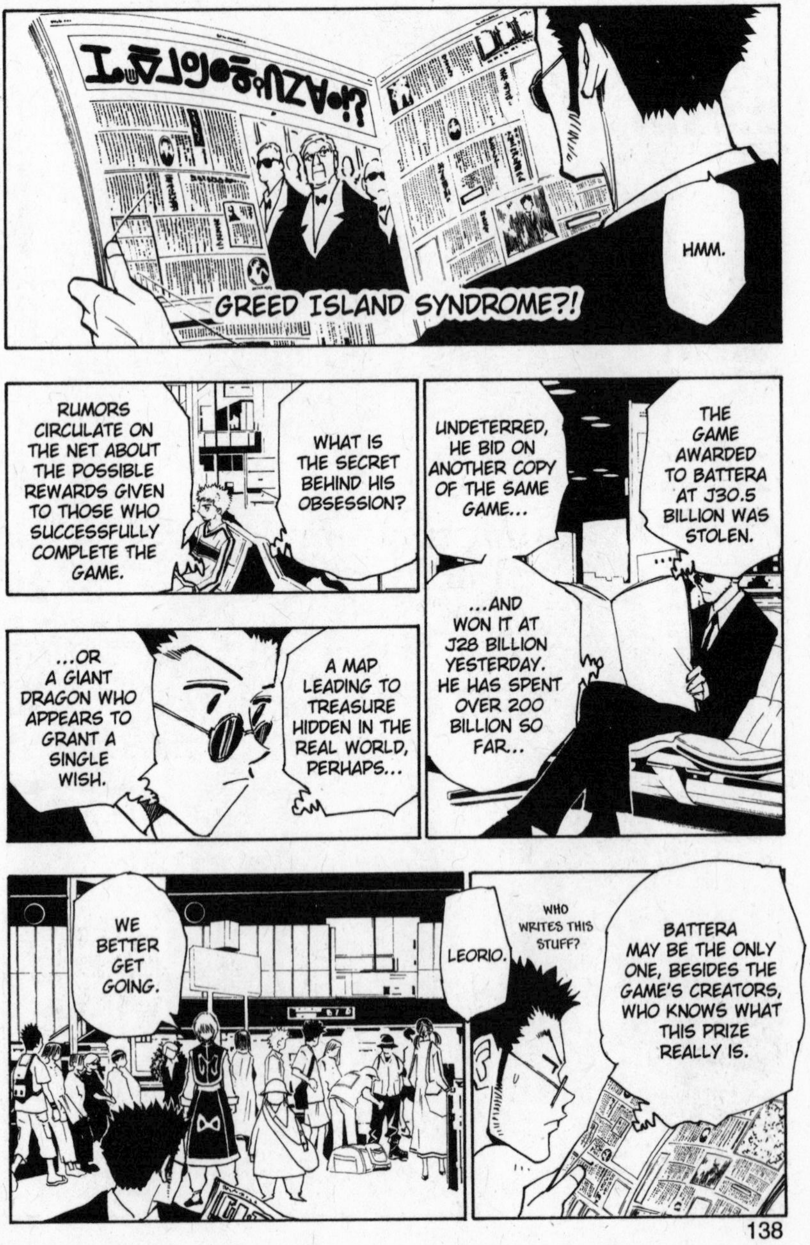
HMM.
GREED ISLAND SYNDROME?!
THE GAME AWARDED TO BATTERA AT J30.5 BILLION WAS STOLEN.
UNDETERRED, HE BID ON ANOTHER COPY OF THE SAME GAME...
...AND WON IT AT J28 BILLION YESTERDAY. HE HAS SPENT OVER 200 BILLION SO FAR...
WHAT IS THE SECRET BEHIND HIS OBSESSION?
RUMORS CIRCULATE ON THE NET ABOUT THE POSSIBLE REWARDS GIVEN TO THOSE WHO SUCCESSFULLY COMPLETE THE GAME.
A MAP LEADING TO TREASURE HIDDEN IN THE REAL WORLD, PERHAPS...
...OR A GIANT DRAGON WHO APPEARS TO GRANT A SINGLE WISH.
BATTERA MAY BE THE ONLY ONE, BESIDES THE GAME'S CREATORS, WHO KNOWS WHAT THIS PRIZE REALLY IS.
WHO WRITES THIS STUFF?
LEORIO.
WE BETTER GET GOING.

READ THIS WAY

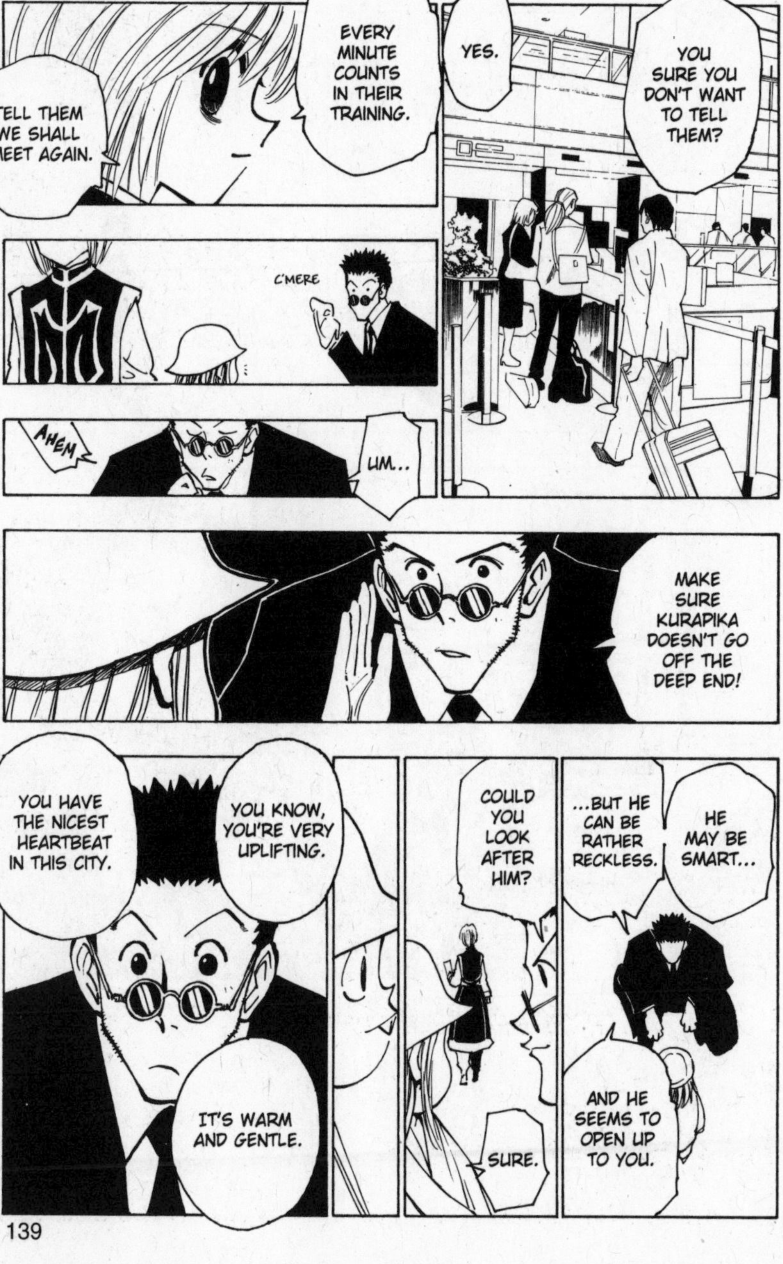
YOU SURE YOU DON'T WANT TO TELL THEM?
YES.
EVERY MINUTE COUNTS IN THEIR TRAINING.
TELL THEM WE SHALL MEET AGAIN.
C'MERE
UM...
AHEM
MAKE SURE KURAPIKA DOESN'T GO OFF THE DEEP END!
HE MAY BE SMART...
...BUT HE CAN BE RATHER RECKLESS.
AND HE SEEMS TO OPEN UP TO YOU.
COULD YOU LOOK AFTER HIM?
SURE.
YOU KNOW, YOU'RE VERY UPLIFTING.
YOU HAVE THE NICEST HEARTBEAT IN THIS CITY.
IT'S WARM AND GENTLE.

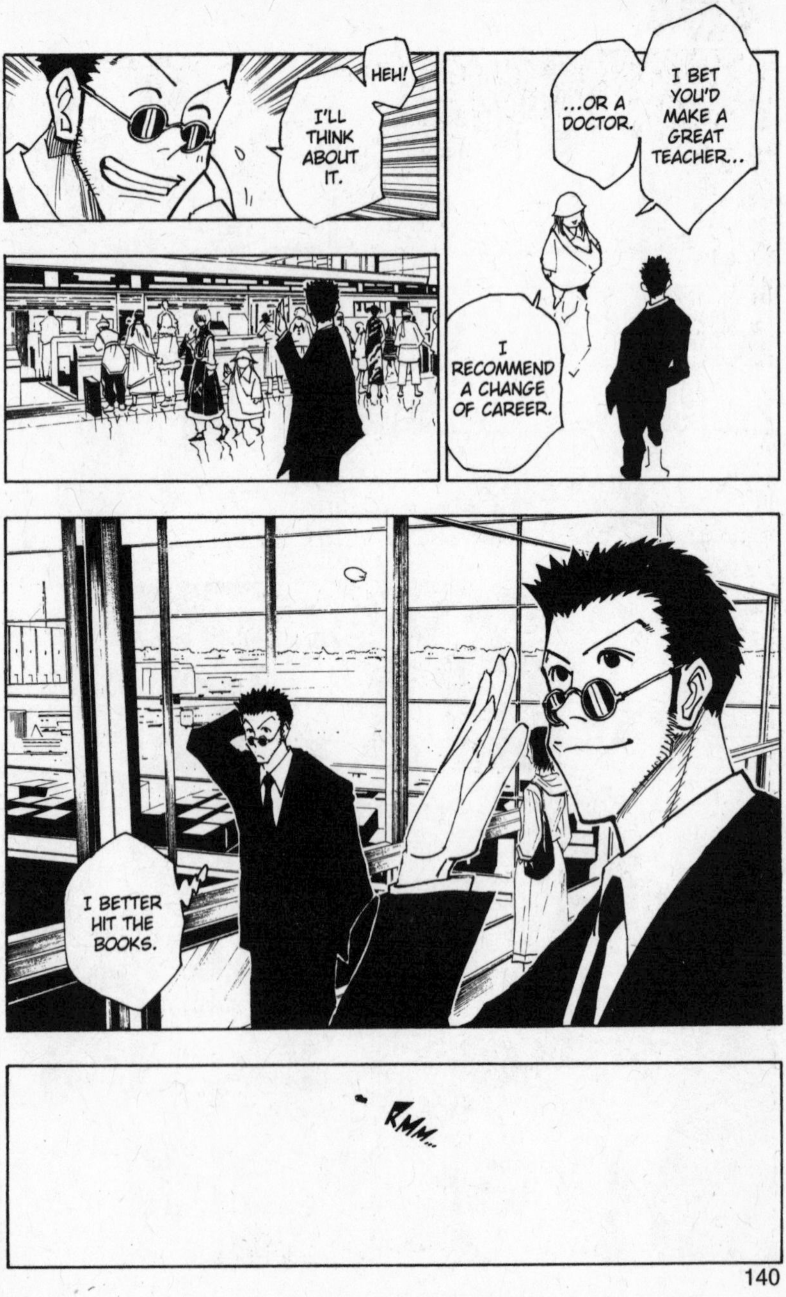
I BET YOU'D MAKE A GREAT TEACHER...
...OR A DOCTOR.
I RECOMMEND A CHANGE OF CAREER.
HEH!
I'LL THINK ABOUT IT.
I BETTER HIT THE BOOKS.
RMM...

READ THIS WAY

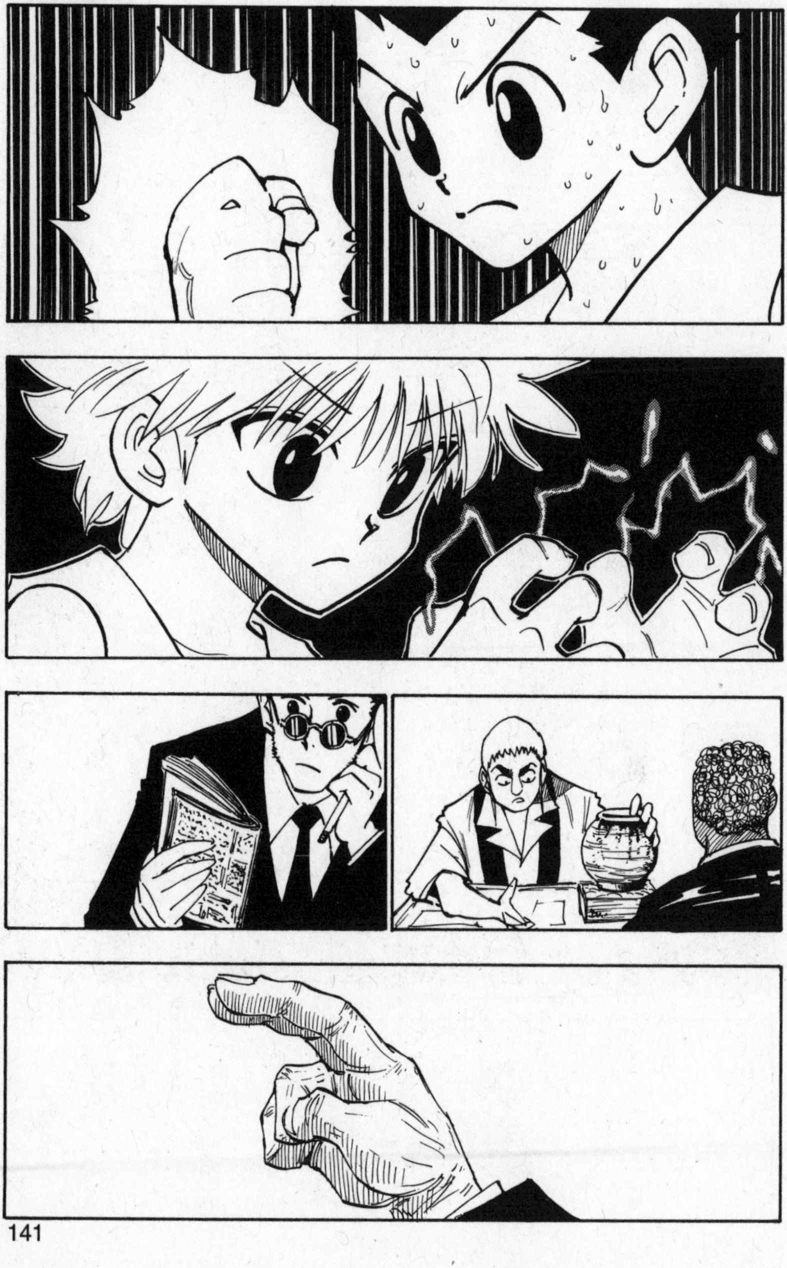

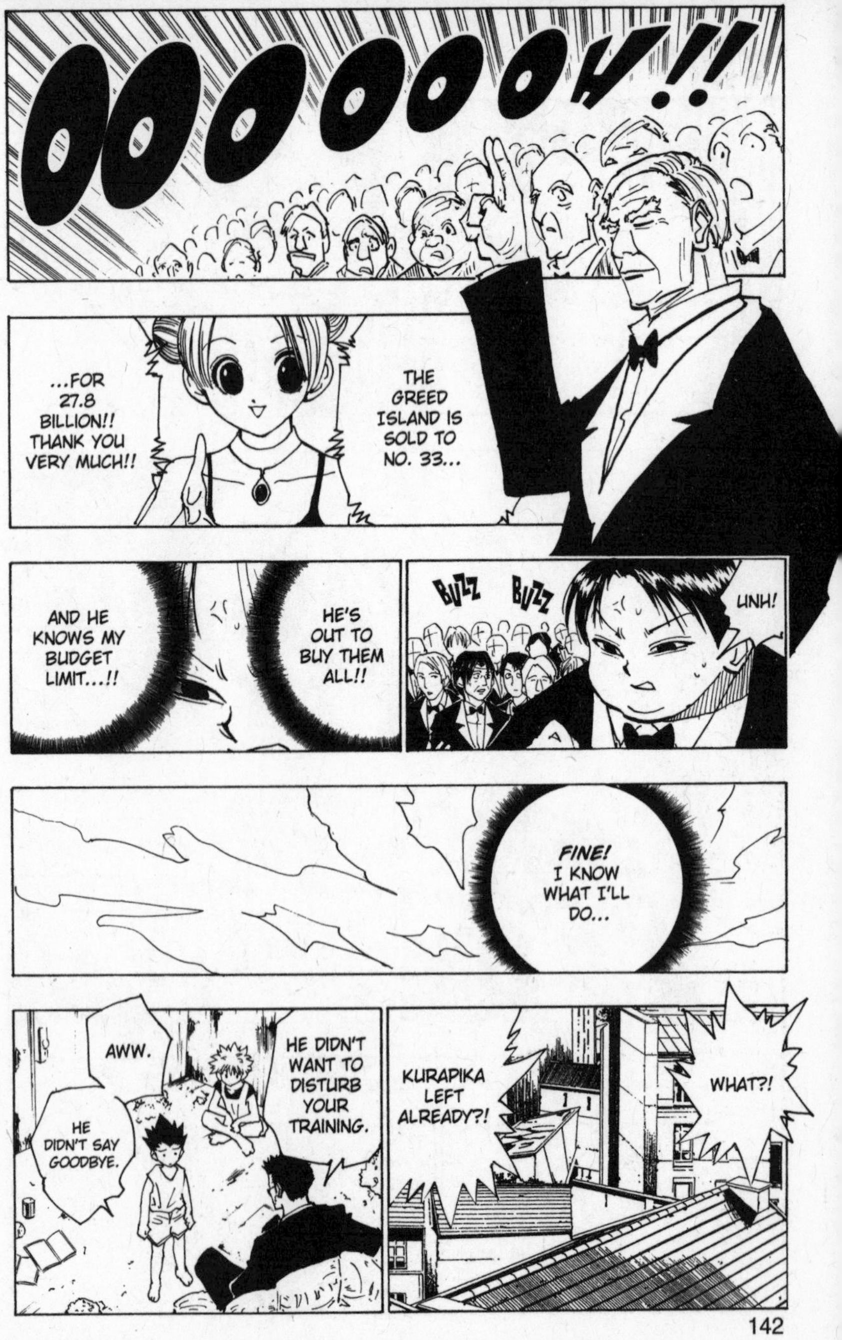
OOOOOOH!!
THE GREED ISLAND IS SOLD TO NO. 33...
...FOR 27.8 BILLION!! THANK YOU VERY MUCH!!
UNH!
BUZZ
BUZZ
HE'S OUT TO BUY THEM ALL!!
AND HE KNOWS MY BUDGET LIMIT...!!
FINE! I KNOW WHAT I'LL DO...
WHAT?!
KURAPIKA LEFT ALREADY?!
HE DIDN'T WANT TO DISTURB YOUR TRAINING.
AWW.
HE DIDN'T SAY GOODBYE.

READ THIS WAY

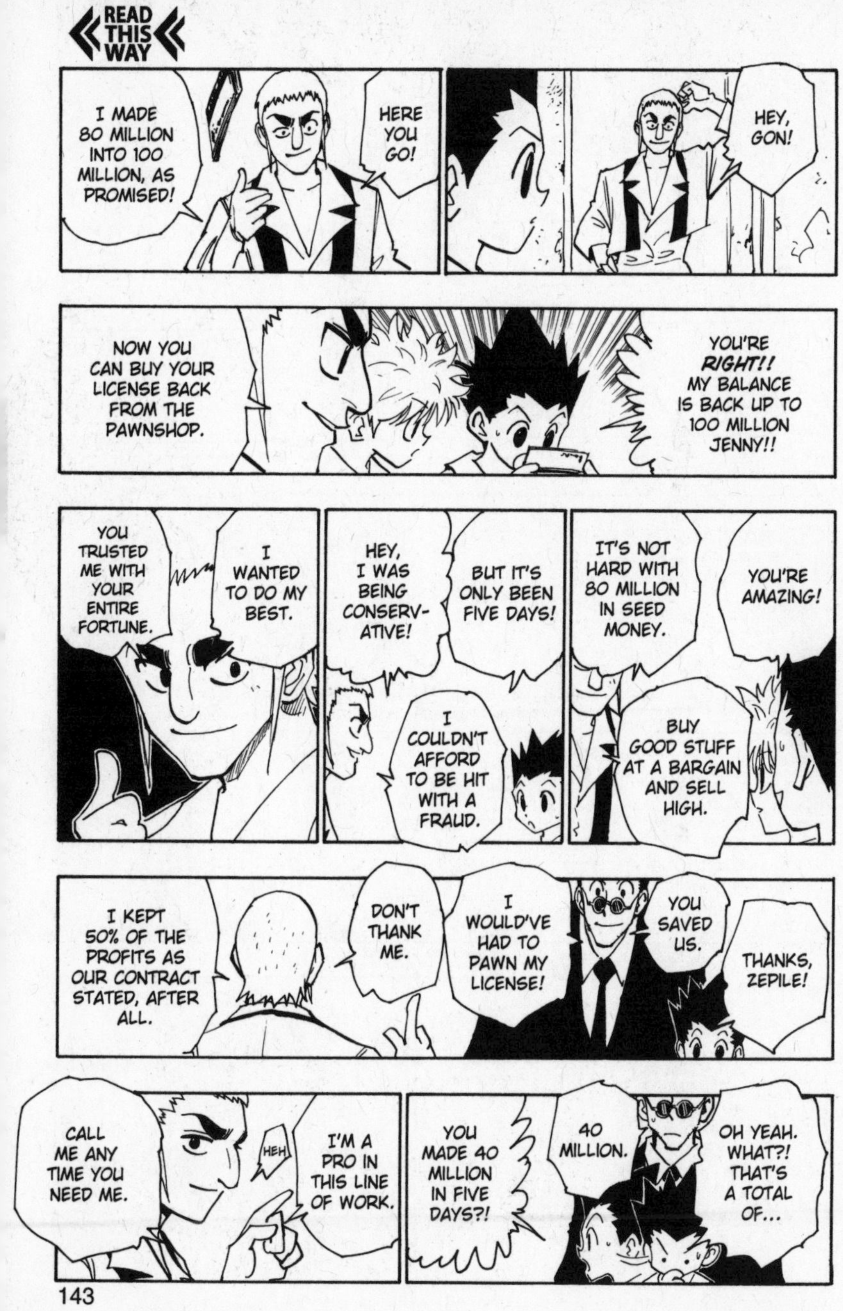
HEY, GON!
HERE YOU GO!
I MADE 80 MILLION INTO 100 MILLION, AS PROMISED!
YOU'RE *RIGHT!!* MY BALANCE IS BACK UP TO 100 MILLION JENNY!!
NOW YOU CAN BUY YOUR LICENSE BACK FROM THE PAWNSHOP.
YOU'RE AMAZING!
IT'S NOT HARD WITH 80 MILLION IN SEED MONEY.
BUY GOOD STUFF AT A BARGAIN AND SELL HIGH.
BUT IT'S ONLY BEEN FIVE DAYS!
HEY, I WAS BEING CONSERV-ATIVE!
I COULDN'T AFFORD TO BE HIT WITH A FRAUD.
I WANTED TO DO MY BEST.
YOU TRUSTED ME WITH YOUR ENTIRE FORTUNE.
THANKS, ZEPILE!
YOU SAVED US.
I WOULD'VE HAD TO PAWN MY LICENSE!
DON'T THANK ME.
I KEPT 50% OF THE PROFITS AS OUR CONTRACT STATED, AFTER ALL.
OH YEAH. WHAT?! THAT'S A TOTAL OF...
40 MILLION.
YOU MADE 40 MILLION IN FIVE DAYS?!
I'M A PRO IN THIS LINE OF WORK.
HEH
CALL ME ANY TIME YOU NEED ME.

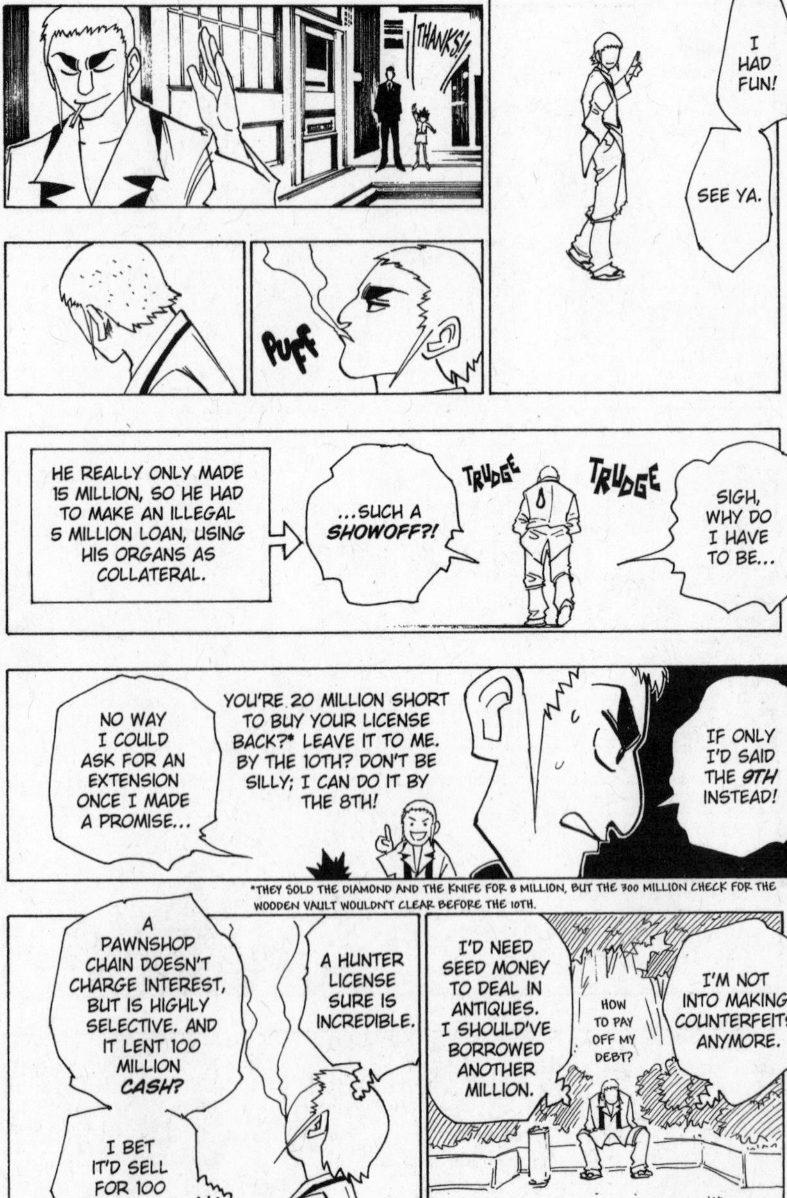
I HAD FUN!
SEE YA.
THANKS!!
PUFF
SIGH, WHY DO I HAVE TO BE...
TRUDGE
TRUDGE
...SUCH A *SHOWOFF?!*
HE REALLY ONLY MADE 15 MILLION, SO HE HAD TO MAKE AN ILLEGAL 5 MILLION LOAN, USING HIS ORGANS AS COLLATERAL.
IF ONLY I'D SAID THE *9TH* INSTEAD!
YOU'RE 20 MILLION SHORT TO BUY YOUR LICENSE BACK?* LEAVE IT TO ME. BY THE 10TH? DON'T BE SILLY; I CAN DO IT BY THE 8TH!
NO WAY I COULD ASK FOR AN EXTENSION ONCE I MADE A PROMISE...
I'M NOT INTO MAKING COUNTERFEITS ANYMORE.
HOW TO PAY OFF MY DEBT?
I'D NEED SEED MONEY TO DEAL IN ANTIQUES. I SHOULD'VE BORROWED ANOTHER MILLION.
A HUNTER LICENSE SURE IS INCREDIBLE.
A PAWNSHOP CHAIN DOESN'T CHARGE INTEREST, BUT IS HIGHLY SELECTIVE. AND IT LENT 100 MILLION *CASH?*
I BET IT'D SELL FOR 100 TIMES AS MUCH.

*THEY SOLD THE DIAMOND AND THE KNIFE FOR 8 MILLION, BUT THE 300 MILLION CHECK FOR THE WOODEN VAULT WOULDN'T CLEAR BEFORE THE 10TH.

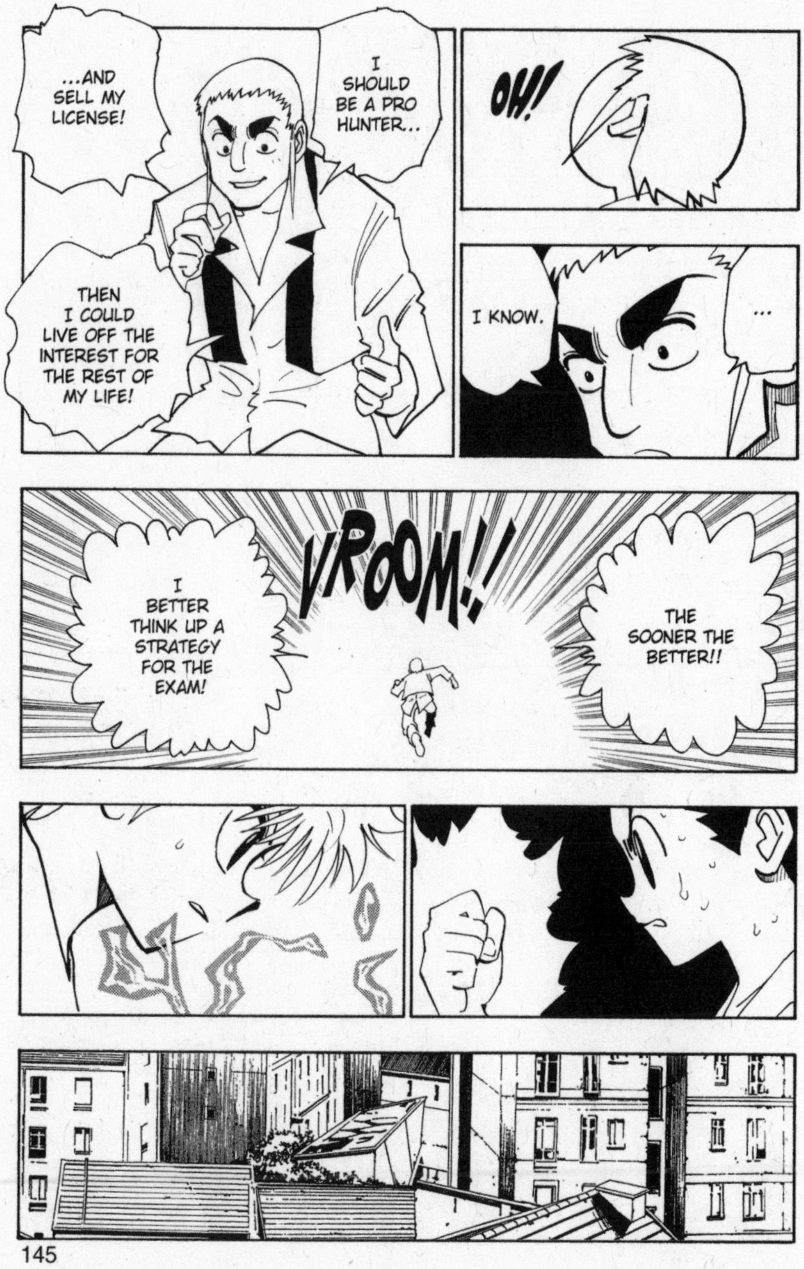
OH!
...
I KNOW.
I SHOULD BE A PRO HUNTER...
...AND SELL MY LICENSE!
THEN I COULD LIVE OFF THE INTEREST FOR THE REST OF MY LIFE!
THE SOONER THE BETTER!!
VROOM!!
I BETTER THINK UP A STRATEGY FOR THE EXAM!

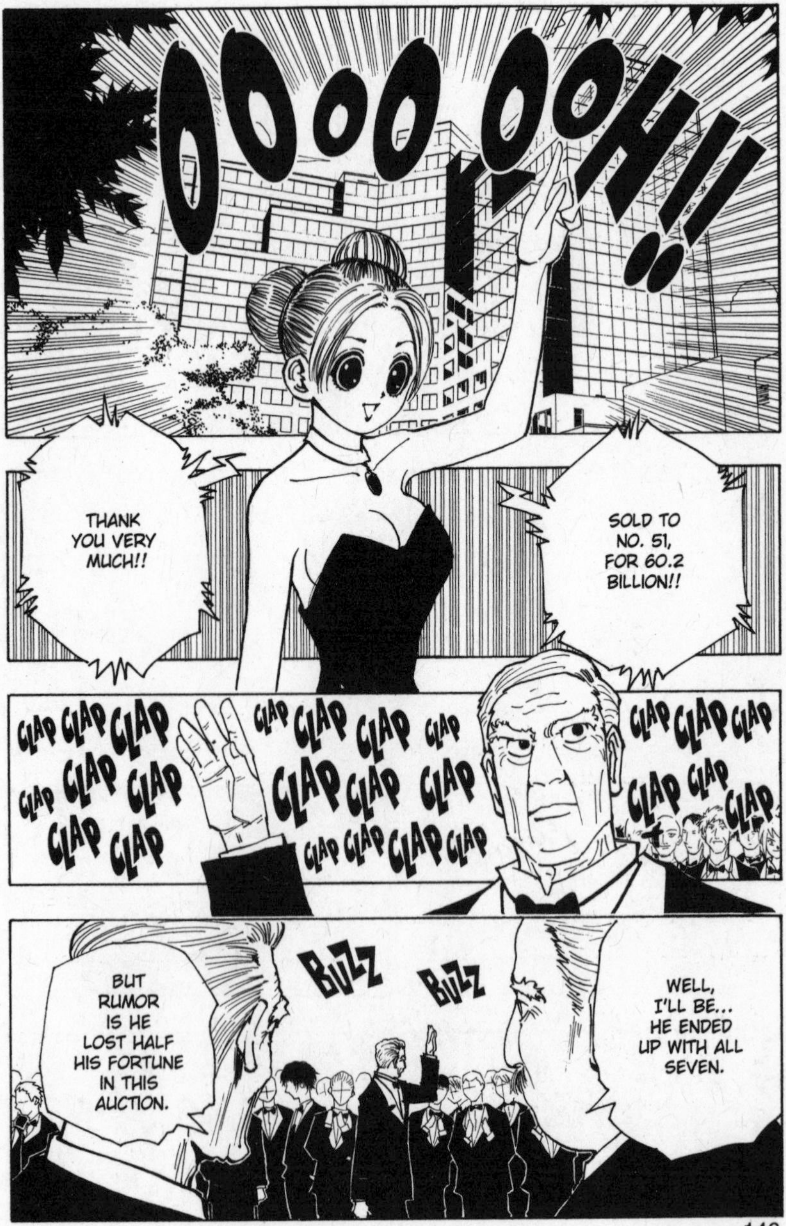
OOOO OOH!!
SOLD TO NO. 51, FOR 60.2 BILLION!!
THANK YOU VERY MUCH!!
CLAP CLAP CLAP CLAP CLAP CLAP CLAP
CLAP CLAP CLAP CLAP CLAP CLAP CLAP CLAP CLAP CLAP CLAP CLAP
CLAP CLAP CLAP CLAP CLAP CLAP CLAP CLAP CLAP
WELL, I'LL BE... HE ENDED UP WITH ALL SEVEN.
BUZZ
BUZZ
BUT RUMOR IS HE LOST HALF HIS FORTUNE IN THIS AUCTION.

READ THIS WAY

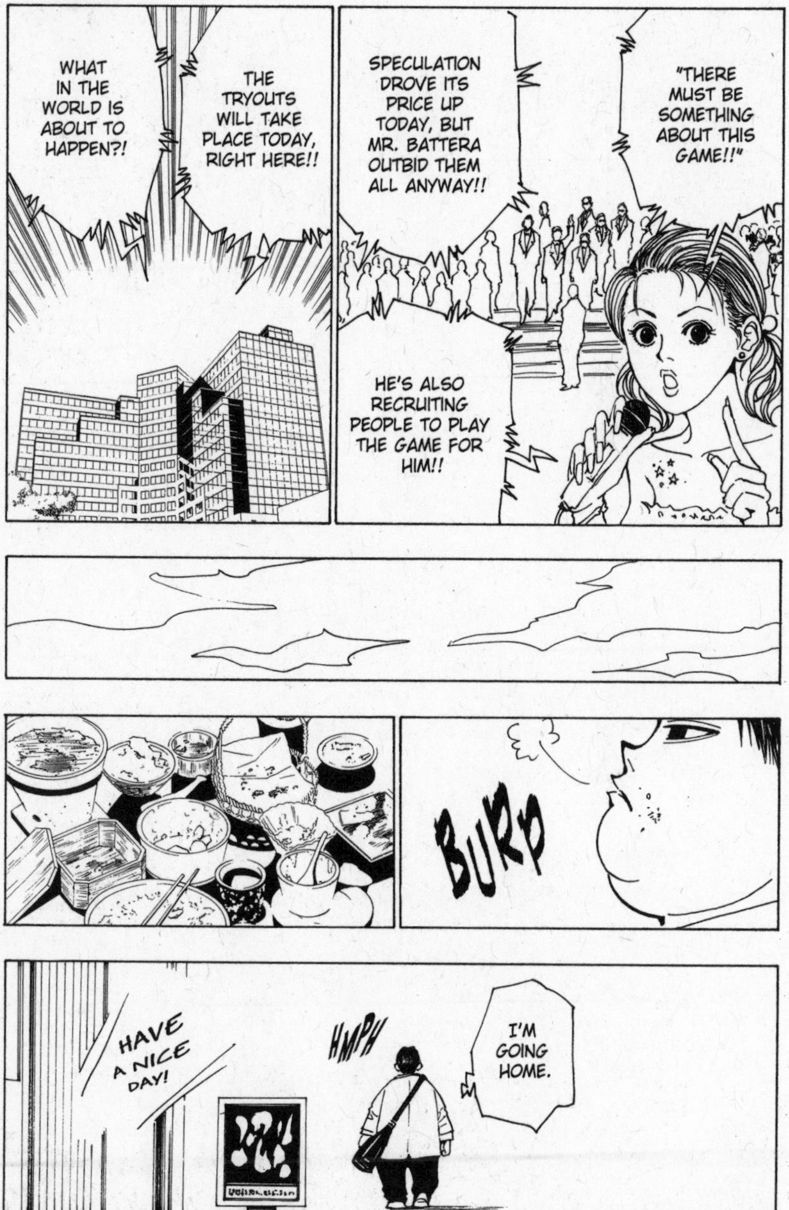
"THERE MUST BE SOMETHING ABOUT THIS GAME!!"
SPECULATION DROVE ITS PRICE UP TODAY, BUT MR. BATTERA OUTBID THEM ALL ANYWAY!!
HE'S ALSO RECRUITING PEOPLE TO PLAY THE GAME FOR HIM!!
THE TRYOUTS WILL TAKE PLACE TODAY, RIGHT HERE!!
WHAT IN THE WORLD IS ABOUT TO HAPPEN?!
BURP
I'M GOING HOME.
HMPH
HAVE A NICE DAY!

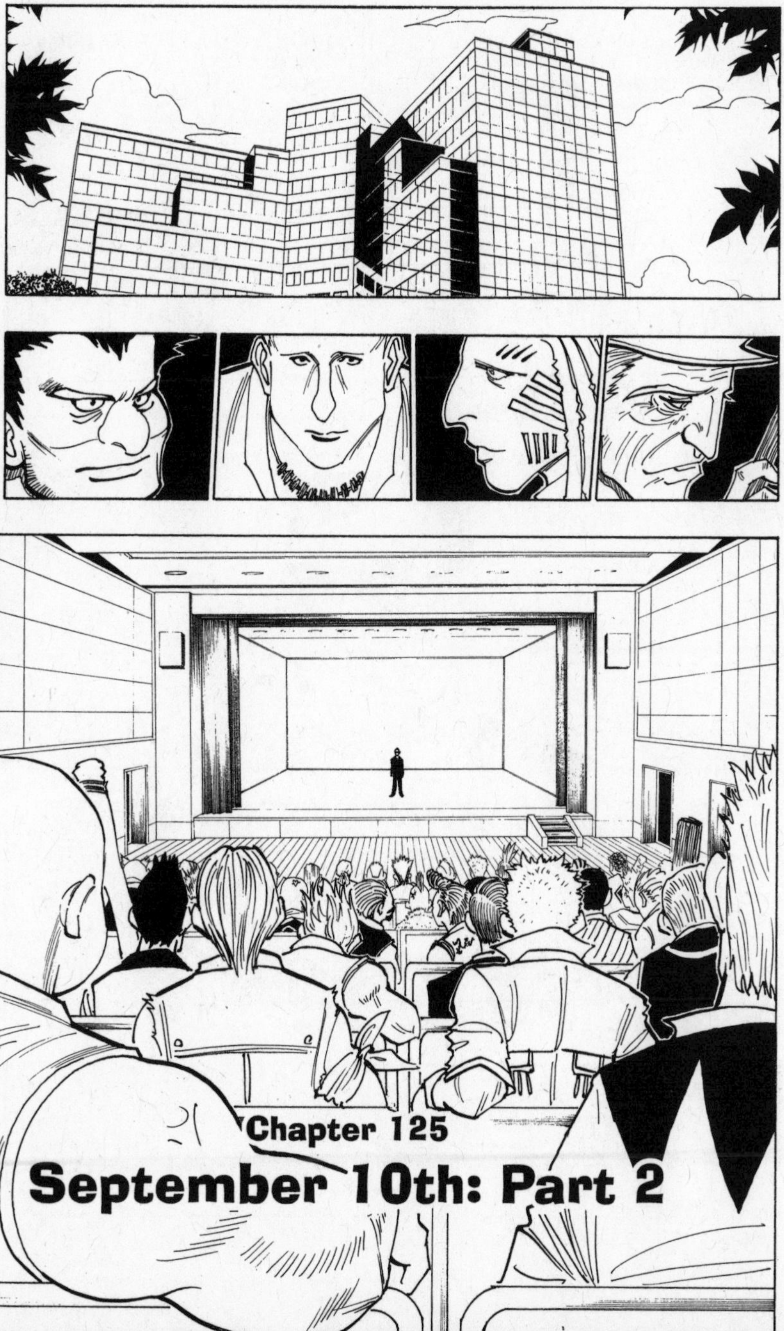
Chapter 125
September 10th: Part 2

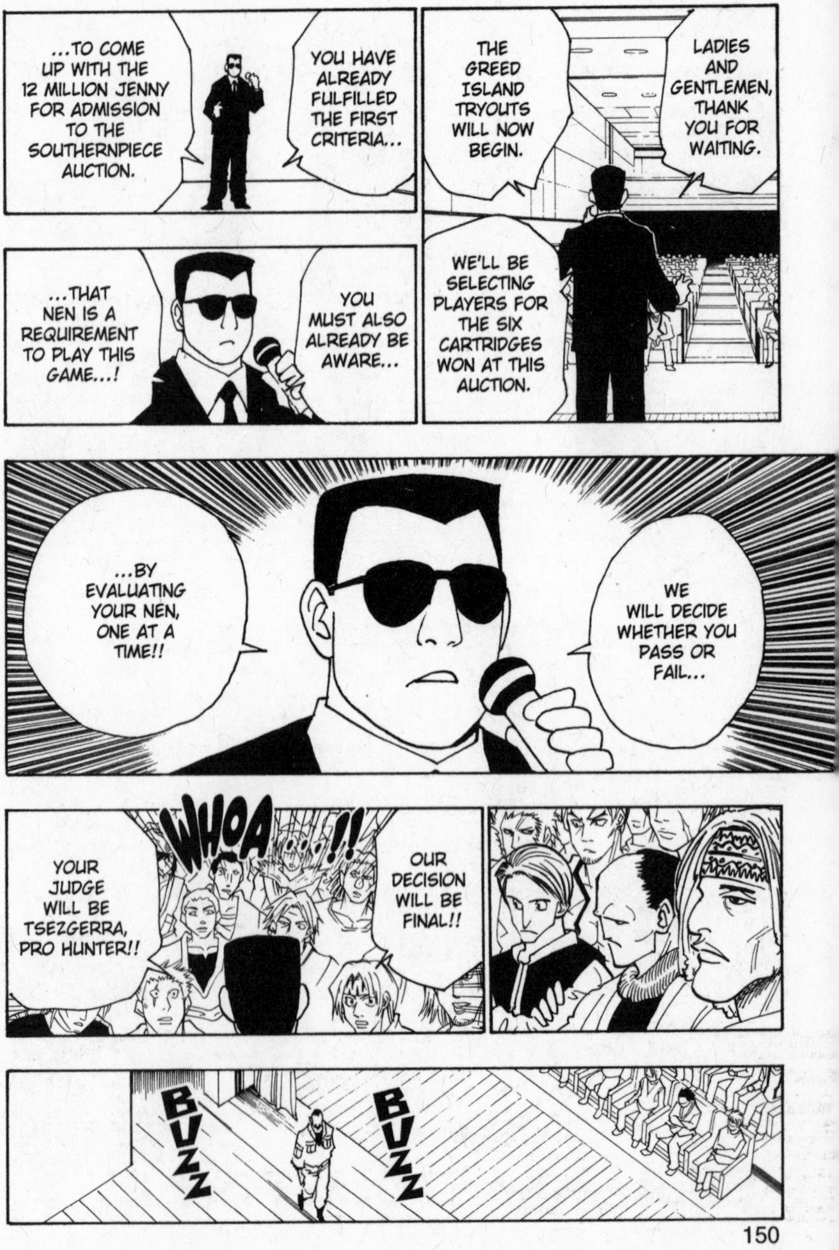
LADIES AND GENTLEMEN, THANK YOU FOR WAITING.
THE GREED ISLAND TRYOUTS WILL NOW BEGIN.
WE'LL BE SELECTING PLAYERS FOR THE SIX CARTRIDGES WON AT THIS AUCTION.
YOU HAVE ALREADY FULFILLED THE FIRST CRITERIA...
...TO COME UP WITH THE 12 MILLION JENNY FOR ADMISSION TO THE SOUTHERNPIECE AUCTION.
YOU MUST ALSO ALREADY BE AWARE...
...THAT NEN IS A REQUIREMENT TO PLAY THIS GAME...!
WE WILL DECIDE WHETHER YOU PASS OR FAIL...
...BY EVALUATING YOUR NEN, ONE AT A TIME!!
OUR DECISION WILL BE FINAL!!
WHOA!!
YOUR JUDGE WILL BE TSEZGERRA, PRO HUNTER!!
BUZZ
BUZZ

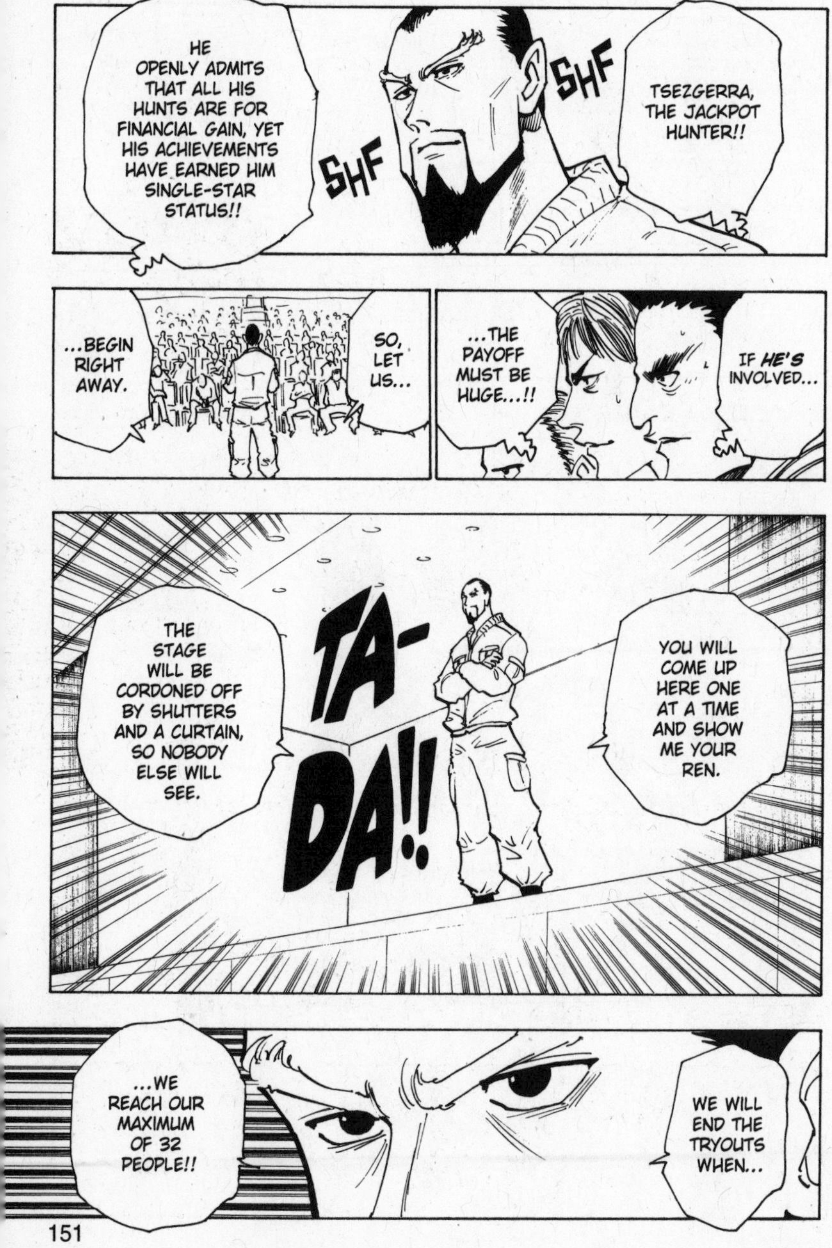
TSEZGERRA, THE JACKPOT HUNTER!!
SHF
SHF
HE OPENLY ADMITS THAT ALL HIS HUNTS ARE FOR FINANCIAL GAIN, YET HIS ACHIEVEMENTS HAVE EARNED HIM SINGLE-STAR STATUS!!
IF *HE'S* INVOLVED...
...THE PAYOFF MUST BE HUGE...!!
SO, LET US...
...BEGIN RIGHT AWAY.
YOU WILL COME UP HERE ONE AT A TIME AND SHOW ME YOUR REN.
TA-DA!!
THE STAGE WILL BE CORDONED OFF BY SHUTTERS AND A CURTAIN, SO NOBODY ELSE WILL SEE.
WE WILL END THE TRYOUTS WHEN...
...WE REACH OUR MAXIMUM OF 32 PEOPLE!!

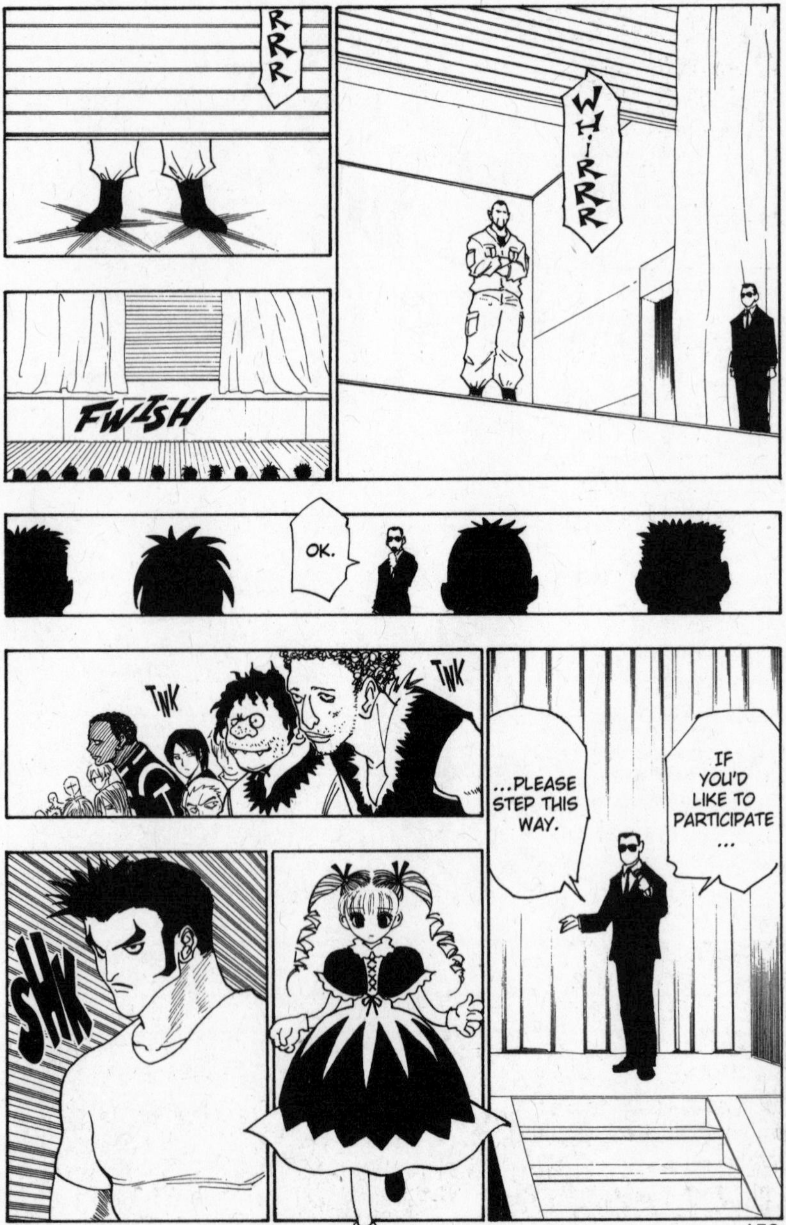
WHIRRR
RRR
FWISH
OK.
IF YOU'D LIKE TO PARTICIPATE ...
...PLEASE STEP THIS WAY.
TNK
TNK
SHK

READ THIS WAY

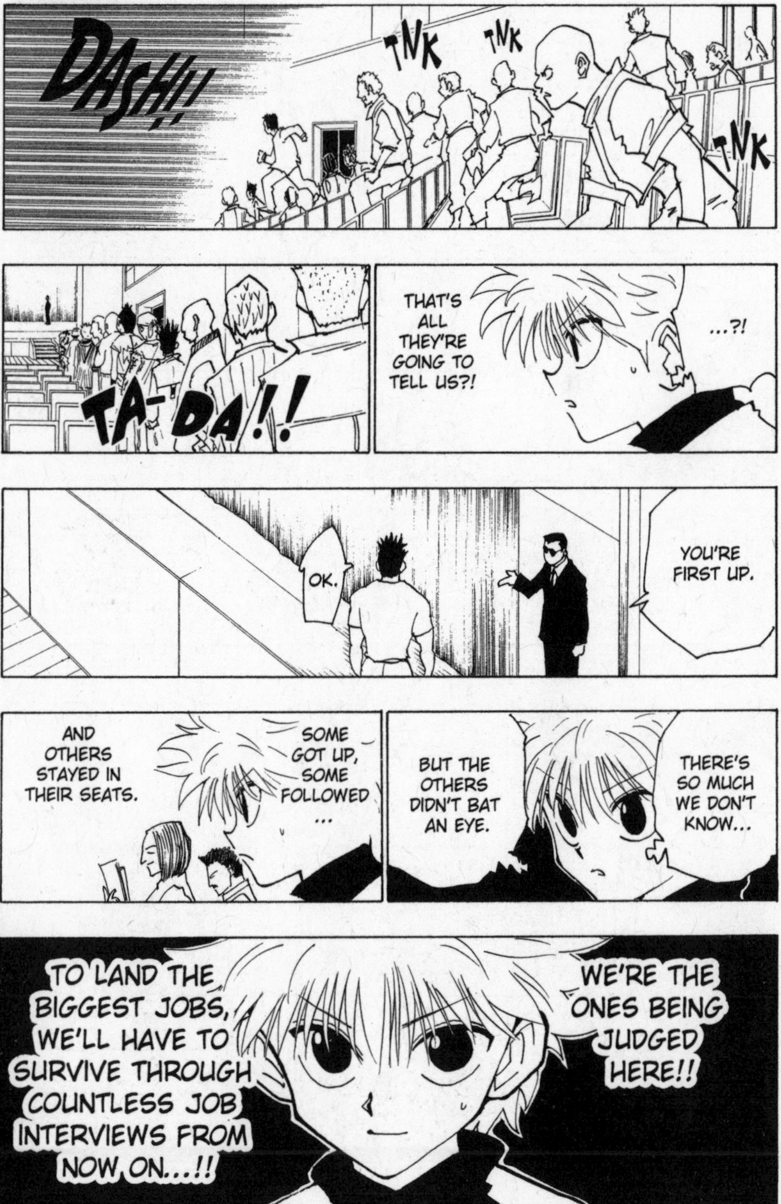
TNK
TNK
TNK
DASH!!
...?!
THAT'S ALL THEY'RE GOING TO TELL US?!
TA-DA!!
YOU'RE FIRST UP.
OK.
THERE'S SO MUCH WE DON'T KNOW...
BUT THE OTHERS DIDN'T BAT AN EYE.
SOME GOT UP, SOME FOLLOWED...
AND OTHERS STAYED IN THEIR SEATS.
WE'RE THE ONES BEING JUDGED HERE!!
TO LAND THE BIGGEST JOBS, WE'LL HAVE TO SURVIVE THROUGH COUNTLESS JOB INTERVIEWS FROM NOW ON...!!

THE OTHERS ALREADY KNOW THIS!! THEY DON'T NEED TO ASK QUESTIONS, BECAUSE THEY KNOW THEY WON'T GET ANY ANSWERS...!
THEY'VE BEEN THROUGH IT ALL MANY TIMES...!!
WE HAVE TO TAKE WHAT WE GET AND INFER THE REST...AND FIGURE OUT THE BEST MOVE...!!
WHAT WE DECIDE TO DO...
...IS ALSO PART OF THE TEST!!
THERE ARE ABOUT 200...
...APPLICANTS IN THIS HALL.
ABOUT 100 ARE IN LINE, WAITING THEIR TURN...!
MORE THAN 50 CLUSTER AROUND, LOOKING FOR A CHANCE.
ABOUT 20...
...HAVEN'T MOVED.

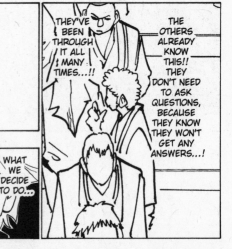

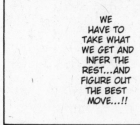

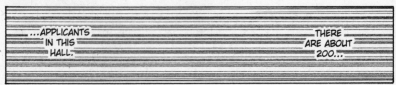

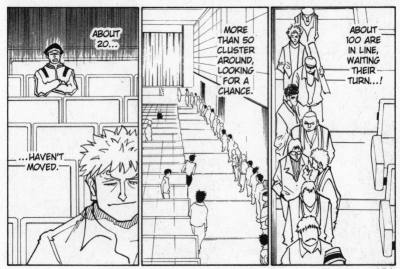

READ THIS WAY

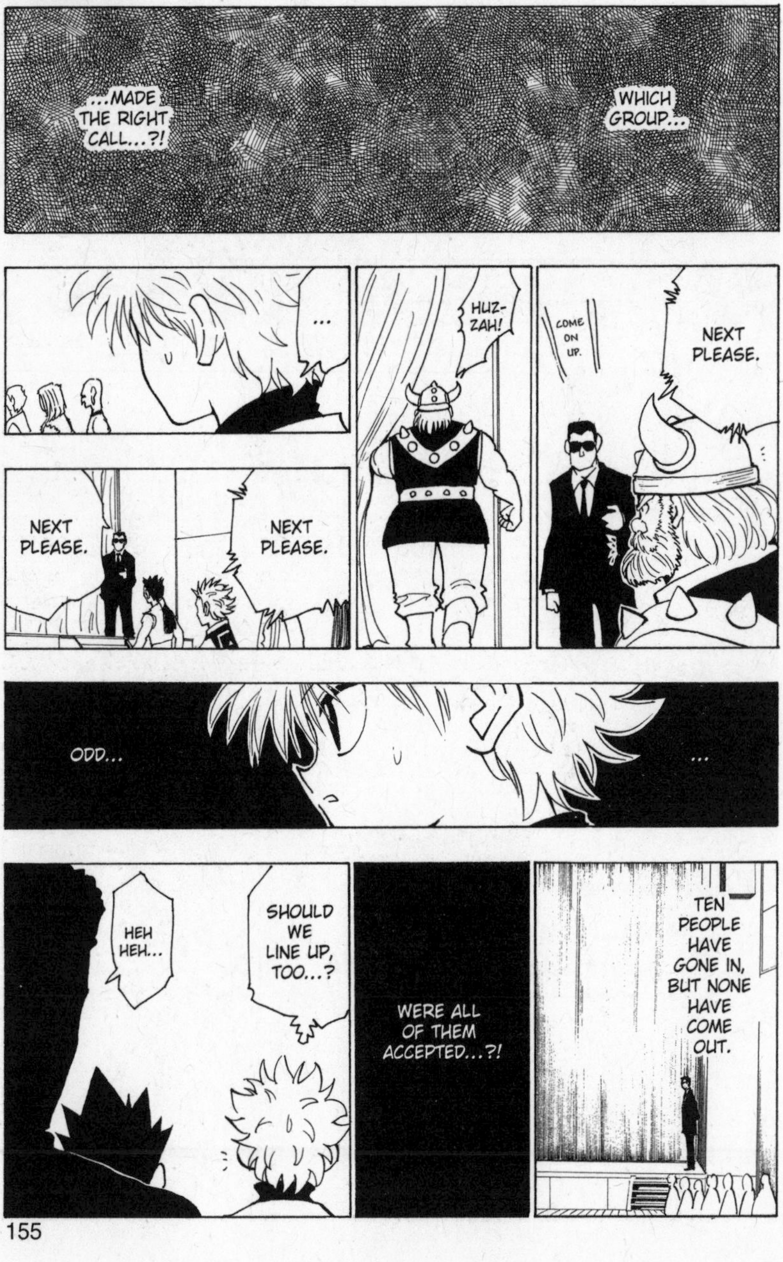
WHICH GROUP...
...MADE THE RIGHT CALL...?!
NEXT PLEASE.
COME ON UP.
HUZ-ZAH!
...
NEXT PLEASE.
NEXT PLEASE.
...
ODD...
TEN PEOPLE HAVE GONE IN, BUT NONE HAVE COME OUT.
WERE ALL OF THEM ACCEPTED...?!
SHOULD WE LINE UP, TOO...?
HEH HEH...

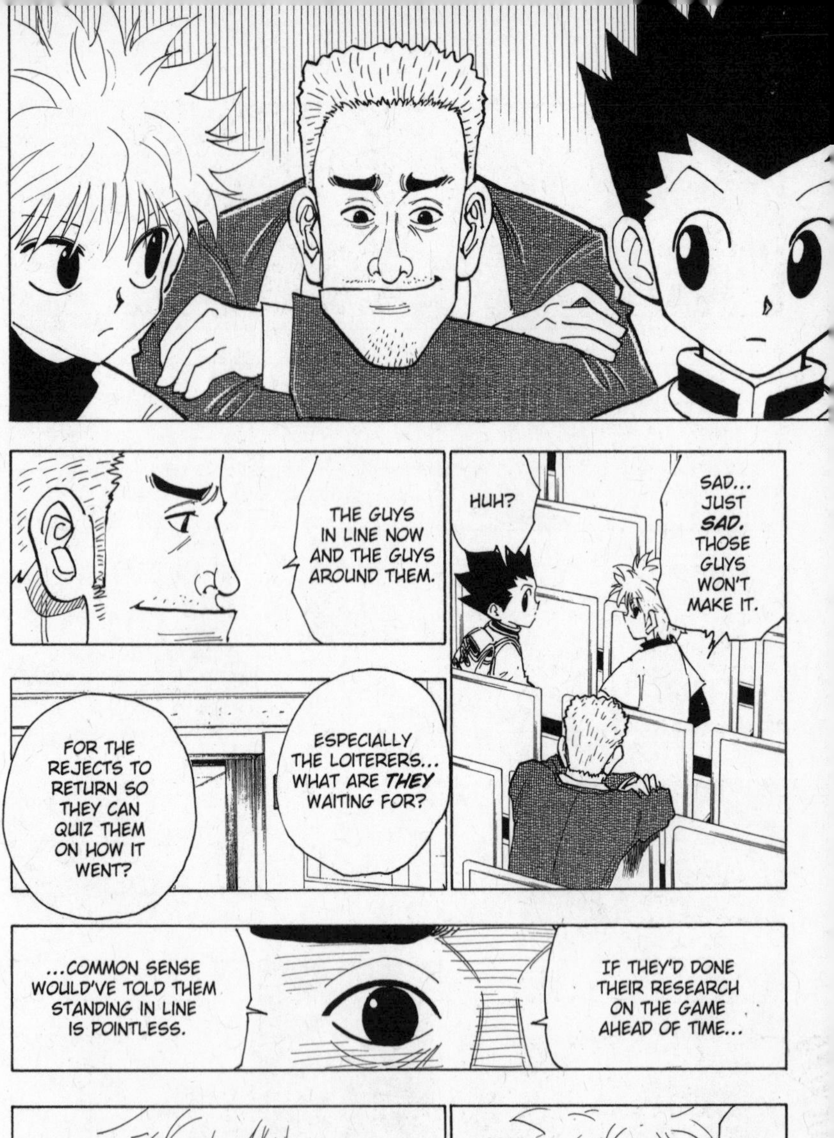
SAD... JUST *SAD.* THOSE GUYS WON'T MAKE IT.
HUH?
THE GUYS IN LINE NOW AND THE GUYS AROUND THEM.
ESPECIALLY THE LOITERERS... WHAT ARE *THEY* WAITING FOR?
FOR THE REJECTS TO RETURN SO THEY CAN QUIZ THEM ON HOW IT WENT?
IF THEY'D DONE THEIR RESEARCH ON THE GAME AHEAD OF TIME...
...COMMON SENSE WOULD'VE TOLD THEM STANDING IN LINE IS POINTLESS.
...
WHAT DOES HE MEAN...?
WE MUST BE CAREFUL IN OUR SELECTION.
WE WILL END THE TRYOUTS WHEN...

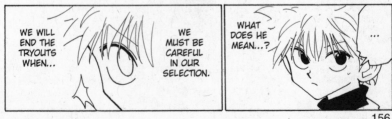

READ THIS WAY

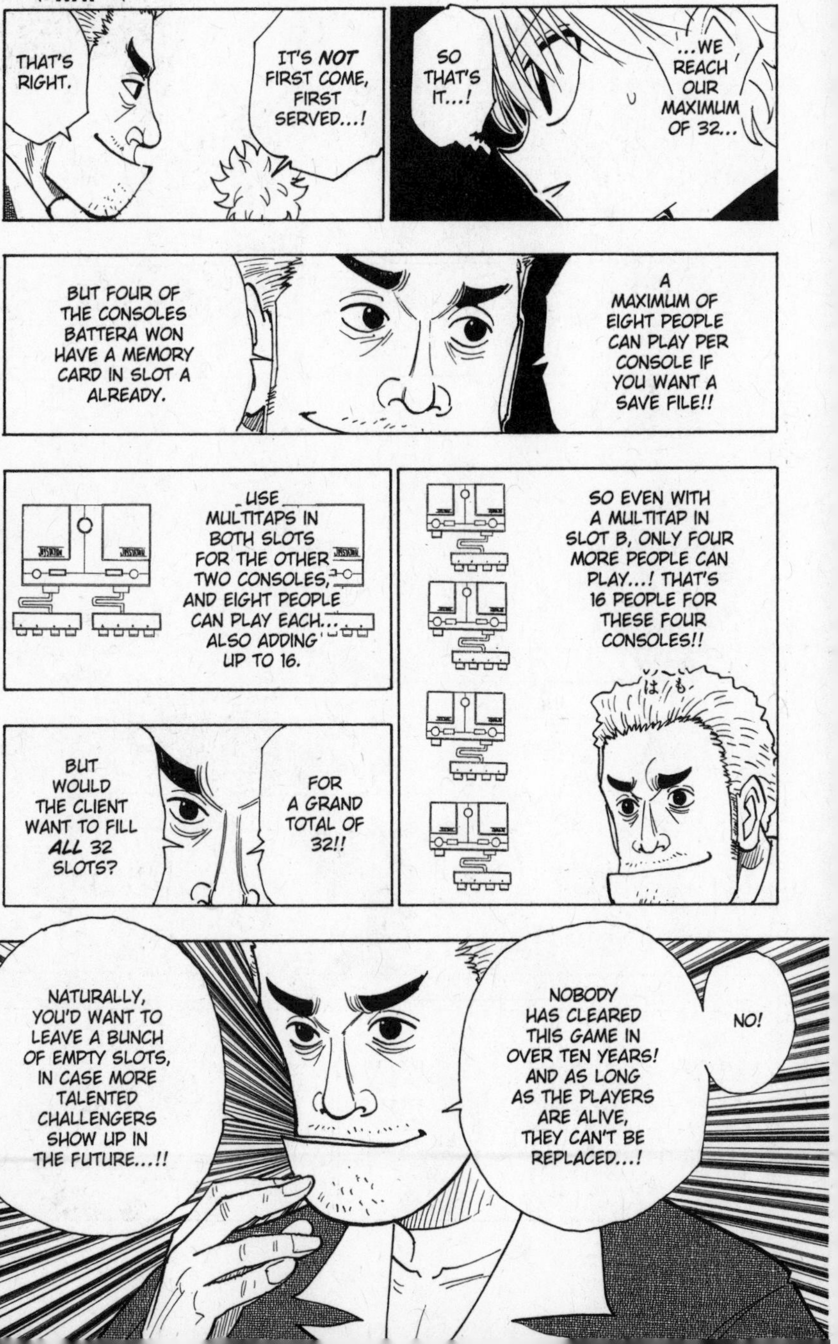
...WE REACH OUR MAXIMUM OF 32...
SO THAT'S IT...!
IT'S NOT FIRST COME, FIRST SERVED...!
THAT'S RIGHT.
A MAXIMUM OF EIGHT PEOPLE CAN PLAY PER CONSOLE IF YOU WANT A SAVE FILE!!
BUT FOUR OF THE CONSOLES BATTERA WON HAVE A MEMORY CARD IN SLOT A ALREADY.
SO EVEN WITH A MULTITAP IN SLOT B, ONLY FOUR MORE PEOPLE CAN PLAY...! THAT'S 16 PEOPLE FOR THESE FOUR CONSOLES!!
USE MULTITAPS IN BOTH SLOTS FOR THE OTHER TWO CONSOLES, AND EIGHT PEOPLE CAN PLAY EACH... ALSO ADDING UP TO 16.
FOR A GRAND TOTAL OF 32!!
BUT WOULD THE CLIENT WANT TO FILL ALL 32 SLOTS?
NO!
NOBODY HAS CLEARED THIS GAME IN OVER TEN YEARS! AND AS LONG AS THE PLAYERS ARE ALIVE, THEY CAN'T BE REPLACED...!
NATURALLY, YOU'D WANT TO LEAVE A BUNCH OF EMPTY SLOTS, IN CASE MORE TALENTED CHALLENGERS SHOW UP IN THE FUTURE...!!

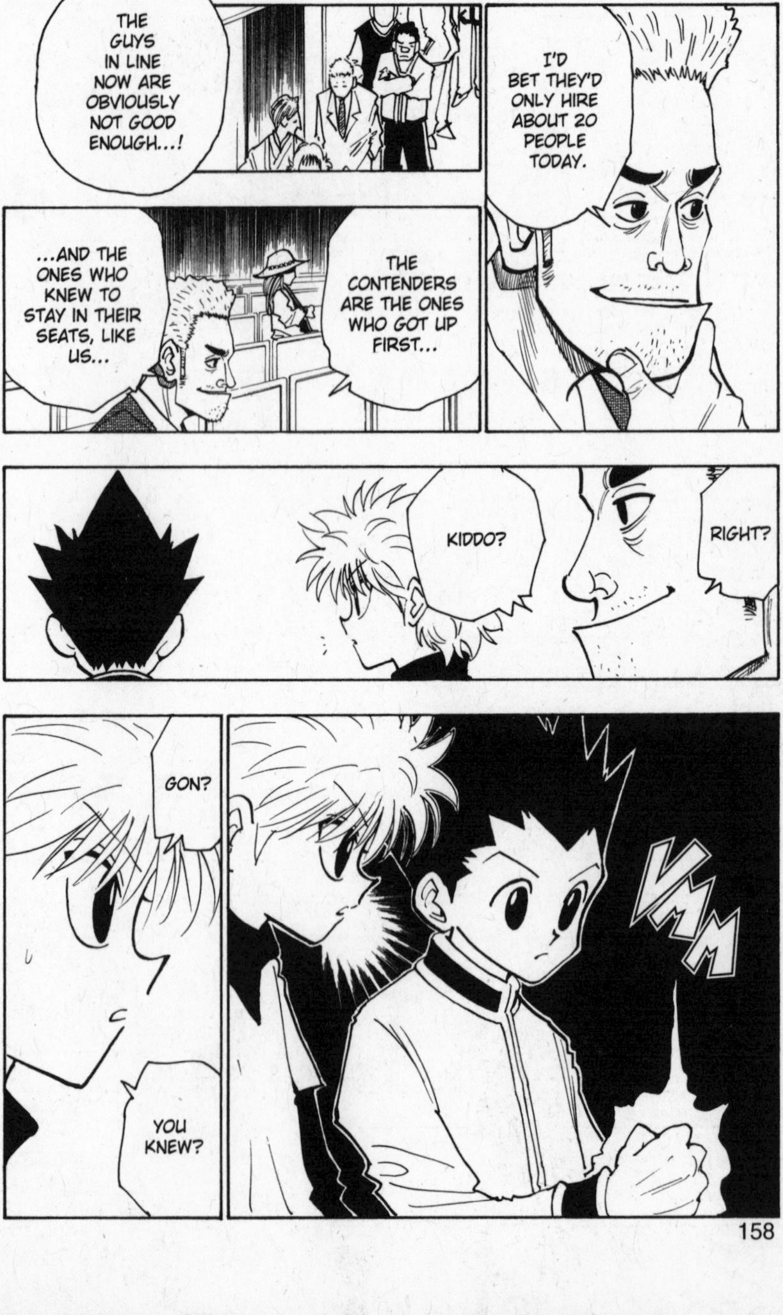
I'D BET THEY'D ONLY HIRE ABOUT 20 PEOPLE TODAY.
THE GUYS IN LINE NOW ARE OBVIOUSLY NOT GOOD ENOUGH...!
THE CONTENDERS ARE THE ONES WHO GOT UP FIRST...
...AND THE ONES WHO KNEW TO STAY IN THEIR SEATS, LIKE US...
RIGHT?
KIDDO?
VMM
GON?
YOU KNEW?

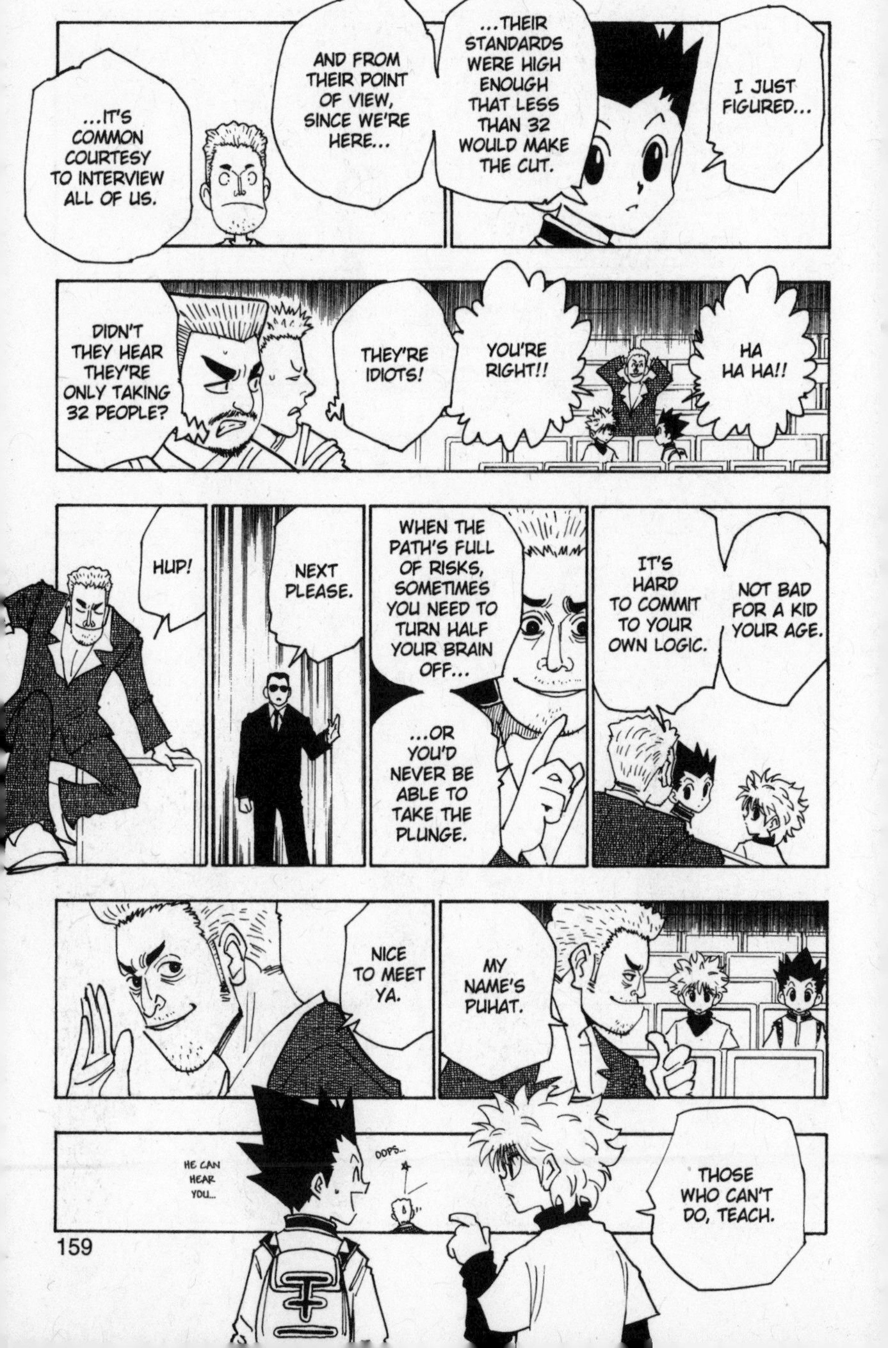
I JUST FIGURED...
...THEIR STANDARDS WERE HIGH ENOUGH THAT LESS THAN 32 WOULD MAKE THE CUT.
AND FROM THEIR POINT OF VIEW, SINCE WE'RE HERE...
...IT'S COMMON COURTESY TO INTERVIEW ALL OF US.
HA HA HA!!
YOU'RE RIGHT!!
THEY'RE IDIOTS!
DIDN'T THEY HEAR THEY'RE ONLY TAKING 32 PEOPLE?
NOT BAD FOR A KID YOUR AGE.
IT'S HARD TO COMMIT TO YOUR OWN LOGIC.
WHEN THE PATH'S FULL OF RISKS, SOMETIMES YOU NEED TO TURN HALF YOUR BRAIN OFF...
...OR YOU'D NEVER BE ABLE TO TAKE THE PLUNGE.
NEXT PLEASE.
HUP!
MY NAME'S PUHAT.
NICE TO MEET YA.
THOSE WHO CAN'T DO, TEACH.
OOPS...
HE CAN HEAR YOU...

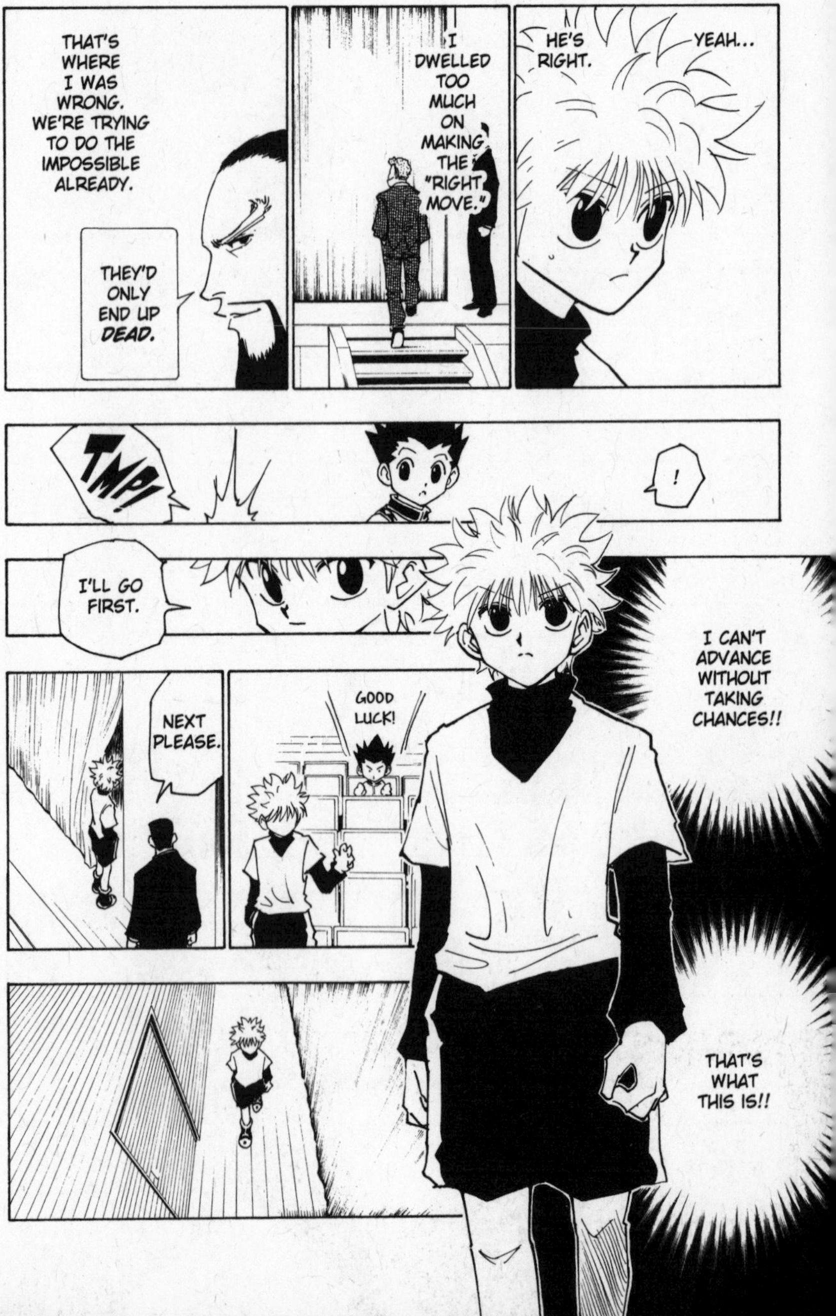
YEAH...
HE'S RIGHT.
I DWELLED TOO MUCH ON MAKING THE "RIGHT MOVE."
THAT'S WHERE I WAS WRONG. WE'RE TRYING TO DO THE IMPOSSIBLE ALREADY.
THEY'D ONLY END UP DEAD.
!
TMP!
I CAN'T ADVANCE WITHOUT TAKING CHANCES!!
THAT'S WHAT THIS IS!!
I'LL GO FIRST.
GOOD LUCK!
NEXT PLEASE.

READ THIS WAY

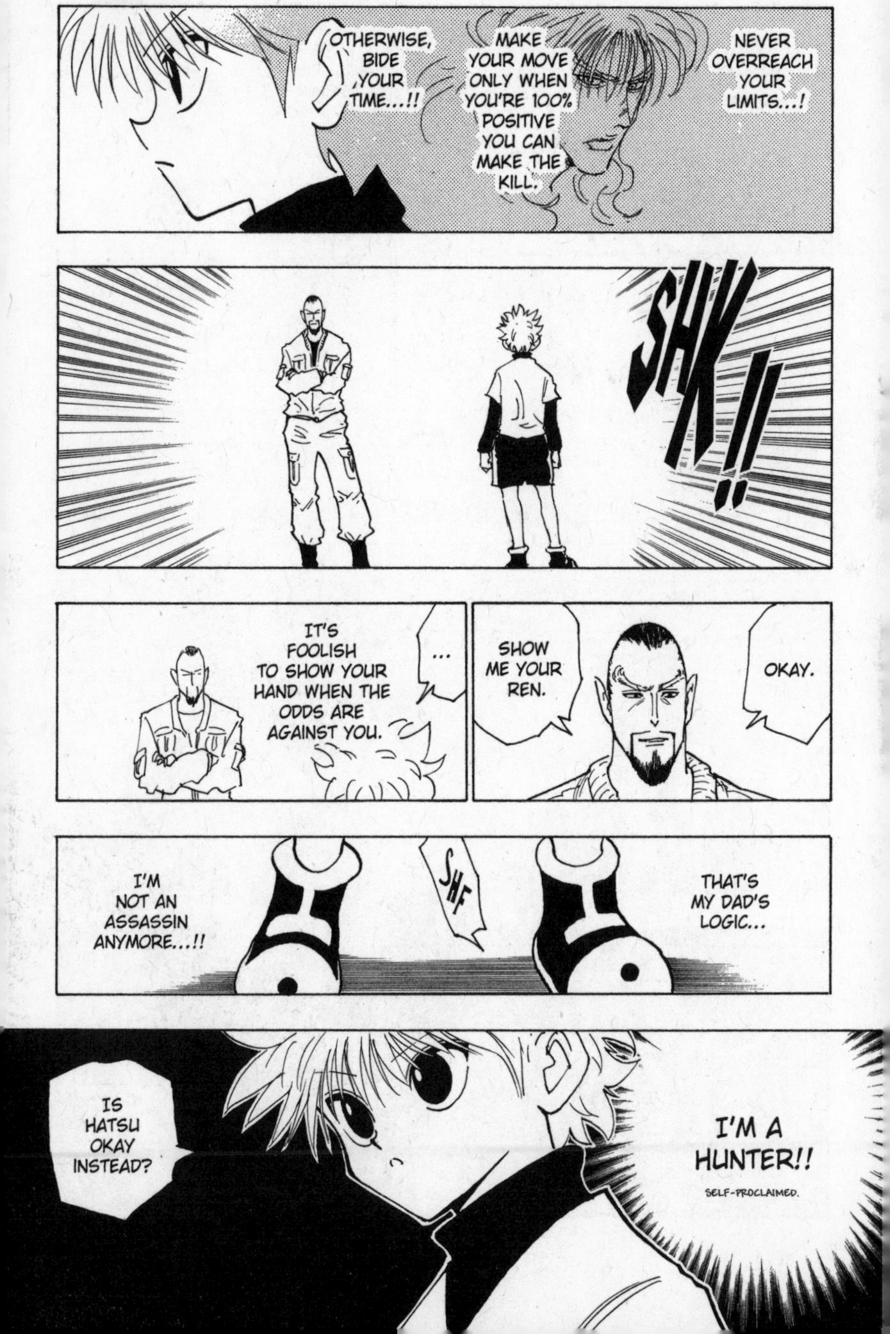
NEVER OVERREACH YOUR LIMITS...!
MAKE YOUR MOVE ONLY WHEN YOU'RE 100% POSITIVE YOU CAN MAKE THE KILL.
OTHERWISE, BIDE YOUR TIME...!!
SHK!!
OKAY.
SHOW ME YOUR REN.
...
IT'S FOOLISH TO SHOW YOUR HAND WHEN THE ODDS ARE AGAINST YOU.
THAT'S MY DAD'S LOGIC...
SHF
I'M NOT AN ASSASSIN ANYMORE...!!
I'M A HUNTER!!
SELF-PROCLAIMED.
IS HATSU OKAY INSTEAD?

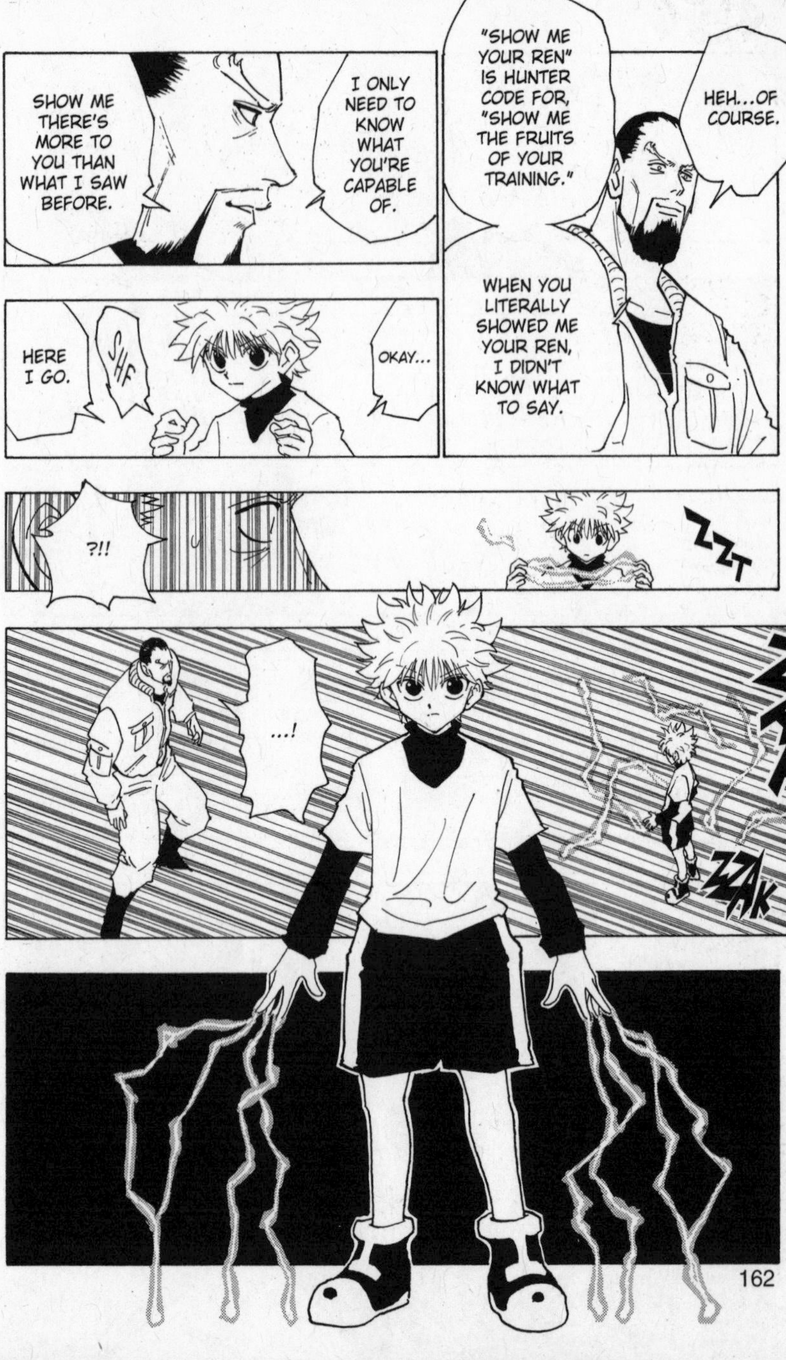
HEH...OF COURSE.
"SHOW ME YOUR REN" IS HUNTER CODE FOR, "SHOW ME THE FRUITS OF YOUR TRAINING."
WHEN YOU LITERALLY SHOWED ME YOUR REN, I DIDN'T KNOW WHAT TO SAY.
I ONLY NEED TO KNOW WHAT YOU'RE CAPABLE OF.
SHOW ME THERE'S MORE TO YOU THAN WHAT I SAW BEFORE.
OKAY...
SHF
HERE I GO.
ZZT
?!!
ZAP
ZZAK
...!

READ THIS WAY

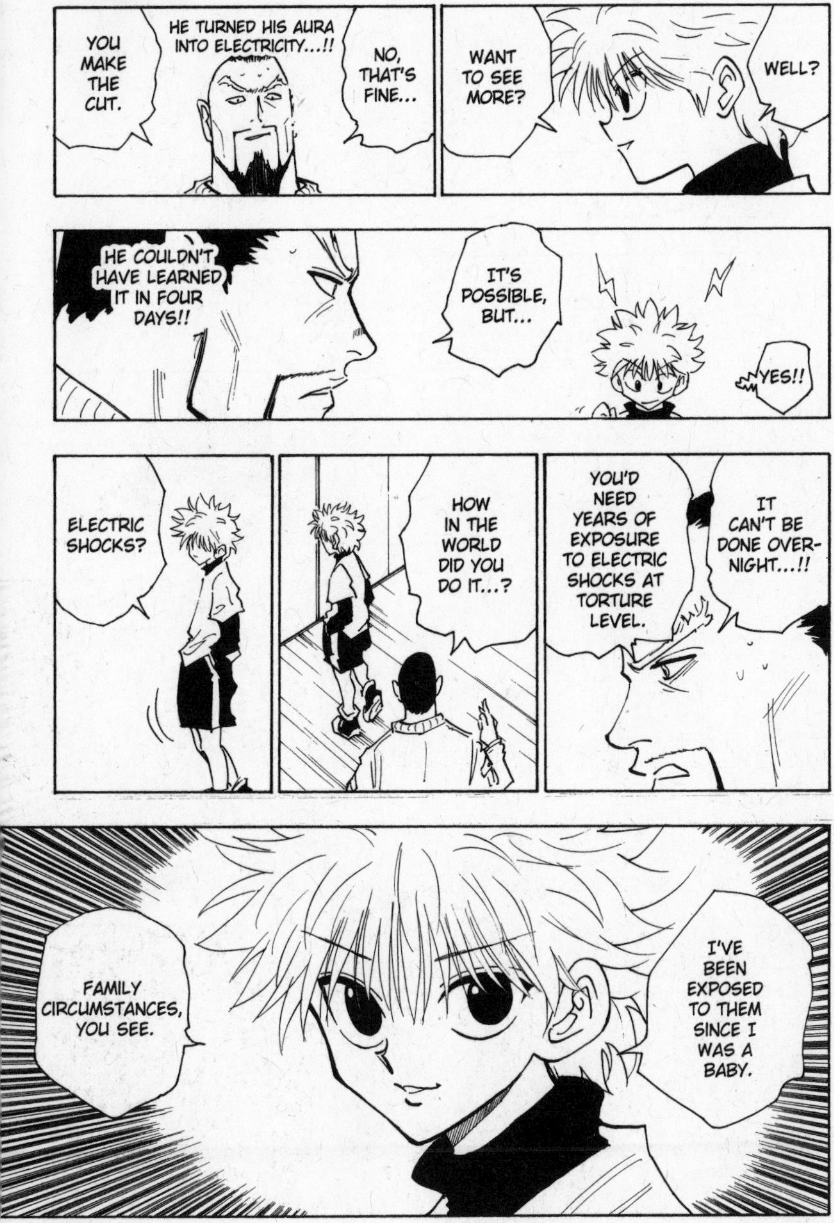
WELL?
WANT TO SEE MORE?
NO, THAT'S FINE...
HE TURNED HIS AURA INTO ELECTRICITY...!!
YOU MAKE THE CUT.
YES!!
IT'S POSSIBLE, BUT...
HE COULDN'T HAVE LEARNED IT IN FOUR DAYS!!
IT CAN'T BE DONE OVER-NIGHT...!!
YOU'D NEED YEARS OF EXPOSURE TO ELECTRIC SHOCKS AT TORTURE LEVEL.
HOW IN THE WORLD DID YOU DO IT...?
ELECTRIC SHOCKS?
I'VE BEEN EXPOSED TO THEM SINCE I WAS A BABY.
FAMILY CIRCUMSTANCES, YOU SEE.

Chapter 126 September 10th: Part 3

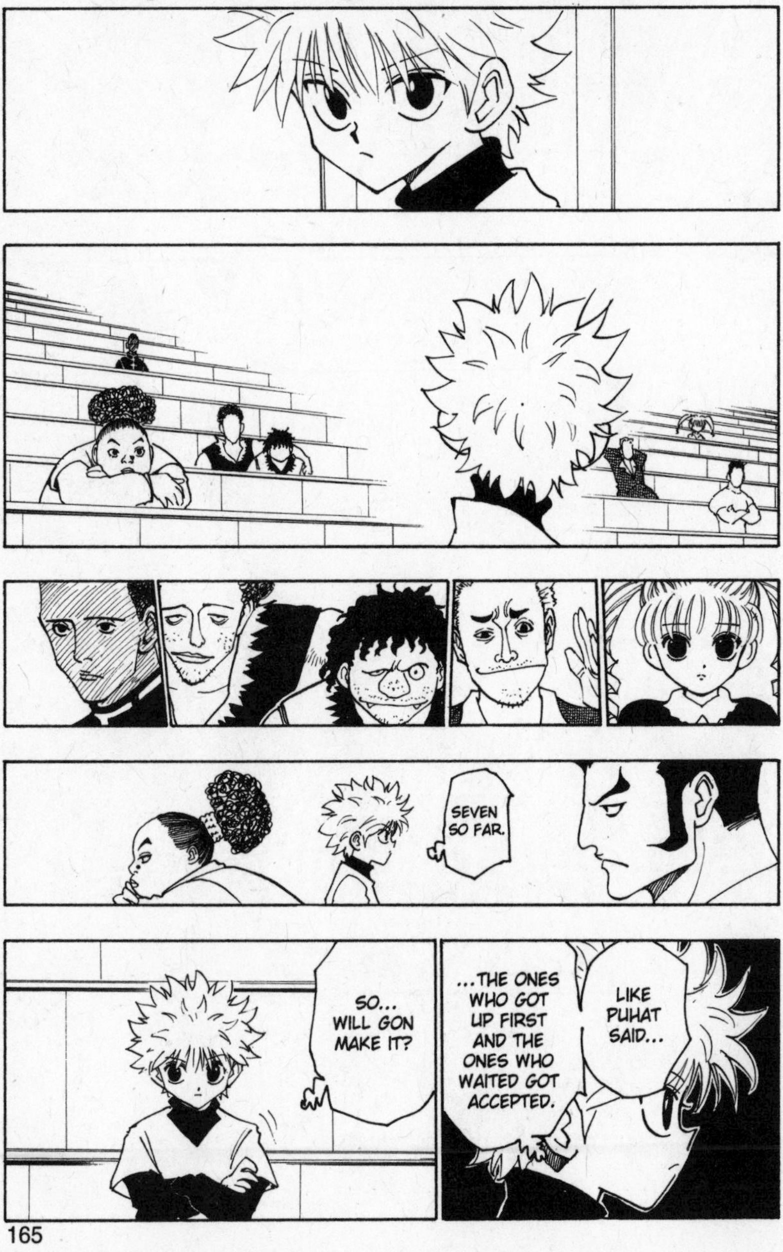
SEVEN SO FAR.
LIKE PUHAT SAID...
...THE ONES WHO GOT UP FIRST AND THE ONES WHO WAITED GOT ACCEPTED.
SO... WILL GON MAKE IT?

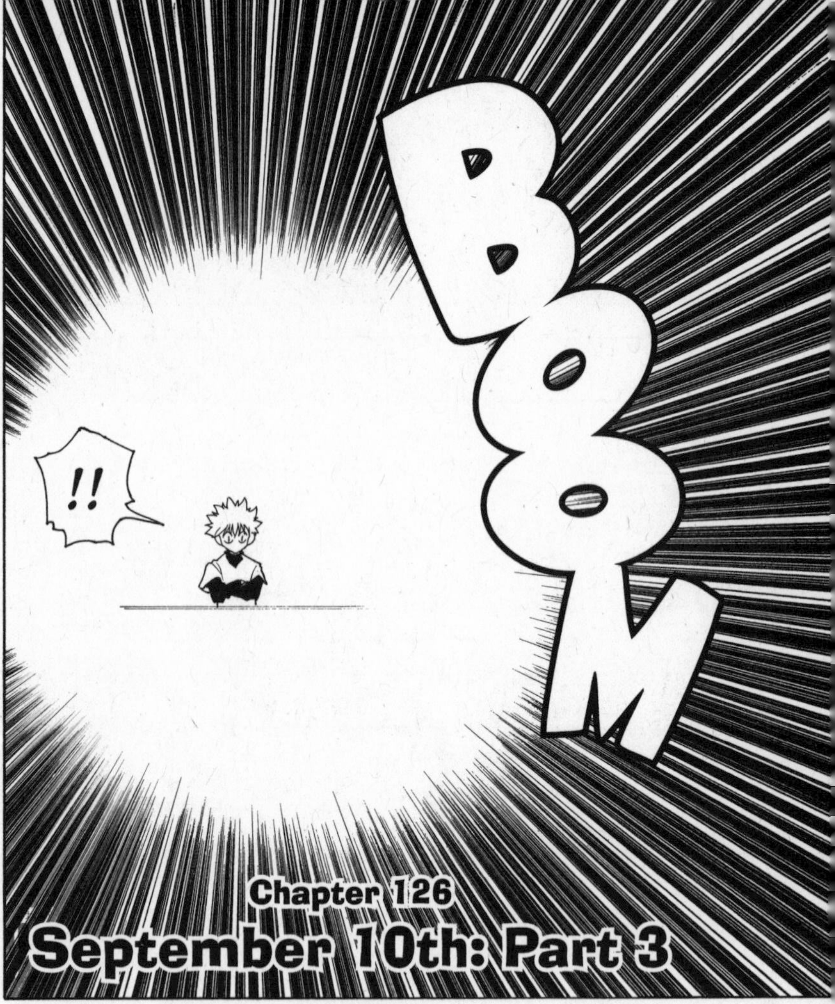
BOOM
!!
Chapter 126
September 10th: Part 3
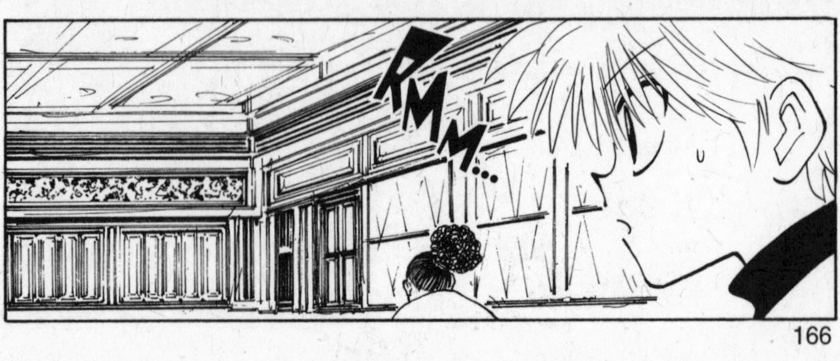
RMM...

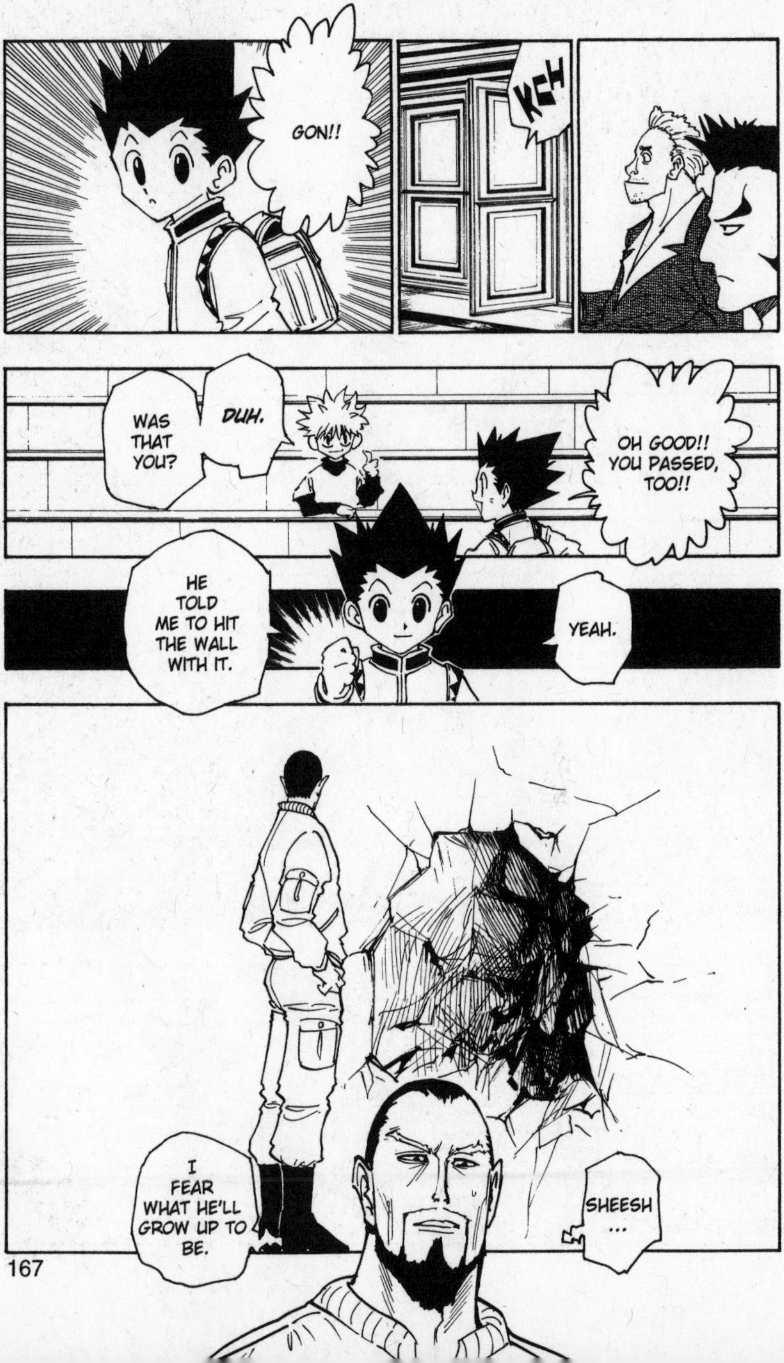
KCH
GON!!
OH GOOD!! YOU PASSED, TOO!!
DUH.
WAS THAT YOU?
YEAH.
HE TOLD ME TO HIT THE WALL WITH IT.
SHEESH...
I FEAR WHAT HE'LL GROW UP TO BE.

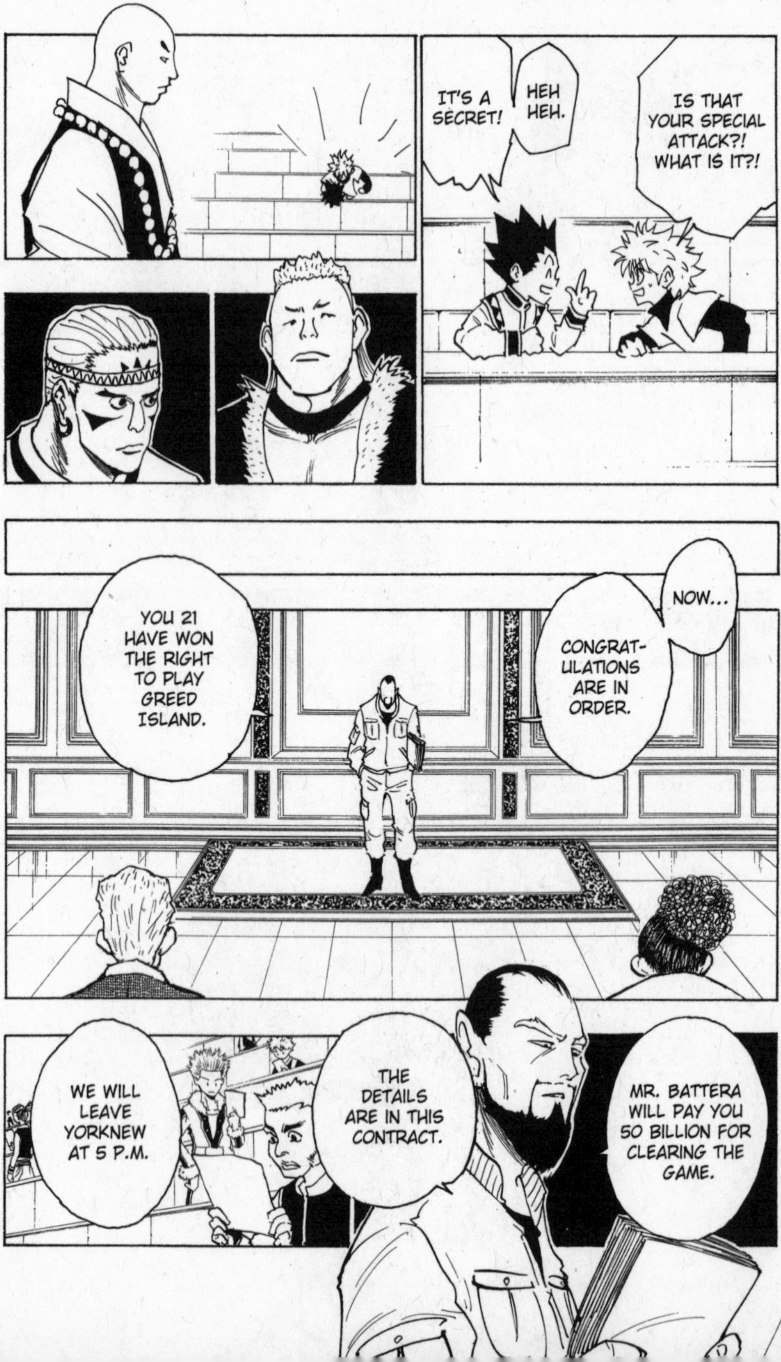
IS THAT YOUR SPECIAL ATTACK?! WHAT IS IT?!
HEH HEH.
IT'S A SECRET!
NOW...
CONGRAT-ULATIONS ARE IN ORDER.
YOU 21 HAVE WON THE RIGHT TO PLAY GREED ISLAND.
MR. BATTERA WILL PAY YOU 50 BILLION FOR CLEARING THE GAME.
THE DETAILS ARE IN THIS CONTRACT.
WE WILL LEAVE YORKNEW AT 5 P.M.

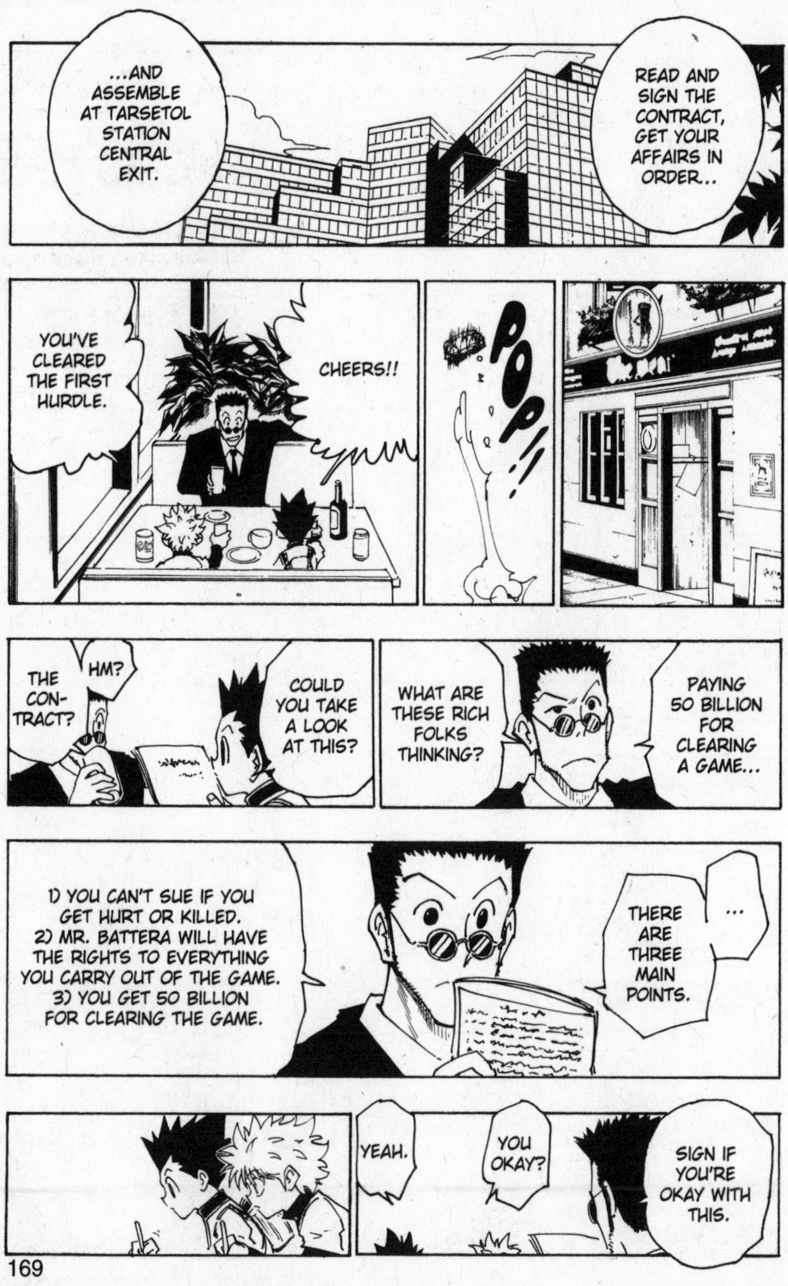
READ AND SIGN THE CONTRACT, GET YOUR AFFAIRS IN ORDER...
...AND ASSEMBLE AT TARSETOL STATION CENTRAL EXIT.
YOU'VE CLEARED THE FIRST HURDLE.
CHEERS!!
POP!!
PAYING 50 BILLION FOR CLEARING A GAME...
WHAT ARE THESE RICH FOLKS THINKING?
COULD YOU TAKE A LOOK AT THIS?
HM?
THE CONTRACT?
...
THERE ARE THREE MAIN POINTS.
1) YOU CAN'T SUE IF YOU GET HURT OR KILLED. 2) MR. BATTERA WILL HAVE THE RIGHTS TO EVERYTHING YOU CARRY OUT OF THE GAME. 3) YOU GET 50 BILLION FOR CLEARING THE GAME.
SIGN IF YOU'RE OKAY WITH THIS.
YOU OKAY?
YEAH.

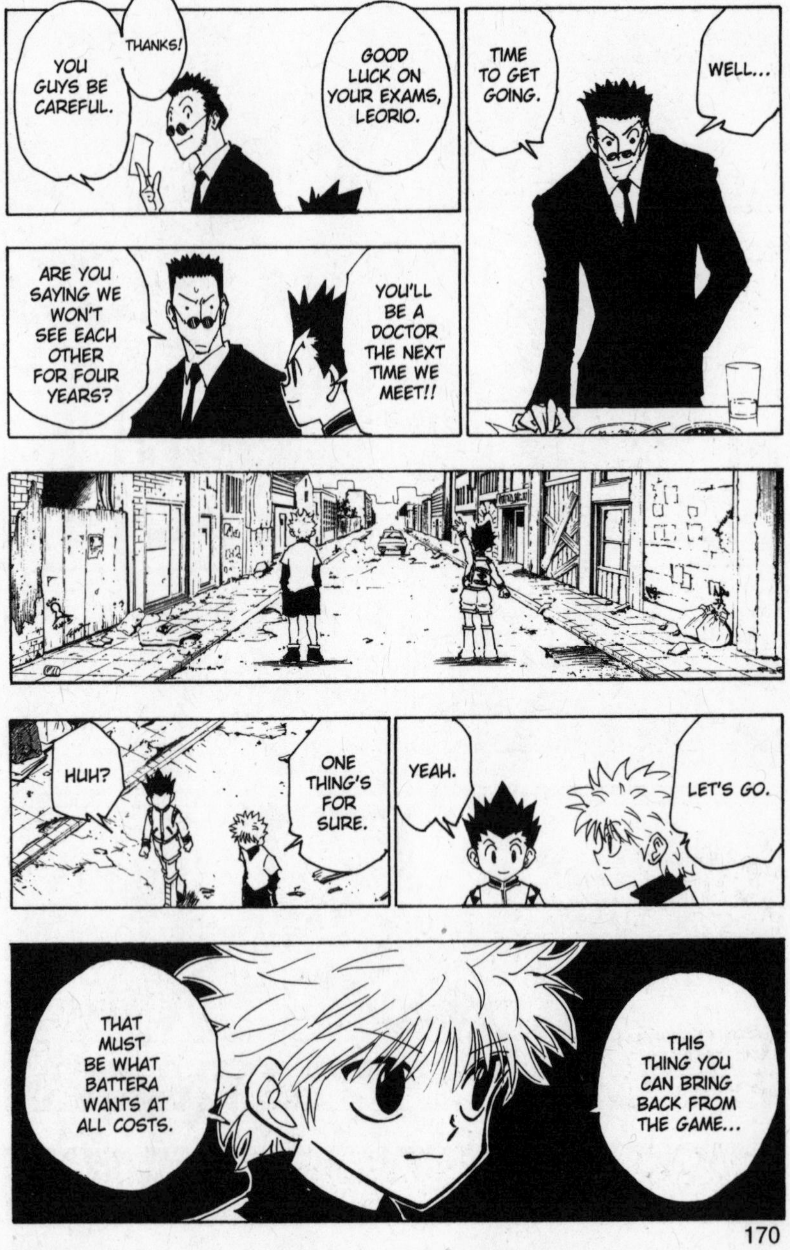
WELL...
TIME TO GET GOING.
GOOD LUCK ON YOUR EXAMS, LEORIO.
THANKS!
YOU GUYS BE CAREFUL.
YOU'LL BE A DOCTOR THE NEXT TIME WE MEET!!
ARE YOU SAYING WE WON'T SEE EACH OTHER FOR FOUR YEARS?
LET'S GO.
YEAH.
ONE THING'S FOR SURE.
HUH?
THIS THING YOU CAN BRING BACK FROM THE GAME...
THAT MUST BE WHAT BATTERA WANTS AT ALL COSTS.

READ THIS WAY

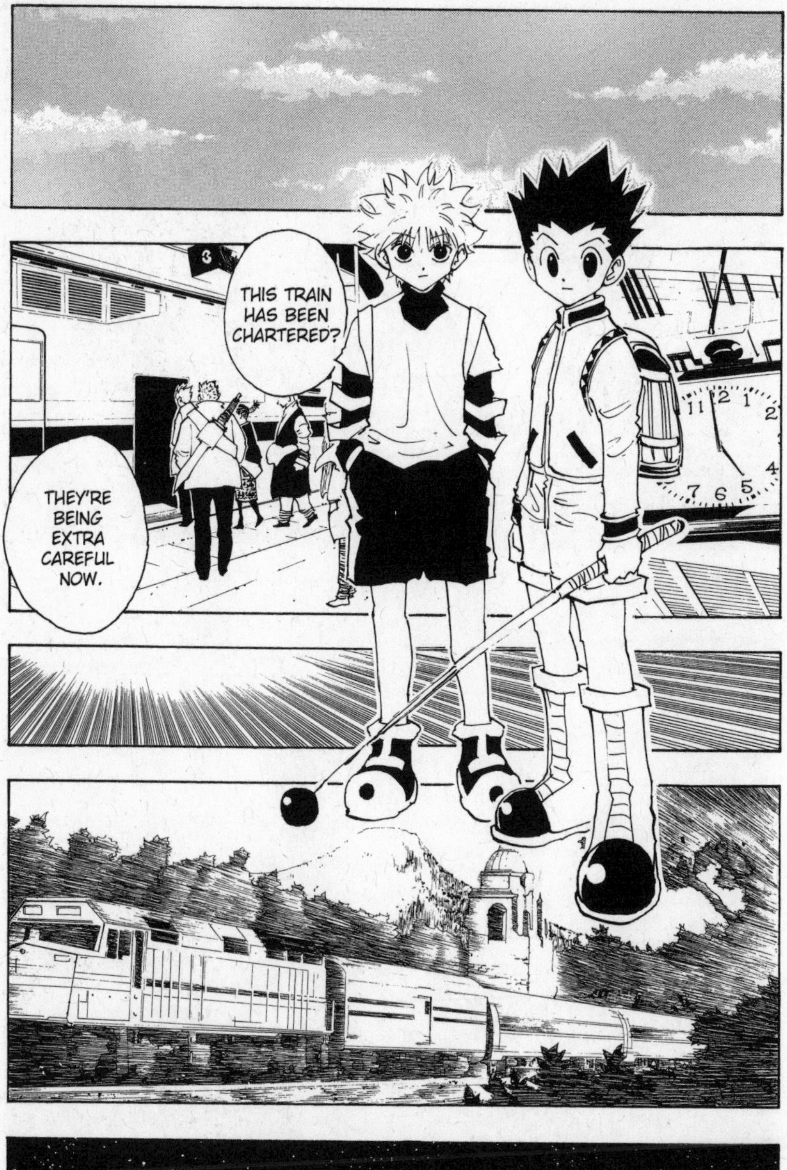
THIS TRAIN HAS BEEN CHARTERED?
THEY'RE BEING EXTRA CAREFUL NOW.

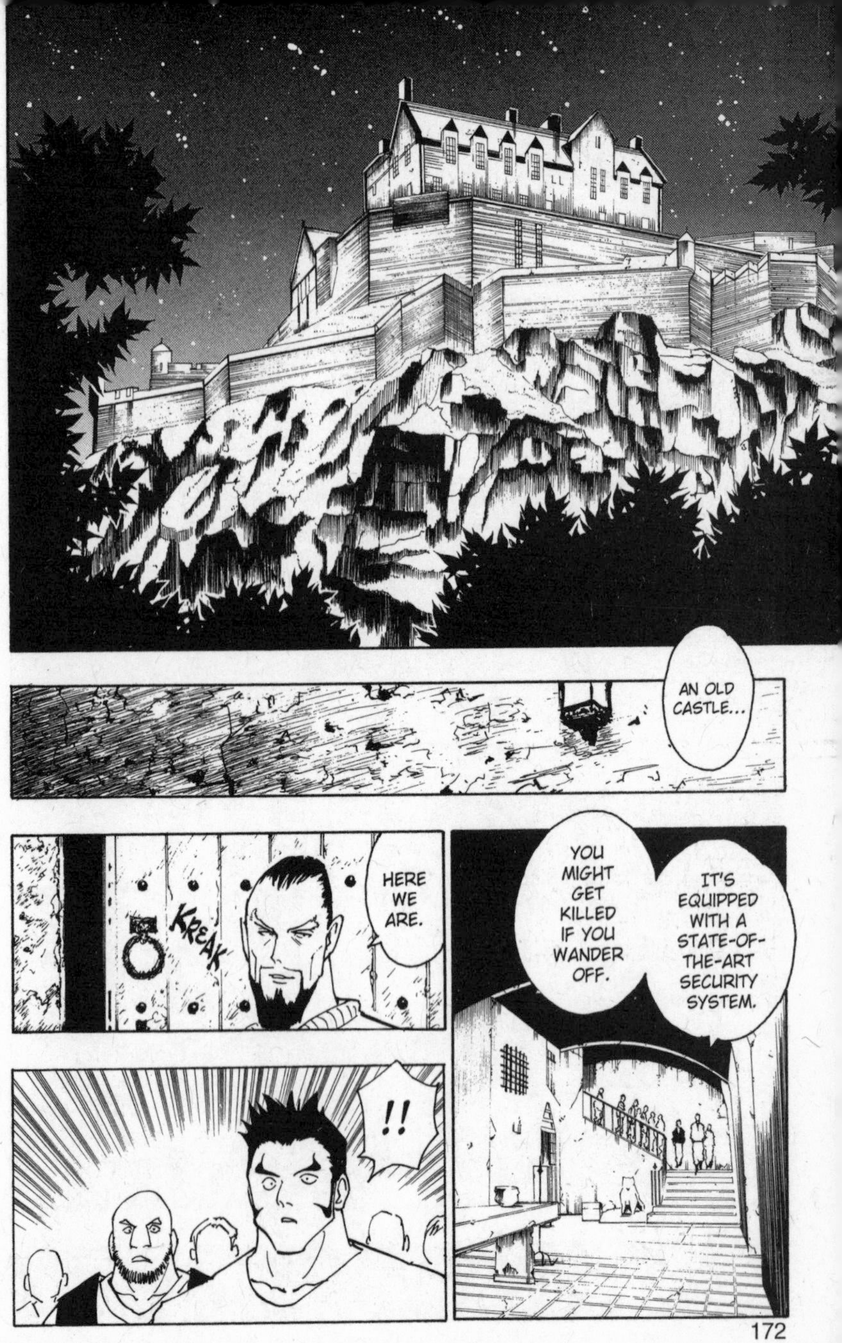
AN OLD CASTLE...
IT'S EQUIPPED WITH A STATE-OF-THE-ART SECURITY SYSTEM.
YOU MIGHT GET KILLED IF YOU WANDER OFF.
HERE WE ARE.
KREAK
!!

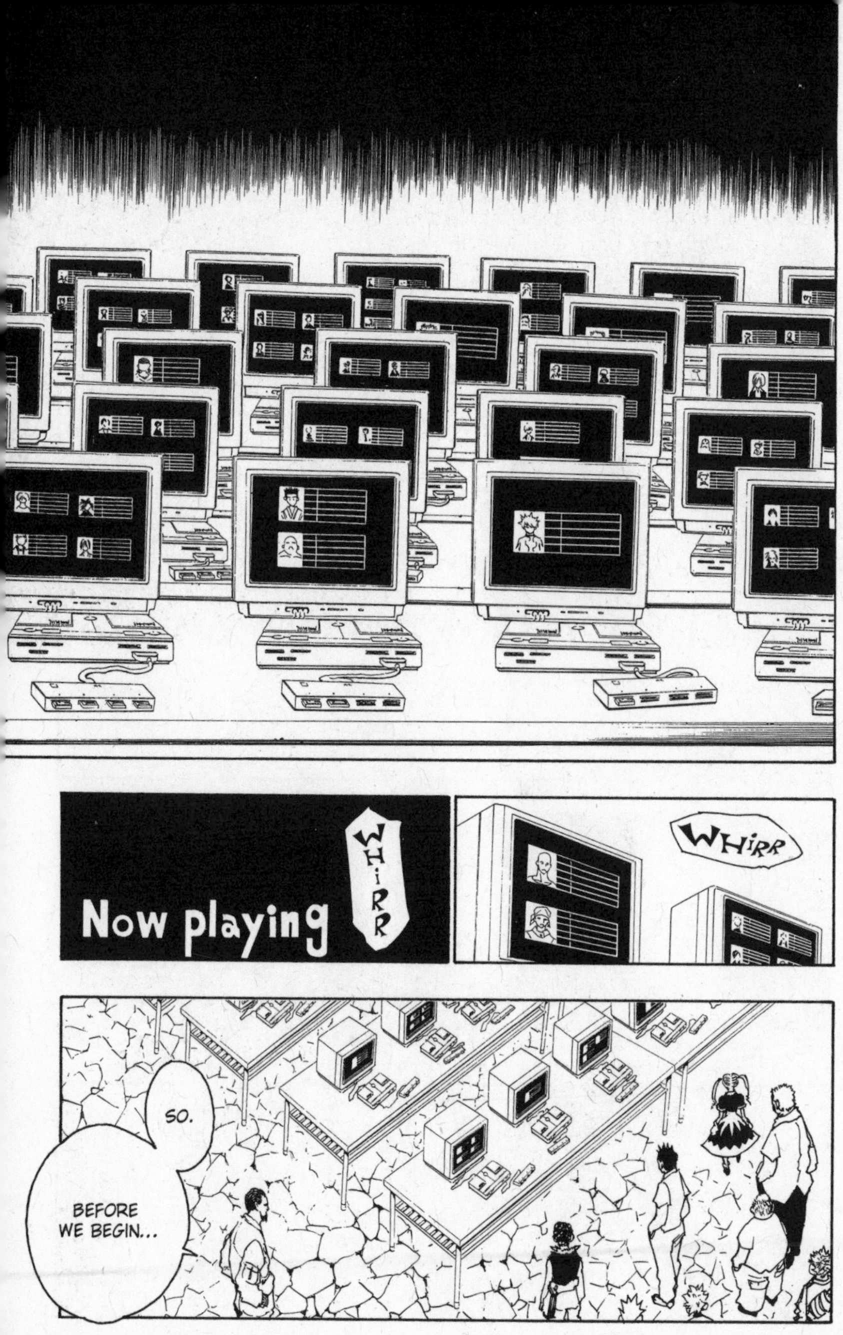
WHiRR
Now playing
WHiRR
SO.
BEFORE WE BEGIN...

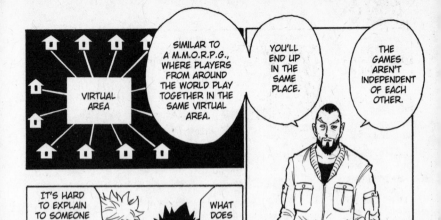

THE GAMES AREN'T INDEPENDENT OF EACH OTHER.
YOU'LL END UP IN THE SAME PLACE.
SIMILAR TO A M.M.O.R.P.G., WHERE PLAYERS FROM AROUND THE WORLD PLAY TOGETHER IN THE SAME VIRTUAL AREA.
VIRTUAL AREA
WHAT DOES THAT MEAN?
I DON'T GET IT.
IT'S HARD TO EXPLAIN TO SOMEONE WHO'S NEVER PLAYED VIDEOGAMES.
BASICALLY, EVERYONE CAN PLAY IN THE SAME SPACE.
HUH?
ISN'T THAT OBVIOUS? THE CONSOLES ARE RIGHT HERE.
THAT'S NOT WHAT HE MEANS.
I'LL HAND OUT THE MEMORY CARDS, THOUGH MOST OF YOU PROBABLY HAVE YOUR OWN.
YOU CAN BEGIN PLAYING RIGHT AWAY...
BUT WE NEED TO CHOOSE THE ORDER YOU'LL GO IN.
ORDER?
YOU WILL FIRST GET AN EXPLANATION OF THE SYSTEM...
...BUT ONLY ONE PERSON CAN HEAR IT AT A TIME.

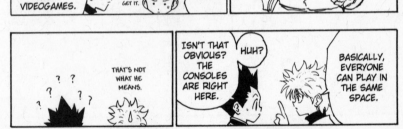

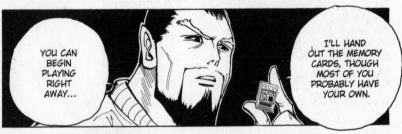

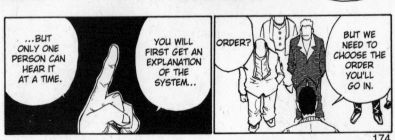

READ THIS WAY

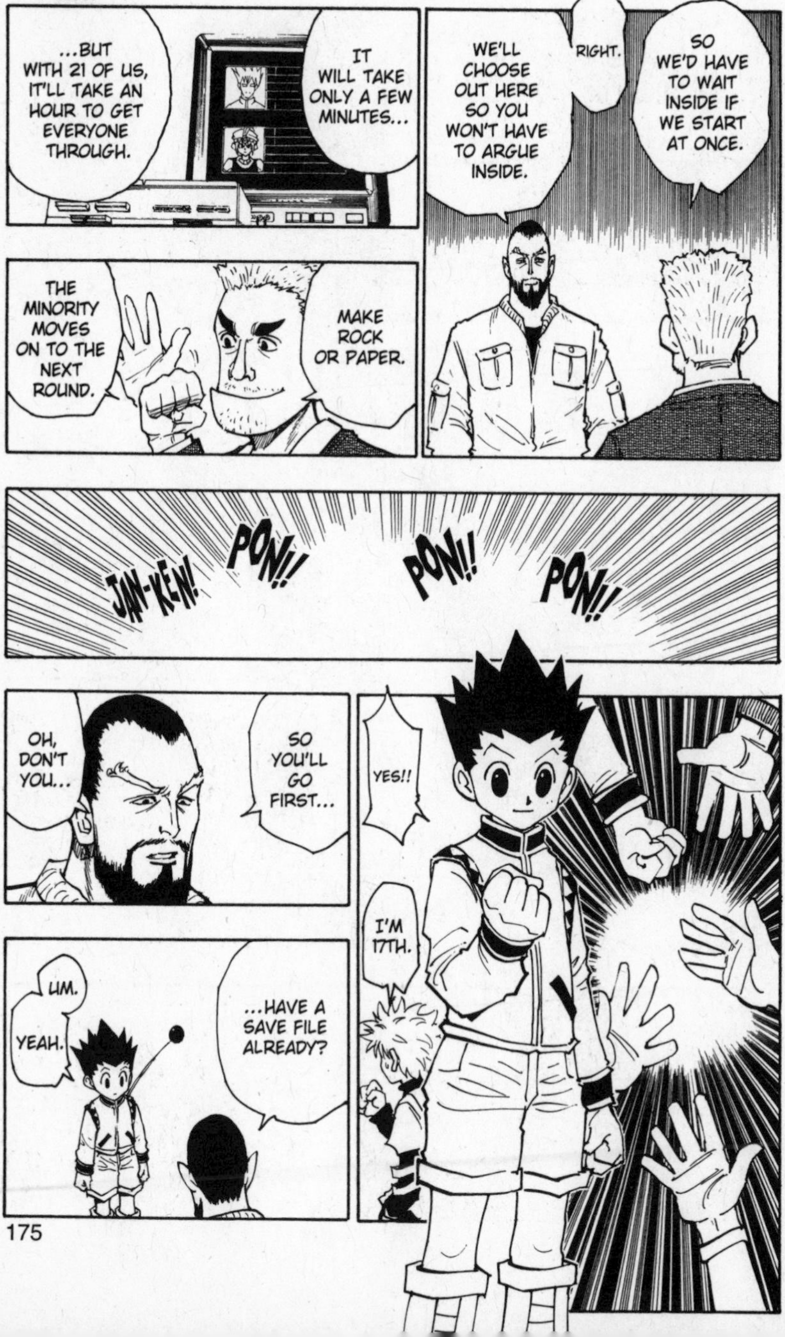

SO WE'D HAVE TO WAIT INSIDE IF WE START AT ONCE.
RIGHT.
WE'LL CHOOSE OUT HERE SO YOU WON'T HAVE TO ARGUE INSIDE.
IT WILL TAKE ONLY A FEW MINUTES...
...BUT WITH 21 OF US, IT'LL TAKE AN HOUR TO GET EVERYONE THROUGH.
MAKE ROCK OR PAPER.
THE MINORITY MOVES ON TO THE NEXT ROUND.
JAN-KEN!
PON!!
PON!!
PON!!
YES!!
I'M 17TH.
SO YOU'LL GO FIRST...
OH, DON'T YOU...
...HAVE A SAVE FILE ALREADY?
UM.
YEAH.

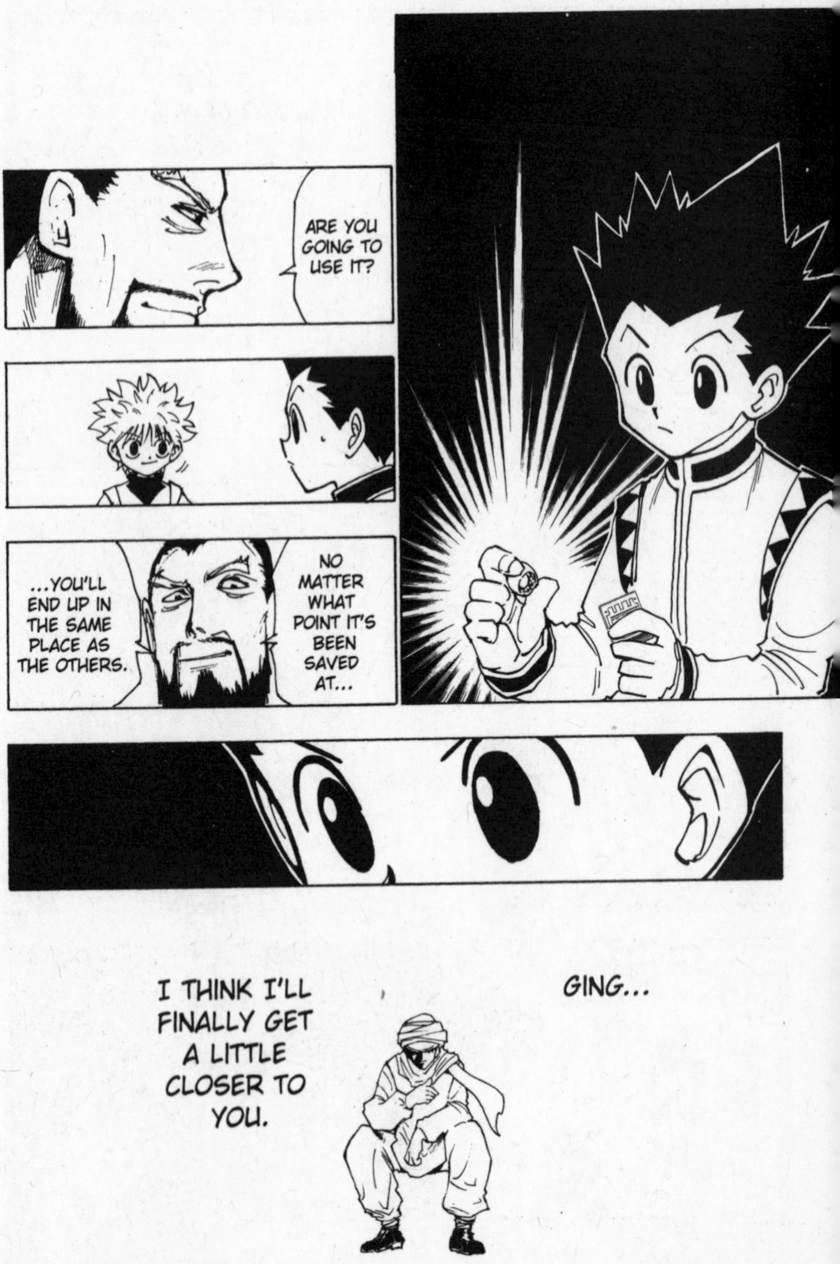
ARE YOU GOING TO USE IT?
NO MATTER WHAT POINT IT'S BEEN SAVED AT...
...YOU'LL END UP IN THE SAME PLACE AS THE OTHERS.
GING...
I THINK I'LL FINALLY GET A LITTLE CLOSER TO YOU.

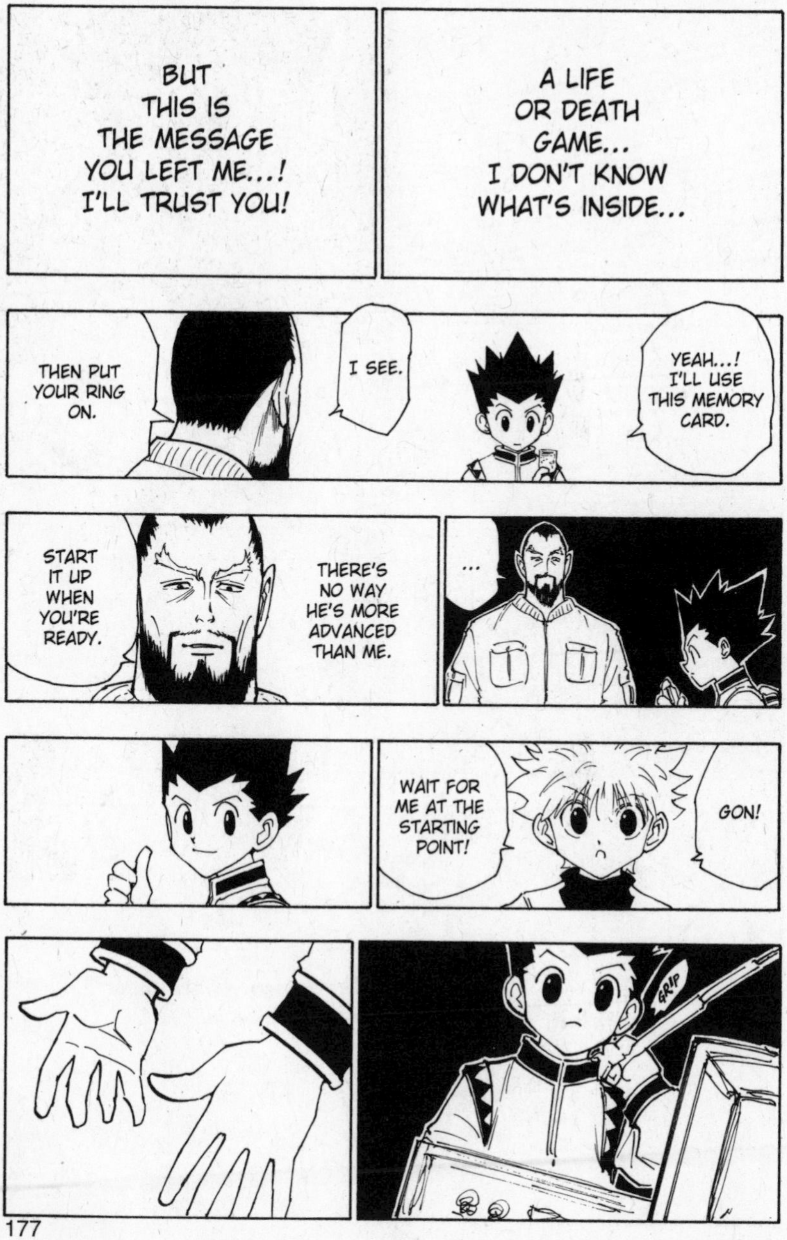
A LIFE OR DEATH GAME... I DON'T KNOW WHAT'S INSIDE...
BUT THIS IS THE MESSAGE YOU LEFT ME...! I'LL TRUST YOU!
YEAH...! I'LL USE THIS MEMORY CARD.
I SEE.
THEN PUT YOUR RING ON.
...
THERE'S NO WAY HE'S MORE ADVANCED THAN ME.
START IT UP WHEN YOU'RE READY.
GON!
WAIT FOR ME AT THE STARTING POINT!
GRIP

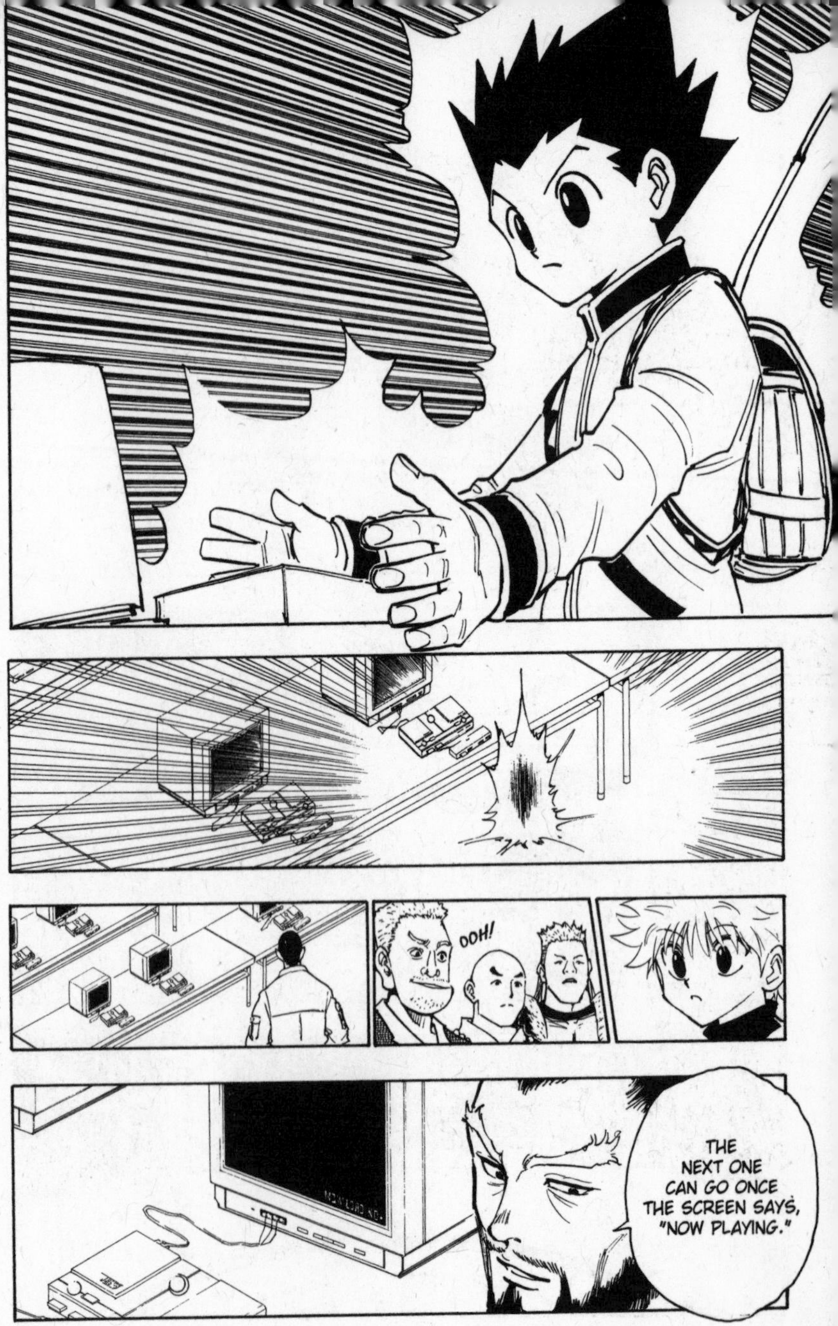
OOH!
THE NEXT ONE CAN GO ONCE THE SCREEN SAYS, "NOW PLAYING."

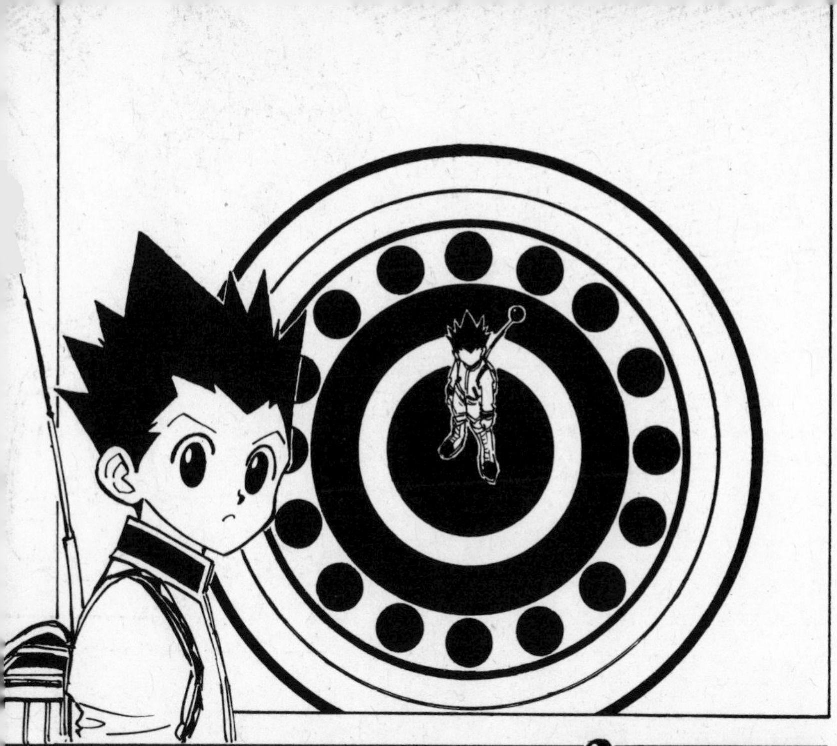

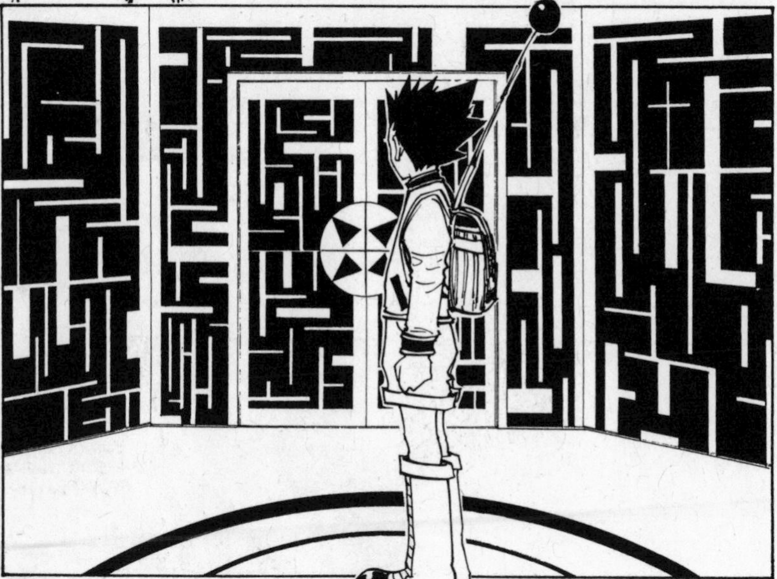

Chapter 127
September 10th: Part 4

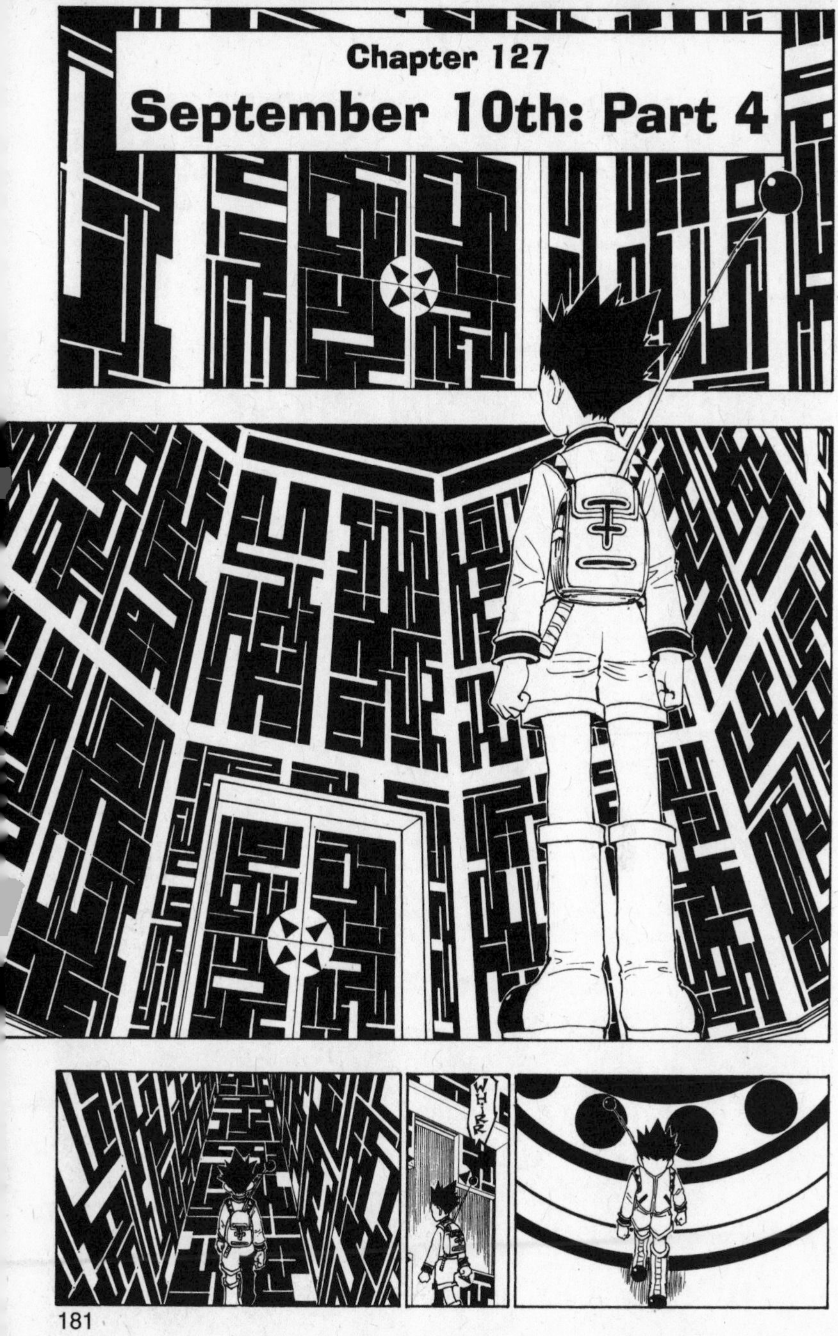
WHIRR

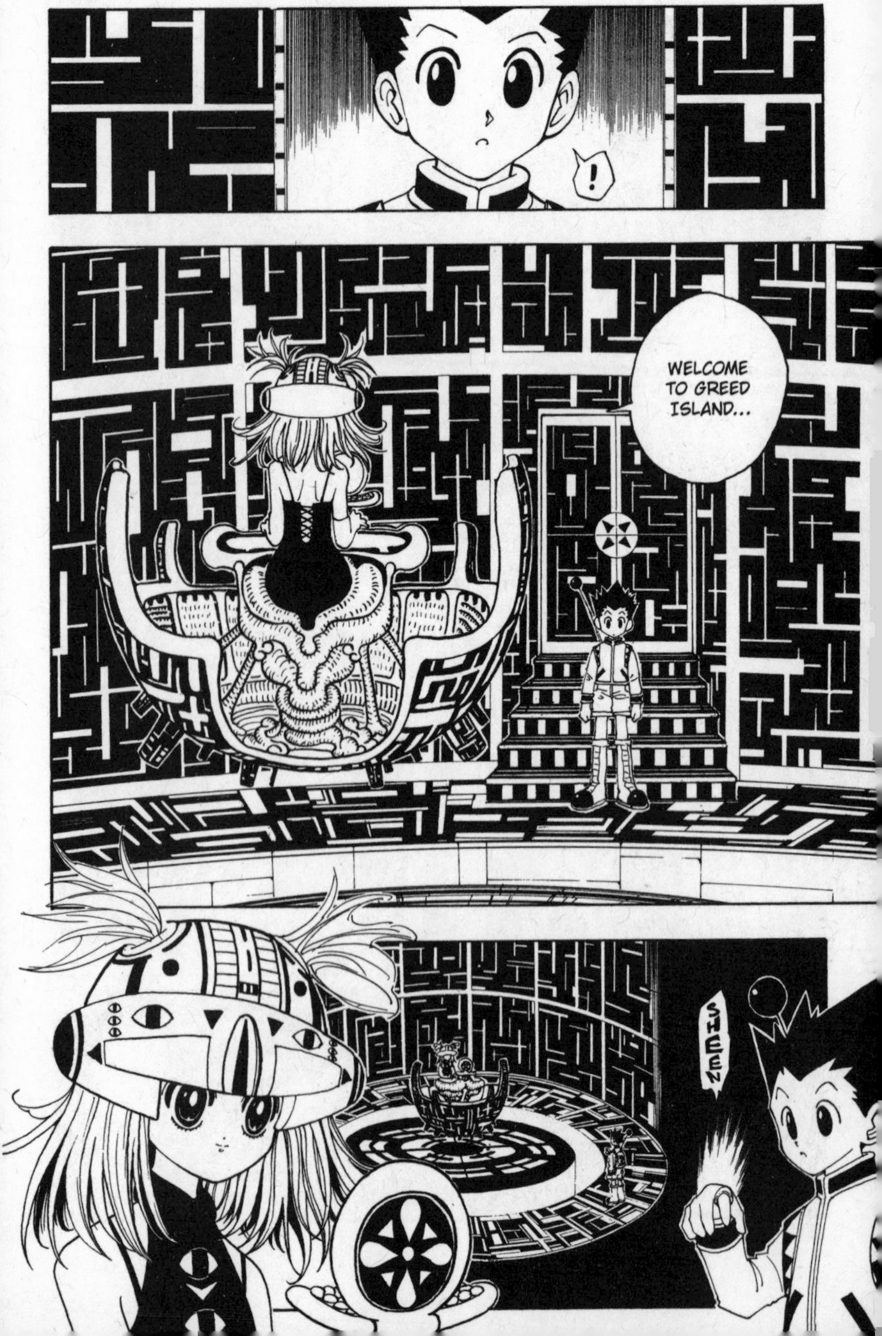
!
WELCOME TO GREED ISLAND...
SHEEN

READ THIS WAY

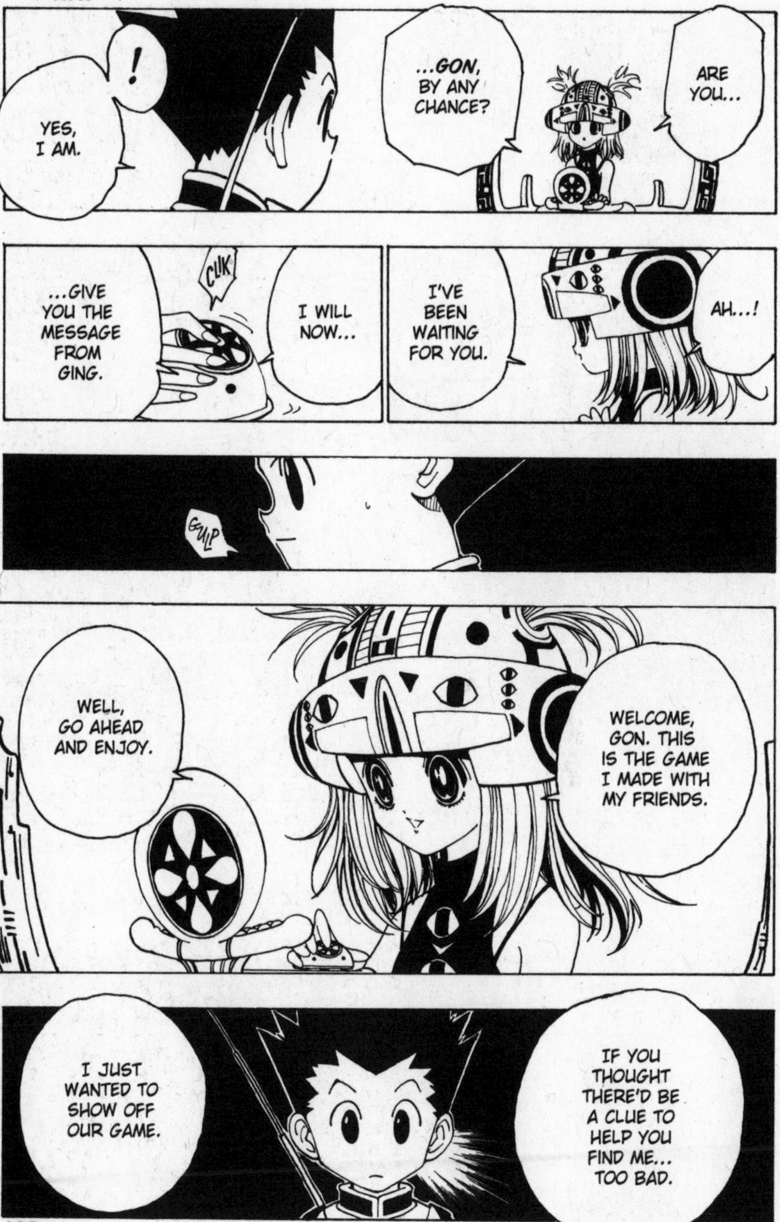
ARE YOU...
...GON, BY ANY CHANCE?
!
YES, I AM.
AH...!
I'VE BEEN WAITING FOR YOU.
I WILL NOW...
CLIK
...GIVE YOU THE MESSAGE FROM GING.
GULP
WELCOME, GON. THIS IS THE GAME I MADE WITH MY FRIENDS.
WELL, GO AHEAD AND ENJOY.
IF YOU THOUGHT THERE'D BE A CLUE TO HELP YOU FIND ME... TOO BAD.
I JUST WANTED TO SHOW OFF OUR GAME.

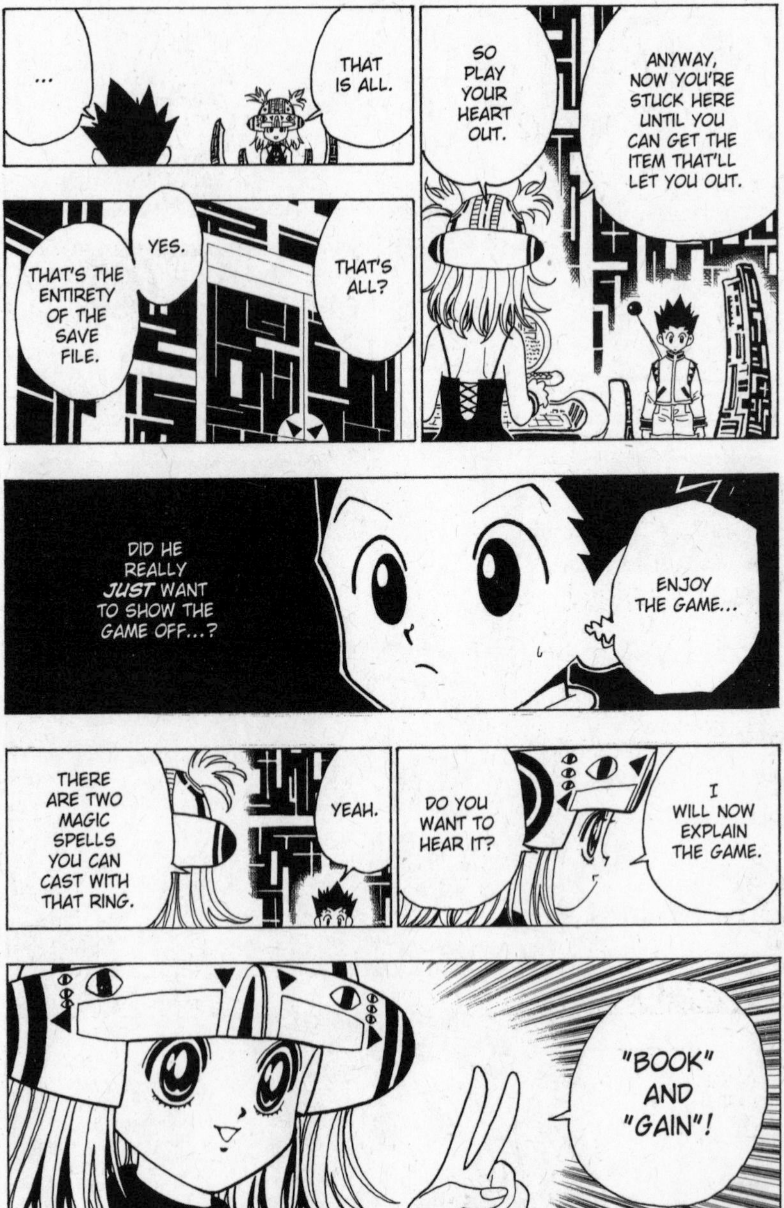
ANYWAY, NOW YOU'RE STUCK HERE UNTIL YOU CAN GET THE ITEM THAT'LL LET YOU OUT.
SO PLAY YOUR HEART OUT.
THAT IS ALL.
...
THAT'S ALL?
YES.
THAT'S THE ENTIRETY OF THE SAVE FILE.
ENJOY THE GAME...
DID HE REALLY *JUST* WANT TO SHOW THE GAME OFF...?
I WILL NOW EXPLAIN THE GAME.
DO YOU WANT TO HEAR IT?
YEAH.
THERE ARE TWO MAGIC SPELLS YOU CAN CAST WITH THAT RING.
"BOOK" AND "GAIN"!

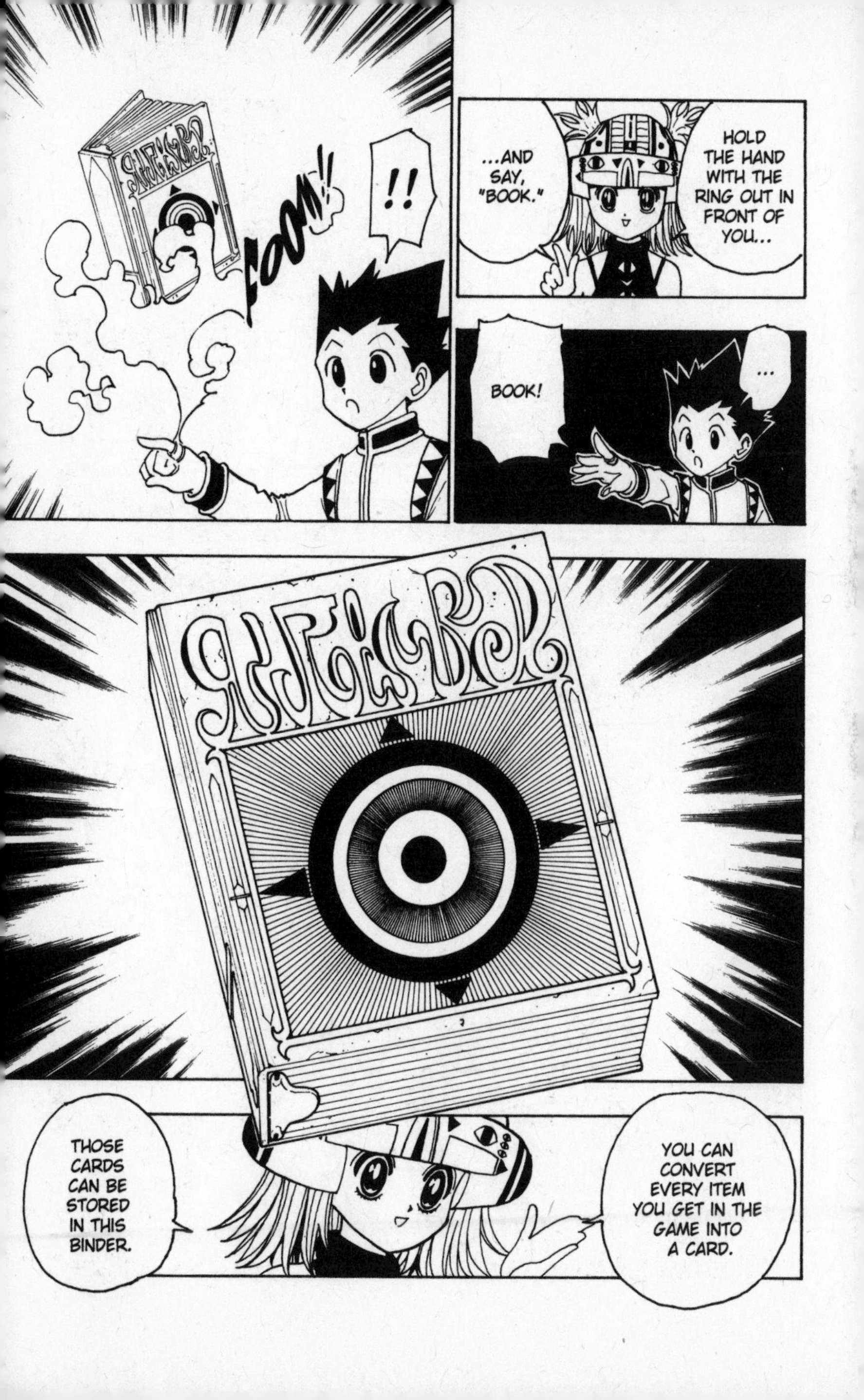
HOLD THE HAND WITH THE RING OUT IN FRONT OF YOU...
...AND SAY, "BOOK."
...
BOOK!
!!
FOOM!!
YOU CAN CONVERT EVERY ITEM YOU GET IN THE GAME INTO A CARD.
THOSE CARDS CAN BE STORED IN THIS BINDER.

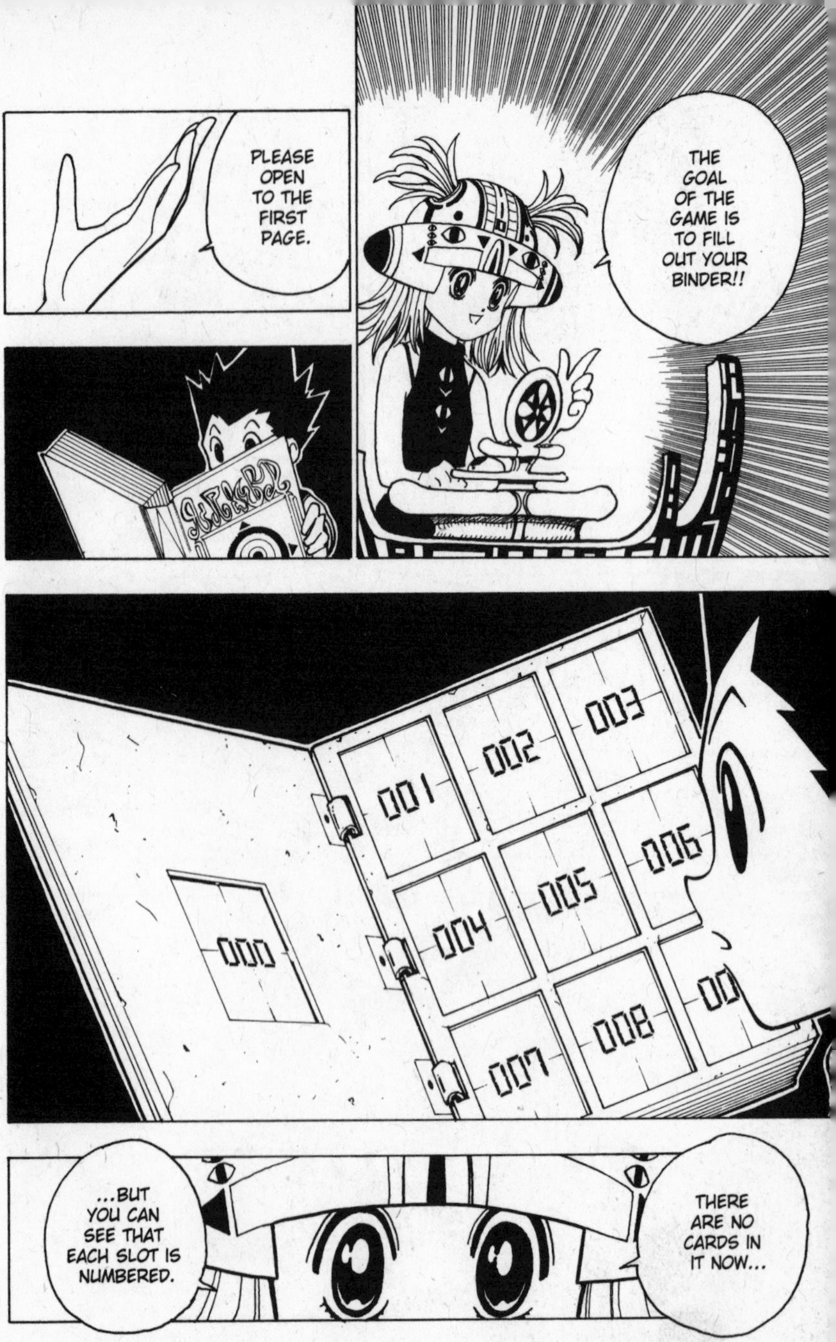
THE GOAL OF THE GAME IS TO FILL OUT YOUR BINDER!!
PLEASE OPEN TO THE FIRST PAGE.
THERE ARE NO CARDS IN IT NOW...
...BUT YOU CAN SEE THAT EACH SLOT IS NUMBERED.

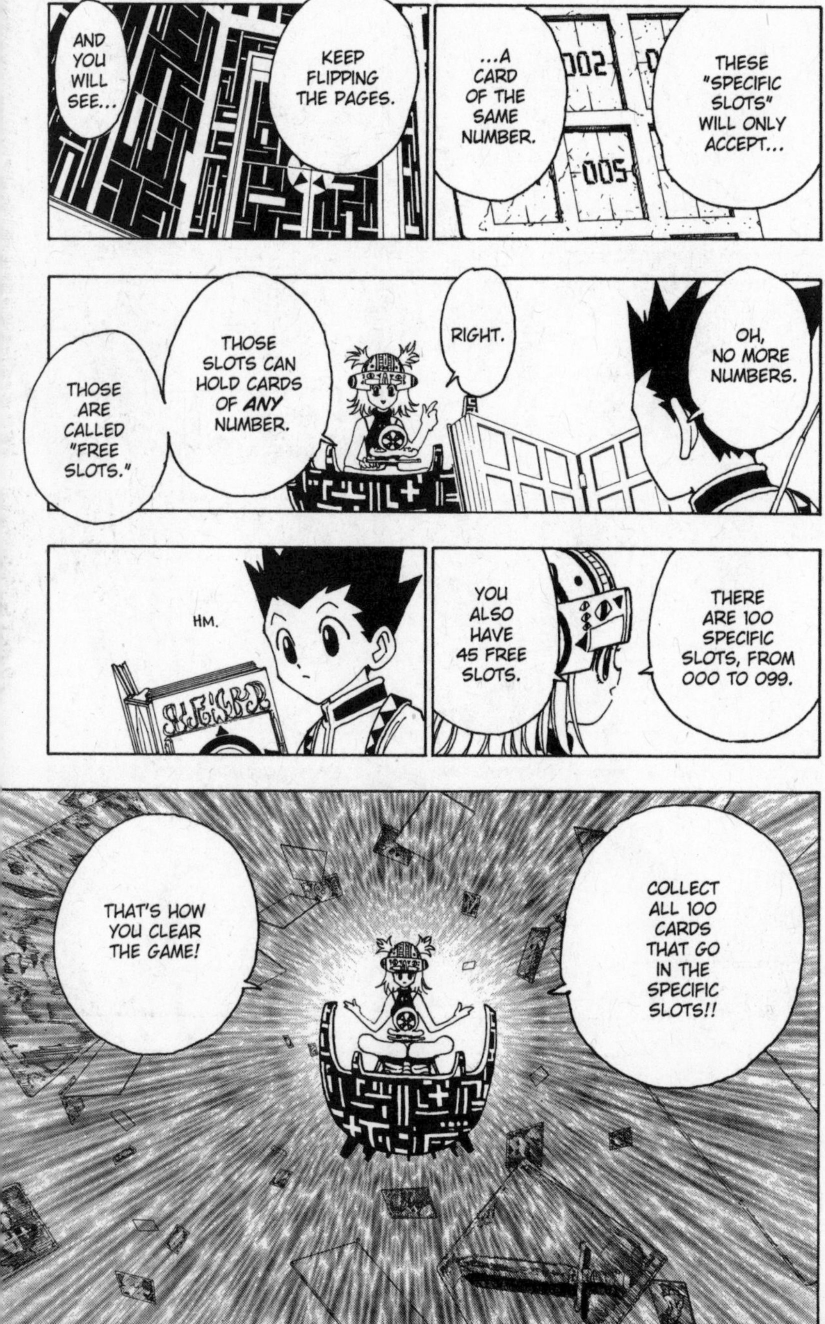
THESE "SPECIFIC SLOTS" WILL ONLY ACCEPT...
...A CARD OF THE SAME NUMBER.
KEEP FLIPPING THE PAGES.
AND YOU WILL SEE...
OH, NO MORE NUMBERS.
RIGHT.
THOSE SLOTS CAN HOLD CARDS OF *ANY* NUMBER.
THOSE ARE CALLED "FREE SLOTS."
THERE ARE 100 SPECIFIC SLOTS, FROM 000 TO 099.
YOU ALSO HAVE 45 FREE SLOTS.
HM.
COLLECT ALL 100 CARDS THAT GO IN THE SPECIFIC SLOTS!!
THAT'S HOW YOU CLEAR THE GAME!

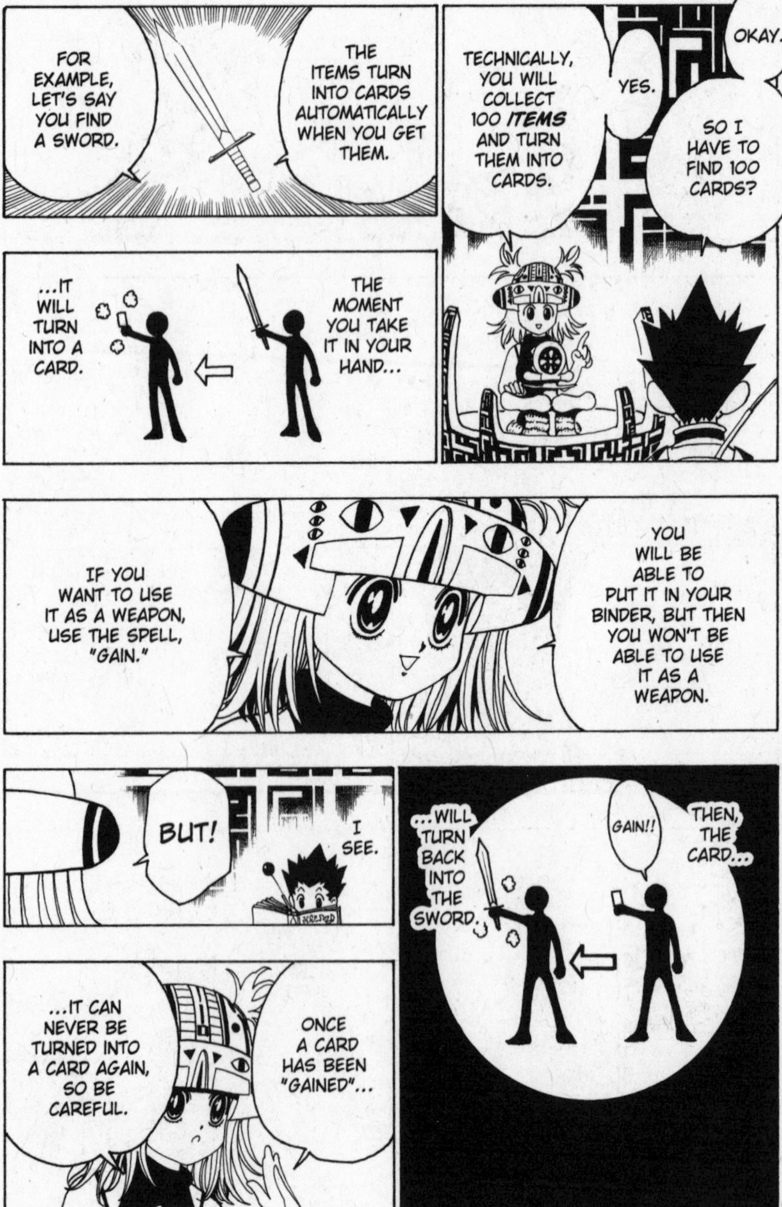
OKAY.
SO I HAVE TO FIND 100 CARDS?
YES.
TECHNICALLY, YOU WILL COLLECT 100 *ITEMS* AND TURN THEM INTO CARDS.
THE ITEMS TURN INTO CARDS AUTOMATICALLY WHEN YOU GET THEM.
FOR EXAMPLE, LET'S SAY YOU FIND A SWORD.
THE MOMENT YOU TAKE IT IN YOUR HAND...
...IT WILL TURN INTO A CARD.
YOU WILL BE ABLE TO PUT IT IN YOUR BINDER, BUT THEN YOU WON'T BE ABLE TO USE IT AS A WEAPON.
IF YOU WANT TO USE IT AS A WEAPON, USE THE SPELL, "GAIN."
THEN, THE CARD...
GAIN!!
...WILL TURN BACK INTO THE SWORD.
I SEE.
BUT!
ONCE A CARD HAS BEEN "GAINED"...
...IT CAN NEVER BE TURNED INTO A CARD AGAIN, SO BE CAREFUL.

READ THIS WAY

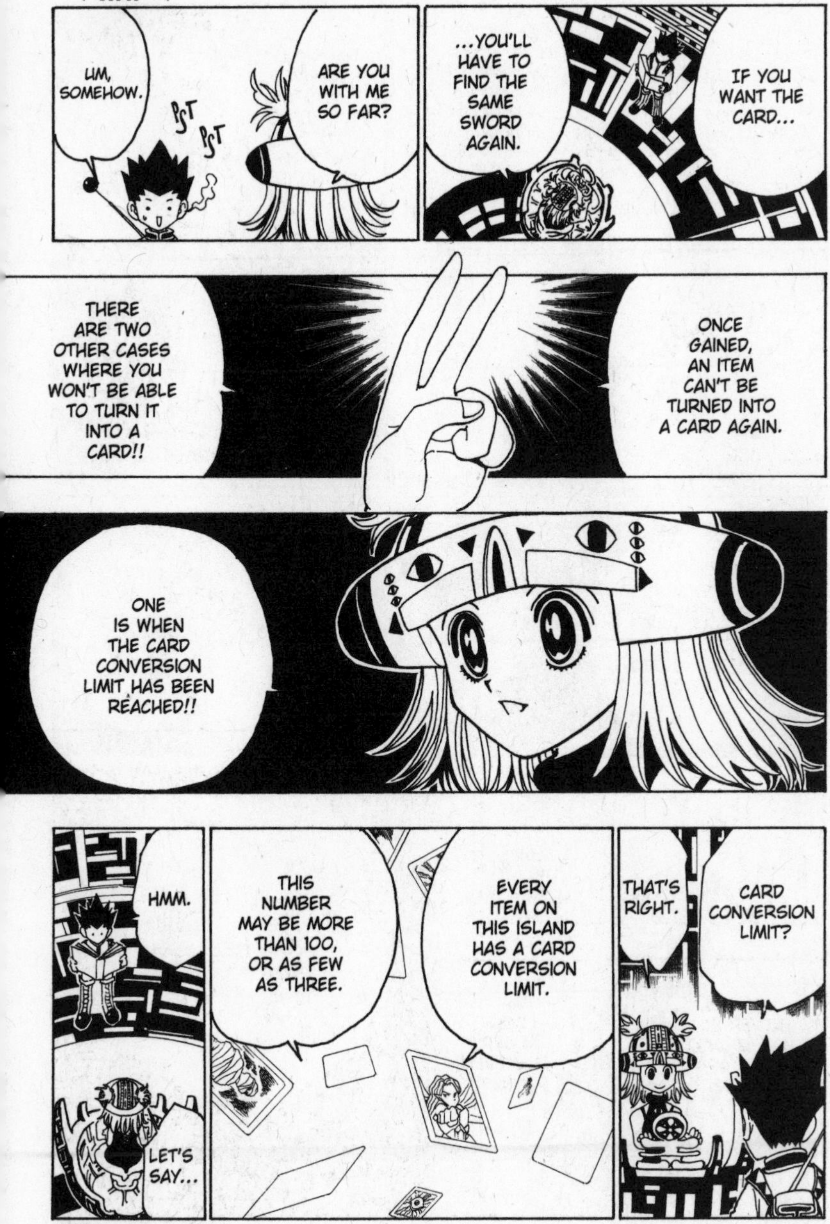
IF YOU WANT THE CARD...
...YOU'LL HAVE TO FIND THE SAME SWORD AGAIN.
ARE YOU WITH ME SO FAR?
UM, SOMEHOW.
PST PST
ONCE GAINED, AN ITEM CAN'T BE TURNED INTO A CARD AGAIN.
THERE ARE TWO OTHER CASES WHERE YOU WON'T BE ABLE TO TURN IT INTO A CARD!!
ONE IS WHEN THE CARD CONVERSION LIMIT HAS BEEN REACHED!!
CARD CONVERSION LIMIT?
THAT'S RIGHT.
EVERY ITEM ON THIS ISLAND HAS A CARD CONVERSION LIMIT.
THIS NUMBER MAY BE MORE THAN 100, OR AS FEW AS THREE.
HMM.
LET'S SAY...

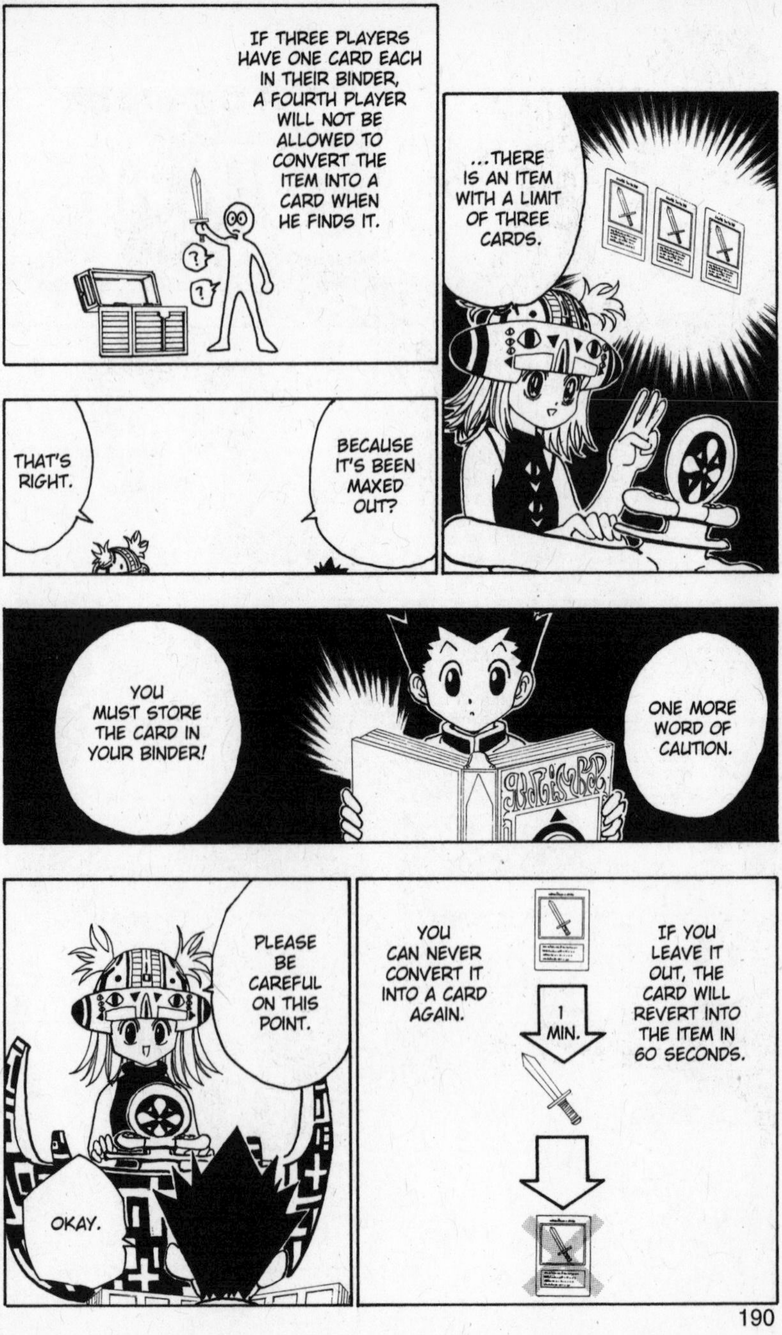
...THERE IS AN ITEM WITH A LIMIT OF THREE CARDS.
IF THREE PLAYERS HAVE ONE CARD EACH IN THEIR BINDER, A FOURTH PLAYER WILL NOT BE ALLOWED TO CONVERT THE ITEM INTO A CARD WHEN HE FINDS IT.
?
?
BECAUSE IT'S BEEN MAXED OUT?
THAT'S RIGHT.
ONE MORE WORD OF CAUTION.
YOU MUST STORE THE CARD IN YOUR BINDER!
IF YOU LEAVE IT OUT, THE CARD WILL REVERT INTO THE ITEM IN 60 SECONDS.
1 MIN.
YOU CAN NEVER CONVERT IT INTO A CARD AGAIN.
PLEASE BE CAREFUL ON THIS POINT.
OKAY.

READ THIS WAY

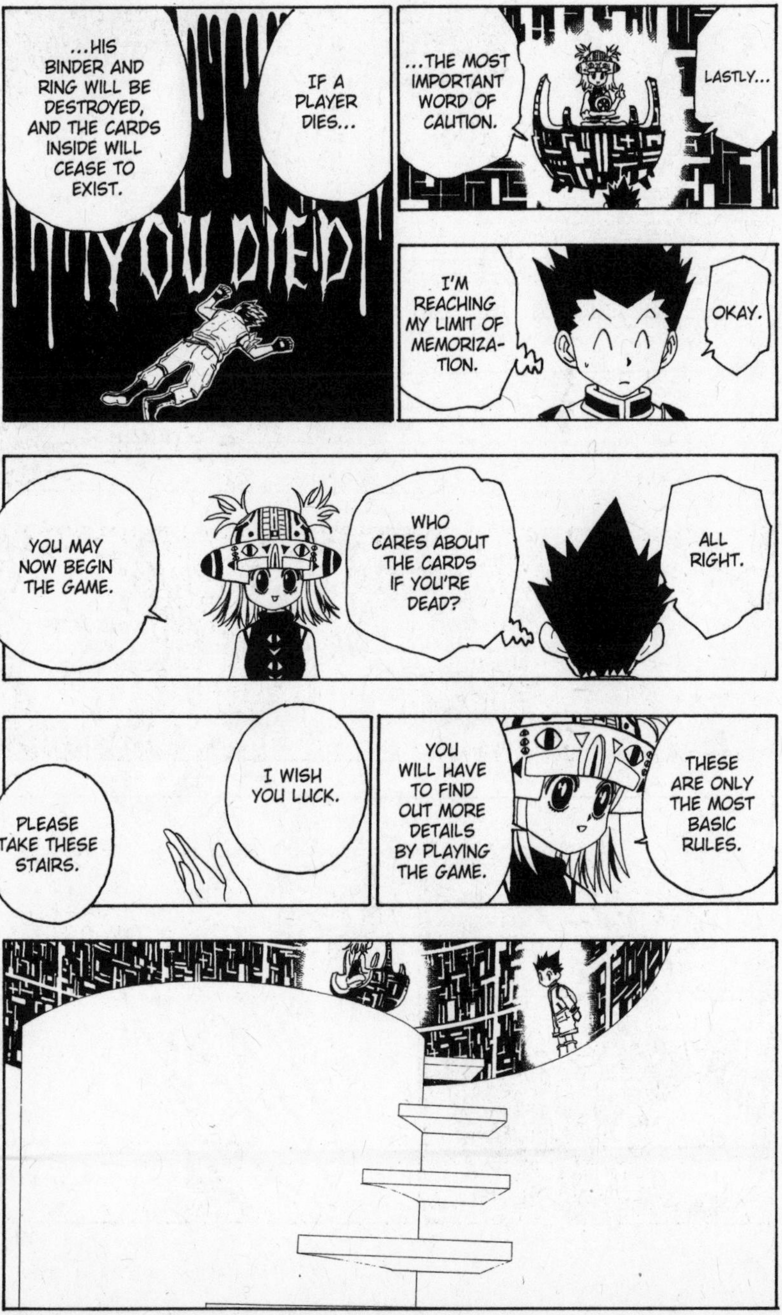
LASTLY...
...THE MOST IMPORTANT WORD OF CAUTION.
OKAY.
I'M REACHING MY LIMIT OF MEMORIZA- TION.
IF A PLAYER DIES...
...HIS BINDER AND RING WILL BE DESTROYED, AND THE CARDS INSIDE WILL CEASE TO EXIST.
YOU DIED
ALL RIGHT.
WHO CARES ABOUT THE CARDS IF YOU'RE DEAD?
YOU MAY NOW BEGIN THE GAME.
THESE ARE ONLY THE MOST BASIC RULES.
YOU WILL HAVE TO FIND OUT MORE DETAILS BY PLAYING THE GAME.
I WISH YOU LUCK.
PLEASE TAKE THESE STAIRS.

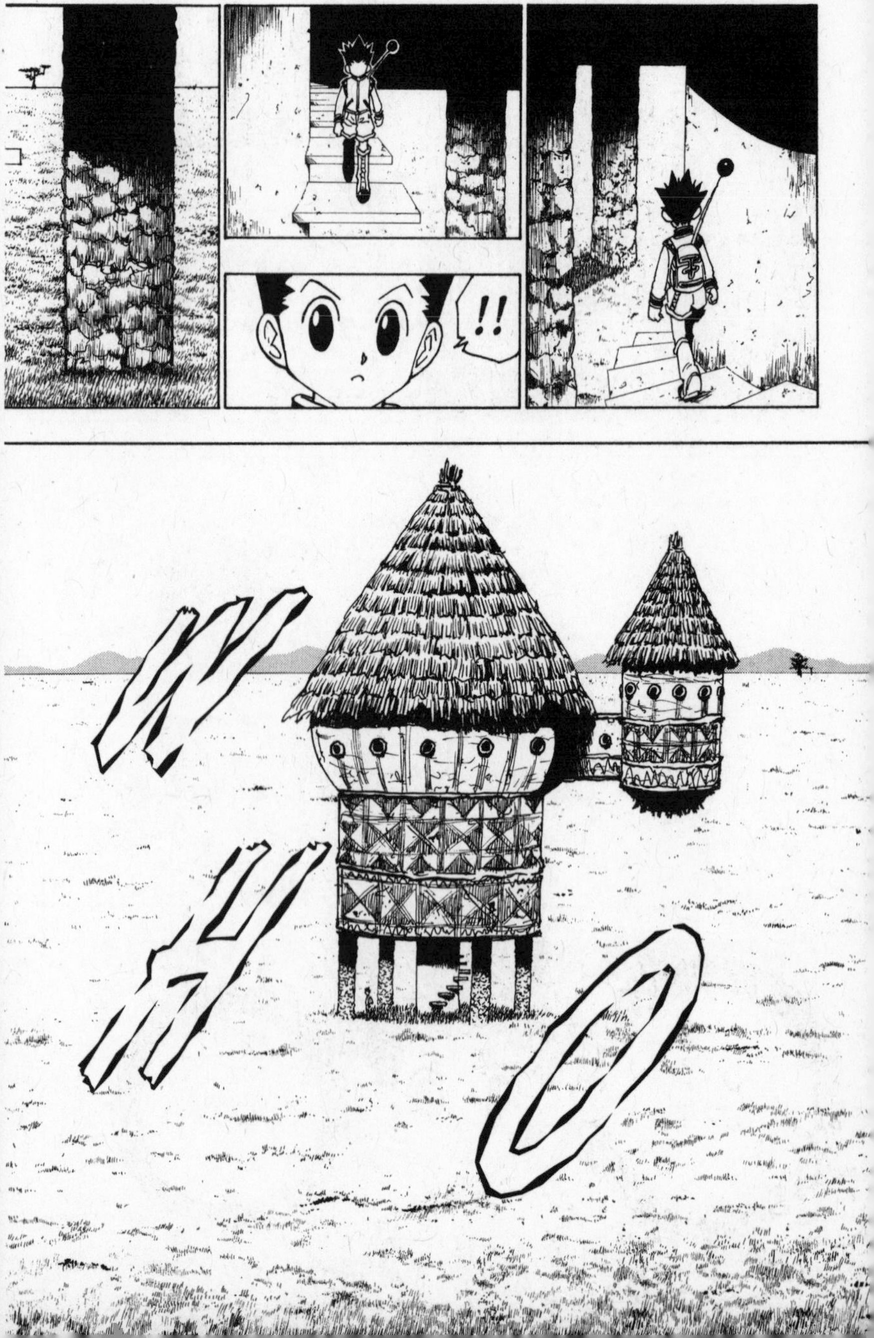
!!

READ THIS WAY

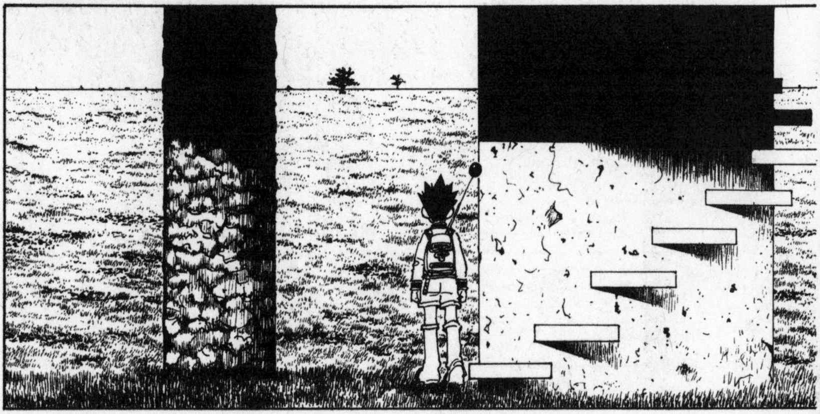

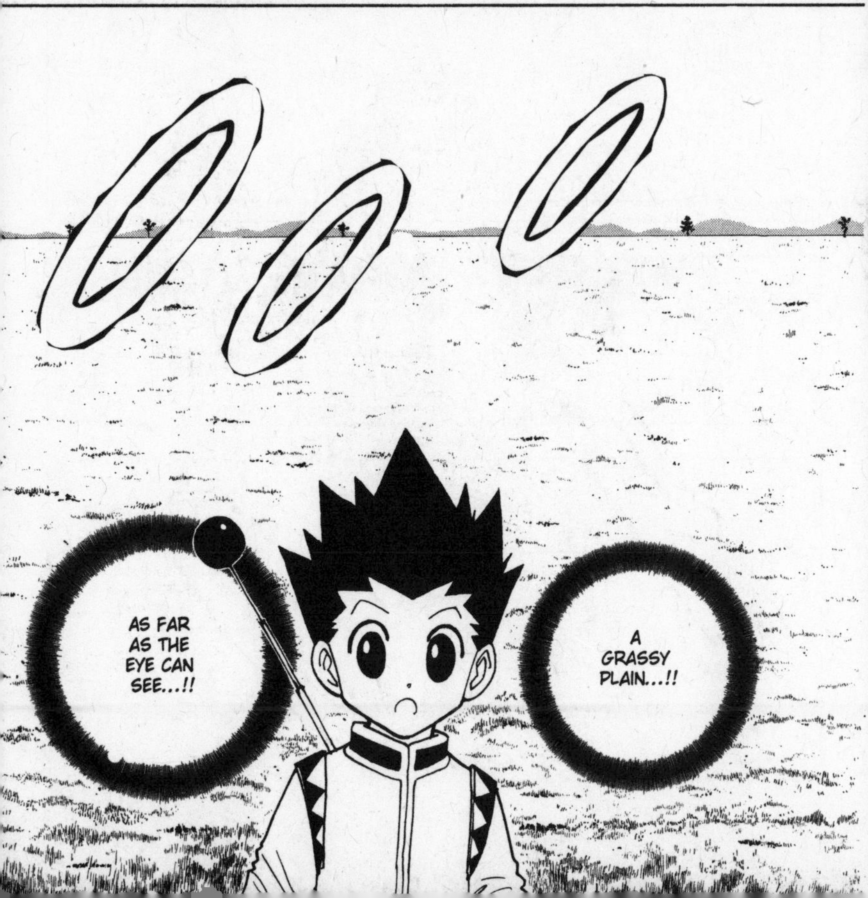
A GRASSY PLAIN...!!
AS FAR AS THE EYE CAN SEE...!!

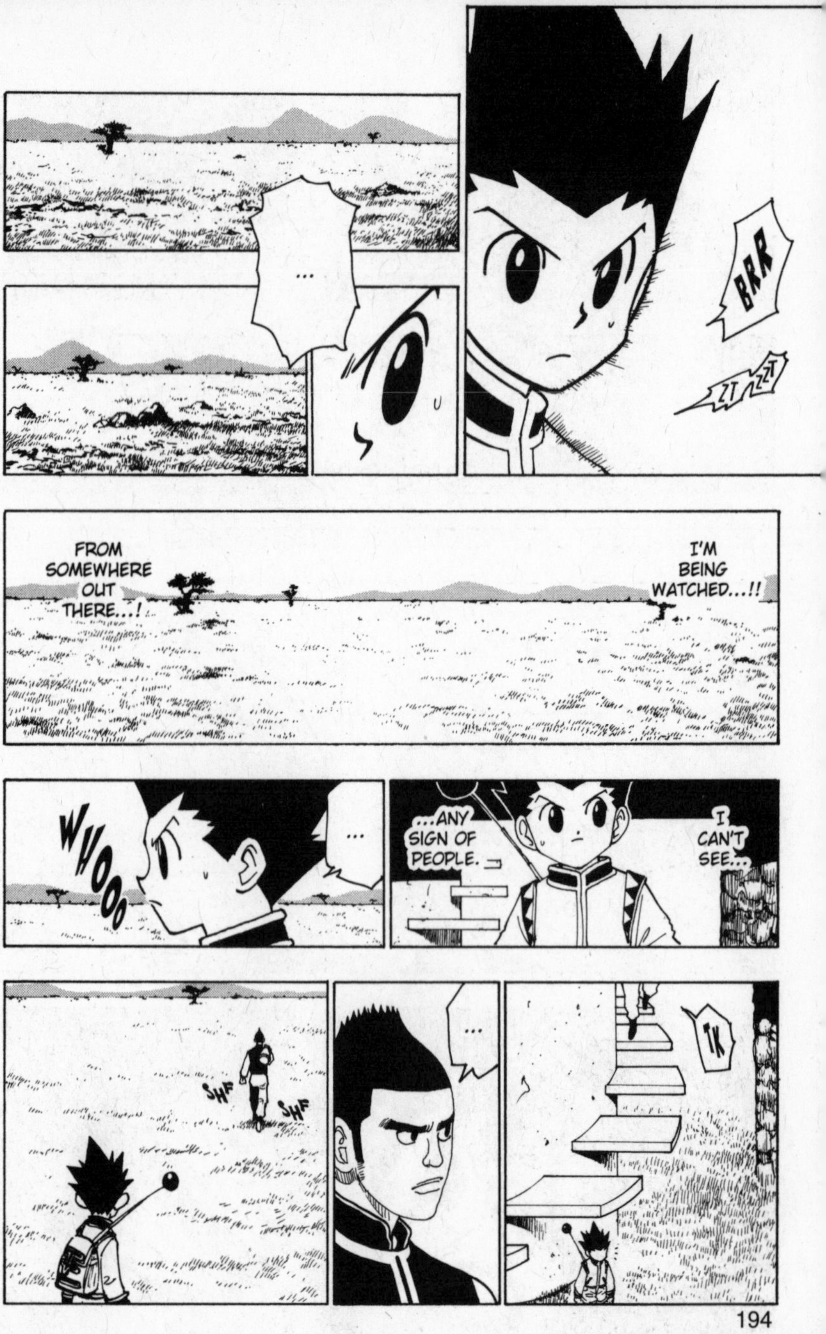
BRR
ZZT
ZT
...
I'M BEING WATCHED...!!
FROM SOMEWHERE OUT THERE...!
I CAN'T SEE...
...ANY SIGN OF PEOPLE.
...
WHOOO
TK
...
SHF
SHF

READ THIS WAY

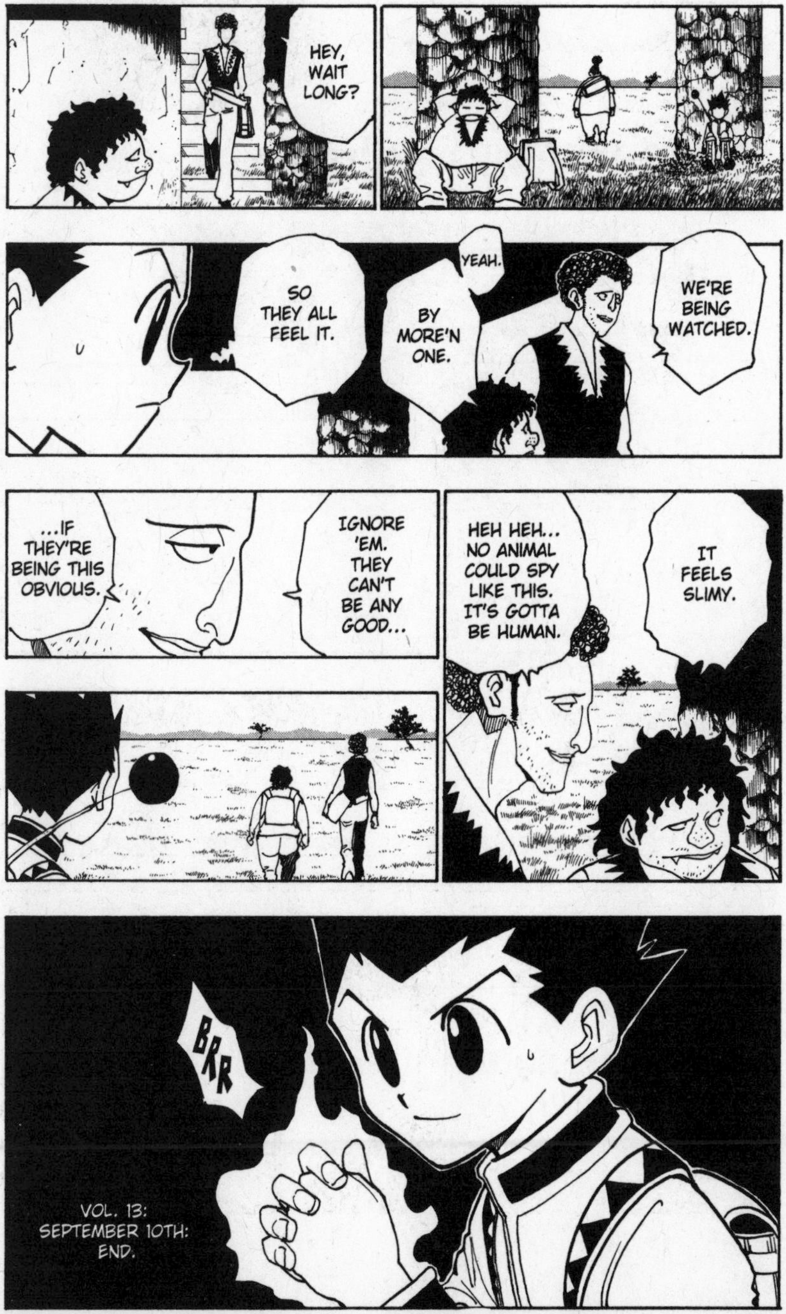
HEY, WAIT LONG?
WE'RE BEING WATCHED.
YEAH.
BY MORE'N ONE.
SO THEY ALL FEEL IT.
IT FEELS SLIMY.
HEH HEH... NO ANIMAL COULD SPY LIKE THIS. IT'S GOTTA BE HUMAN.
IGNORE 'EM. THEY CAN'T BE ANY GOOD...
...IF THEY'RE BEING THIS OBVIOUS.
BRR
VOL. 13: SEPTEMBER 10TH: END.

Coming Next Volume...

The *Greed Island* video game has some nasty surprises in store for Gon and Killua, including a dangerous player called "The Bomber" who is killing off the competition to free up more cards. There's also the matter of some monsters, but help comes from an unexpected source.

Available now!

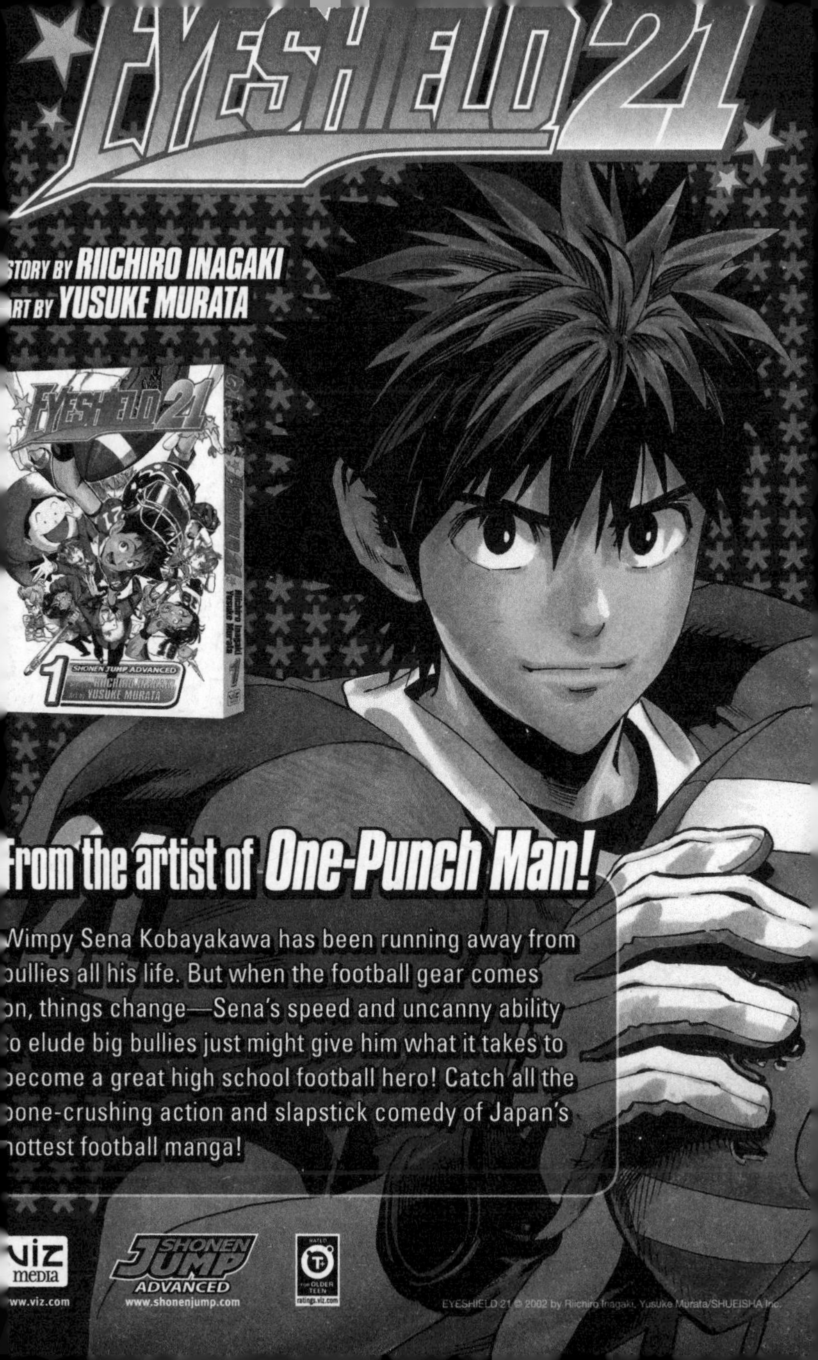
EYESHIELD 21
TORY BY RIICHIRO INAGAKI
RT BY YUSUKE MURATA
EYESHIELD 21
1 SHONEN JUMP ADVANCED RIICHIRO INAGAKI YUSUKE MURATA
rom the artist of One-Punch Man!
Wimpy Sena Kobayakawa has been running away from
ullies all his life. But when the football gear comes
n, things change—Sena's speed and uncanny ability
o elude big bullies just might give him what it takes to
ecome a great high school football hero! Catch all the
one-crushing action and slapstick comedy of Japan's
ottest football manga!
viz media
ww.viz.com
SHONEN JUMP ADVANCED
www.shonenjump.com
RATED T+ FOR OLDER TEEN
ratings.viz.com
EYESHIELD 21 © 2002 by Riichiro Inagaki, Yusuke Murata/SHUEISHA Inc.

You ...he ...!

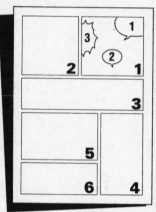

Whoops! Guess what? You're starting at the wrong end of the comic!

…It's true! In keeping with the original Japanese format, **Hunter x Hunter** is meant to be read from right to left, starting in the upper-right corner.

Unlike English, which is read from left to right, Japanese is read from right to left, meaning that action, sound effects and word-balloon order are completely reversed… something which can make readers unfamiliar with Japanese feel pretty backwards themselves. For this reason, manga or Japanese comics published in the U.S. in English have sometimes been published "flopped"—that is, printed in exact reverse order, as though seen from the other side of a mirror.

By flopping pages, U.S. publishers can avoid confusing readers, but the compromise is not without its downside. For one thing, a character in a flopped manga series who once wore in the original Japanese version a T-shirt emblazoned with "M A Y" (as in "the merry month of") now wears one which reads "Y A M"! Additionally, many manga creators in Japan are themselves unhappy with the process, as some feel the mirror-imaging of their art skews their original intentions.

We are proud to bring you Yoshihiro Togashi's **Hunter x Hunter** in the original unflopped format. For now, though, turn to the other side of the book and let the adventure begin…!

—Editor